MW01267622

Davidson
2004

LIES LIKE TRUTH

Lies Like Truth

SHAKESPEARE, MACBETH,
—— and the ——
Cultural Moment

Arthur F. Kinney

WAYNE STATE UNIVERSITY PRESS   DETROIT

Copyright © 2001 by Wayne State University Press
Detroit, Michigan 48201. All rights are reserved.
No part of this book may be reproduced without formal permission.
Manufactured in the United States of America
05 04 03 02 01   5 4 3 2 1

Library of Congress Cataloging-in-Publication Data

Kinney, Arthur F., 1933–
Lies like truth : Shakespeare, Macbeth, and the cultural moment / Arthur F. Kenney.
p. cm.
Includes bibliographical references and index.
ISBN 0-8143-2965-9 (cloth : alk. paper) — ISBN 0-8143-2966-7 (paper: alk. paper)
1. Shakespeare, William, 1564–1616. Macbeth.   2. Shakespeare, William,
1564–1616—Stage history—To 1625.   3. Macbeth, King of Scotland, 11th cent.—In
literature.   4. Literature and society—England—History—17th century.   5. Literature and
history—England—History—17th century.   6. English language—Early modern,
1500–1700—Semantics.   7. Theater audiences—England—History—17th century.
8. Shakespeare, William, 1564–1616—Language.   9. Culture in literature.
10. Historicism.   I. Title.
PR2823 .K56 2001
822.3'3—dc21   00-012159

The frontispiece of King James I on horseback appears courtesy of The Royal Collection
© 2000, Her Majesty Queen Elizabeth II.

The illustration on page 32 is from *The Large, The Small, and the Human Mind* by Roger
Penrose and is reprinted with the permission of Cambridge University Press.

For James M. Dutcher

The role of literature is what a period thinks of itself.

Pierre Macherey

Contents

Preface

Not until the middle of the twentieth century would technology
open up new opportunities for intellectual discovery on the
same scale as it had in the Renaissance with the simultaneous
emergence in Europe of clocks, printing, and algebra.

James Bailey

Revolutions are . . . taken to be those non-cumulative developmental episodes in which an older paradigm is replaced in
whole or in part by an incompatible new one.

Thomas S. Kuhn

When I first began this book with a university-wide lecture at the
invitation of the chancellor of the University of Massachusetts, Amherst, the question I sought to answer was as simple as it was absorbing:
how did Shakespeare come to mean in his own time—or, to make the
important issues more lucid and direct, what did *Macbeth* mean to the
audience that first saw the play at the Globe Theater in 1606? For four
centuries now, *Macbeth* has remained one of the most read, most studied,
and most performed of Shakespeare's plays, and it has been reinterpreted
by countless directors and actors on countless stages. In classrooms, the
play has been a moral allegory about the fall of a good man, the psychology
of ambition, the evil of ambitious wives, or the crime of demonology and
its punishment; the portrayal of a heroic but tragically flawed villain; the
dangers of a savage or military culture. But not all of those meanings were
equally accessible—or at least equally urgent—to playgoers in 1606, and
some of them were arguably not available at all. Other events were: the
Powder Plot, which threatened a stable monarchy, if believed; the potential
dangers of a foreign or even alien king; a religious debate in which one

branch of Christians—the Calvinists—believed in the absolute reprobate; a king who seemed to argue absolute rule but denied the possibility of its collapse into tyranny; the increasing frequency of rebellion by discontented London citizens helpless at the mercy of weather and threatened by a fundamental shift in economic practices; an endangered honor code as the basis of social position and behavior; unexpected acts of witchcraft or the swift, random attack of epidemics of plague. Cognizant that "All the world doth practice stageplaying," as Florio's Montaigne puts it in the English translation of 1603,[1] used by the Globe Theater as its motto, *Totus mundus agit histrionem,* which, if any of these matters, did *Macbeth* address, head-on or by implication, intended or not? Was the play inviting particular reactions as Shakespeare reshaped his sources and brought contemporary affairs into the play? What, in fact, was the text of a play at once so popular that it stayed in production and yet—astonishingly, given its timeliness—was not published until the great First Folio of 1623, as if it might contain hidden or dangerous matter or was especially liable to piracy? Is the 1623 text we have anything like the 1606 performance text?

At once, then, I had more questions than before and no indications of any answers. I wanted to follow the aim of historical criticism that J. R. deJ. Jackson, in *Historical Criticism and the Meaning of Texts,* defines as trying "to read past works of literature in the way in which they were read when they were new,"[2] and who also sketches a methodology for this:

> If the aim of the recovery is to know a past literary environment as it was known in its own time so that reference to it in particular works will be comprehensible, three aspects will need to be considered: the range of works that existed; the portion of that range that was well enough known for authors to be able to take it for granted; and the way in which that portion was understood, in so far as it differs from the way in which a modern reader might be expected to understand it. (109)

My original title—subsequently used by Lee Patterson for his book on Chaucer long before I had completed my own—was *Macbeth and the Subjects of History,* using *subject* to mean topic and one of the governed as well as *subject to; history* meaning the historical Macbeth of the tenth century, Holinshed's history of Macbeth, the character in Shakespeare's play, and the matters of 1606. At that point, and after, I turned, as many researchers might turn, to the extant documentary evidence. I studied the statutes, laws, and regulations in place in early Stuart England; I read the calendar of state papers and chased down fugitive papers and diaries summarized there, as well as other manuscript letters and commonplace books; and I set about systematically to read every extant book and pamphlet printed or circulating in England from 1600 to 1606 because they were surely abroad, publicly, read or waiting to be read at the time *Macbeth* was first seen. I studied the theatrical conditions in 1606, from the composition of Shakespeare's acting company and its repertoire of plays to the size and shape of his stage and the demographic composition of his public (and private) audiences. Following the lead of Marc Bloch and the Annales school of history, I sought to know the culture deeply and widely at the originary moment of *Macbeth;* to "bring a world to presence," as Ned Lukacher memorably puts it,[3] would tell me, a literary historian, something about the meaning, function, and place of literature and about the forces of history that I might not otherwise discover. I might even find a somewhat different play.

But the Annales school believes in the *longue durée* as well as *l'histoire événmentielle*—that nothing happens in a split second; that there is no such thing as an originary moment but only a slicing into history, or time, which is more reliably a process; as Patterson also realized, "an originary moment, a moment set outside and against history, is an impossible delusion."[4] And friends who followed my work noted that the spectators at the first *Macbeth* would recall events and ideas and even pamphlets that stuck in their minds from well before 1600, and that other forces only in print in, say, 1610 were already being formulated and even discussed in 1606, leading me to understand and more deeply appreciate critic Raymond Williams's sense of residual, dominant, and emergent forces in a culture which showed that culture as always dynamic, caught only artificially in the midst of movement and change.[5] On the one hand, the New Historicism taught me (once said, it seemed only common sense) that a number of cultural practices could be "read" as texts are read in literary classes—that they used some of the same techniques and signs to confer meaning. On the other hand, cultural materialism taught me (although it then seemed only common sense) that material artifacts of a culture—such as the anachronistic twofold balls and treble scepter, the "Horrible sight: Now I see 'tis true" (4.1.122; 1669) that Macbeth is shown in the conjuration scene—made the play contemporary to 1606 as well as historical.

Whatever *Macbeth* meant in 1606, then, was richly complicated and not always easily, or perhaps ever wholly, recoverable; it would surely go beyond what any current production or even textbook was providing or any recent treatise such as that connecting the play to the Powder Plot or to witchcraft.[6] Such an understanding would need to recover the cultural moment which, as Howard Felperin has pointed out, is "laden with the traces of earlier and the latencies of subsequent moments,"[7] and it would have to accommodate, as Clifford Geertz has warned, "a situation at once fluid, plural, uncentered, and ineradicably untidy."[8]

Yet while it now seemed increasingly urgent for me to know more about what *Macbeth* meant to the playgoers at the Globe Theater in 1606, I began to realize that dissatisfactions with past literary and historical practices that have led to an anxious and persistent interrogation by current postmodernist theorizing were most revelatory of all. Matters such as episteme, rupture, and aporias; unfixed boundaries and textual instabilities; traces and supplements—these, I believe, register through heteroglossia or polysemy that kind of indeterminacy or irresolution that anticipates what Thomas S. Kuhn describes in *The Structure of Scientific Revolutions*: that our culture is in the throes of a fundamental paradigm shift in the way we understand our past and present culture and in the ways literature functions as a participant in it. The current crisis in literary studies—in research in the humanities and social sciences generally—is, I believe, a natural reflection and necessary corollary to recent fundamental revolutions in the physical sciences and attuned to recent writings in cognitive science. Moving from a material to a service economy is in keeping with an electronic revolution we have yet to confront, register, and apply adequately, but as I hope to begin to show in the monograph that follows, these are deeply linked to the changes in critical theory and the rise of cultural studies. Just as literary history was born in an age of socialism and New Criticism was practiced during years of recuperation and stabilization after a worldwide holocaust, so the advent of the computer and virtual reality has fundamentally changed the way we think, investigate, and learn. We will not—we soon *cannot*—practice formalist literary criticism in the way we once did. The "intellectual impact" of "the true electronic computing revolution," James Bailey has acknowledged, "will be greater than anything since the Renaissance, possibly greater than anything since the invention of language,"[9] and we may add to this the announcement by Princeton University scientists in October 1999 that the brain, once thought to atrophy in later age, actually continues to develop with the addition of new neurons—quite possibly thousands a day.[10]

To begin to answer my questions about *Macbeth* and to begin to understand this epistemological revolution in literary and cultural studies signaled by rapid changes in technology are the reasons why I have written this book. Chapter 1 draws on early modern treatises of cognitive science available to Shakespeare and his audiences as well as those of our own time; chapter 2 records cultural practices fundamentally and inherently in play with any reader or performer of a dramatic text in 1606 as well as any playgoer. Both chapters conclude in chapter 3, which sets out a new way of reading and a new way of practicing a hermeneutics of indeterminacy that, I will argue, gets us closer to early modern texts as they were understood in Shakespeare's age, and, at the same time, closer to the way dramatic plays such as *Macbeth* were understood from early modern times to beyond the present technological revolution.

Washington, D.C.
Cortland, New York
Amherst, Massachusetts
September 2000

Acknowledgments

Plus ça change, plus c'est la même chose: no new undertaking is ever really new. Some time after beginning work on this book, I recalled one of my mentors in graduate school, Frank Livingstone Huntley, insisting that in each class we should dig vertically and deeply to understand the meaning of literature; his instances were *Religio Medici* and *Urne Buriall.* His argument was against the broad sweep of intellectual history as a dominant means of study and of partial excerpts in literary anthologies that made connections and built "movements" only by skimming the surfaces of things. So this book, in a way, began decades ago in graduate school. Much, much later the Chancellor and a faculty committee of my university asked me to deliver one of the Chancellor's Lectures. I chose as my subject " 'Present Fear' and 'Horrible Imaginings': Re-visiting *Macbeth,*" and a student and friend, Edward H. Curran, and I began to do intensive research. Some of that still resides in what follows.

During the interim and especially in the past few years, it seems as if everyone actively working in the areas of this book contributed to it through ideas, reprints of their own work, or suggestions by phone or letter for my own further research, and although I tried to keep a running ledger of debits, probably only a fraction survived my aberrant bookkeeping. Hoping those who supported this work that are not mentioned will excuse my oversight and accept my genuine appreciation, I do want to list here those survivors in my accounts book: Ted Curran, Paul Yachnin,

David Norbrook, Edward Chaney, Brian Morris, Frances Teague, Harry Berger Jr., Kirby Farrell, Carl Swanson, Richard Burt, Jenny Wormald, Leah Marcus, James Bulman, Annabel Patterson, Brian Gibbons, A. R. Braunmuller, Cedric Brown, Christopher Martin, John T. Matthews, James Siemon, Ian Donaldson, Alistair Fox, Lois Potter, Andrew Gurr, David Bergeron, Jay L. Halio, Tim Murray, David Harris Sacks, Stanley Archer, Douglas Lanier, Paul Zolrod, Lorraine Helms, Peter Blayney, Bernice S. Kilman, William Long, Edward M. Jayne, Florence Sandler, Eugene D. Hill, Daniel Amneus, Peter Stallybrass, Kenneth Gross, R. Malcolm Smuts, Scott Lucas, the Rev. John Mark Jones, Linda Pollock, R. B. Parker, Linda Peck, Sheldon Zitner, Robert N. Watson, Tom Dughi, Winfried Scleiner, Roderick Lyall, Jean R. Brink, Lena Cowen Orlin, Lynda Boose, Carole Levin, Phyllis Rackin, Jean Howard, Barbara H. Traister, R. B. Shand, Lois Schwoerer, Gordon J. Schochet, William Woodson, James Dutcher, Elizabeth Story Donno, Derek Alwes, Barbara Everett, Craig A. Bernthal, Ronald M. Meldrum, F. W. Brownlow, Stanley Wells, Richard F. Hardin, Brian F. Levack, A. L. Beier, Robert Hume, Rick Smith, Ronald Levao, Leeds Barroll, Kate Clarke, Leland Estes, Louis Montrose, Peter Medine, Richard Strier, David Lee Miller, Gary Taylor, Jodi Mikalachki, Eric S. Mallin, Lloyd Davis, David S. Linton, Julie R. Solomon, David Cressy, Stanley Stewart, Steven Mullaney, Richard Helgerson, Clifford Davidson, Anne Lancashire, Phillipa Pattison, Sasha Roberts, Ann Thompson, M. K. Bennett, Donald Foster, B. J. Sokol, Normand Berlin, Paul Werstine, Stuart Kurland, Barbara Freedman, and Emrys Jones.

I am grateful to Arthur B. Evans, Director of Wayne State University Press, for his unfailing support of this project. Sara Berger prepared the manuscripts; two anonymous readers helped to improve it; Adela Garcia saw it through the publishing process; and Jonathan Lawrence copyedited it. Nat Herald read an early version with great acuity, care and guidance. Tom Broughton-Willett has supplied the index. I would also like to thank Stan Sherer for preparing the photographs of the illustrations and designs appearing throughout the book.

The University of Massachusetts provided me with generous leave time, teaching schedules, and research aid; in addition, I received considerable support, and at critical times, from the National Endowment for the Humanities, the Folger Shakespeare Library, and the Huntington Library and Art Gallery. The staffs of these libraries—especially Betsy Walsh and Mary Wright—have my lasting gratitude; I received considerable guidance and support as well from the Bodleian Library; the British Library; the Public Records Office in Chancery Lane, London; the Olin Library, Cornell

University; the W. E. B. DuBois Library at the University of Massachusetts; and the libraries of the Shakespeare Institute, Stratford-on-Avon, and the Shakespeare Birthplace Trust (and the assistance of Marion Pringle).

Finally, I share the sentiments of the printer of the first English edition of Boccaccio's *Decameron* (1620): "Bookes (Courteous Reader) may be rightly compared to *Gardens;* wherein, let the painfull Gardiner expresse never so much care and diligent endevour; yet among the very fairest, sweetest and freshest Flowers, as also Plants of most precious Vertue; ill savouring and stinking Weeds, fit for no use but the fire or mucke-hill, will spring and sprout up. So fareth it with Bookes of the very best quality, let the Author bee never so indulgent, and the printer vigilant; yet both may misse their ayme, by the escape of Errors and mistakes, either in sense of matter, the one fault ensuing by a ragged Written Copy; and the other through want of wary correction. If then the best Bookes cannot be free from this common infirmity; blame not this then, of farre lighter argument, wherein thy courtesie may helpe us both: His blame, in acknowledging his more sufficiency then to write so grosse and absurdly: and mine, in pardoning unwilling Errours committed, which thy judgment finding, thy pen can as easily correct" (ii, sig. A4).

A Note on the Text

Since the argument of this book hopes to recover as much as possible the conditions of life and thought at the Globe Theater in 1606, I have used the only early authoritative text we have of *Macbeth*—the First Folio of 1623. All quotations to this play, and the other plays of Shakespeare, are in the spelling of the First Folio with references to the Through Line Numbers, preceded by references to the New Arden editions. For other works of the period, I have used first editions and original documents wherever possible, giving references to the texts by folio or signature number as more reliable than pagination. All dates are New Style, with the calendar year beginning on January 1.

I have incorporated some of my remarks in earlier essays: "Speculating Shakespeare, 1605–1606" in *Elizabethan Theater: Essays in Honor of S. Schoenbaum*, ed. R. B. Parker and S. P. Zitner (Newark: University of Delaware Press, 1996) 252–70; "Imagination and Ideology in *Macbeth*" in *Ideological Approaches to Shakespeare: The Practice of Theory*, ed. Robert P. Merrix and Nicholas Ranson (Lewiston: The Edwin Mellen Press, 1992) 57–85; "Shakespeare's *Macbeth* and the Question of Nationalism" in *Literature and Nationalism*, ed. Vincent Newey and Ann Thompson (Liverpool: Liverpool University Press, 1991) 56–75; "Scottish History, the Union of the Crowns and the Issue of Right Rule: The Case of Shakespeare's *Macbeth*" in *Renaissance Culture in Context: Theory and Practice*, ed. Jean R. Brink and William F. Gentrup (London: Scolar Press, 1993) 18–53; and a revision of "Imagination and Ideology in *Macbeth*" in *The Witness of Times: Manifestations of Ideology in Seventeenth-Century England,* ed. Katherine Z. Keller and Gerald J. Schiffhorst (Pittsburgh: Duquesne University Press, 1993) 148–73. I am grateful to these editors and publishers for the re-use of some of my material.

The single crown shown throughout the book is the imperial crown as it appears on the proclamation of James I announcing the Powder Plot. The design incorporating both rose and thistle first appeared on the title page of Robert Fletcher, *A Briefe and Familiar Epistle Shewing His Maiesties Most Lawfvll, Honovrable and Ivst Title to All His Kingdomes* (London, 1603). The frontispiece is an engraving of James I on horseback by Francis Delaram, updated, but about 1610. The Globe Theater (center forefront) is depicted as a circular structure. Other buildings displaying flags are presumably the Beargarden to the left and the Rose (pulled down in 1605) or the Swan Theater. The large church seen between the horse's legs is St. Mary Overie, and to the right the entrance to London Bridge is studded with poles bearing the heads of traitors. The verses celebrating the king express confidence in the monarch.

CHAPTER ONE

MACBETH AND THE CULTURAL MOMENT

I have a taste for reading even torn papers lying in the streets.
Don Quixote

Modernity begins with the recognition that the object before me is not a sign but a random particle. And it is all there is; nothing is behind or beyond it, nor is anything underneath. It is opaque and irreducible, one singularity among others multiplied excessively in every direction. The universe is made of such things. The historic task of modernity, starting in the seventeenth century and continuing to this day, has been to develop a theory of rationality adequate to a universe of randomness—and not only a theory but a program of strategic operations capable of entering into the heterogeneity of things and bringing it under control. . . . A poetic universe is, philosophically speaking, a universe of correspondences. In a poetic universe, every fragment is a luminous detail. It resonates with the supersensuous. It is in perpetual transport from the everydayness of its material appearance to the sphere of the transcendental where it is really located, and its impact upon consciousness constitutes a moment of vision or the sense of embracing the totality of all that is. There are overarchings everywhere.
Gerald L. Bruns

A literary work is not an object that stands by itself and that offers the same view to each reader.
Hans Robert Jauss

Everyone who has seen or read *Macbeth* knows what the play is about, except that for different spectators and different readers it is about different things. "As actors, directors, audiences, and critics all testify," Michael J. Collins writes, "*Macbeth* is a complex, ambiguous, unsettling play."[1] "What bears in on us in the opening scenes," adds Graham Bradshaw, "is something terrifyingly inchoate."[2] The play opens amid "Hurleyburley" where battles unresolved, perhaps irresolveable, are never "lost, and wonne" (1.1.3–4; 5–6)[3] but, answering regicide with regicide, are open to the possibility of continuing bloodshed at the play's end. *Macbeth* is not only puzzling but, even more than *Hamlet,* a deliberately interrogative play. The first four scenes begin with questions: "When shall we three meete againe?"; "What bloody man is that?"; "Where hast thou beene, Sister?"; "Is execution done on *Cawdor*?" and throughout the Folio text, key moments stop short at questionings:

> I know I am *Thane* of Glamis, / But how, of Cawdor? (1.3.71–72; 171–72)
>
> Why doe you dresse me in borrowed Robes? (1.3.108–9; 215)
>
> If ill / Why hath it giuen me earnest of successe, / Commencing in a Truth? (1.3.131–33; 243–44)
>
> If we should faile? (1.7.59; 539)
>
> Is this a Dagger, which I see before me, / The Handle toward my Hand? . . . / or art thou but / A Dagger of the Minde, a false Creation, / Proceeding from the heat-oppressed Braine? (2.1.33–39; 613–19)
>
> But wherefore could I not pronounce Amen? (2.2.30; 687)
>
> Will all great *Neptunes* Ocean wash this blood / Cleane from my Hand? (2.2.59–60; 721–22)
>
> Ride you this afternoon? (3.1.19; 1004)
>
> Which of you haue done this? (3.4.48; 1316)
>
> Who was't came by? (4.1.140; 1692)
>
> Wherefore was that cry? (5.5.15; 2336)

Each question interrupts the developing narrative; catches short the characters; breaks open the play and forces playgoers to realign events.

Such an observation is not especially surprising; what is surprising is that traditional literary criticism has failed to confront such issues as simultaneous, contradictory, independent, or unresolved meaning. What we need, then, and what I propose, is a newly realized hermeneutics of indeterminacy that, based in the cultural moment in which the play was written and first performed, both extends and complicates its historically verifiable meanings. In 1606 playgoers confronting such questions might have turned to the well-known story of Macbeth in Francis Thynne's account of Scottish history found in the widely known *Chronicles* attributed to Raphael Holinshed. But the differences between Holinshed's history and Shakespeare's play might only generate more questions. In Holinshed, Duncan denies any election of his successor by tanistry after his death by naming Malcolm Prince of Cumberland, thus performing an act of tyranny before that of Macbeth. Shakespeare's play does not reveal that both Macbeth and Lady Macbeth have strong claims to the throne of Scotland—both stronger than Duncan's, or Malcolm's—since they are both descended from royalty, Lady Macbeth having both maternal and paternal royal ancestors. Shakespeare omits any direct mention of Lulach, Lady Macbeth's son by her first marriage, while retaining a reference to this in her knowing what it is to suckle a babe: it is Lulach, in fact, Macbeth's foster son, who succeeds him to the throne of Scotland in Holinshed's account. In Holinshed (but not in Shakespeare) Banquo openly allies himself with Macbeth in the murder of Duncan, which occurs on an open field of battle; it is Macbeth, not Duncan, who is the popular leader of the northern Scottish clans. According to the Holinshed account, Macbeth was properly elected, ruled peacefully for ten years (setting a precedent), and visited the Pope in Rome (bringing Christianity to Scotland); Macduff, however, rebelled against Macbeth by refusing, unlike the other thanes, to help the King build a new castle at Dunsinane. In contradicting received history, then, Shakespeare raises other questions in the course of his play in 1606, rupturing the narrative playgoers might have known and expected.

Scenes, too, were problematic in 1606. The Porter's brief scene—he has only 34 of the play's 2,167 lines in the Folio text—opens with a monologue that he delivers as a dialogue:

> Here's a knocking indeede: if a man were Porter of Hell Gate, hee should haue old turning the Key. *Knock.* Knock, Knock, Knock. Who's there i'th' name of *Belzebub*? Here's a Farmer, that hang's himselfe on th' expectation of Plentie: Come in time, haue Napkins enow about you, here you'le sweat for't. *Knock.* Knock, knock. Who's there in th'other Deuils Name? Faith here's an equiuocator, that could sweare in both the Scales against eyther Scale, who committed Treason enough for Gods sake, yet could not equiuocate to Heauen: oh come in, Equiuocator. *Knock.* Knock, Knock, Knock. Who's there? 'Faith, here's an English Taylor come hither, for stealing out of a French Hose: Come in Taylor, here you may rost your Goose. *Knock.* Knock, Knock. Neuer at quiet: What are you? but this place is too cold for Hell. Ile Deuill-Porter it no further: I had thought to haue let in some of all Professions, that goe the Primrose way to th'euerlasting Bonfire. *Knock.* Anon, anon, I pray you remember the Porter. (2.3.1–22; 744–62)

The Porter raises questions by dispersing his visitor into various vocations and then re-membering them in his role as the keeper of Hell Gate. Nineteenth- and twentieth-century commentators have suggested that such a rupture in the unfolding plot—ruptured by an unannounced character

25

and by an unforeseen tone of satire—is a matter of comic relief for the playgoers of 1606 as much as for ourselves and that, moreover, this sudden delay in the action heightens suspense while allowing the actors playing Macbeth and Lady Macbeth to change costumes. Then as now it may also give pause so that playgoers can dwell inwardly on the enormity of the Macbeths' crime.

But in 1606 other responses were also available. A commonplace advanced by Henry Peacham, Thomas Nashe, John Taylor the Water-Poet, and Ben Jonson was that of the crafty farmer who cornered the grain harvests in the early 1600s and then hanged himself when prices tumbled; Joseph Hall's *Virgidemiarum* anticipates this:

> Ech Muck-worme will be rich with lawlesse gaine
> Altho he smother vp mowes of seven years graine
> And hang'd himself when corne grows cheap again (iv.6)

Unforeseen economic conditions in an unstable time could victimize men whose plight was ignored by a seemingly disinterested government.[4] In 1961, John B. Harcourt suggested in *Shakespeare Quarterly* another potent meaning in 1606.

> The farmer has, through his hoarding, acted detrimentally to the well-being of society: private gain has prevailed over the public interest. The equivocator has committed treason; the tailor has stolen from clothing that properly belongs to another. If we consider that Macbeth, driven by a ruthless personal ambition, has committed the ultimate in treason, regicide, and has seized the crown and royal robes that were not his by right, it becomes evident that the Porter's three examples were chosen not at random, but precisely because of their relevance to the dramatic situation.[5]

Nor is Harcourt done. A few pages later he writes,

> In addition, two of the three references to hell-bent souls have distinct scatological innuendoes. "Haue Napkins enow about you, here you'le sweat for't" no doubt serves primarily to establish the temperature of hell; yet *sweat,* a curious verb in this connection, is easily explained through its secondary denotation—the sweating-tub as standard Elizabethan therapy for venereal disease [or perhaps the fatal sweating sickness described by Thomas Nashe in 1594 in *The Unfortunate Traveller*]. "Here you may rost your Goose" carries a triple implication: in this overheated place, a goose may be roasted, a tailor may heat his iron, a syphilitic lesion may be treated. And if Hilda Hulme is correct in her surmise that *tailor* is a euphemism for *penis*, the whole line takes on a consistent underground meaning easily conveyable through gesture: an English "tailor" steals out of a fashionable French garment and contracts the

Gallic pox. Even the phrase "euerlasting Bonfire" (2.3.21; 761) continues in the same frame of reference. Although the term in Shakespeare is generally festive in its implication, as in modern usage, its original sense was *bone-fire, corpse-fire*, so that the image of an everlasting funeral pyre is particularly appropriate to suggest the torment of Hell. Something of this double-sense, half-joking, half-grim, may be noted in Bedford's boastful promise:

Farewell my Masters, to my Taske will I.
Bonfires in France forthwith I am to make,
To keepe our great Saint *Georges* Feast withal.
Ten thousand Souldiers with me I will take,
Whose bloody deeds shall make all Europe quake. (*1 Henry IV,* 1.1.152–56;
164–68)

But whatever Shakespeare's knowledge of the etymological significance of the word, I would argue that *bone-fire* continues the clinical undercurrent of the passage; bone-ache is after all a recognized symptom of the pox, and Pandarus and Thersites [in *Troilus and Cressida*] alone can provide us with adequate supporting references. A heavy, leering emphasis on the part of the Porter could quickly convey this meaning to the audience. (398–99)

Such various signals lay strong claims on the Porter's first speech at the Globe in 1606, yet one tends to modify or cancel another. Such conflicting independent responses, in fact, are more nearly related to Michel Foucault's sense of competing discourses and his associated theory of the individual as the site on which competing discourses play, and are played out. This is why "we should think of the play not as an encoded message but as a highly organized and powerfully generative matrix of meaning, or field of forces," as Graham Bradshaw writes of another Shakespearean play of the period.[6]

Other scenes engender the same multiplicity. As long ago as 1935, Beatrice Daw Brown noted an association between the scene of Lady Macbeth's sleepwalking and a popular tale in 1606 found in the collection known as the *Gesta Romanorum*. She summarizes the Latin *Gesta* (no. 13 in Oesterley's edition) this way: "A woman of queenly station and hitherto of blameless report murders, in the interests of her own security, an innocent person. The blood of her victim falls upon her hand, and although she makes repeated efforts to remove the stain, it remains. Oppressed by the burden of her guilty secret, she finally makes confession to a priest and the stain vanishes." Brown notes that "in each case . . . the victim is a person innocent of wrong-doing against the murderess, and there is a further associative link in the *modus operandi* of the crime—the victim is in both cases killed by the letting of blood."[7] But association would also require dissociation: the familiar story in 1606 features a priest, while Shakespeare's more pagan world has only a doctor quite aware of the state to which Dunsinane has fallen: "infected mindes / To their deafe pillowes will discharge their secrets: / More needs she the Diuine, then the Physitian" (5.1.69–71; 2164–66). In the associative/dissociative *Gesta*, moreover, the blood is from the wounds of Christ instead of Duncan (whose sacrifice may therefore be made holy). This too is the force of the recollected *Gesta*: "She loked on her hande, and it was all blody, that no hote watyre ne couthet ne no nothere licoure myght washe it away." "What, will these hands ne'er be cleane?" asks Lady Macbeth and then answers her own question: "all the perfumes of Arabia will not sweeten this little hand" (5.1.42, 48–49; 2135, 2143–44). Thus by allusion the killing of Duncan is connected with the crucifixion of Christ and his suffering made futile. But Brown notes that the irremovable bloodstain is also associated with the "mark of Cain" (706) and with the bloody hands of Pilate that Shakespeare had also signaled in *Richard III* (1.4.261–63; 1105–7) and *Richard II* (4.1.239–42: 2161–64).

For many of us at the close of the twentieth century, such connections may seem too pious and particularized. But they are among the most likely responses in 1606 when there was mandatory attendance at church each week, the Bible was the most popular household book, and where the first sight across the Thames upon leaving the Globe was that of St. Paul's Cathedral. Indeed, the playgoer at the Globe in 1606 who came to *Macbeth* after attending morning prayer might see Macbeth's regicide as breaking one of the commandments and as violating Mosaic law in a way that guarantees he is a reprobate. Another playgoer, arriving from the Inns of Court to witness the same performance, might see the instruments of death and the bloody hands afterward as sign of justifiable or unjustifiable homicide, while a playgoer who had recently consulted Holinshed would be looking for ways in which the play veers toward and departs from the accepted facts, and, further, might see that the cowardly "milk-soppe" Duncan in Holinshed's portayal of Scottish rulers preceding England's James I is here given more respect while the succeeding Scottish king—known to history as a peacemaker—is very quickly a tyrant. Each playgoer attends the same performance of the same play, and each has sensible, accurate, but quite divergent views of what is being shown onstage, drawing on different if simultaneous cultural forces and ideas. Sensory data are ordered and colored by the imposition of additional attitudes and data (from Scripture, court practices, Holinshed) to isolate different kinds of signals and different neurological processes, registering quite different thoughts, answering differing needs, and charging images with differing meanings that render any single meaning of the play—and even any single dominant meaning of the play—untenable. Such cultural perspectives and cultural practices thus greatly enrich a play like *Macbeth,* both potentially and actually, but they challenge the older critical paradigm that argued for a single, or dominant, meaning for the play.

This sense of a text proposed through a hermeneutics of indeterminacy suggested by the cultural moment—in this case a playtext or a literary dramatic text—is one that calls up, suspends, and disperses cultural beliefs, forces, and practices at a moment in time. This is not the way we have been trained to understand literature. Traditionally, literary and cultural studies have been analogous to the field theory of the sciences: seeing how particles adhere in a radioactive field, for instance, is similar to understanding how images cohere to "make" a poem or play. The result is a kind of unity and organicism that, long before the New Critics—as far back, in fact, as Plato—have been determining factors in our understanding and appreciation of texts such as *Macbeth.* Field theory illuminates such unity by metaphorically combining discrete materials (and referents) as constituents of a greater whole. The view is essentially Kantian, attacking problems and conducting investigations by observing correspondences and by attending to matters of relationship. But, in fact, in Shakespeare's time, words and phrases took on their *own* material and even emblematic meanings; they mattered, as Judith H. Anderson puts it, "as currency and commodity; as vow, memento, inspiration, and sacrament; they matter as graphic character, as icon, as template, as *topos* or 'place.' "[8] Such powerful words could disunify the text too.

The New Critics' use of the instance for the whole, working at first as a particular idea or image for a larger system of simulated reality, has worked remarkably well because it is both resilient and durable. The very richness of potential interactions permits self-organizing systems that are complex, adaptive, and dynamic. In language study, Saussure proposed in his posthumous *Cours de linguistique generale* (1916) that a language system (*la langue*) should not be considered simply as a collocation of discrete semantic units but rather seen as a unified system that supplied meaning through the relational *exchanges* between signs (*les paroles*). Both in its conception and its operation, Sausserian linguistics finds an analogy in Einstein's then-contemporary theory of relativity, which argues for the all-embracing lawfulness that continually manifests itself in the physical universe. Words, like atoms, are objective correlatives, to use Eliot's term,[9] are components of the larger work—they literally "com-pose" it. Such field study places single works in still larger unified fields: for literature, those of period, nation, and genre, as Eliot placed individual talent within a larger Western tradition.[10] These fields of understanding, often nesting within one another, have long reinforced the understanding of a single work of literature—like *Macbeth*—as harmonious, organic, and finally transcendentally singular in pattern, meaning, and effect.

But subsequent neuroscience, which deals with cognitive theory and should have as its purpose the development of a coherent epistemology, has found such field study difficult if not untenable. Neuroscientists such as Erich Harth claim that the physical model of the mind as a place where cognitive functions unify disparate stimuli is based on a false analogy with a person as a single receptor who combines the acts of seeing, hearing, and thinking. Actually, he says, sensory data is widely scattered, and messages picked up from the outside world as images or neural codes are subjected to a wide variety of hierarchies of neural analyzers. A special brain center is concerned with discriminating colors visually perceived; another brain center deals with motions; and still another with shape-specific stimuli. Some neurons or neuron groups signal the presence of a single line segment of a particular orientation, while others seek complex patterns. The eye picks up a complete replica of an outside scene but disperses it among many different neural centers in the brain, deconstructing the field pattern of the initial visual image among many centers before sending it, by alternative, simultaneous routes, to the highest neural levels in the cerebral cortex. Some philosophers interpret this process, Harth writes, as a kind of "theater, a stage, populated by many actors presenting many scripts, all of it unified through the eyes of the observer. . . . But if there is a stage, the single observer of it all is missing."[11] The strong belief that *sensory perceptors* unify and assemble data into thoughts and associations, says Harth, "is nothing but a figment of our imagination" (xxii).

Harth may represent our current thinking in cognitive science, but his basic formulations were already present in the works of Aristotle and developed further by Galen. Galen placed the faculties of the mind in lateral ventricles, or a band across the brain, where several rooms or cells were collapsed into a single space. According to Galen, sensory data is collected in the first room, as the site of common sense, *sensus communis*, where they are integrated across the modalities. Such sensations are capable of yielding images, and he consequently locates fantasy and imagination in the first room too. The second or middle room is the site of cognitive processes, such as reasoning, judgment, and thought, while the third cell or ventricle is where memory is located. In Shakespeare's time, this commonly accepted physiology of the brain was pictured in various books such as the *Margarita Philoosophica* of G. Reische (1503) shown here:

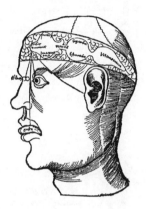

In Reische's drawing, taste, smell, sight, and hearing are all combined in the first ventricle of common sense, alongside fantasy and imagination, before passing through the vermis to the second ventricle, where thought and judgment reside, and so on into memory; the various curved lines within the band may represent cerebral convolutions. Leonardo also popularized this concept of cognition. In 1543 Vesalius, condemning drawings such as Reische's as crude, redrew the brain from the perspective of a horizontal dissection in which the ventricular structures remain detailed and essentially unchanged, although the surrounding cortex is rudimentary.

Not only Shakespeare but also at least some in his audiences shared such an understanding of cognition, for one of his characters in *Love's Labor Lost* remarks on "A foolish extravagant spirit, full of forms, figures, shapes, objects, ideas, apprehensions, motions, revolutions. They are begat in the ventricle of memory, nourished in the womb of pia mater" (4.2.61–64).

Subsequent centuries of cognitive science have only made this basic understanding of the brain's operations more detailed in the way the brain's neurons, as agents of energy, work. We now know that the human brain has approximately 10 billion neurons tightly interconnecting trillions of synapses—perhaps as many as 10 trillion. In a mature brain, a single neuron may communicate with thousands of others simultaneously. Neurons also receive data from other parts of the body, such as the bloodstream. But they are not terminal. They transmit through a neural net that connects them from dendrites and along neural pathways or axons that carry information to the brain.[12]

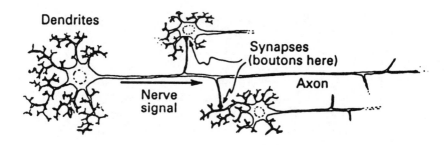

When we put together the incoming sensory pathways with the outgoing motor ones, we have a reliable picture of what the brain does: it functions not unlike a computer in sifting and analyzing data and arriving at appropriate responses. "Thus, if a woman in a red dress were to move across your field of vision," Harth writes, "there would be appropriate activity in the region of V3 where form is detected; in the region V4, which contains feature extractors for color; and in the region V5, which is sensitive to motion. We look in vain for a center where all these bits of information are reassembled into a perceptual whole. The woman in the red dress has disappeared and is replaced by a variety of coded symbols that are scattered over different parts of the brain" (61). On the stage of the Globe in 1606, by analogy, playgoers might see the Porter, hear a heavy and insistent knocking, see the door at the back of the stage from which the Macbeths might at any moment appear, or perceive a stage largely empty.

These images might all be present: sequential as I have had to list them, but also possibly simultaneous, instantaneous, scrambled, or recurring.

Moreover, scrambling may take place in time as well as in space. Because different signals travel at different times and along different pathways as they go from one level to the next, time may be distorted, earlier events may appear later, and vice versa in analogy to Raymond Williams's notion of emergent, dominant, and residual processes occurring simultaneously within a culture. Watching the Porter struggle toward the door, the playgoers at the Globe in 1606 might also, at the same time, be recalling the hasty departure of Macbeth and Lady Macbeth seconds before and perhaps their bloody hands just before that, or they may be concerned instead with who is on the other side of the door, pounding on it, and what they will say once they are admitted to Inverness Castle. Or the playgoers may recall the proleptic witches and assess whether events are proving them right or wrong and, now that their predicted titles have proven likely to be true, whether they will reappear. Playgoers' active receptivity of stimuli, processed neurally and in conjunction with the imagination, may also make Macbeth more attractive, since it is his imagination that has prompted some recent events onstage; or, from another perspective, the present situation with the Porter may recall Macbeth's willful ambition: or, with the comic actions of the Porter, render previous action in the play momentarily irrelevant. Competing but quite independent meanings, then, can be assigned to particular passages or scenes in *Macbeth,* with ideas and materials that could have easily been applied in 1606, along several individualized, discrete neurological pathways: each playgoer could, theoretically (and no doubt did actually), use quite different synapses, in anyone's choice of 10 trillion, from those employed by the person in the next seat. Even without the aid of neuroscience, this seems inescapably true on the surface of it. But it is just as true that the time-honored methods of field study are inadequate to deal with such competing or parallel possibilities and discourses.

I think it is no coincidence that as the modern era has perceived an increasing fragmentation of experience in cognitive science, such postmodernist ideas as deconstruction have emerged as a natural corollary. Profoundly aware of rupture and in search of those deep and hidden structures that might anneal divisions of experience and textual aporias, our turn to Marxist theory of a divided society or Freud's (or Lacan's or Winnicott's) theories of the disintegrated personality has revealed a deep distrust of organicism and an equally deep distrust of reconciliation, of any quick fix. It is every bit as revealing, I think, to witness the indisputable, ineluctable rise of computer technology as just as crucial and necessary a corollary. The notion of databases—which can store indefinitely an unlimited amount of related and totally unrelated material to be recalled on command and, as importantly, in any combination or in several or competing combinations—belies this intellectual revolution, this fundamental shift of paradigms for the humanities that Thomas S. Kuhn located in the sciences with Copernicus, Newton, and Lavoisier. Knowledge is stored now in bytes as well as components. Storage is wholly independent of composition or recomposition, constitution and reconstitution. Assemblages and recall can be virtually random and arbitrary at a real level of activity: creativity through coincidence and through juxtaposition as well as through chosen instances or lexias, the creation of sequential and cognitively relevant bundles of bytes. In the revolution of the late twentieth century, pattern has been displaced by the menu, field study by hypertext.

Just so: hypertext reconfigures the way we conceive of texts, seeing them as reworkings of lexias, such as the *Gesta* in connection with Lady Macbeth's sleepwalking, or in chains of related lexias such as her bloody hands with those of Cain and Pilate. Such linkages—electronic in the case of the computer and hypertext—are not such a stranger to literary criticism as we might first think. "Electronic linking, which provides one of the defining features of hypertext," Gunnar Liestøl observes, "also embodies Julia Kristeva's notion of intertextuality, Mikhail Bakhtin's emphasis upon multivocality, Michel Foucault's conceptions of networks of power, and Gilles Deleuze and Felix Guattari's ideas of rhizomatic, 'nomad thought.' . . . [E]ven thinkers like Hélène Cixous, who seems resolutely opposed to technology, can call for ideas, such as *l'écriture feminine,* that appear to find their instantiation in this new information technology."[13]

Rather than setting out to establish large patterns, as the earlier field study did, the increasingly dominant practice of hypertext is nodal and relational. It focuses on connecting individual pathways of sensory relationships or discrete bits of information following work by Donald Hebb, a Canadian psychologist, who in 1949 demonstrated that we store memories not in individual cells of the brain but in cell assemblies, in strings of cells. Every time an electric current passes from one neuron to another across one of our synapses, it establishes a connection and makes it easier for a current to pass that way another time. As Daniel McNeill and Paul

Freisberger phrase it, "A synapse is like a tollbooth at a bridge, but a special, friendly kind where the toll decreases the more often you cross."[14] "Some synapses," Roger Penrose adds, "are excitatory in nature, with neurotransmitters which tend to enhance the firing of the next neuron and others are inhibitory, tending to suppress the firing of the next neuron. We can refer to the reliability of a synapse in passing the message from one neuron to the next as the strength of the synapse" (125), those frequently used establishing what we term memory. Thus a frequent path will constitute a cell assembly, a memory, allowing the brain to locate quick combinations of understanding for *rectangle, cow,* or *moon.* At a far simpler level, abstract algebra was developing an analogical understanding, moving in ordered sets of recorded data from chain sets, which most of us learned as linear records in elementary algebra classes, to tree sets, which can be represented like this:

Such strings of data (lexias) resemble not only the electronic linking of hypertext, the operation of a menu on CD-ROM, but, just as effectively, Beatrice Daw Brown's chain of sets from the *Gesta* through the Bible to *Macbeth.* (It can also carry us from prostitution to tub to the penis.)

As I was revising this book, Steven Pinker's *How the Mind Works* was published; he makes the same associations:

> The computational theory of mind has quietly entrenched itself in neuroscience, the study of the physiology of the brain and nervous system. No corner of the field is untouched by the idea that information processing is the fundamental activity of the brain. Information processing is what makes neuroscientists more interested in neurons than in glial cells, even though the glia take up more room in the brain. The axon (the long output fiber) of a neuron

is designed, down to the molecule, to propagate information with high fidelity across long separations, and when its electrical signal is transduced to a chemical one at the synapse (the junction between neurons), the physical format of the information changes while the information itself remains the same. And . . . the tree of dendrites (input fibers) on each neuron appears to perform the basic logical and statistical operations underlying computation. Information-theoretic terms such as "signals." "codes," "representations," "transformations," and "processing" suffuse the language of neuroscience.[15]

Somewhat later, Pinker talks of the way we perceive and conceive—the way playgoers at the Globe in 1606 saw and how (if not what) they understood—by using a term common to cognitive science, computers, and hypertext: access.

Access-consciousness has four obvious features. First, we are aware, to varying degrees, of a rich field of sensation: the colors and shapes of the world in front of us, the sounds and smells we are bathed in, the pressures and aches of our skin, bone, and muscles. Second, portions of this information can fall under the spotlight of attention, get rotated into and out of short-term memory, and feed our deliberative cogitation. Third, sensations and thoughts come with an emotional flavoring: pleasant or unpleasant, interesting or repellent, exciting or soothing. Finally, an executive, the "I," appears to make choices and pull the levers of behavior. Each of these features discards some information in the nervous system, defining the highways of access-consciousness. And each has a clear role in the adaptive organization of thought and perception to serve rational decision making and action. (138–39)

Since the patterning of computer programs is modeled upon the way the mind functions, it is no surprise that, by extension, hypertext responds to the same conceptual organization of providing linked sequences that the synapses of the brain are most accustomed to contribute. But the four kinds of access-consciousness that Pinker describes confirm our suspicions that different spectators see or hear (and surely think or recall) somewhat different things. Processing identical information (the appearance of the Porter or witches, Macbeth's knife or Lady Macbeth's burning taper), they will (1) record them differently as images; (2) give them and surrounding images different preferential orders of attention; (3) judge their effects; and (4) combine or recombine them in different ways. Thus by focusing on some images (or sounds) rather than others and omitting some altogether—we never recall fully every scene and every line having seen a play once or even twice—we make important those matters our worn synapses are most accustomed to transporting to "hold in our minds," and we take those matters, as bytes, and make of them connected sequential strings, or lexias, to form our interpretation, to "make" "meaning."

Shakespeare and his contemporaries learned to compose in just this way, by combining bytes of data known as *sententiae*—*loci* or *loci communes* that, as useful phrases, were kept in individual commonplace books, stringing them into orations and even dialogue. The terms were originally not precisely synonymous; *loci* were categories of argumentation, and *loci communes* referred to common sayings such as proverbs. They were stored under abstract headings in commonplace books to use as initiating ideas or illustrations, but the age was one absorbed in list making and data collecting (of dictionaries and encylopedias), with lexical, herbal, and zoological listings among the most frequent. Such lists served as their own retrievable data banks. They could be highly specialized. In his *Treatise of Schemes and Tropes* (around 1550), Richard Sherry divided such bytes into seven "kyndes": common moral sentences; common rules; proverbs; chrias ("short exposicion[s] of any dede or words wyth the name of the author recited"); enthymemes ("sentence[s] of contraries"); aenos (sayings or sentences "taken out of a tale"); and commandments (92–93). Erasmus had recorded many of then in his *Adagia* of 1500, which perpetually grew in subsequent editions, anticipating the later growing editions of essays by Montaigne and Bacon. The *Adagia* was a favorite text in English grammar schools, but so was Erasmus's later work (also of many editions), the *De duplici capia verborum ac rerum,* which built whole speeches out of trains of variations on a single byte or phrase and employed them in sequential lexias. Works were thus linear, accumulative, Erasmus laying the groundwork, Terence Cave tells us, for "a theory of writing as an activity at once productive and open-ended, escaping the limits which formal treatises of rhetoric and dialectic attempt to impose on it."[16] Writing by assemblage was a process analogous to that of hypertext. English humanists who wrote by employing phrases or events from ancient texts—as Shakespeare will turn to chronicles of the ancient Macbeth—saw literature, according to Mary Thomas Crane, "as the collection and redeployment of those fragments and not, in many cases, as the assimilation and imitation of whole works."[17] Indeed, "literary texts were imagined as fields or containers from which fragments of matter could be gathered" (52). Painters also worked in a way we might call hypertextual. According to James Elkins, "Drawings of objects set against indeterminate or empty backgrounds, as was the practice, appear ready to be inserted in paintings whenever a painter might want."[18]

The term *hypertext* was first used by Theodor H. Nelson in 1965, but the origin of the idea is generally credited to Vannevar Bush, whose 1945 essay "As We May Think" provides a possible solution to the scientist's problem of keeping abreast with increasing amounts of research by using a "sort of mechanized private file and library," a machine that could store, annotate, retrieve, and link information: the *memex*.[19] While Bush emphasized the "trail"—the linear ordering of related items from the "maze of materials available," such as Brown assembles data from stories in the *Gesta* and the Bible—he allows side excursions, as in the tree set pictured above. (This allows Brown to move from bloodletting to handwashing.) Such an idea is the basis for Borges's story of a library with no agreed-upon center but with innumerable connected corridors of related books. By analogy, George P. Landow has argued that with hypertext "we must abandon conceptual systems founded upon ideas of center, margin, hierarchy, and linearity"—this is where the Kuhn-like revolution occurs—"and replace them with ones of multilinearity, nodes, links, and networks."[20] Independently, in *S/Z*, Roland Barthes has seen text as composed of blocks of words (or images)—let us call them lexias—electronically linked by multiple chains, paths, or trails in an open-ended, perpetually unfinished textuality. "In this ideal text," says Barthes, "the networks are many and interact, without any one of them being able to surpass the rest"; it is like so many neural pathways transmitting images to and from the cerebral cortex: "this text is a galaxy of signifiers, not a structure of signifieds," and "it has no beginning; it is reversible; we gain access to it by several entrances, none of which can be authoritatively declared to be the main one." (Can we now determine the *single* way to enter into completely understanding—if that were ever possible—the significance of the Porter's scene?) "The systems of meaning," continues Barthes, "can take over this absolutely plural text, but their number is never closed, based as it is on the infinity of language."[21] Foucault, in *The Order of Things,* also points to the "frontiers of a book" that "are never clear-cut" because "it is caught up in a system of references to other books, other sentences: it is a node within a network . . . [a] network of references."[22] Texts, then, may be built (or understood) by chains of lexias (blocks of texts) but also multilinearly and multisequentially (the farmer, tailor, and Porter all equivocate; so does Macbeth in a separate chain of lexias). Such concurrent multiperspectives are likened by George Puttenham in his *Arte of English Poesie* (1579) to various reflections that might be seen in a mirror or glass, "whereof there be many tempers and manner of makinges, as the *perspectiues* doe acknowledge, for some be false glasses and shew thinges otherwise than they be in deede, and others right as they be in deede, neither fairer nor fouler, nor greater nor smaller. There be againe of these glasses that shew thinges exceeding faire and comely, others that shew figures very monstrous & illfauoured" (sigs. D2v–D3).

Bytes of data seemed, like atoms, to be too random; they had to be placed in lexias to gain usefulness. The first major rhetorician to make this point strongly was Peter Ramus. In *La dialectique* of 1555, he set up such strings of data by what he terms method: "Method is the disposition by which, when several things are considered, the first of note is put first, the second second, the third third, and so on. . . . That which is naturally more evident must take precedence in the order and exposition of doctrine, just as causes must come before effects and, in symbols, the general and universal must come before the specific and particular."[23] The same sense of sequentiality as necessary to meaning held true, he claims, for art: "This method of art seems to me to be a long golden chain, such as Homer imagined, and whose links are so interdependent and intertwined, that none can be taken away without breaking the order and integrity of the whole" work created by the poet (3–4), just as playgoers in 1606 would put into sequence a scene's conversation or the progression of a character's thoughts or actions. In 1577 Henry Peacham visualized just such a method in defining rhetorical figures as bifurcating chains in *The Garden of Eloquence:*

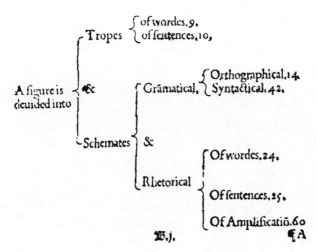

39

transporting into English more complicated menus of thought and understanding that Ramus had earlier published in his *Dialectique:*

Dialectic, 'the art of discussing well,' is divided into:

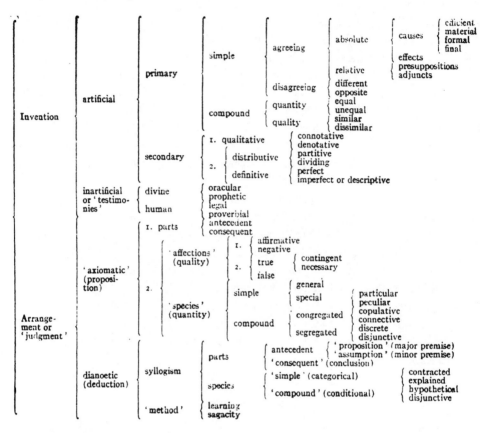

Ramus proceeded to do the same for the other fundamental branches of
learning—grammar and logic—and his followers carried such cognitive
acts into other fields. Dudley Fenner, for instance, in *Certain Godly and
Learned Treatises* (1592), attempts to make baptism comprehensible and
mnemonic in just such a fashion of lexia making:

The persons		Infantes
therfore are	the baptized	Men of discretion
of 2. sortes,		The parents of the Infants.
	others	The whole body of the Congregation.
		(sig. L6v)

40

Still, the most complicated set of lexias developed by one of Shakepeare's contemporaries is the four-page foldout chart that John Dee provides in his preface to H. Billingsley's translations of the geometry of Euclid in 1570 (between sigs. A4v and B1).

Such an understanding of the ways texts function allows each playgoer to receive a performance of *Macbeth* individually and variously at both the visual and verbal levels—spectral and memorial—simultaneously, as playgoers could and doubtless did at the Globe in 1606. The familiar computer practice of navigation is also a meaningful one for hypertextual criticism, as is that of coterminous instantiation. A student using a CD-ROM of *Macbeth,* for example, might watch a film clip at the same time he or she hears a sound track or, on a split screen, reads annotations to the dialogue. If we extend the visual and verbal dimensions of *Macbeth* into other areas of simultaneous understanding—such as the legal and medical ramifications of murder, as we will do in chapter 2—we will approximate the hypertextual practice of criss-crossing, or surfing, "with many thematic dimensions serving as routes of transversal," as Rand J. Spiro and his coauthors put it. "The treatment of an irregular and complex topic *cannot be forced in any single direction* without curtailing the potential for transfer," he writes. "If the topic can be applied in many different ways, none of which follow[s] in rule-bound manner from the others"—as the Porter may be focusing on equivocation, abundant harvests, or syphilis—"then limiting oneself in acquisition to, say, a single point of view or a single system of classification, will produce a relatively *closed* system instead of one that is open to context-dependent variability. By criss-crossing the complex topical landscape, the twin goals of highlighting multifacetedness and establishing multiple connections are attained."[24]

In hypertext, relevant ideas can often be represented best by an associative network, or web, specifying meaning by multiple relationships that move off sequentially in various directions. The hypertext format introduces context but liberates that context from being arranged with a specific ordering; thus hypertext is analogous to the associative networks of neuroscientific understanding, as Ramon y Cajal and Harth have made clear. The center of interest now, as in a moment in *Macbeth,* is not its relationship to the margins, or to the beginning and the ending, but to a web of meaningful interrelations that are mutually enhancing at any nodal point in the play. Such networking comprehension is not new, of course; another common practice in Shakespeare's time was biblical exegesis and biblical typology or the disruption of texts by marginal glosses, what Erasmus referred to as "speaking alongside."

Closer to us in time, Derrida, in *Speech and Phenomena,* uses the principle of assemblage: "The word 'assemblage' seems more apt for suggesting that the kind of bringing-together proposed . . . has the structure of an interlacing, a weaving, or a web, which would allow the different threads and different lines of sense or force to separate again, as well as being ready to bind others together."[25] Thais E. Morgan contends that intertextuality, when translated to signifying practices of such assemblages, refocuses the old triad of author/work/tradition—the triad Eliot based his literary criticism on and on which the German philologist Jakob Burckhardt plotted the Italian Renaissance—to text/discourse/culture, thus releasing the symbols and signs from deterministic patterns and allowing them free play: it moves signs (or words, or symbols, or metaphors), that is, to Bakhtinian dialogic and heteroglossia.[26] Just because assemblages move out from different centers, or foci, like the neural networks having no outer margins because no final terminals (will there ever be a final and ultimate performance or meaning of *Macbeth*?), *the* system is infinitely re-centerable. We can revisit the play with a seminal or central focus on the witches, or on Duncan, or on Lady Macbeth, or Malcolm or Rosse; on the military code, the honor code, or the code of revenge; on success, succession, or surcease; on dangers, swords, or possets. Or we can impose on the play more or less informal meanings of our own.

Partial and imposed meaning is precisely what characterizes the only eyewitness reports of performances of early modern English drama before *Macbeth* that are known to survive. Norman Jones and Paul Whitfield White have recently discovered a manuscript account of a performance of *Gorboduc* staged at the Inner Temple during the Christmas season of 1561. This play—long thought by critics to be a kind of *ur-Lear* concerned with the transfer of rule—was not seen by a contemporary that way at all. Rather, four dumb shows and the play were registered as "whereby was ment that yt was better for the Quene to marye with the L[ord] R[obert] Dudley, the Queen's Master of Horse] than with the K. of Sweden [Eric XIV],"[27] confirming independent observations by Marie Axton that marriage negotiations for the Queen and for Dudley were pressing issues at the Inner Temple revels.[28] The other extant report is recorded by John Manningham in his diary. He saw Shakespeare's *Twelfth Night* at the Middle Temple in February 1602—shortly before the staging of *Macbeth*—but he saw it not as a romance or a story of twins but as a stock Italian farce about a widow being wooed by her servant.[29]

Playgoers at the Globe, then, could enter into an interpretation of the Porter by his many-layered speech, but in 1606 they could just as well enter by observing his costume, listening to his intonations of speech, focusing on what he carries, or realizing that this very Elizabethan English servant has somehow wound up in an early medieval Scottish castle. As an active imaginary, the functioning playgoer and the playwright may merge in using similar cognitive processes. Together or apart, they realize particular dimensions of their shared cultural moment.

In physics, a moment is that fulcrum where many dispersed forces come to equate each other; conversely, in mathematics no moment can be perceptually isolated, since a moment like a single degree on the circumference of a circle is known only by what surrounds it. A cultural moment is a point in time where both obtain: the balance and the surround. Within such a broad framework, we can introduce Vincent B. Leitch's understanding that "the task of cultural criticism is to analyze and assess the social roots, institutional relays, and ideological ramifications of communal events, institutions, and texts" of all kinds, "high" and "low,"[30] and, I would add, the sights and sounds, reading and experience which together constitute a place and time. Certain new understandings are possible if we look at a text like *Macbeth* with such lateral lexias, if, as Pierre Bourdieu has argued in his *Outline of a Theory of Practice,* we see the potential meanings of a text "not as a question of decoding . . . but of restoring its practical necessity by relating it to the real conditions of [and at] its genesis."[31] In effect, such a task reorients and significantly widens any sense of intertextuality, since all areas of a culture's self-expression may be incorporated in conveying any particular part or act of that culture—just as the circumference of a circle helps us to any particular degree on that circumference. Such a task moves outward from a point or moment in the play to related thoughts or images (i.e., lexias) which in sequence initiate meaning for one or more scenes in the play or even the play as a whole.

Kenneth Muir seems to have such a procedure in mind when, in discussing sources for *Macbeth* in the introduction to his New Arden edition, he writes that

> Sir James Fergusson of Kilkerran, Bart., *Shakespeare's Scotland* (1957), p. 6, points out that the Table of all the Kings of Scotland was reprinted in London in *Certeine Matters concerning the Realme of Scotland* (1603). He also suggests that *Macbeth* may have been influenced by some details in the career of James Stewart of Bothwellmuir, who fell from power in 1585 and met his death in 1595. He became Earl of Arran and was spurred on by the ambition of a

wicked wife. The "highland oracles" had shown her that "Gowrie shouid be ruined," but she "helped the prophecy forward as well as she could." Stewart was slain by a kinsman of the Regent Morton

> of whose ruin and death he had been the primary agent; he too tried to avoid the circumstances which it had been prophesied would attend his death; and his "cursed head," like Macbeth's, was cut off by his slayer and set on a pole.

> Stewart's wife was suspected of trafficking with witches and she was described as "a meete matche for such a spouse, depending upon the response of witches, and enemie of all human societie" (Wardlaw MS, 182). Shakespeare may have been ignorant of these matters but they provide further evidence that the atmosphere of the play was not alien to Shakespeare's contemporaries. (xxxvi)

Indeed, these bytes or lexias suggest particular moments in the play by giving them a surround outside it. We can add related lexias of our own by looking at other, related incidents. Closer to home and nearer in time (1606) was the sensational multiple murder by one Walter Calverley, who in an insane fit killed two of his children and wounded his wife, a crime that later (1608) would serve as the basis for another popular play in London, *A Yorkshire Tragedy*. But 1605 was also the time of great storms, of economic unrest, and of the Powder Plot to blow up the royal family, the Crown's officers and the officers of the Established Church, and both houses of Parliament. In 1605 King James saw a play on his own family lineage as well as his claim for the new triple title, heard a debate on the powers of the imagination, and examined young Anne Gunter, who could cast pins from her mouth and who was accusing some of her older neighbors of being witches. In 1606 Edward Forset published *A Comparative Discourse of the Bodies Natural and Politic*, arguing the duties of subjects and the rights of a sovereign according to natural law as well as the laws of human societies, and Jean Bodin's influential treatise on sovereignty was finally translated into English as *Six Bookes of a Commonweal*. On November 22, 1605, a man named Whitehead was tried in Star Chamber for forging letters of the Earl of Salisbury and Sir John Fortescue which had commanded the justices of Essex to remove from the bench Sir Thomas Gardener, but Whitehead was discovered to be a student of magic who had learned in Germany how to conjure and how to baptize a dog; he was sentenced to stand in the pillory at two locations, to lose both his ears, and to suffer perpetual imprisonment. Three days later "certain insolent priests" caused a riot in Southwark.

These are particular instances, but sights and sounds are fundamental constituents of the cultural moment, providing other lexias and sequences of lexias, and although, as Louis A. Montrose warns, "we can have no access to a full and authentic past, a lived material existence, unmediated by the surviving textual traces of the society in question,"[32] such ordered sets of what we can recover, mutually reinforcing, mutually corrective, can nevertheless lead us toward dimensions of *Macbeth* playing at the Globe in 1606. Shakespeare's play opens with the apparition of the weird sisters; in January 1605 Sir Dudley Carleton of London wrote Ralph Winwood of other apparitions and battles: "There was lately an apparition near Berwick of armies and fighting-men on Holydown-hills, which gave the alarm to the town, and frighted those of the Scottish Border,"[33] clearly rumor and gossip, if distant, worth recording. John Chamberlain notes another sight in his letters. In the midst of a sermon by John Milward, chaplain to King James, on April 28, 1605, "a cuckowe came flienge over the pulpit, (a thing I never saw nor heard of before) and very lewdly called and cried out with open mouth";[34] this finds resonance in the "Owle that shriek'd" (2.2.3; 650), disturbing Lady Macbeth at the time of Duncan's death, and in the unnatural "Mowsing Owle" (2.4.13; 939) that disturbs the Old Man and Rosse in the aftermath of that death. Tombs and memorial stones with carved pictures of the dead were commonplace; pictures were also painted on flags and banners to honor those portrayed. But such banners were also used as advertisements under other conditions and to show grotesques in freak shows, something Macduff recognizes when taunting Macbeth: "Wee'l haue thee, as our rarer Monsters are / Painted vpon a pole" (5.8.25–26; 2465–66). Macbeth will be shown not simply as a monster, but as a traitor, an example, a memento mori.

Other visual configurations, other sights, might be recalled by playgoers at the Globe to see *Macbeth* in 1606. There were the visual reminders of the earlier morality plays, for instance: Herod's attempt to murder the Magi and his anxiety to murder all children who might come to rule is reconceived in Macbeth's attempt to murder Banquo and Fleance as well as Macduff's family. Macbeth's anguished remark to Lady Macbeth, "O, full of Scorpions is my Minde, deare Wife" (3.2.36; 1194), his very posture, might remind playgoers at the Globe of the soldier in the play of Pharaoh: "Greatte mystis [of gnats], sir, there is both morn and noyn, / byte us full bytterly." From a different angle of vision, Macbeth's rumination on killing Duncan—"If it were done when 'tis done, then 'twere well, / It were done quickly" (1.7.1–2; 475–76), echoing Jesus to Judas at the Last Supper ("That thou doest, do quickly"; John 13:27)—confirms Lady Macbeth's plans to deny Duncan another day of life. There were properties, too, with clear symbolic value, such as the dagger, which often signaled assassination or (as in *The Spanish Tragedy* and *Doctor Faustus,* both plays in recent revivals) could not mean death so much as despair: it does double duty in Macbeth's hallucination. More specifically, the anonymous *Faire Maid of Bristow,* played at Hampton Court before King James and Queen Anne and published in 1605, shows the murder of a man asleep and an innocent associate smeared with blood to suggest his guilt (sig. D2v). The 1604 Lord Mayor's Show, entitled *The Triumphs of Re-United Brittania,* also printed in 1605, presented a show of eight kings, but the sponsoring Merchant Taylors company, inviting the King to join them, left a vacant place in the chariot for James.

Sounds were also important constituents, and so potential lexias for understanding, of any cultural moment. The German visitor Paul Hentzner records in his *Itinerary* for 1598 that the English are "vastly fond of great noises that fill the ear, such as the firing of cannon, drums, and the ringing of bells, so that it is common for a number of them, that have got a glass in their heads, to go up in some belfry, and ring the bells for hours together," while Thomas Dekker records that in London "hammers are beating in one place, Tubs hooping in another, Pots clinking in a third, water-tankards running at tilt in a fourth" and carts were incessantly clattering on the cobblestone streets; in addition, the buzzing of conversations in many languages in the markets and at Paul's made London into the "Tower of *Babell* newly to be builded up."[35] A bell summons Macbeth to murder Duncan, reinforcing the special significance church bells had as signs of plague and death, while the passing bell was thought to deter demons about someone who was dying—to protect them as well as announcing their death. But bells could be variously interpreted and used in constant stories and rumors. In 1606 word spread through London and nearby shires that hundreds of sheep had been found slaughtered, with nothing taken but tallow and giblets, whole carcasses with their fleece still on them piling up in the pastures.[36] In his addition to the annals of John Stow, Edmond Howes writes about the spring of 1606 that "Satterday, the 22d of March, about halfe an howre before seven a clocke in the morning, was suddenly spread throughout the Court and the Cittie of London, for certaine newes that the King was slaine at Oking."[37] Such rumors were often curtailed by public readings of royal proclamations at the sounding of the herald's bell; on March 22, just such a proclamation by the heralds announced the King's safety. An earlier proclamation, transferring the spoken word into fact and law, announced the accession of James in 1603, explaining the choice of the Privy Council by interpreting James's ancestry and establishing through his present rule in Scotland the fact of empire, "Prologues to the swelling Act / Of the Imperiall Theame" (1.3.128–29; 239–40)—a phrase anachronistic in *Macbeth*—which was further guaranteed by breaking precedent to affix on the proclamation a picture of the *imperial* crown. From Windsor on July 2, 1603, there came yet another warning and command: "It hath bene discouered to Vs by seuerall persons, that one *Anthony Copley*, the yonger brother of one *Copley* that is lately returned from forreine parts into this Countrey, hath dealt with some to be of a conspiracie to vse some violence vpon our Person" (sig. C2), the first of many such proclamations concerning attempts to kill the King.

The sounds of sermons bring ideas and images even closer to *Macbeth* in 1606. Anthony Moxley anticipated both the Powder Plot and the play in a royal sermon at Greenwich on March 26, 1605, and published later that year. It would seem, in fact, to provide an outline for viewing the play:

> Now, when the action of sinne is committed, there doth not presently follow *Hardening*: for, if the heart doe melt and thaw, if the soule doe giue and resolue into teares of repentance for the same, then there is no *Hardening*. But, if from one action committed, wee come vnto another, and so to the custome and continuance in sinne, then are wee snared with the cordes of our owne iniquity, and fettered with this chaine against the generall day of Gods Iudgement.

"At the first it is importable," according to the Reverend Moxley; "it doth strike such an horror into him, that he is in a wofull taking and greiuously tormented," but this is followed by a heaviness of heart, then a lightness resulting from being accustomed to sin, succeeded by a state in which the sinner "is *insensible, past feeling*," and still a fifth state which he calls "*Delectable*": "When men take pleasure in sinne (as *Solomon* saith) *They reioyce* in *doing* euill and *delight in wickedness*" (sig. C4). "If a man giue ouer himselfe vnto sinne, so that it take deep roote in the heart, and be setled in the soule," he concludes, "hee shall neuer be able to pull it vp, nor to arise from the death of sinne" (sig. E2); the consequence is despair, "The way to dusty death" (5.5.23; 2344). In another sermon, published as his *Confvtation of Atheism* (1605), preacher John Dove likened the soul to a candle. He tells of a preacher who "caused a candle to bee lighted and brought it to the Table, hee blew it out, and sayd: Your soule is no more then the flame of that candle, you see an ende of that, it is blowen out, and so shall it be with your soule when you die" (sig. I4v). Lady Macbeth's flickering taper is a visual sign of her endangered life, too. It finds further resonance in Banquo's earlier remark that "There's Husbandry in Heauen, / Their Candles are all out" (2.1.4–5; 577–78).

Quite other sets of lexias available in 1606 may be found in the printed records, books, pamphlets, and even broadsides and ballads—the most ephemeral of publications and now largely lost. *A Kalender, or Table, comprehending the effect of all the Statutes that haue beene made and put in print* was published in 1606, and for playgoers of that year, several laws might serve as an ordered sequence of lexias alongside plays. In 25 Edward 3.2, for instance, still in force, we read in part, "It is high Treason to compass or imagine the death of the King, the Queene his wife, or of their eldest Sonne and heire" (sig. 3Y6v). A later statute or related lexia added, "Concealment or keeping secret of any high Treason, shalbe deemed & taken onely misprision of Treason" (sig. 3Z1). By such laws, not only Macbeth and Lady Macbeth, but also Banquo, Malcolm, and Macduff are traitors in Shakespeare's play. The book also contained "An Acte against Coniuration, Witchcrafte and dealinge with evill and wicked Spirits" renewed in 1603 as 1 James c.22. It applied to those who "use, practise or exercise any Invocation or Conjuration, of any evill and wicked Spirit, or shall consult, covenant with, entertaine employ feede or rewarde any evil and wicked Spirit to or for any intent or purpose; or take up any dead man woman or child out of his her or theire grave, or any other place where the dead bodie resteth, or the skin bones or any other parte of any dead person, to be imployed or used in any manner of Witchcrafte Inchantment Charme or Sorcerie wherebie any person shalbe killed destroyed wasted consumed pined or lamed in his or her bodie, or any parte thereof,"[38] joining Macbeth with the three sisters in his practices in 4.1. Other statutes in the cultural moment of 1606 concern the succession, descent, and right of the Crown (1); Jesuits, seminary priests, and recusants (4); the punishment of rogues, vagabonds, and sturdy beggars (7); and inordinate haunting and tippling in inns, alehouses, and other victualling houses (9).

Books served as identification and sometimes as pedigree. In the popular opinion of 1606 in London, John Knox was the best-known Scotsman, standing for stout and conservative Calvinism. His authority came partly from his writing, including the *Book of Discipline* that formed the basis of the Scottish Church. In addition, his *History of the Reformation in Scotland* is a personal history best known in 1606 for his accounts of interviews he held with Mary Stuart, James's mother, in which he argued that the church was independent of secular governmental authority and that his own conscience presented to him the superior law. So popular a preacher was Knox, and so powerful, that Mary could not make an accusation of treason stick: he acted out the theories of popular resistance promoted by other Scottish historians—John Major and Hector Boece before him, and George Buchanan, James's first tutor, after. Knox also held that God and the Bible argued women rulers were unnatural; he had in mind Mary Stuart herself, Mary Guise of France, and Mary Tudor of England, all of them despised, all of them Catholic. His attack was published in his *First Blast of the Trumpet against the Monstrous Regiment of Women* (1558), unfortunately released just after Mary Tudor's death. Taken by the English to refer, therefore, to Elizabeth I, it had by 1606 become a notorious if legendary book. But its argument outlines the career of Lady Macbeth which Shakespeare first supplies to that Scottish historical narrative. Knox opens with his premise: "To promote a woman to beare rule, superioritie, dominion or empire aboue any realme, nation, or citie, is repugnant to nature, contumelie to God, a thing most contrarious to his reueled will and approued ordinance, and finallie it is the subuersion of good order, of all equitie and iustice" (sig. B1), adding, "For their sight in ciuile regiment, is but blindnes: their strength, weaknes: their counsel, foolishnes: and iudgement, phrensie, if it be rightlie considered" (sig. B1v). He goes on,

> Nature, I say, doth paynt them furthe to be weake, fraile, impacient, feble, and foolishe: and experience hath declared them to be vnconstant, variable, cruell, and lacking the spirit of counsel and regiment. And these notable faultes haue men in all ages espied in that kinde, for the wiche not onlie they haue remoued women from rule and authoritie, but also some haue thought that men subiect to the counsel or empire of their wyues here vnworthie of all public office. For thus writeth Aristotle in the seconde of his Politikes: what difference shal we put, saith he, whether that women beare authoritie, or the husbandes that obey the empire of their wyues, be appointed to be magistrates? For what insueth the one, must nedes folowe the other, to witte, iniustice, confusion and disorder. . . . Yes, and some haue killed with crueltie their owne husbandes and children. (sigs. B2, B4v)

Knox suggests the pattern of Lady Macbeth's life in his pattern of the woman ruler, moving from unaturalness to cruelty and ending in madness ("phrensie").

George Buchanan's Latin account of Scottish history, circulating as contraband in London in 1606, diverges from Knox in its specificity and from Holinshed in its narrative. Buchanan observes that both Duncan and Macbeth have hereditary claims to the throne of Scotland since both are sons-in-law of Malcolm II. The rule first passes to Duncan, but he is a weak king—like Shakespeare's Duncan, and Holinshed's—and his excessive clemency, and naïveté, exacerbated by his nomination of his own son Malcolm as his successor in spite of the customary law of tanistry, bring on Macbeth's murder of him. But this is a death both known and sanctioned by the Scottish nobility because Macbeth, through his mother, has greater claim on the throne and holds the promise of being a stronger and more effective ruler. The reason for Macbeth's ascendancy, then, is not ambition but ability. Yet after ten years of peaceful rule, Macbeth grows increasingly tyrannical—just as Buchanan said would happen with primogeniture—and he is deposed in favor of Malcolm III, with the help of disappointed nobility. This too smacks in time of tyranny for Buchanan; he remarks that Malcolm sealed his power by appointing a number of his allies to new positions with, Buchanan says, "barbarous" titles, such as James I was doing in London in 1606. In fact, the title of "thanus," Buchanan writes, sometimes gave way to the title of "Stuartus." At this point of slander against James's hereditary line, Buchanan's strongly polemical purpose finally surfaces: he wrote his history as an ideological justification for the Presbyterian coup d'état that deposed Mary Queen of Scots in favor of her year-old son, James. For Buchanan, however, it meant potential parallels between the story of Macbeth and the story of Mary Stuart—and was the stuff of London rumor and gossip.

If we choose contemporary histories as lexias, which in sequence instantiate meaning, Buchanan's detailed double account of Mary, in his *Rerum Scoticarum Historia* (Book 18) and in his *Detectio Mariae Reginae Scotorum*, provides the portrait of an evil regicide that may well have contributed to playgoers' sense of the character and significance of Lady Macbeth. This in turn might suggest, in 1606, that the royal play of *Macbeth* had behind it (as Ralegh's later *History of the World* would in 1616) persons nearer to hand. Buchanan's story of Mary, Bothwell, and Darnley (James's father) bears some lexial resemblance to the assemblage of Lady Macbeth, Macbeth, and Duncan. Buchanan's Latin *Historia* recounts how Mary's husband, Henry Darnley, not yet fully recovered from illness (probably syphilis) at Stirling Castle, was brought at her direction to Edinburgh on a litter. With the aid of her lover, the Earl of Bothwell, she prepared for him a house called Kirk o' Fields which was then deserted, standing next to the city walls not far from the palace. It was, says Buchanan, in "a desolate place between two ruined churches, where neither outcry nor disturbance could be overheard."[39] The Queen visited him often during his continuing illness so as to avoid any suspicions, according to Buchanan, and set about "spies on all his sayings and doings" (111).

The Queen and Bothwell then turned all their attention to the murder-plot, and how they could transact the business most secretly. The Queen pretended love for her husband, and oblivion of past offences. She ordered her own bed to be brought from the palace and placed in the chamber below that of the King. There she lay for several nights, sitting up late in conversation with him. Meanwhile she did not cease to think up every method possible of turning the blame of the crime, once it had been committed, on her brother James and the earl of Morton. For when those two, whom she feared and hated on account of their integrity and authority, had been eliminated, everything else, she assured herself, would arrange itself. (113)

On Sunday, February 9, 1567,

The Queen, who had planned the murder for that day, wanted to seem wholly at her ease, so she attended the marriage of Bastien, one of her singers, during the day, in the palace. Having spent the evening in games and celebration, she came to visit her husband with a fairly large following. There she spoke with him, more cheerfully than usual, for a few hours. She often kissed him, and she gave him a ring. After the Queen had gone away, the King talked over the events of the day with the few servants who remained. Among other remarks calculated to raise his spirits, he remembered a few words which somewhat spoiled his enjoyment. For, either because her expectation of accomplishing the crime made her unable to conceal her exultation, or because the words slipped out unintentionally, she let fall the remark that it was about that time last year that David Riccio had been murdered. No one liked this unmeet recollection of past crime [for Darnley had been implicated in the killing of her private secretary, out of jealousy], but the night was far spent, and the next morning was to be devoted to games and amusements, so they went quickly off to bed.

Meanwhile in the room below gunpowder had been placed to blow up the house. Everything seemed to have been arranged carefully and cunningly, but they let circumstance reveal no trivial indication of the crime. For the bed in which the Queen had slept for some nights was carried away, and an inferior one substituted in its place—amid such notorious extravagance, they grudged a trifling sum of money! In the middle of the evening's proceedings, the Frenchman Paris, one of her rascally servants, entered the King's chamber and placed himself, silently, so that he could be seen by the Queen. That was the signal agreed upon, that everything was ready. As soon as she saw Paris, the Queen pretended that she had just remembered Bastien's wedding, and blamed herself for her negligence, because she had not gone to the masked ball that evening as she had promised, and had not seen the bride to her bed, as was the custom. With this remark she rose and went home. On her return to the palace, she spoke for a considerable time with Bothwell. He was at length dismissed. He returned to his own chamber, changed his clothes, put on a military cloak, and passing through the guard, returned to the town with a few attendants. Two other groups of the conspirators came to the appointed place by different routes. A few of them went into the King's chamber, the keys of which, as I said before, were in their possession. They fell upon him as he slumbered, and strangled him, along with one of his servants, who slept on a little bed nearby. They carried the strangled bodies through a postern which they had made through the town wall for this purpose and into an adjacent garden. Then they set fire to the gunpowder, and blew up the house from its foundations, with so great an explosion that several neighbouring houses were shaken, and people who slept in the furthermost parts of the town were awakened, bewildered and alarmed. After the crime, Bothwell left by way of the ruined town walls, and returned by a different route from that by which he had come, through the guard of the palace. . . . Bothwell returned home, and with feigned amazement carried the news to the Queen, who went to her chamber, and for much of the next day she lay in deep and tranquil sleep.

Meanwhile rumours had been spread by the regicides to the effect that the King had been murdered by means of Moray and Morton. (115–16)

Buchanan says that "the story was carried to the English border before dawn" (117), but people thought that James's mother had killed his father.

The nobles at court decided to give him a rich and honourable funeral. But the Queen caused him to be buried by porters during the night, without funeral honours. And the general indignation was greatly increased because he was buried near to the grave of David Riccio, as if she offered her husband's corpse as an appeasement to the manes of that foul villain.

Two incidents occurred at this time which I think are worth relating here. One of them happened a short time before the murder. James Loudon, a gentleman of Fife, who had long lain stricken with fever, about noon on the day before the King's death raised himself up in his bed in alarm, and loudly called on those present to come to the aid of the King, "for the murderers are upon him!" Then a little after he cried in a mournful voice, "You are too late: he is dead!" And it was not long after this before he himself gave up the ghost. The other incident happened at the very time of the murder. Three familiar friends of the Earl of Atholl, relations of the King and men of integrity and rank, dwelt not far from the King's lodging. As they were sleeping in the middle of the night, someone seemed to approach Dugald Stewart, who lay next to the wall, and drew his hand lightly over his beard, and so awakened him, saying, "Arise, for they bring you violence!" He sat up suddenly, and was musing on his vision when all at once another cried from the other bed, "Who is kicking me?" Dugald replied, "The cat, perhaps, who walks by night." Then the third man, who had not yet been roused, suddenly threw himself from his bed on to his feet, asking, "Who struck me on the ear?" As he spoke, a figure was seen to go out of the door, making some noise. And while they spoke together of what they had seen and heard, they were all alarmed by the noise of the destruction of the King's house. (118–19)

Later, Buchanan adds wryly, "a certain tailor, who was altering the King's clothes to suit Bothwell, was bold enough to remark that it was only right, and well in accordance with the custom of the land, for the clothes of the deceased to be given to the executioner" (122). Like Macbeth, Bothwell is dressed "in borrowed Robes" (1.3.109; 215). Although copies of Buchanan's *Historia* were known to be circulating in Latin throughout England in the 1590s and on into James's reign, in 1584, two years after Buchanan's death, this work along with Buchanan's political philosophy was censured in the Scottish Parliament as "not meet to remain for records of truth to posterity," and the owners of the printed copies were required to turn them in to be purged of "the offensive and extraordinary matters among the contents."[40]

Although parallels are far from exact, the ways in which Mary Stuart enacts the kind of assassinations that tainted the reputation of her Scottish predecessor James I elongates the story of Macbeth into a more generalized story of Scotland—and with Mary Stuart involved, one which is also very much concerned with Lady Macbeth. Naomi Liebler argues that the play is deliberately incomplete at two points. Donalbain disappears from the play after the murder of Duncan with an ominous speech—"The neere in blood, the neerer bloody" (2.3.140–41; 915)—and the play ends with Scotland about to be annexed to England.[41] "Let us add one final twist," says Michael Hawkins, proposing his own reordering of these particular lexias: "Those who left a performance of *Macbeth* interested enough to pursue the study of Scottish history would soon discover that Malcolm's son is murdered by the Donalbain who disappeared to Ireland in Act II. The despised 'kerns and gallowglasses' of the Celtic reaction thus got some revenge on the Anglo-Scottish political establishment, but not even Shakespeare would have dared to show that in the decade of the Plantation of Ulster."[42] The time may have thought otherwise. "The players do not forbear to represent upon their stage the whole course of this present time," George Calvert writes around 1606, "not sparing either king, state, or religion, in so great absurdity, and with such liberty, that anybody would be afraid to hear them."[43]

The year 1606 was characterized by books on history and political theory that provided sequenced meaning departing from the play only to lead back to it, but the bookstalls in Paul's Churchyard offered a variety of fare for a public growing in literacy. There were numerous publications of strong religious controversy, following on the heels of the Powder Plot. William Perkins's *Whole Treatise of the Cases of Conscience* was issued by Cambridge University Press, as was an edition of his book on predestination. There was Lucas Osiander's *Manvell Or briefe volume of Controuersies of Religion between the Protestants and the Papists,* Oliver Ormerod's satirical *Pictvre of a Papist,* and Matthew Sutcliffe's *Abridgement Or Svruey of Poperie,* "Containing," according to the title page, "a compendious declaration of the grounds, doctrines, beginnings, proceedings, impieties, falsities, contradicting absurdities, fooleries, and other manifold abuses of that religion [in a way that would do honor to Ramus], which the Pope and his complices doe now maintaine, and wherewith they haue corrupted and deformed the true Christian faith, Opposed vnto Matthew Kellisons Suruey of the new Religion, as he calleth it, and all his malicious inuectiues and lies." A number of other books dealt with medicine. There is a translation of Christoph Wirsung's *General Practise of Physicke* and Thomas Cogan's *Hauen of Health,* where Cogan notes that one thing "to be regarded in preseruing of health, is Sleepe, which after *Aristotle* is defined to be *an impotencie of the senses.* Because in sleepe the senses be vnable to execute their office, as the eye to see, the eare to heare, the nose to smell, the mouth to tast, and all sinowy parts to feele. So that the senses for a time may seeme to be tyed or bound, and therefore sleepe is called of some *the bonde of the senses*" (sig. P4). But a short time later he adds that sleep is "the Image of death" (sig. P4v). William Ram's translation and condensation of the medical work of Dr. Reinhert Dodson, called *Rams little Dodson,* defines henbane—Banquo's "insane Root, / That takes the Reason Prisoner" (1.3.84–85; 186–87?)—as one of the "simples and plants [that] are not to be taken into the body, without great *skill* and good correction, by the learned and skilfull Phisicions" (sig. A3v). He also supplies several treatments for the King's Evil when the Royal Touch is unavailable, alluded to at *Macbeth* 4.3.146–56; 1978–88 (sig. O6v; cf. sig. M4v). At the same time, the playgoer who frequented the bookstalls could see or purchase *The Ivdgement, or exposition of Dreames* by Artimodorus, who notes that oracles can distract (sig. A8v), and *A Profitable Booke, declaring diuers aprooued Remedies to take out spots and staines in Silkes, Veluets, Linnen and Woollen Clothes.*

Still another chain of lexias to provide *Macbeth*'s primary meaning for those who went to the Globe in 1606 were other plays staged publicly and privately in the early years of James's reign. Fulke Greville's *Mustapha* (written in the 1590s, staged in the early 1600s, and printed in 1609) has in Soliman's wife, Rossa, who persuades her husband that their son threatens his life and then kills Soliman's daughter Camena, declare Achmat a traitor; she is in many ways a simpler version of Lady Macbeth. Ben Jonson's *Sejanus,* the last play in which we have records that Shakespeare acted, performed in 1603 and printed in 1605, concerns the corrupt, tyrannical ways in which Sejanus rises to power during the absence of Tiberius and how, in the end, he is outmaneuvered and killed by Macro: in outline, a coarser version of the outline of *Macbeth.* Thomas Kyd's *First Part of Hieronomo* was printed in 1605; it deals with an absolutist government that leads to corruption; a hired murderer makes an honest mistake because another man wears the victim's disguise, and he allows Andrea to flee much as Fleance seizes the opportunity to take flight in *Macbeth. Part II* of Christopher Marlowe's *Tamburlaine,* reprinted (and probably restaged) in 1605, has bloody and savage battles similar to the ones reported in *Macbeth* 1.2, overvaulting ambition in Tamburlaine, a study of conscience in his son Calyphas, the sudden death of Zenocrate after a talk with her physician (cf. *Macbeth* 5.1), and Tamburlaine's last dogged fight to the end. "Murdrous fates throwes all his tryumph downe," says the prologue (sig. A2). Shakespeare used directly the anonymous *True Chronicle History of King LEIR* (printed in 1605) as a source for his own play of *Lear,* but there are also moments that give pause: Ragan, for instance, adumbrates Macbeth—"I feele a hell of conscience in my brest" (sig. H4v)—and Lady Macbeth: "A shame on these white-liuered slaues, say I, / That with fayre woris so soone are ouercome. / O God, that I had bin but made a man; / Or that my strength were equall with my will!" (sig. I1). In Shakespeare's *Richard III,* Clarence tells Richard at the play's opening that the King "harkens after prophecies and dreames" (sig. A2v), and Gloster talks with his executioners of Clarence as Macbeth talked with his chosen murderers of Banquo (sig. C3v), likewise suffering the untrammeled consequences:

> *Cla.* Oh, I haue past a miserable night,
> So full of vgly sights, of gastly dreames,
> That as I am a Christian faithfull man,
> I would not spend another such a night,
> Though t'were to buy a world of happie dayes,
> So full of dismall terror was the time . . .
> My soule is heauie, and I faine would sleepe. (sigs. C4–C4v)

The scene of Lady Macduff and her son (4.2) may have had its original in Shakespeare's conception of the Duchess of Yorke with the two children of Clarence (2.l): young Yorke's jesting about weeds and herbs is similar to Lady Macduff's discussion with her son about thieves and traitors (sigs. D4v–E1). And the ghosts of royalty and nobility who appear to Richard on Bosworth Field (5.3) stand behind the show of eight kings in *Macbeth* (4.1). Yet the play most like *Macbeth* is *Julius Caesar*, which had shortly preceded it. After much inner conflict and a nightmarish period of anticipation, which is described in very similar terms in the soliloquies of Brutus (2.1.61–69; 682–90) and Macbeth (1.3.137–42; 248–55), each, about halfway through the play, murders the ruler of the state who had especially loved and favored him. This violation of the body politic leads to unnatural and prodigious happenings in the macrocosm. Both plays are about that act and futile attempts to trammel up the consequences; both involve soothsayers or witches, dreams, and ghosts, and a willed death that is, literally and figuratively, suicidal.

Other lexias could conspire for playgoers then and for us, building chains of referential meaning, now. Samuel Daniel's *Certain Small Poems, Lately Printed* (1605) includes his closet drama *Cleopatra*. In act 2 we read,

> If we vnto ambition tend,
> Then doest thou draw our weakenesse on,
> With vaine imagination
> Of that which neuer hath an end . . .
> Ambition is a Vulture vile.
> That feedes vpon the heart of pride:
> And finds no rest when all is tride.
> For worlds cannot confine the one,
> Til other, lists and bounds hath none.
> And both subuert the minde, the state,
> Presure destruction, enuie, hate. (sig.2E2)

For the cultural moment was keenly attuned to the destructive power of the imagination. The Geneva Bible in many households, especially the Old Testament, always uses *image* and *imagination* as evil, as in "When the Lord sawe that the wickedness of man was great in the earth, and all the imaginations of the thoughts of his heart were onely euill continually, (6) Then it repented the Lord, that hee had made man in the earth, and he was sorie in his heart" (sig. A3). William Lambarde points to the legal force of the imagination when he records that the Tudor law of treason—perhaps the very *donée* of *Macbeth* for playgoers in 1606—was "imagining and compassing of the death of a king." Montaigne's essay on the force of the imagination in Florio's 1603 translation collates. In writing of Gallius

Vibius, he notes that "Some there are, that through feare anticipate the hangmans hand; as he did, whose friends having obtained his pardon, and putting away the cloth wherewith he was hood-winkt, that he might heare it read, was found starke dead upon the scaffold, wounded only by the stroke of imagination."[44] Such resonances seem uncanny. "Wee sweat, we shake, we grow pale, and we blush at the notions of our imaginations; and wallowing in our beds we feele our bodies agitated and turmoiled at their apprehensions, yea in such manner, as sometimes we are ready to yeeld up the spirit" (97). Lady Macbeth is thus encapsulated too. He continues:

> We cannot command our haire to stand an end, nor our skinne to startle for desire or fears. Our hands are often carried where we direct them not. Our tongue and voice are sometimes to seeke of their faculties, the one loseth her speech, the other her nimblenesse. . . . It is very likely that the principall credit of visions, of enchantments, and such extraordinary effects, proceedeth from the power of imaginations, working especially in the mindes of the vulgar sort, as the weakest and seeliest, whose conceit and beleefe is so seized upon, that they imagine to see what they see not. (104–5, 99)

Peter De Loier's *Treatise of Specters or straunge Sights, Visions, and Apparitions appearing sensibly unto men* (1605), translated from the French and printed in London by Valentine Simmes, also seems to have been a communally shared reference. De Loier defines first "what a Specture is": "*A Specter, or Apparition, is an Imagination of a substance without a Bodie, the which presenteth it selfe sensibly vnto men, against the order and course of nature, and maketh them afraid* . . . the Imagination hath sometimes taken the name of a Specter, or strange sight: of a Phantosme, & of a visiō . . . a Phantosme . . . is an imagination of thinges which are not indeede, and doth proceede of the senses being corrupted" (sigs. B1–B1v, 2B4v). What De Loier proceeds toward is not simply a physical, but a medical description of illnesses of the imagination. One especially telling moment, which some playgoers might have shared with Shakespeare, is this: "But this is certaine, that there be some glasses which will represent seaven or eight faces, of which some will seeme dead, and others will shew as if they were going out of the glasse, not without great woonder" (sig. Q2).

So, too, others. *The Second Part of the French Academie* by Pierre de la Primaudaye was published in 1605, and there some of the playgoers at the Globe might have read

> that in trueth, *fantasie* is a very dangerous thing. For it bee not guided and brideled by reason, it troubleth and moueth all the sence and vnderstanding, as a tempest doeth the sea. For it is easily stirred vp not onely by the externall

sences, but also by the complexion and disposition of the body. Heereof it proceedeth that euen the spirits both good and bad haue great accesse vnto it, to stirre it either to good or evill, and that by meanes vnknowen to vs. (sig. K6v)

His cautions are even more resonant with Lady Macbeth: "This facultie of the fantasie is sudden, and so farre from stayednes, that euen in the time of sleep it hardly taketh any rest, but is alwaies occupied in dreaming & doting, yea euen about those things which neuer haue bene, shalbe, or can bee" (sig. K6). Francis Bacon provides still another 1605 lexia. In *The Twoo Bookes of Francis Bacon: Of the proficiencie and aduauncement of Learning, diuine and humane* he lists the three distempers of learning: "The first fantastical learning: The second contentious learning, & the last delicate learning, vaine imaginations, vaine Altercations, & vain affectatiõs" (sig. E2v). The third is, of course, the most apposite for *Macbeth:*

For the third vice or disease of Learning, which concerneth deceit or vntruth, it is of all the fowlest; as that which doth destroy the essentiall fourme of knowledge; which is nothing but a representation of truth; for the truth of being, and the truth of knowing are one, differing no more than the direct beame, and the beame reflected. This vice therefore brauncheth it selfe into two sorts; delight in deceiuing, and aptnesse to be deceiued, imposture and Credulitie: which although they appeare to be of a diuers nature, the one seeming to proceede of cunning, and the other of simplicite; yet certainely, they doe for the most part concurre. (sig. F2)

Most importantly and finally, he remarks, "High and vapourous imaginations, in steede of a laborious and sober enquirie of truth shall beget hopes and Beliefes of strange and impossible shapes" (sig. 2H4v).

Such lexias are always already performative, theatrical, deconstructive, and infinitely reconstitutive. Rather than pull the play together into a singular unity, they take us off in tree-shaped sets of our own making. There is no way to dismiss the textual aporias that are there in our received text of *Macbeth*—and that may or may not have been there in similar fashion in 1606—but we can find as reliable guides to 1606 those cultural pressures, cultural artifacts, and cultural practices that together make up the cultural moment that spoke to *Macbeth* and that *Macbeth* spoke to. We will now investigate various chains of hypertextual lexias that will show us how before turning, in chapter 3, to a poetics for the computer age of hypertext, a poetics of the multiple and indeterminate.

CHAPTER TWO

CULTURAL PRACTICES

We cannot separate literature and art from other kinds of social practice, in such a way as to make them subject to quite special and distinct laws. They may have quite specific features as practices, but they cannot be separated from the general social process.

Raymond Williams

My main assumption is that, as Shakespeare wrote the plays for a definite audience at a definite point of time, we cannot hope to understand them fully without asking first and foremost what they would mean for that audience. A dramatic poet appeals first and foremost to the mentality of his audience and it is through the mentality of his audience that his plays must consequently be interpreted.

Lilian Winstanley

Of his time, Shakespeare was also in time; his plays bear witness to many historical moments, and to the forces of historical change. To acknowledge this unwieldy complexity of the historical is to begin to understand the meanings of history in and for his drama.

Douglas Bruster

All events become part of the conditions for producing texts.
Meredith Skura

"Great drama," Curtis C. Breight writes, "is energized by cultural turbulence, not quiesence":[1] life in London in 1606 was troubled and troubling. Stability had never really returned after the great threat of the armada from Spain in 1588; although strong winds and good fortune had defeated that Catholic invasion, another had been under active preparation in Spain in the 1590s. King James's right to be ruler—to be absentee ruler, since he spent more time at his hunting lodges than at court—was still being questioned. Spies were everywhere. "The peace of the City streets was disturbed by repeated scuffles between apprentices and gentle-men's servants," Ian Archer tells us; "Londoners rioted against the Inns of Court, the pretensions and immunities of whose denizens angered them; and during the 1590s the aldermen repeatedly had occasion to complain about the reluctance of gentlemen to contribute towards extraordinary military rates." By the time John Stow completed his *Survay of London* in 1598, Archer continues,

> the farm at the Minories had been let out for garden plots, while the bedrid-den people of the cottages of Houndsditch had been replaced by "brokers, sellers of old apparel, and such like." It was typical of what he saw as a collapse of community spirit. . . . Stow also mourned the damage done to the physical fabric of the City over the course of his lifetime, the result of the twin pressures of population growth and the Reformation. The capital's growing population had been housed by a combination of the subdivision of existing properties and the proliferation of alleys. As the nobles moved away to the more fashionable west, the once grand mansions of nobles had been con-verted into petty tenements. Thus Suffolk House in Southwark had been sold to merchants who pulled it down, "and in place thereof builded many small cottages of great rents to the increasing of beggars in that borough." Worcester House and the Coldharbour underwent a similar fate. . . . The physical space of Stow's London is furthermore hallowed by the dead, not simply by the 1,775 worthy persons whose monuments Stow, astonishingly, identifies by name (the Hebrew Bible, for comparison, contains 1,426 named personages), but also by the "innumerable bodies of the dead" interred, in times of plague, in the mass graves of the suburbs.[2]

One-fifth of Londoners died in the plague of 1603, but before that several years of dearth and an incredible year of harvest had strained the economy, leaving many homeless and many others without sufficient food, work, or income. Bethlem Hospital, for the mentally ill, was always filled. The congested London streets were thronged with pickpockets and other petty criminals; and in November 1605 the Powder Plot to blow up the royal family, as well as all the leaders in government and the church, had very nearly succeeded. The world seemed at sixes and sevens.

The Powder Plot reopened the question of the Stuart succession. There had been a rumor—existing well into the seventeenth century—that Henry IV had never been certain of his right to the crown of England.[3] Perhaps the foreign James had even less claim. In the years immediately preceding 1603, Howard Nenner comments,

> the king of Scots was clearly right to be apprehensive. As long as there was no agreement on the critically important question of how the right to succeed

Elizabeth was to be determined—whether by some principle of heredity, by Henry VIII's will, by an eleventh-hour designation by the queen, or by an equally belated act of parliament—there would be the dangerous possibility of the queen's dying without a known and certain successor, and of a determination having to be made by force of arms. (22)

There was considerable anxiety that Elizabeth I would not name her successor, as Peter Wentworth had been requesting in Commons since the 1580s; his *Pithie Exhortation to her Majestie for Establishing Her Successor to the Crowne,* written in 1587, was published in 1598, long after his death. Wentworth charged that if Elizabeth failed without further delay to name an heir to the throne, her subjects could be in "extreme confusion and desolation."[4] In 1595, R. Doleman, the pseudonym for the Jesuit Robert Persons, published *A Conference About the Next Succession to the Crowne of Ingland.* Working for a Catholic succession that would put the Spanish Infanta Isabella on the throne of England, Doleman meant to raise troublesome questions in his book. An eminent Scottish scholar, Sir Thomas Craig, in *The Right of Succession to the Kingdom of England* (1602), made the case for James's hereditary right to the crown of England. Both Persons and Craig agreed that if a decision was not reached before Elizabeth's death, there would be civil unrest, civil dissension, and quite possibly civil war. According to Nenner, Henry Hooke argued in 1601 that God could ultimately direct the Queen "to nomynate that person, whome in all good conscience shee might designe and make knowne unto her people" as her "right and lawful heire." Others, however, were not at all sure that her nomination would or could settle the matter. Wentworth specifically questioned the wisdom of the Queen's *selecting* her successor, citing the precedents of Henry VIII and Edward VI as the "seede of horrible miseries" (Nenner 20). Sometime after 1650 George Lawson would still look back and find it questionable whether in a hereditary monarchy the Queen had the right to nominate, or the Privy Council to proclaim, a successor to the throne.

We can measure to some degree the breadth of James's interest in the English throne. Through the late 1590s he had secretly allied himself with Essex, but given the volatility of Essex's own career, he seems also to have attempted to make alliances with Spain and surely began courting Cecil. By 1599 there were rumors in England that Scottish war preparations, sometimes thought to have a Danish connection because of James's marriage, were well advanced. The Salisbury Papers contain a letter from G. Coppin to Cecil in August 1599 which claims that it is Coppin's "duty to advertise you of the strange rumours and abundance of news spread abroad in the city, and so flying into the country, as there cannot be laid a more dangerous plot to amaze and discourage our people, and to advance the strength and mighty power of the Spaniard, working doubts in the better sort, fear in the poorer sort, and a great distraction in all, in the performance of their service." Coppin adds that the Spanish were thought to be preparing another armada of fifty thousand soldiers, supported by another hundred ships from Spain; they were planning to invade England "to settle the King of Scots in this realm." The story was so widely accepted that it was "creditably bruited as a preacher, in his prayer before his sermon, prayed to be delivered from the mighty forces of the Spaniard, the Scots and the Danes."[5] Only a month before, Robert Cecil had heard from Sir Edward Coke that he had questioned an Essex supporter named Weyman who gave him "(amongst much refuse) many things worthy of our observation" that could "as much prognosticate a mathematical conquest (which yet may be imagined) as mustering, making of armour, expectation of forces from Denmark, hope of and from Ireland, &c." (9:227). In addition, there is extant a series of letters from 1598 to early 1601 from John Petit in Flanders (also known as J.B.) to Peter Halins (alias Thomas Phelippes) in London; they keep reporting rumors and testifying that James is building a coalition on the Continent to take the English throne if it is not offered to him. By 1599, Petit finds reason to think that Denmark, Germany, Rome, Spain, Brussels, and Paris are all involved; by August 1599 he claims that his letters are being opened and their contents given to James.[6] Before he was named King of England, then, James was not only anxious about the kingship; he was obsessed by it.

For the English in 1603, his election was a mixed blessing. In a way, it fulfilled the prophecy of reuniting Scotland and England—something that seemed a natural conclusion to the much earlier union of Lancaster and York. But for others, James remained an alien, the son of a convicted traitor, and—so a widespread rumor had it—the bastard son of Mary Stuart and David Rizzio. Naming his first son Henry seemed provocative. It was also reported that his queen, Anne of Denmark, had converted to Catholicism, and this appeared to be confirmed when in Rome the Pope began to talk of James's own secret Catholic leanings. The proclamation issued by the Privy Council and others announcing James's succession was as much a proposition: it argued a slender and doubtful legal basis and was quite obviously contrived, for those who cared to study it, in the way it developed James's hereditary claim to the throne through his Tudor great-grandmother Margaret to Henry VII and through his great-great-grandmother Elizabeth of York to Edward IV. There was no mention of James's parentage and no reference to the will of Henry VIII, which had dictated the three previous successions and which, by the terms it laid out, would put Arbella Stuart—from England, not Scotland—next in line. James's ascension to the throne was, for some, similar to the seizure and possession of it that Shakespeare dramatizes in *Macbeth*. Thus it is that despite the splendid pageant that welcomed the new King to London in the summer of 1603, when James was celebrated as King of Great Britain, that scarcely a year later, in 1604, Thomas Dekker could publish his *Seuen Deadlie Sinns of London* locating those sins at the same stations used by the royal entry. Anne of Denmark herself had chosen as her attendants for that occasion women who were all connected to the Essex uprising that challenged the rule of Elizabeth I two years earlier.

A WORLD OF BYTES AND LEXIAS

Such facts, rumors, and interpretations are bytes of data that, sequentially linked, show the turbulence of the years surrounding the writing and staging of *Macbeth*. But unrest was not new in England in 1603 or even in the 1590s. The country had long been accustomed to protests and uprisings, usually over local causes, and to resistance theory begun in the works of John Ponet in the 1550s and later practiced secretly by Catholics. The country was equally aware of Calvin's firm belief in human depravity, and what it was capable of: both were registered in the Powder Plot. Before that, throughout the 1590s, a fresh Spanish invasion had been horrifying to contemplate yet impossible to ignore. Troop movements from Spain into the Low Countries began rumor after rumor, from 1590 through 1598; heightened reports circulated in 1592 and 1594. They were bolstered by actual events: the Spanish made a raid on Cornwall in 1595 and in October of that year sent another armada against England which was turned back by bad weather. In 1596, Spanish cannon firing on Calais could be heard in Greenwich, just outside London. Still a third armada left Spain for England in October 1597, but it too fell victim to storms and turned back.

Nor did threats to English rule end with the accession of James in

1603. Just one month before his coronation, on June 24, Midsummer Day, a plot was discovered to take control of the King and to assassinate him. Subsequent investigation revealed there were actually two plots that had been aborted: the Bye (or Priests) Plot led by two Catholic priests, William Watson and William Clark, along with Sir Griffin Markham and Sir Anthony Copley, and, even more unsettling, the Main Plot in which the conspirators were in part well-connected nobility, including Henry Brooke, Lord Cobham (who, as Warden of the Cinque Ports, was crucial to England's defense), and Thomas Lord Grey of Wilton, a Puritan activist. Cobham's brother implicated him with the archduke of Austria, who was also the Spanish King Philip's son-in-law and ruler of the Spanish Netherlands; both men, along with Sir Walter Ralegh, implicated in turn in Cobham's confession, were sent to the Tower of London. Plague caused the November 1603 trials to be held in Winchester. All the conspirators arrested in the Bye Plot were declared guilty on November 19; the trials of Cobham, Grey, and Ralegh on November 25 and 26 also convicted them. On November 29 Watson and Clark were hanged, drawn, and quartered at Winchester, and the quartered bodies of the two priests were put atop the gates at Winchester, their heads impaled on the first tower of Winchester Castle. Cobham, Grey, and Ralegh were scheduled for beheadings. As Leeds Barroll retells the story:

> James, in a theatrically brilliant manipulation of ritual, arranged for the conspirators to be brought to the scaffold individually, where each bade farewell to friends, said the appropriate prayers, and readied himself for execution. Markham, who went first and was visibly shaken, was told at the moment of execution to return to the castle for further meditation. Lord Grey, who appeared to Dudley Carleton like "a dapper young bridegroom," confessed his crime with a religious fervency, only to be informed that the order of executions had been reversed and he would have to wait another hour. After a similar charade was staged with Cobham, the three conspirators were reunited on the scaffold.[7]

Dudley Carleton reports that "as Grey and Markham, being brought back to the scaffold, as they then were but nothing acquainted with what had passed no more than the lookers-on with what should follow, looked strange one upon the other, like men beheaded and met again in the other world."[8] They were told by the sheriff that the King had countermanded the verdict and allowed them to live. There "was then no need to beg a plaudite of the audience," Carleton continues, "for it was given with such hues and cries that it went from the castle into the town and there began afresh, as if there has been some such like accident. And thus experience was made of the difference of examples of justice and mercy, that in this last no man could cry loud enough God save the King, and at the holding up of Brooke's head [Cobham's younger brother executed earlier], when the executioner began the same cry, he was not seconded by the voice of any one man but the Sheriff" (51). Barroll calls this drama "sensational" (66); but it was also bizarre. King James had managed to insinuate himself into the proceedings at the moment that would demonstrate his greatest power and authority, but his timing largely unsettled what he had meant to control. Cobham, Copley, Grey, Markham, and Ralegh were returned to the Tower. Copley was pardoned on August 18, 1604, subject to exile. Markham was banished on July 16, 1605. These trailing events kept alive the fact of attempted assassination. Ultimately Grey died in the Tower on July 9, 1614; Cobham was allowed to leave in 1617 for medical treatment and died shortly after; Ralegh, released in 1616 to explore for gold in the Amazon, killed some Spaniards on the voyage and when he returned to England was arrested once more and beheaded on October 29, 1618.

In 1606 it was Bate's Case. Under the Elizabethan scheme of monopolies, the Levant company had controlled the trade with Venice on currants and oil; the company paid the Crown £4,000 a year for its charter and recovered its loss by levying a tax of 5s. 6d. a hundredweight on currants and a similar tax on oil for merchants who were not company members. When the attack on monopolies in 1600 occurred, the company surrendered its charter; the Crown, opening sales to everyone, levied the same tax. But in 1606 a Turkish merchant named John Bate or Bates discovered that the custom was illegal and refused to pay it; he was sued in the Court of Exchequer, and the case went before the four Exchequer Barons. Legally, Bates had no case and the decision was found in favor of the Crown, but it established precedent by formulating the doctrine of absolute royal power in the courts. "The revenue of the Crown is the very essential part of the Crown," the judgment reads, "and he who rendeth that from the King pulleth also his crown from his head, for it cannot be separated from the Crown . . . in these cases of prerogative the judgment shall not be according to the rules of the Common Law, but according to the precedents of this Court wherein these matters are disputable and determinable."[9] The King who looked arbitrary was also absolute.

It follows that the atmosphere in 1606 was thick with distrust and conspiracy. As Patricia Parker memorably puts it, this was a "world of informer and spy."[10] The intricate schemes and double agents put in place to trap the imprisoned Mary Stuart in acts of treason in 1585 and 1586 broadened, under Sir Francis Walsingham's direction, into an enviable spy network that operated internationally. "Getting intelligence" was a major preoccupation of Elizabethan government in its final fifteen years, and it became a basic principle of government too with James. In the book of advice to Prince Henry, the *Basilicon Doron,* written in Scotland in 1598 and printed and widely distributed in three editions in England in 1603, James counsels his son to take care always to spy upon his own court and to be ever watchful about what occurs there. The Cecil Papers preserved by the Historical Commission show that Cecil spent much of his time running James's government by working with intelligence and intelligencers. Here are two representative letters abstracted in the papers, the first to Cecil from Sir Peter Manwood, the second from Sir Thomas Smith.

> 1605, Nov. 24.—This day was brought to me Matthew Laurence who has been staying at Dover three weeks to get passage to Lord Arundel; and now returning to London, was last night taken in an alehouse near Canterbury. He is aged about 55, somewhat red faced, blackish hair and beard, somewhat grey, bald headed. At first he told me he had business over, and having spent his money was forced to return; but never confessed to Lord Arundel till upon search these letters from the Baron to him about apparel were found, and a copy of his to his lordship of news from hence; neither did he make any Commissioners at Dover acquainted whither he was going, but being not well and his money spent, he sent over his letters by Michael Clerke, a post. What so great a provision of apparel out of England means, and to be so secretly kept, I understand not, and therefore have sent up the letters and papers taken about him, and have committed him till I know your pleasure whether he shall be sent up or discharged.—My house near Canterbury, 24 Nov. 1605.
>
> [1605], Nov. 25.—I have made as diligent search of Mr. Heriott's lodging and study at Sion as the time would permit. . . . Letters there are few, almost none, and such as are carry an old date. Books of all sorts of learning, and many: of all sorts and professions of religion: but neither one place nor other, though I opened all his chests, has afforded me anything needful to be brought to you. I have therefore sealed up his study close and his chests, to the end there may be a more exact survey if you shall think meet.

The sense of felt danger seems almost palpable. James's own sense of danger, however, was joined with his need for knowledge. When the provincial of the Jesuits in England was testifying in the Powder Plot trials, James himself was present, partially concealed behind a screen of wickerwood where he sat, without respite, from eight in the morning until seven in the evening. In 1607, when he finally decided to bring to heel at last the leading, outspoken Scottish Presbyterian minister Andrew Melville, Knox's successor, he had the Privy Council investigation held where he could overhear it from a secret vantage point within a closet. Melville's biographer comments acidly, "A low trick, and disgraceful to royalty, by which the prisoner was encouraged to use liberties which he would not otherwise have taken, and which were overheard by the person who was to decide upon his fate."[11] With James (as later with Shakespeare's *Macbeth*), perse- ✓ cution and prosecution seem deeply intertwined.

Such cultural practices contributed to the sense of severe instability that characterized London in 1606, a milieu uniquely accessible to theatrical presentation given its own inherent sense of drama, dissimulation, and display. *Macbeth* seems itself an unstable play yearning toward a sense of universal peace. It is not only full of threats and violence, hallucinations, charms, conjurations, and secret plotting; it is also full of rumors and mystery. It is a play that continually interrogates and surprises as it unsettles. "Surprise is continual," G. Wilson Knight writes:

> Macbeth does not understand how he can be Thane of Cawdor (1.3). Lady Macbeth is startled at the news of Duncan's visit (1.5); Duncan at the fact of Macbeth's arrival before himself (1.6). There is the general amazement at the murder; of Lennox, Ross, and the Old Man at the strange happenings in earth and heaven on the night of the murder (2.3; 2.4). Banquo and Fleance are unsure of the hour (2.1). No one is sure of Macduff's mysterious movements. Lady Macbeth is baffled by Macbeth's enigmatic hints as to the "deed of dreadful note" (3.2). The two murderers are not certain as to whom has wronged them, Macbeth or Banquo (3.1); they do not understand the advent of the "third murderer" (3.3). Ross and Lady Macduff are at a loss as to Macduff's flight, and warning is brought to Lady Macduff by a mysterious messenger who "is not to her known" (4.2). Malcolm suspects Macduff, and there is a long dialogue due to his "doubts" (4.3); and in the same scene Malcolm recognizes Ross as his countryman yet strangely "knows him not" (4.3).[12]

But *Macbeth* holds few surprises among the cultural practices of its time. Not one, but two, kings maneuver their way to the throne in this play: like James, Macbeth is obsessed with gaining the crown; like James, Malcolm builds an international force to invade the kingdom and seize it as rightfully his own. The play's king's two bodies are two kings who are its two most vulnerable leaders; they too devise plots, are increasingly anxious for intelligence. Bloody thoughts instigate bloody deeds. The play begins with judgment on Cawdor, after Macbeth rips Macdonwald open on the battle-field; it ends with judgment as the man untimely ripped from his mother's womb kills Macbeth. Above all, at a performance at the Globe of *Macbeth* in 1606, surveillance was increasing inside as well as outside the play-house, even in the unlikeliest of places. Given this atmosphere, Macbeth's counsel to the First Murderer to "Aquaint you with the perfect Spy o' th' time" (3.1.129; 1136), like his revelation to Lady Macbeth that

> I heare it by the way: But I will send:
> There's not a one of them but in his house
> I keepe a Seruant Feed (3.4.129–31; 1413–15),

must have been especially chilling. But it also sheds light on why Rosse, cousin to Lady Macduff, would visit her, warn her against danger, and then leave just as abruptly: he has found out what Macbeth wanted to know, that Macduff has left the kingdom. Elsewhere, too, in scenes where he is silent, listening, or talking, drawing out responses from others, Rosse re-mains a cultural point man until his final defection. In 1606 the troubled and troubling events staged at the Globe in *Macbeth* materially speak to a troubled audience, both confirming their uneasiness and giving them release.

In cognitively understanding the world that created *Macbeth,* and that *Macbeth* reflected, we can turn to one, some, many, or all of the following individual bytes and sets of lexias, as Shakespeare's playgoers surely did. With us, as with them, the play's meaning will depend on our choice(s) and sequence(s). Indeed, we may even reinforce some bytes when we see how they can make cognitive sense in more than one sequence or lexia. Processing neurologically some of the sights, sounds, images, and refer-ences as they might have will bring us as close to those playgoers of 1606 as we can possibly get.

Theatrical Lexias

King James himself recognized theater as an important material prac-tice. Before coming to England he had been a strong proponent of plays: an English company is recorded in Edinburgh in 1593 and 1599, receiving from the King on each visit £333 6s. 8d.; when the Edinburgh preachers strenuously objected, James issued a license allowing public plays and gave the players an additional £40 "to by timber for ye preparatioun of ane hous to thair pastyme."[13] On a third visit in 1601, James gave the players £400 and made the Scotsman Laurence Fletcher, apparently their leading actor, an honorary burgess of Aberdeen. James arrived in London on May 7, 1603; ten days later he issued the Privy Seal for a patent of the Lord Chamberlain's Men, which he renamed the King's Men, and on May 19 they received the new patent obviously following that issued by Elizabeth in 1574, with only a few alterations, with Fletcher given pride of place preceding all including Shakespeare. The company members are

> freely to use and exercise the Arte and facultie of playing Comedies, Tragedies, Histories, Enterludes, Moralls, Pastoralls, Stage plaies, & such other like, as they have already studied, or heerafter shall use or studie, aswell for the recreation of o^r loving subjects, as for o^r solace and pleasure, when we shall thinke good to see them, during o^r pleasure. And the said Comedies, Tragedies, Histories, Enterlude, Morall, Pastoralls, Stage plaies, & such like, To show and exercise publiquely to their best Commoditie, when the infection of the plague shall decrease, as well wthin theire now usuall howse called the Globe, wthin o^r Countie of Surrey, as also wthin anie towne halls, or Mout halls, or other convenient places wthin the lib'ties and freedome of any other Cittie, Univ'sitie, Towne, or Borough whatsoev' wthin o^r said Realmes and dominions.[14]

As servants of the King they were effectually grooms of his chamber, and each member of the company received four and a half yards of red cloth to furnish himself with liveries for royal occasions.

The King thus only strengthened a lively cultural practice even as he attempted to control it. By 1600 the Privy Council had licensed two public theaters (the Fortune and the Globe); other companies staged plays at the Rose, the Boar's Head, and the Curtain; and boys companies performed at St. Paul's and Blackfriars. Thomas Platter, traveling from Germany to England in 1599, has left a firsthand account:

> Daily at two in the afternoon, London has two, sometimes three plays running in different places, competing with each other, and those which play best obtain most spectators. The playhouses are so constructed that they play on a raised platform, so that everyone has a good view. There are different galleries and places, however, where the seating is better and more comfortable and therefore more expensive. For whoever cares to stand below only pays one English penny, but if he wishes to sit he enters by another door, and pays another penny, while if he desires to sit in the most comfortable seats which

are cushioned, where he not only sees everything well, but can also be seen, then he pays yet another English penny at another door.[15]

Comedies were more popular than tragedies; the most popular tragedies were those of revenge, crimes, or domestic conflict: *Macbeth* powerfully combines all three. From 1603 to 1608 the plays of the King's Men drew on the history of Rome (*Sejanus, Antony and Cleopatra, Coriolanus*), ancient Britain (*King Lear*), and Scotland (*Gowrie, Macbeth*). Performances were prohibited during Lent, Shrovetide, and in times of plague, so that a year's season lasted a few weeks after the Christmas season, a short spring term between Easter and the end of Easter law term, the summer months (which might include provincial tours, especially during an epidemic in London), and a full autumn season from the start of Michaelmas Term. But the plague took a considerable toll: while 1604–5 was relatively unaffected, playhouses may have been open for as little as two months in all of 1603–4, three months in 1605–6 (the year of *Macbeth*), one month in 1606–7, and five months in 1607–8; in 1606 plague was recorded from March to December, with a sufficient number of cases to close the theaters in London and Southwark. When plays were performed, they were presented in repertory. Roslyn Knutson has shown that "a typical run is one in which the play was given eight to twelve performances over four to six months."[16] This system made fierce demands on the actors; Bernard Beckerman reckons that an actor mastered a new role every other week while keeping another thirty or forty in mind and that leading actors like Edward Alleyn, in a three-year period, would learn over fifty new parts and retain an additional twenty old ones.[17] The plays they were given were clearly commercial ones; a playwright earned a small fee for the play but also had benefit nights when all the receipts were his, and the popularity of a play thus increased profits. Some playwrights, like Shakespeare, were also shareholders of the company.

In addition, the King's Men uniquely owned their own playhouse. The first Globe Theater was built by the then Lord Chamberlain's Men in the spring of 1599 in Southwark, just 150 yards south of the Thames and a little over a quarter-mile west of London Bridge, immediately south of Maid Lane. It was constructed by Richard and Cuthbert Burbage and their carpenter, Peter Street, from timber used in the old Theatre in Shoreditch, just north of the city walls. Richard Hosley estimates that it was a twenty-four-sided polygon with a diameter of about one hundred feet with two exterior staircases allowing the various entrances that Platter describes. There was a thatched roof over the stage resting on two pillars and, based on an analogy with the Swan Theater, for which a stylized contemporary drawing survives, there was a large rectangular stage jutting halfway into the yard with standing room on three sides. The ceiling of the stage was painted to resemble the Heavens and a central trapdoor on the stage could lead to an area, unseen but signifying Hell, that could also allow spectacular effects such as the appearance and disappearance of the witches in 1.1 and 1.3. Two doors at the rear of the stage led to the tiring (attiring) house where costumes and properties were kept. Over the stage and under the roof was a balcony for limited acting and gentlemen's boxes, but spectators also stood on the ground or sat in the tiered galleries or even at times on the stage itself.[18]

Plays at court or in town halls, guild halls, or the halls of great houses placed the stage at one end and tiers of bleachers on the two sides and at the back with boxes at ground level. At royal performances the best seats were those offering not the best sight lines of the play but the best view of the King; the royal party sat on a raised dais and under a canopy. The Venetian ambassador, Nicolo Molin, wrote about such an arrangement to the Venetian Doge on January 12, 1605: "We entered a box by five or six steps; in it were two chairs; the King took one, the Queen the other, a stool was prepared for me on the King's right, and another for the Duke [of Holst, the Queen's brother] on the Queen's left, but he would not sit down; he preferred to stand uncovered, for three hours."[19] A dispute is recorded over where James should sit at a Christ Church performance at Oxford in August 1605; he was finally placed in the center of the hall so that viewers would see him at the same time they saw the play. Royal performances thus continually realized James's advice to Prince Henry in the *Basilicon Doron* that the prince is always one sitting on a stage for people to behold and admire. This would have been true at royal performances of *Macbeth,* too, where James would be a second king in the sight line toward Duncan, Macbeth, or Malcolm. With James's accession to the throne, in fact, the number of such performances markedly increased. At his first Christmas James is said to have requested thirty plays; Dudley Carleton writes to John Chamberlain on January 15, 1604, "The first holy dayes we had every night a publike play in the great hale, at which the king was ever present, and liked or disliked as he saw cause; but it seems he takes no extraordinary pleasure in them. The Queen and Prince were more the players frends, for on other nights they had them privately, and hath since taken them to theyr protection,"[20] establishing two new companies in the Queen's Men and Prince Henry's Men. A longer Christmas season also provided more plays during the cultural moment of *Macbeth;* according to the Chamber Accounts, the King's Men were paid for eleven court performances in 1603–4 and again in 1604–5, ten in 1605–6, nine in 1606–7, and thirteen in 1607–8; from 1603 to 1616, the King's Men performed 175 times at court, as compared to 118 performances by all the other companies combined. Shakespeare would thus have known as he composed *Macbeth* that the play would likely be seen—in some form—at court.

While acting gained increased respect during James's reign, it was a viable trade as early as the 1570s, when men formed careers on the stage and attempted to learn their many parts. They worked from individual "parts," not seeing the whole script but, in some cases at least, seeing "plots" or "plattes" that outlined the play with cues, entrances, and exits. R. B. McKerrow has written that the original manuscript "was merely the substance, or rather the bare bones, of a performance on the stage, intended to be interpreted by actors skilled in their craft,"[21] marking the instability of the script, the variability of each performance, and the difficulty of recovering with any satisfaction a particular performance of *Macbeth* in 1606. Alan Dessen notes, furthermore, that "many entrances do not specify the exact number of actors to be used but rather call for '*and others as many as can be*' (*Titus Andronicus*, I, i, 72 s.d.) or '*as many as may be*' (*Edward I*, 1. 51, *The Double Marriage*, VI, 400) or '*as many as may be spared*' (*The Tragedy of Hoffman,* 1.1682). . . . [A] stage direction in [Thomas Heywood's] *The Captives* ('*either strikes him with a staff or casts a stone*') . . . was not changed by the theatrical annotator; similarly, the playhouse manuscript of *John a Kent and John a Cumber* includes the call for a figure to come '*out of a tree, if possible it may be*' (1. 836)."[22] The repertory system encouraged a certain flexibility in performance because the actors had specialized roles written for them: Beckerman notes that "Richard Burbage invariably played the leading role, Robert Armin the leading comic role, Robert Cowley played important secondary roles" (134). Contrasted roles of tall and short women in Shakespeare's plays throughout the 1590s argue for at least two boys in the company, one perhaps apprenticing to the other. Such actors would permit the lesser role of Lady Macduff to offset Lady Macbeth and to be seen *with* her when doubling as the waiting-gentlewoman of 5.1. If necessary, gatherers or others could be hired to swell the numbers in crowded scenes.

To aid the staging of crowd scenes, the playwright often resorted to battle reports (as in 1.2) or to having some figures stand for the whole (as in 5.6–8). Dessen adds that "the players made adept use of *alarums* or off-stage sound effects ('a gong insistently clanging, trumpets blaring recognizable military signals, then steel clashing, ordnance firing') and *excursions* ('individual pursuits and combats onstage')" (12). Thus sound played an important part along with the visual; Stephen Orgel notes that courtiers at the Christ Church performance in August 1605 referred to the playgoers as "auditors" rather than "spectators": "What this audience has come to *see* is the king; but their experience of the drama will be—as the terms *auditory* and *audience* suggest—to hear it. Theater in 1605 was assumed to be a verbal medium. And acting . . . was a form of oratory."[23] But the visual was always coordinated with the auditory. Elaborate costumes replaced settings, and hand properties were frequent as well. These too were conventional, so that kings might be identified through crowns and scepters, counselors through their white staffs of office. Bladders or sponges filled with calf's or pig's blood were carried under the armpits and squeezed to produce blood during battle. The fact that much of the action of *Macbeth*—most of it, in fact—takes place at night or in the darkness or semi-darkness may at private theaters increase the reliance on sound and emphasize strained attempts to see both what is and what is not.

The range of characters, staged events, and styles of language deliberately appealed to a heterogeneous audience. Certainly many playgoers were educated gentlemen, nobility, or students from the Inns of Court, what Ann Jennalie Cook has called "privileged playgoers," but there were also, by her own citation, middle and lower classes, including servingmen, applewives, chimney boys, chambermaids, merchants and their factors, apprentices, grooms, whores, porters, yeomen, and feltmakers.[24] Andrew Gurr observes that "a visit to a playhouse or a baiting-house or prize-fight or whorehouse was always within reach for the great majority of the working population as well as the wealthy."[25] An artisan could earn six or seven shillings a week, and a play cost a penny while a quart of good ale could cost four pence, and dinner anywhere from three to eighteen pence. About fifteen hundred attended a public performance, or as many as eighteen thousand a week at the Globe alone—a large number as well as a large cross section of the urban population. The consequent hurly-burly there, John L. McMullan tells us, was considerable:

> In the boxes and the pit were to be found the best of the [criminal] profession: the vizards and tongue pads. In the galleries the bulkers or common trulls trafficked. The galleries were noted for their roaring and brawling; there an assortment of bullies, sharpers, and sots advertised their women, sought out

clients, and staged thefts and confidence cheats. A regular feature was the orange girls who operated as intermediaries negotiating discreet acquaintances between male admirers and actresses and prostitutes.[26]

It is not surprising, then, that McMullen adds later that "Edward Alleyn, an actor and man of property, . . . owned and operated three brothels. Indeed, at the time of his second wife's death he paid out a bawd's rent as a form of charity to the worthy poor" (139). Such large crowds, cross sections of the nation's largest and busiest city, served as a public forum not only of entertainment but of opinion. Plays provided for the literate and illiterate alike the stories and editorials similar to our newspapers through enactments of the past and present. In many ways, theater was the *central* cultural practice when *Macbeth* was performed at the Globe in 1606. But we can understand more thoroughly the force and reception of *Macbeth* in 1606 by following lexias of contemporary references it could arouse, consciously or not, in the playgoers during and after such performances.

ROYAL LEXIAS

As a chief reflection and commentary on its cultural moment— especially with Duncan, Macbeth, Banquo, and Malcolm as the historical subjects—Shakespeare's play incorporates near and distant references to James. The one king living in 1606 who appears in *Macbeth* at the Globe (4.1), James I and VI had his own well-developed sense of theater, as did most royalty. An anonymous Spanish account from 1604, for example, describes the "Banquet and Entertainment Given by James I to the Constable of Castile at Whitehall Palace, on Sunday, Aug. 19" as royal theater; such events can put the banquet scene in *Macbeth* (3.2) in better perspective.

> The dishes were brought in by gentlemen and servants of the King, who were accompanied by the Lord Chamberlain, and before placing them on the table they made four or five obeisances. The Earls of Pembroke (*Panbrue*) and of Southampton officiated as gentlemen-ushers. Their Majesties with the Prince [Henry] entered after the Constable and the others, and placed themselves at their throne, and all stood in a line to hear the grace said; the Constable being at the King's side and the Count de Villamediana on the Queen's. Their Majesties washed their hands in the same basin, the Lord Treasurer handing

the towel to the King, and the High Admiral to the Queen. The Prince washed in another basin, in which water was also taken to the Constable, who was waited upon by the same gentlemen. They took their seats in the following manner: their Majesties sat at the head of the table, at a distance from each other, under the canopy of state, the Queen being on the right hand, on chairs of brocade with cushions; and at her side, a little apart, sat the Constable, on a tabouret of brocade with a high cushion of the same, and on the side of the King the Prince was seated in like manner. . . . There was plenty of instrumental music, and the banquet was sumptuous and profuse. The first thing the King did was to send the Constable a melon and half a dozen of oranges on a very green branch, telling him that they were the fruit of Spain transplanted into England; to which the latter, kissing his hand, replied that he valued the gift more as coming from his Majesty than as being the fruit of his own country; he then divided the melon with their Majesties, and Don Blasco de Aragon handed the plate to the Queen, who politely and graciously acknowledged the attention. Soon afterwards the King stood up, and with his head uncovered drank to the Constable the health of their Spanish Majesties, and may the peace be happy and perpetual![27]

Behind James's performance (as behind Macbeth's banquet) is one of James's chief policies—that of a permanent peace with Spain—and within it one of his chief roles, the royal peacemaker come to unify countries, bound here publicly by oath and ceremony. This unmistakably staged event also incorporates as witnesses and participants everyone present: for a brief moment as chorus, the audience too are actors.

Indeed, the *Basilicon Doron,* written to Prince Henry, is a theatrical manual.

> Be also moderate in your raiment, neither ouer superfluous, like a deboshed waster; nor yet ouer base, like a miserable wretch; not artificially trimmed and decked, like a Courtizane, nor yet ouer sluggishly clothed, like a countrey clowne, nor ouer lightly like a Candie souldier, or a vaine young Courtier; nor yet ouer grauely, like a Minister: but in your garments be proper, cleanely, comely and honest, wearing your clothes in a carelesse, yet comely forme: keeping in them a middeforme, *inter Togatos & Paludatos,* betwixt the grauitie of the one, and lightnesse of the other: thereby to signifie, that by your calling yee are mixed of both the professions; *Togatus,* as a Iudge making and pronouncing the Law; *Paludatus,* by the power of the sword . . . framing euer your gesture according to your present actions: . . . Remember also, to put a difference betwixt your forme of language in reasoning, and your pronouncing of sentences. (*Workes,* sig. Q2v)

In formulating such practices, James is as canny and self-conscious as Shakespeare's Macbeth; with him, policy and principle are performative. "I bid you," he tells Henry elsewhere in the *Basilicon Doron,* "know all

75

crafts: For except ye know euery one, how can yee controll euery one, which is your proper office?" (sig. P4).

But performance—not to say theatricality—marked many events of his public life and some of his private moments as well. History records that James was born on June 19, 1566, the son of Mary, the daughter and only living child of James V, and Henry Stuart, Lord Darnley, a bare three months after Darnley and others had killed Mary's secretary, David Rizzio, who was taking supper with her in her private chambers. That fact was known in England in 1606, as was the persistent rumor that James was actually the bastard child of Rizzio; James may even make public reference to this in his comment about the "Bastard of *Normandie*" in his *Trew Law of Free Monarchies* (1598, 1603; *Workes,* sig. R5v). Mary's final days of pregnancy were spent in a cramped room where her labor was long and difficult; James was born with a caul of membranes over his head. This meant that his brain did not receive the normal supply of oxygen in the first hours of his life and probably contributed to his weak and misshapen body and stooped posture in later years. Rumor persisted, however, that this was a magical sign giving him a charmed life, a special gift for prophecy: he too was not *naturally* born of woman. Then, scarcely a year later, Mary was expelled from rule after a flight to England, and at little more than a year of age, James was crowned King of Scotland on July 29, 1567, with the fiery John Knox preaching his coronation sermon, establishing in that very fact the conversion of the nation's religion from Mary's Catholicism to Knox's own Genevan brand of presbyterianism. Of the royal namesakes who preceded him as James VI, two had been assassinated by their subjects and three more had died in or as a result of war with England; of the four regents who would govern Scotland during James's minority, only one would die a natural death.

A playwright and humanist scholar, George Buchanan, was James's primary teacher in childhood. Buchanan was especially stern and did not hesitate to whip and punish his student when he thought it necessary. Later, in England, James would boast of having Buchanan as his tutor—but he also had nightmares of Buchanan and vivid memories of his radical thought and dictatorial manner. James reached his majority and was crowned in October 1579 with a royal entry pageant in Edinburgh that included scenes from religion, history, mythology, and allegory in its theatricality. At the West Port, for instance, James witnessed a tableau on the "Wisdom of Solomon" meant to characterize his own later self-inscription. At the old Tolbooth, Justice, Peace, Plenty, and Policy greeted him, and Religion led him to St. Giles Cathedral for the actual service. Leaving

church, he was confronted with Bacchus and a fountain flowing with cele-
bratory wine, but like the ceremony of peace with Spain in 1604, there
were other potent theatrical symbols: along Canongate he saw a tableau of
the abolition of the pope and the Mass and before he arrived at the palace
of Holyroodhouse, he saw his own show of kings of Scotland.[28] That year
he also met his first male favorite, Esmé Stuart d'Aubigny, his French
cousin, whose strong effects on James ended when the Ruthven family
ambushed the two men in 1582, holding James prisoner and forcing Esmé
into permanent exile. James was held hostage for the better part of a year.
He later managed to escape and in 1584 executed William, the first Earl
Gowrie, who had led the kidnapping. In 1600 James again accused the
Ruthven family of kidnapping him and attempting to assassinate him; this
he explained in a pamphlet published in Edinburgh and London that same
year. One or both of these incidents was doubtless the subject of the lost
play of *Gowrie* performed twice by the King's Men in 1604 before it was
removed from the stage. But as Alvin Kernan has recently recounted,

> Death also pursued with extraordinary thoroughness all those lords . . . who
> had been involved in one way or another in the murder of Darnley [at Kirk
> o' Fields in February 1567 by James's mother Mary and the Earl of Bothwell,
> according to Buchanan] and in the subsequent deposition of Mary. James,
> earl of Moray, was assassinated; Archbishop Hamilton was hanged; the earl of
> Lennox was stabbed in the back by his jailer; William Maitland, "Secretary
> Lethington," poisoned himself to avoid trial; John Stuart, 4th earl of Athol,
> was poisoned at a banquet; George Gordon, 6th earl of Huntly, had a seizure
> at a football game and died seeing ghosts; the earl of Argyll died in agony
> from the stone (gallstones); Kircaldy of Grange was hanged; and the brutal
> Gilbert Kennedy, 4th earl of Cassilis, was fatally thrown from his horse.
> James's hand was not always visible in these deaths, but the revenge was
> spectacularly gory and complete.[29]

Even James's yearlong attempt to fetch his bride, Anne of Denmark, and
marry her was delayed and threatened by storms at sea for which a witches'
coven at North Berwick and a wizard earl associated with the Gowries
claimed responsibility.

On April 5, 1603, James began another series of theatrical performances—the public duties of a king—as he made his way from Edinburgh
to London following his election as James I. He was accompanied by a
large number of Scots—virtually the entire administration of his government in Edinburgh: his close cousin Ludovic Stuart, duke of Lennox, by
title a descendant of the Lenox in *Macbeth* (2.3ff.), and others soon to
become central at his court in England. His younger son, Charles, was left

behind in the charge of Lord President Seton, the descendant of Macbeth's Seton in act 5. The entourage stopped at each village and hamlet to pronounce union and peace, justice, and clemency, the king-becoming graces listed in *Macbeth* (4.3.91ff.; 1917ff.). They reached the fortress town of Berwick on April 6, Newcastle on April 9, Durham on April 13, and York on April 16, where a "Conduit all the day long ran white and claret vine, every man to drinke as much as he listed."[30] Then, it is recorded, he was entertained as Shakespeare's Macbeth entertains in 3.4:

> The 21st, being Thursday, his Highnese tooke his way towardes New-warke-upon-Trent, where that night he lodged in the Castle, being his owne house, where the Aldermen of New-warke presented his Majestie with a faire gilt cup, manifesting their duties and loving hearts to him, which was very kindly accepted. In this Towne, and in the Court, was taken a cut-purse doing the deed; and being a base pilfering theefe, yet was a Gentleman-like in the outside. This fellow had good store of coyne found about him; and upon examination confessed that he had from Barwick to that place plaied the cut-purse in the Court. His fellow was ill mist, for no doubt he had a walking mate; they drew togither like coach horses, and it is pitie they did not hang togither; for his Majestie hearing of this nimming gallant directed a warrant presently to the Recorder of New-warke, to have him hanged, which was accordingly executed. . . . The King, ere he went from New-warke, as he had commanded this silken base theefe in Justice to be put to death, so in his benigne and gracious mercie, he gives life to all the other poore and wretched Prisoners, clearing the Castle of them all.[31]

For many, this was a severity not unlike Macbeth's that in its punishment decreed without fair trial and the liberty given to prisoners demonstrated an arbitrary, potentially absolutist ruler. The progress concluded, after a visit to Master Oliver Cromwell at Hinchingbrooke Priory on April 27, with hospitality and entertainment by James's new principal secretary, Robert Cecil, at his country house of Theobalds beginning on May 3.

Plague in London precluded immediate coronation, which was postponed, as things turned out, to March 15, 1604. In the meantime, on July 17, the new King performed another surprising act: he issued a general summons offering knighthood to all persons who had £40 a year in land, either to come and receive the honor or to compound with the King's commissioners: like Shakespeare's Duncan and Malcolm, he attempted to secure rule (and revenues) through awarding titles. Creative in raising money, he spent it lavishly. On July 20 he established a separate residence for Prince Henry and his sister Lady Elizabeth at Oatlands and appointed 70 servants to assist them; a few weeks later the number was increased to

104, and before the year was out it was augmented to 141. On July 21 he elevated others: Charles Blount, Lord Mountjoy, was created earl of Devonshire; Sir Thomas Egerton, Lord Chancellor, was created baron Ellesmere; Sir William Russell, lord Russell of Thornhaugh; Sir Henry Grey, lord Grey of Groby; Sir John Petre, lord Petre of Writtle; Sir John Harington, lord Harington of Exton; Sir Henry Danvers, lord Danvers of Dauntsy; Sir Thomas Gerard, lord Gerard of Gerard's Bromley; Sir Robert Spencer, lord Spencer of Wormleighton; and—more ominously—Henry Wriothesley, earl of Southampton, once Shakespeare's patron and condemned as a traitor in the Essex rebellion of 1601, earl of Southampton restored and newly created; and Thomas lord Howard of Walden, one of the Howards who had led the Catholic opposition to Elizabeth I, newly created earl of Suffolk (cf. Malcolm at 5.9.28–29; 2515–16). Finally, "On the 23rd of July," the record continues, "not less then 300 Gentlemen reaped the fruits of his Majesty's laborious exertions; and were dubbed Knights in the Royal Garden at Whitehall. Among these, were such of the Judges, Serjeants at Law, Doctors of the Civil Law, and Gentleman Ushers, as had not before received that honour. The majority attended according to the Summons" (Nichols, *Progresses,* 9:205).

All this preceded the coronation of James in Westminster Abbey on July 25, 1603. The script of that performance is extant, if absent from the extant script of *Macbeth* and so there to be imagined. The King and Queen crossed Westminster Bridge to enter the church by the west door; they proceeded down the aisle to a hymn, were shown to the people who acclaimed their allegiance, and then a second anthem was followed by the King and Queen offering a pall and a pound of gold each at the altar. There followed a prayer by the Archbishop of Canterbury, his sermon, and his administering of the oath. Then came the sacred Investiture with sword, ring, scepter, and imperial crown.[32]

With James's Archbishop of Canterbury replacing Macbeth's Thane of Fife, James became history's first king to be seated on the Stone of Scone in Westminster Abbey wearing the crown of Edward the Confessor (*Macbeth* 2.4, 4.3, 5.8). In his subsequent sermon on the coronation, Lancelot Andrewes speaks of James's descendants, not ancestors, "who shall (wee trust, and pray they may) stretch their line to the world's end,"[33] anticipating Shakespeare's Macbeth, whose own "Line" will "stretch out to'th'cracke of Doome" (4.1.117; 1664). For Michael Drayton, the moment of coronation only fulfilled past prophecy:

> Two famous Kingdoms separate thus long,
> Within one iland, and that speake one tongue,

Since *Brute* first raign'd, (if men of *Brute* alow)
Neuer before vnited vntill now. ("To the Maiestie of King IAMES," sig. B2v)

For Drayton, Scripture and history meet in a moment of triumphal epiph-
any. Within a year, William Willymat reissued the *Basilicon Doron* as *A
Prince's Looking-Glass* made material by Shakespeare in 4.1. Willymat followed this with his own, *A Loyal Subject's Looking-Glass*, where, conversely,
he pronounces pride, ambition, and envy the chief vices of subjects and
the chief causes of rebellion. "All three," M. C. Bradbrook observes wryly,
"animate Macbeth."[34]

The cold winter of 1603–4 brought the plague to a halt, and by March
it was thought safe for King James and Queen Anne to make their delayed
journey through the city of London. On March 12, 1604, James, Anne,
and Prince Henry arrived at the Tower of London, the traditional starting
place for the royal processional. James, who was fascinated by lions, took
the family to see the fiercest of them and decided it would be fine sport to
put a dog in the same cage. Three followed in succession; only one lived,
and Henry, countering the joy of his father's cruelty, took the survivor to
St. James's Palace where he had it cared for. It was a strange, if widely
broadcast, prelude to the royal entry itself on March 15. That day festivities
included a river pageant, a display of fireworks, and the building of seven
great arches. It was "one of the two or three greatest spectacles of early
seventeenth century England," according to R. Malcolm Smuts, "an event
staged before tens of thousands of spectators, involving hundreds of participants and a massive display of ostentation. Expenditures by the Crown
alone amounted to over £36,000—a sum comparable to the cost of twenty
court masques, or roughly double that of constructing the Whitehall Banqueting House. London's guilds contributed £4100 more, while the Bor-
ough of Westminster and the many peers and gentry who marched in the
royal procession invested unknown but substantial sums":[35] among them
were the King's Men in their new red livery. James was first greeted by St.
George and St. Andrew ("the Patrons of both Kingdomes"), who met on
horseback "to testifie their leagued combination, and newe sworne brotherhood."[36] They were admonished by the Genius Loci:

And when soft-handed Peace so sweetly thrives,
That bees in souldiers' helmets build their hives;
When Joy a tip-toe stands on Fortune's wheale,
In silken roabes; how dare you shine in steele? (340)

It also resembled theater: "The streets seemed to be paved with men;
stalles, instead of rich wares, were set out for children; open casements

filed up with women—. Even children, might they have bin suffred, would gladly have spent their little strength about the engines that mounted up the frames" (342). A chorister of Paul's proclaimed the

Great Monarch of the West, whose glorious stem
Doth now support a triple diadem, . . .
. . . .
Wearing above Kings now, or those of olde,
A double crowne of lawrell and of gold (357),

alluding to James the King and James the Poet, and, somewhat later, "a chorus in full voices" sang to "make Heaven ring, / His welcomes shouted loudlie / For Heaven itselfe lookes proudly, / That Earth has such a King" (366–67). Large, triumphal arches, under the direction of Ben Jonson, declared those attributes for which James wished to be known; on one section of one arch, for instance, *Genius Urbis* was dressed in a mantle of purple, holding in one hand a goblet and in the other a "branch full of little twigs, to signifie increase and indulgence."[37] The six daughters of Genius, descended from *Monarchia Britannica*, were Gladness, Loving Affection, Unanimity, Veneration, Promptitude, and Vigilance. At another, the Nova Felix Arabia Arch, the carving of nine muses and seven liberal arts emphasized intellectual and literary achievement.

At a time laden with anxiety, conducive to unsettled drama and performance, James reinforced the cultural pronouncements of the royal entry with some political pronouncements of his own: he quartered into the Great Seal the arms of Cadwallader and Edward the Confessor to underscore his notion of Great Britain; he pointed with pride to his own descent from Henry Tudor as the grandson of Henry's sister Margaret; and he even intimated that this was the reason he had named his first son—and England's first heir in a half-century—Henry and his daughter Elizabeth. Others continued his creations. Robert Wakeman, in his *Sermon Preached Before the Kings Maiestie at None-Such April. 30. 1605,* calls attention to "that happy vnion of these famous kingdomes, of England and Scotland vnder one Soveraigne, so that of them it is verified, which was spoken of the tribes in the *prophecie* of *Ezechiel*" (sig. A8). In 1606, perhaps after seeing the show of eight kings in *Macbeth* 4.1, H. R. (Henry Roberts) comments of James in his account of *The Most royall and Honourable entertainment, of the famous and renowned King, Christien the fourth, King of Denmarke,* a show put on when King Christian, Queen Anne's brother, arrived from Denmark on July 16, 1606, that he was "the mirrour of all honour" (sig. B2v). For "When it pleased GOD, to place the Imperiall crown of this most blessed, and famous kingdome, on the head of our most glorious and renowned soueraigne King *Iames,* it was not a little admired amongst the commons of this land" (sig. A4). Shakespeare figures the King in the mirror of the eighth spectral king (4.1.119; 1666), and James enlarges on this trope, amphibologically, in his speech to the Lords and Commons at Whitehall on Wednesday, March 21, 1609: "As ye made mee a faire Present indeed in presenting your thankes and louing dueties vnto mee: So haue I now called you here, to recompence you againe with a great and a rare Present, which is a faire and a Christall Mirror; Not such a Mirror wherein you may see your owne faces, or shadowes; but such a Mirror, or Christall, as through the transparantnesse thereof, you may see the heart of your King. The Philosophers wish, That euery mans breast were a Christall, where-through his heart might be seene, is vulgarly knowne" (*Workes,* sig. 2X6), and concludes,

> Yee know that principally by three wayes yee may wrong a Mirrour. First, I pray you, looke not vpon my Mirrour with a false light: which yee doe, if ye mistake, or mis-vnderstand my Speach, and so alter the sence thereof.
>
> But secondly, I pray you beware to soile it with a foule breath, and vn-cleane hands: I meane, that yee peruert not my words by any corrupt affections, turning them to an ill meaning, like one, who when hee heares the tolling of a Bell, fancies to himselfe, that it speakes those words which are most in his minde [cf. *Macbeth* 2.1].
>
> And lastly, (which is worst of all) beware to let it fall or breaks; (for glasse is brittle) which ye doe, if ye lightly esteeme it, and by contemning it, con-forme not your selues to my perswasions. (sigs. 2Z4–2Z4v)

That moments of the royal triumphal entry into London remained emblematic is also shown by their reappearance in Henry Peacham's book of emblems, the *Minerva Britannia,* in 1612. His first emblem shows a crown held above by a divine hand, illustrating the divine will and James's divine right to rule (but, for those of a more skeptical cast of mind, also reminiscent of a similar suspended crown, attached to the Gowrie crest and associated with the Gowrie conspiracy against the King's life in 1600). Another emblem in Peacham's collection shows the lions of Scotland and England holding up the crown of Great Britain with this prophecy:

> BELLONA henceforth bounde in Iron Bandes
> Shall kisse the foote of mild triumphant PEACE,
> Nor Trumpets sterne, be heard with their landes
> Envie shall pine and all old grudges cease[38]

—a feat assigned by Shakespeare's Rosse (without any other known reference) to Macbeth as "*Bellona's* Bridegroome, lapt in proofe" (1.2.55; 79).

Still another of Peacham's emblems shows a thistle and rose growing on the same stalk, watered by God's hand, with the motto "*Quae plantavi irrigabo*" (What I have planted, I shall water). It is accompanied by a verse reiterating the rule of James as the providence of the Lord, much as the Captain makes Macbeth's battle akin to victory at Golgotha (1.2.41; 61).

Yet "all the motifs of these verses had appeared in some form or other on the triumphal arches of 1604," Graham Parry remarks (24); and all were seen by the King's Men as they marched through the streets of London toward Westminster. Indeed, Jonson reused these motifs, and others similar to them, in his masque *Hymenaei,* performed in court on January 5, 1606, just as Shakespeare was beginning *Macbeth.* This elaborate court presentation, Jonson's first, is patterned after a Roman wedding ceremony (denoting James's love of imperial motifs, the swelling acts of *his* imperial theme). The show opens with an enthroned "Juno, whose great name / Is UNIO, in the anagram" (11. 231–32), but as Parry writes elsewhere, "the masque spreads out to illuminate political and philosophic truths. . . . So in the climactic tableau Jonson links the marriage of Essex and Suffolk [in whose honor it is staged] to the royal marriage of James and Anne, to the union of the kingdoms, to the union of the elements of human nature under the government of Reason, and to the union of heaven and earth effected by the love of God."[39]

But, again amphibologically, all this theatricality had its dark side as well. Sir Anthony Weldon's later description of James, perhaps recording oral reports, tells of the results of his unfortunate birth:

> The king's character is much easier to take than his picture, for he could never be brought to sit for the taking of that. . . . He was of a middle stature, more corpulent through his cloathes then in his body, yet fat enough, his cloathes ever being made large and easie, the doublets quilted for steletto proofe, his breeches in great pleits and full stuffed: he was naturally of a timorous disposition, which was the reason of his quilted doublets; his eyes large, ever rowling after any stranger that came in his presence, inasmuch as many for shame have left the roome, as being out of countenance; his beard was very thin; his tongue too large for his mouth, which ever made him speak full in the mouth, and made him drink very uncomely, as if eating his drink, which came out into the cup of each side of his mouth . . . his legs were very weake, having had (as was thought) some foul play in his youth, or rather before he was born, that he was not able to stand at seven years of age, that weaknesse made him ever leaning on other mens shoulders; his walk was ever circular, his fingers ever in that walke fiddling about his codpiece.[40]

This James resembles more the weaker Duncan, while John Davies, in his *Microcosmos,* printed in 1603 and reissued in 1605, comments on the two-edged sword of Jacobean ideology, on policy and tyranny (sig. Q1v), and

Sir Walter Ralegh alludes to the same amphibology more subtly in his posthumous *Prerogative of Parliaments in England:* "That which is done by the King, with the aduice of his priuate or priuie Councell, is done by the Kings absolute power" (sig. Il). Again like Duncan, one of James's first acts in 1603 was to abolish the law of tanistry; like Macbeth, James inherited the throne by a double claim of father and mother and cousin-marriage, while Malcolm's psychological cruelty with Macduff in 4.3 seems reworked in the theatrical executions, or temporary stays of execution, from those involved in the Bye and Main Plots in 1604. James shares with Macbeth an ambitious imperialism and with Duncan the pronouncement of the death sentence without trial, as he shares with Malcolm the desire to unify Scotland and England. James made a similar royal entry into London following the Powder Plot in 1606.

At the time of *Macbeth* in 1606, then, there was much cause to be concerned about the new ruler who preached nationalism and international unity. He had, for one thing, displaced many Englishmen with Scots officers in the government and in the household—158 in all.[41] He put five Scotsmen on the Privy Council shortly after his arrival and put only Scotsmen next to him in the royal bedchamber. So the caustic jingle:

> Hark! Hark!
> The dogs do bark,
> The beggars have come to town.
> Some in rags,
> And some in tags,
> And some in velvet gowns.[42]

Garters were awarded to Lennox and Mar; "No Englishman, be his rank what it may, can enter the Presence Chamber without being summoned," the Venetian agent wrote in May 1603, "whereas the Scottish lords have free entrée of the privy chamber, and more especially at the toilette."[43] "The intrusion into court life of a group of Scots," writes Pauline Croft, led to "a complete change in court routine."[44] It is not surprising, with this sudden influx of new men, that Shakespeare's contemporary Arthur Wilson adds, "the streets swam night and day with bloody quarrels" between the English and Scots.[45]

But the Scots had the reputation of being quick of temper, and hot. John Major records in the history available to Shakespeare, and to his playgoers:

> At the first word of the presence of the foe, each man before midday is in arms, for he keeps his weapons about him, mounts his horse, makes for the

enemy's position, and, whether in order of battle or not in order of battle, rushes on the foe, not seldom bringing destruction on himself as well as on the invader. . . . They are full of mutual dissensions, and war rather than peace is their normal condition. The Scottish kings have with difficulty been able to withstand the inroads of these men. . . . They are armed with bow and arrows, a broadsword, and a small halbert. They always carry in their belt a stout dagger, single-edged, but of the sharpest.

In 1527 Boece had added:

The injure done to ony ane of thaim, was repute so common to thaim al, that thay wald nevir evoid the displeseir thairof out of thair hertis, quhill the samin war recompanist with the blude of thair ennimes. . . . The nobilis and commonis contendit quhay suld be maist faithful to othir; and quhen the capitane, throw his fers spreit and hardines, apperit in ony extreme dangeir of ennimes, all the band that was of his opinion, ruschit sa fersly to his defence, that othir thay deliverit him out of that present dangeir, or ellis all at anis lois thair lives with him,[46]

while Shakespeare's contemporary William Harrison adds, following Holinshed's *Chronicle,* that "the Scots, a people mixed of the Scithian and Spanish blood, . . . that unto our time [Ireland] cannot be cleansed of them. I find also that . . . these Scots were reputed for the most Scithianlike and barbarous nation."[47]

But "central and local [Scottish] records are full of references to 'murder, burning, ravishing of women, violent reif, slaughter, common theft and reset of theft,'" W. Croft Dickinson sums, showing the quick-tempered nature of the Scots at sharp disagreement with James's theatrical postures of peace, patience, and understanding, "or, more frequent still, 'wrangous, violent and masterful spoilation.'"[48] In 1590, James was himself unable to control the Highlands, where, Dickinson records, "certain of 'the wicked clan Gregor,' continuing in 'blood, slaughters, herschips, reifs and stouths,' had murdered the king's forester in Glenartney, and then, according to the accepted account, had cut off the dead man's head and had carried it to their young chief in Balquhidder" (389), much as Macduff longs to hold the tyrant Macbeth's head aloft; "Wee'l haue thee, as our rarer Monsters are / Painted vpon a pole, and vnder-writ, / Heere may you see the Tyrant'" (5.8.25–27; 2465–67). The cruelty of Macbeth, Duncan's "valiant Cousin, worthy Gentleman" (1.2.24; 43) because he took the enemy and, says the Captain, "with bloody execution, . . . / he vnseam' d him from the Naue to th' Chops" (1.2.18, 22; 37, 41), would confirm popular expectations of James and the Scots, and popular fears.[49]

"The union of the crowns was thus seen to hold in itself the seeds of its own destruction," Bruce Galloway tells us; "a great advancement for the Stuarts, but a great danger to their secure hold over either kingdom."[50] In *Macbeth* it is Banquo who introduces this metaphor, and it comes at a crucial moment—when the investigative, interrogative Banquo ("How farre is't called to [Forres]?" [1.3.39; 138]) suddenly *commands* the three sisters:

> . . . he seemes wrapt withall: to me you speake not.
> If you can looke into the Seedes of Time,
> And say, which Graine will grow; and which will not,
> Speake then to me, who neyther begge, nor feare
> Your fauors, nor your hate (1.3.57–61; 157–61),

although his dispassion is something he feigns, as he reveals a short time later ("haue we eaten on the insane *Root*" [1.3.84; 186; my italics]). When Macbeth attempts to counter Banquo's doubt ("Your Children shall be Kings" [1.3.86; 188]), it is Banquo who, in retrospect, confirms the witches and so first encourages Macbeth's hopes and fears, simply and declaratively: "You shall be King" (1.3.86; 189).

POLITICAL LEXIAS

Other proposed strings of lexias also associate King James with a Globe performance in 1606. Shakespeare's play rises with Macbeth's vision of "the swelling Act / Of the Imperiall Theame" (1.3.128–29; 239–40) and takes its descent with his later recognition in the vision the three sisters provide him: "some I see, / That two-fold Balles, and trebble Sceptres carry. / Horrible sight" (4.1.120–22; 1667–69). Yet to playgoers at the Globe in 1606 both observations would be current ones, and sharply discrepant, anachronistic to the historical Macbeth of the eleventh century. They use the actual language of James VI and I, bringing him verbally as well as visually, through the use of the mirror, into the play. Just as *Macbeth* shares James's theatricality, so it also builds on his political practices, subtle and shadowy lexias of his theoretical pronouncements about right rule. To establish cultural practices that constitute the cultural moment of *Macbeth* in 1606, I will at times need to cite primary documents at considerable length. If I were to paraphrase them, counter to the ways bytes lead to lexias, I would reduce the documents to impose my own lexias, while the real point of this chapter is to provide readers with bytes of various tones and subtlety so that they, too, may build their own lexias of reaction to *Macbeth* as the earliest spectators might have.

For instance, John King's sermon before James at Hampton Court on September 30, 1606, Kenneth Fincham and Peter Lake comment,

> proclaimed that "our Solomon or *Pacificus* liveth." . . . The sermon was the last in a series of four preached—and later printed—at the king's behest before an unwilling audience of Scottish Presbyterians. The quartet outlined James's standing as a ruler by divine right and laid down the conceptual foundations of the Jacobean church. A godly prince, exercising his divinely ordained powers as head of church and state, advised by godly bishops, themselves occupying offices of apostolic origin and purity, would preside over a new golden age of Christian peace and unity. . . . James I was *rex pacificus,* a new Constantine, a truly godly prince.[51]

All three—King, Fincham, and Lake—catch the mood James wished to have prevail in 1606. Tired of Scottish clan feuds and the strident opposition of the Scottish kirk, James saw in his accession to the English throne an opportunity for peace and harmony.

The message is central to his maiden speech to Parliament, on its first day, March 19, 1604:

> The first then of these blessings, which God hath ioyntly with my Person sent vnto you, is outward Peace: that is, peace abroad with all forreine neighbours: . . . the second great blessing that GOD hath with my Person sent vnto you, is Peace within, and that in a double forme. First, by my descent lineally out of the loynes of *Henry* the seuenth, is reunited and confirmed in mee the Vnion of the two Princely Roses of the two Houses of LANCASTER and YORKE. . . . But the Vnion of these two princely Houses, is nothing comparable to the Vnion of two ancient and famous Kingdomes, which is the other inward Peace annexed to my Person. (*Workes,* sigs. 2S3v–2S4)

Later, in his *Meditation upon the Lord's Prayer,* James struck a quite different pose: "I know not by what fortune, the *dicton* of PACIFICUS was added to my title, at my coming into England; that of the Lion, expressing true fortitude, having been my *dicton* before: but I am not ashamed of this addition; for King Salomon was a figure of CHRIST in that he was a king of Peace."[52] Others joined the chorus. Samuel Daniel, in his "Panegyricke Congratulatorie" published in *Certaine Poems* (1603; collected 1605), observes that

> What heretofore could neuer yet be wrought,
> By all the swords of powre, by blood, by fire,

By ruine, and destruction, here is brought
To passe, with peace, with love, with ioy, desire:
Our former blessed vnion hath begot. (sig. A3v)

In *The Ioiefvll and Blessed Revniting the two mighty & famous kingdomes, England & Scotland into their ancient name of great Britaine* (1605), John Bristoll adds, "King *Iames* doue-like bringeth the Oliue branch, sheweth that the waters are abated, anger appeased, dangers escaped, sorrows fled, and that salvation, and ioy entereth the Arke of great Brittaine" (sig. K4v).

James set out, then, to realize the kind of peace sought by Duncan and Malcolm in Shakespeare's play. A royal proclamation on May 17, 1603, had confronted the war-torn border country between the two nations that had been the site of feuding, and his efforts soon renamed this land the middle shires, known for peace. He tackled external peace in a proclamation of June 23, 1603, promising to return any captured Spanish ships "without any long or chargeable suit of Law" (sig. B6v). The *Calendar of State Papers, Domestic* shows a flurry of actions toward peace: James moved to dissolve the garrison at Berwick on December 4, 1603; he reduced the troops in Ireland on December 12; and, more locally and chauvinistically, on April 15 of the following year he ordered Lord Chief Justice Popham to apprehend all those who sought to cause disturbances against Scotsmen. He further saw to it that the 1604 Articles of Peace with Spain was published in 1605. While most of the treatise is concerned with international commerce, the *Articles of Peace, Entercovrse and Commerce* also pursued his public stance as peacemaker: article 8 refused assistance to "the *Hollanders,* or other enemies of the King of Spaine" (sig. B4v), while article 28 released "such as hae been taken in warre, and are captives on either part" (sig. E2v). In the earliest years of the Jacobean reign, then—before *Macbeth* reached the Globe in 1606—James was putting an end to the antagonism with Spain that had begun with the death of Mary Tudor and the coronation of her Protestant sister, been exacerbated in 1570 by the excommunication of Elizabeth I by Pope Pius V, and deepened with Spanish armadas and English piracy. James was announcing a whole new era in history, as Malcolm does, with a government ruled by the "Grace of Grace" (5.9.38; 2525).

The strategic cornerstone of James's rule was, from the start, the union of the crowns, the establishment of Great Britain, bringing together the two nations, which Malcolm, in league with the English Northumberland, achieves in act 5 of *Macbeth*. But it was not easy to persuade the English whose dislike of the Scots had been exercised in centuries of minor skirmishes along their common border and only culminated in the massacre at Flodden Field. The poet-scholar-king thus showed ingenuity as well. He began, in his March 19, 1604, speech to Parliament, by using Elizabeth I's own posture and language, changing only the gender:

> What God hath conioyned then, let no man separate. I am the Husband, and all the whole Isle is my lawfull Wife; I am the Head, and it is my Body: I am the Shepherd, and it is my flocke: I hope therefore no man will be so vnreasonable as to thinke that I that am a Christian King vnder the Gospel, should be a Polygamist and husband to two wiues; that I being the Head, should haue a diuided and monstrous Body; or that being the Shepheard to so faire a Flocke (whose fold hath no wall to hedge it but the foure Seas) should haue my Flocke parted in two . . . as God hath made *Scotland* the one halfe of this Isle to enioy my Birth, and the first and most vnperfect halfe of my life, and you heere to enioy the perfect and the last halfe thereof; so can I not thinke that any would be so iniurious to me, no not in their thoughts and wishes, as to cut asunder the one halfe of me from the other (*Workes,* sigs. 2S4v–2S5),

or some of the language finding haunting resonance in *Macbeth.* He returned to the notion of partnership in marriage in his speech to Parliament at Whitehall the year after *Macbeth* first went onstage, on March 31, 1607:

> Vnion is a mariage: . . . Is it the readiest way to agree a priuate quarell betweene two, to bring them at the first to shake hands, and as it were kisse other, and lie vnder one roofe or rather in one bedde together, before that first the ground of their quarell be communed vpon, their mindes mitigated, their affections prepared, and all other circumstances first vsed, that ought to be vsed to proceed to such a finall agreement? (*Workes,* sig. 2V5)

James's proposal follows, closely at times, that of Protector Somerset in 1547, in his "Epistle Exhortation"—"we will haue a mariage and no conquest, wee wishe peace and amitie, we are wery of bataill and miserie"[53]—which Roger A. Mason has found "loaded with connotations of English hegemony."[54] One of James's Scottish preachers, John Gordon, even found a creative etymology in the Bible:

> This name of *Brittania,* or *Brettania* cometh from the name of such a one of the posterity of Japhet [Genesis 10], that did first divide the Isles of the Gentiles, unto whom by lot this Island did fall. Therefore it is most certain that as the rest of the name of the kingdoms of Europe, did take their original name from the sons of Japhet: even so we must seek the etymology of Brittania, out of the Hebrew language, which is Brit-an-iah, and doth consist of three words. BRIT signifieth, *foedus,* a covenant; AN, *ibi,* there; IAH, *Dei,* of

God. Which three being conjoined in one, do signify, that THERE IS THE COVENANT OF GOD, that is, in this Island the covenant of God was to be established,

augmenting James's proposal that Britain was derived from the island's conqueror Brut, while in a court sermon of 1604 John Hopkins finds in the union of Israel with Judah a prototype of Anglo-Scottish union.[55]

There was very little if anything original about James's posture, but he was able to succeed where others attempting union before him had failed because of the convergence of forces few if any could predict: previous dynastic marriages; Elizabeth I's failure to produce an heir; discontent in Scotland with French interventions; the Protestant Reformation; and the defeat of the Catholic Mary Stuart, causing James to be reared, like Elizabeth, a Protestant. We can judge the popularity of James's position—at least with some—by the visual and verbal presentation to the royal family when they first arrived at the Tower of London preceding the coronation in Westminster. As the orator put it publicly: "The partition-wall betweene these two Kingdomes by the finger of God at your coming to the crowne is gone."[56]

And once more deeds confirmed words. On January 1, 1604, the court saw a masque uniting Chinese and Indian knights. On January 6, Samuel Daniel's masque of *The Vision of Twelve Goddesses* assembled them at the Temple of Peace. In 1604 a new common coinage of both kingdoms featured the title "king of Great Britain." The five-shilling piece, or sixty shillings Scots, displayed a rose or thistle on the housings of a horse being ridden by James with the inscription, "QVAE DEUS CONIVNXIT NEMO SEPARET" ("What God has joined together let no man separate"). In 1604 there was also a thistle crown with its reverse motto Ezekiel 37:22: "FACIAM EOS IN VNAM" ("I will make them one nation in the land, on the mountains of Israel. There will be one king over all of them and they will never again be two nations or be divided into two kingdoms").[57] In October 1604 James showed his determination that Parliament accept the union of the crowns by using the royal prerogative to alter his title to "King of Great Britain, France and Ireland"—the new "trebble Sceptres"—and gained some support from Sir Edward Coke, who devised a British coat of arms. William Drummond of Hawthornden made reference to "the King of Great Britain (for so I must now, for distinction of two Kings in one Island, call him),"[58] and other Scots writers joined in. For the poet Robert Ayton the Tweed was seen as "Fair famous flood, which sometyme did devyde / But now conjoyns, two Diadems in one," and Alexander Craig styled James as "a father and a famous prince / . . . Keepes Britaine whole, least it be over throwne."[59]

There were also sound tactical reasons for pursuing unification. With the two countries joined, James could strengthen his own dynasty, improve political stability and administrative efficiency, aid both economies, and even use the harmonizing polity of the English church to help settle down the unruly, independent kirks. The final reason for advocating union was, as Brian P. Levack has it, "the fulfilment of a historical and divinely inspired plan. Because it was commonly believed that the two nations had been united in the murky medieval past," he remarks, "because many previous attempts had been made to recover that unity, especially in the sixteenth century, and because the actual Union of the Crowns appeared to be the work of Divine Providence, unionists in the early seventeenth century considered the further union of the two kingdoms to be a divine mission" (7). It realized, in a wonderfully fortunate way, a harmonious era for what was widely regarded as the coming apocalypse, so that, as Shakespeare's Macbeth prophesies, James's "Line [will] stretch out to'th'-cracke of Doome" (4.1.117; 1664). This scriptural notion also caught fire: "Have wee not a Christian king going before us to fight the Lords battell, hazarding all that he hath for the welfare of Jerusalem?" asked William Cowper. "Then blest the time wherein great James began," wrote the poet James Maxwell, "T'unite the Crowns of this great Ile of Man." John Russell, the Scottish lawyer, agreed: "For as under Lucius, Britanie was the first pairt that banischit gentilisme, Inlymaner God raysit *vp* of the same Ile, Constantine the great quha expellit Romaine Idolatrie, furth of all the wther provinces of the habitable warld."[60] It became a new marriage now: not Scotland and England but Christianity and empire. Shakespeare's play addresses them both.

Macbeth's "Imperiall Theame" (1.3.129; 240) in time becomes Malcolm's "Imperiall charge" (4.3.20; 1836). But like union, empire was not a new concept. The preamble to Henry VIII's Act in Restraint of Appeals (1533) claimed that "this realm of England is an empire,"[61] while in 1547, drafting his will, he wrote, "a full and plain gift disposition assignement declaration limitation and appoinctement wt' what conditions our doughters Mary and Elizabeth shall severally have hold and enjoye the sayd imperial Crowne and other the premiss's after our deceasse and for default of issue and heyres of the severall bodyes of us and of our sonne prince Edward lawfully begotten and his heyres."[62]

The imperial crown became Tudor property. The first edition of John

Foxe's *Actes and Monuments* (1563) compares the early sufferings of Elizabeth I with the Marian persecution of Reformed martyrs and her reign to
that of Constantine, the Church's first emperor: to make it mnemonic, he
placed a portrait of the Queen within the capital *C* of Constantine.[63] When
James passed under seven memorial arches in his royal entry into London,
the first of the seven designed by Ben Jonson recalled this with a figure
representing the monarchy of Britain sitting below the crowns of England
and Scotland, with the motto, "Orbis Britannicus, Divisus ab orbe," which,
Jonson said, was "to shew that this empire is a world divided from the
world." He was referring to James as Augustus.[64] John Russell wrote a
treatise called "the happie and blissed Unioun betuixt the tua ancienne
realmes of Scotland and Ingland . . . presently undir the gratious mon-
archie and impyir of our dread soverane, King James the Sixt of Scotland,
First of Ingland, France and Ireland," and James was given an accession
medal that read "Emperor of the whole island of Britain." Elizabeth I had
seen a model for her civilized rule in the achievements of Rome, and analogies of early Stuart rule under Rome continued: it helps to explain the
numerous Roman plays of the period, including *Antony and Cleopatra* and
Coriolanus as well as *Sejanus* and *Catiline His Conspiracy*. But James continued to give pride of place to his own imperialism, in part because it reinforced his desire to reunite Scotland and England. He used the imperial
crown wherever possible—in speeches, proclamations, and documents—
where it often replaces the royal crown and on the most significant proclamations it appears just above "By the King." In a proclamation on the
Powder Plot, it even *replaces* "By the King."

In an inventory the following year—in fact, in 1606, the year of *Macbeth*—James records:

> The Imperiall Diadem and Crowne, and other Roiall and Princely orna-
> ments and Jewells to be indyvidually and inseparably for ever hereafter an-
> nexed to the Kingdome of this Realme.
>
> Imprimis, the Imperiall Crowne of this Realme, of gould, the border
> garnished with seaven ballaces, eight saphiers, five pointed diamonds, twenty
> rubies (two of them being craised [broken]), nineteen pearles; and one of the
> crosses of the same Crown garnished with a great sapphire, an emoralde
> crased, four ballaces and nyne pearles not all of one sort.[65]

But not everyone had the same high praise for imperialism. In his essay
"Of Empire," Francis Bacon concludes, "All precepts concerning Kinges
are in effect comprehended in these two remembrances. *Memento quod es
homo,* and *Memento quo es Deus,* or *Vice dei:* The one to bridle their

power, & the other their will" (11.9; 1612 edition, sig. I8v), a reference, according to Ernst H. Kantorowicz, to the new Roman emperor en route to the Capitol, who is told by his slave, "Look behind thee. Remember thou art a man."[66]

The Macbeths share James's view as they reach out for the power and the glory. Lady Macbeth would keep her husband from "All that impeides thee from the Golden Round, / Which Fate and Metaphysicall ayde doth seeme / To haue thee crown'd withall" (1.5.28–30; 375–77), and Macbeth would wear his "Golden Opinions" in "their newest glosse" (1.7.33–34; 509–10); what he fears most is the devaluation and mockery of that crown as seen in Banquo's threat to his position: then "Vpon my Head they plac'd a fruitlesse Crowne, / And put a barren Scepter in my Gripe" (3.1.60–61; 1051–52). Garments are equally symbolic, equally important. At first, Macbeth is surprised at the new title of Cawdor—"Why doe you dresse me in borrowed Robes?" (1.3.108–9; 215)—and Banquo too remarks, "New Honors come vpon him / Like our strange Garments, cleaue not to their mould, / But with the aid of vse" (1.3.145–47; 258–60). But once he is "drest" in royal hopes (1.7.36; 513), he is alert to Duncan's "Siluer skinne lac'd with his Golden Blood" and daggers "Vnmannerly breech'd with gore" (2.3.112–16; 877–81). Later, merely now an actor in the part, a king when life is but "a walking Shadow, a poore Player, / That struts and frets his houre vpon the Stage, / And then is heard no more" (5.5.24–26; 2345–47), he realizes Cathnes's prophecy—"He cannot buckle his distemper'd cause / Within the belt of Rule"—and Angus's agreement: "Now do's he feele his Title / Hang loose about him, like a Giants Robe / Vpon a dwarfish Theefe" (5.2.15–16, 20–22; 2192–93, 2198–2200).

Those witnessing *Macbeth* at the Globe in 1606 who wished to know more about James's own political theory did not have far to look: his statements were readily available. *Basilicon Doron* went through eight distinct editions, impressions and issues in London in 1603 and a ninth edition in Edinburgh: twelve thousand copies in less than a month, selling at 5½d.[67] This book, James writes in the epistle "To the Reader," *must be taken of all men, for the trew image of my very minde*" (*Workes*, sig. N2). While the strategies James proposes may involve dissimulation and theatricality, the philosophy is straightforward: kings rule men absolutely, yet are in turn absolutely ruled by, and accountable to, God. In essence, he will not depart from that belief, although he will seek the limits of its possibility for kingcraft. Willymat's *A Loyal Subjects Looking-Glasse* argues for the complementary obedience of all citizens; they must refrain "from taking in hand or intermeddling with any part of the Magistrates office," attending "only each of them his owne private busines according as his owne place, function, and calling requireth" (47–49, 58–59). Fulke Greville concurs in his *Treatise of Monarchy,* arguing that monarchy is the best form of government: the king's authority ascertained the public good, and even if he degenerated into a tyrant, it was not the place of the people (but only of God) to resist him. Gentillet's *Discourse,* translated into English by Simon Patericke in 1602, amended this only slightly by urging princely counsel: "A Prince, how prudent soever he be, ought not so much to esteeme of his owne wisedome, as to despise the counsell of other wise men, *Salomon* despised them not, and *Charles the wise* alwaies conferred of his affaires with the wise men of his Counsell" (sigs. B2–B2v).

James further elaborated on his theory and strengthened his own position as ruler in *The Trew Law of Free Monarchies: Or the Reciprock and Mvtvall Dvetie Betwixt a Free King, and His Naturall Subiects,* which went through one edition in 1598 and two more in 1603. The basic proposition immediately unsettled: "Kings are called Gods by the propheticall King *Dauid,* because they sit vpon GOD his Throne in the earth, and haue the count of their administration to giue vnto him" (*Workes,* sig. R1v). For James the pamphlet defended the divine right of kings, but for many of his subjects it proclaimed absolutism. In either event, it proceeds rationally and logically, arguing an understanding of right rule from scriptural, legal, and natural grounds. His own example of the first was, surprisingly, Samuel's prophecy of the tyrant Saul, whom he defends before arguing more generally, building on 1 Samuel:

> Now then, since the erection of this Kingdome and Monarchie among the Iewes, and the law thereof may, and ought to bee a paterne to all Christian and well founded Monarchies, as beeing founded by God himselfe, who by his Oracle, and out of his owne mouth gaue the law thereof: what liberty can broiling spirits, and rebellious minds claime iustly to against any Christian Monarchie; since they can claime to no greater libertie on their part, nor the people of God might haue done, and no greater tyranny was euer executed by any Prince or tyrant [than Saul], whom they can obiect, nor was here fore-warned to the people of God, (and yet all rebellion countermanded vnto them). (sig. R4)

He was equally unforgiving when it came to the law of the state:

> The kings . . . in *Scotland* were before any estates or rankes of men within the same, before any Parliaments were holden, or lawes made: and by them was the land distributed (which at the first was whole theirs) states erected and decerned, and formes of gouernement deuised and established: And so it

followes of necessitie, that the kings were the authors and makers of the Lawes, and not the Lawes of the kings. (sig. R5)

Thus "ye see it manifest, that the King is ouer-Lord of the whole land: so is he Master ouer euery person that inhabiteth the same, hauing power ouer the life and death of euery one of them" (sig. R6). He finds final support in natural law:

> And the proper office of a King towards his Subiects, agrees very wel with the office of the head towards the body, and all members thereof: For from the head, being the seate of Iudgement, proceedeth the care and foresight of guiding, and preuenting all euill that may come to the body or any part thereof. The head cares for the body, so doeth the King for his people. . . . And for the similitude of the head and the body, it may very well fall out that the head will be forced to garre cut off some rotten member (as I haue already said) to keepe the rest of the body in integritie: but what state the body can be in, if the head, for any infirmitie that can fall to it, be cut off, I leaue it to the readers iudgment. (sigs. R6v, S1)

And if the argument is raised that a wicked man may become king or tyrant, then that, James continues, is as it should be:

> Whereunto for answers, I grant indeed, that a wicked king is sent by God for a curse to his people, and a plague for their sinnes: but that it is lawfull to them to shake off that curse at their owne hand, which God hath laid on them, that I deny, and may so do iustly. . . . As for vindicating to themselues their owne libertie, what lawfull power haue they to reuoke to themselues againe those priuiledges, which by their owne consent before were so fully put out of their hands? for if a Prince cannot iustly bring backe againe to himself the priuiledges once bestowed by him or his predecessors vpon any state or ranke of his subiects; how much lesse may the subiects reaue out of the princes hand that superioritie, which he and his Predecessors haue so long brooked ouer them? (sigs. S1v–S2)

Later, in *A Speach in the Starre-Chamber,* delivered on June 20, 1616, he went even further, to the secret knowledge, the *arcani imperii,* available only to kings: "It is Athiesme and blasphemie to dispute what God can doe: . . . so, it is presumption and high contempt in a Subiect, to dispute what a King can doe, or say that a King cannot doe this, or that" (*Workes,* sig. 3A3).

James concludes in *A Trewe Lawe,* "And it is here likewise to be noted, that the duty and alleageance, which the people sweareth to their prince, is not only bound to themselues, but likewise to their lawfull heires and posterity, the lineall successiõ of crowns" (sig. S3). Together, the two statements come close to the medieval theory of the king's two bodies, promulgated in 1606 by Richard Knolles's translation of Jean Bodin as *Sixe Bookes of a Commonweale:* "It is an old prouerbe with vs, That the king doth neuer die, but that so soone as he is dead, the next male of his stocke is seised of the kingdome, and in possession thereof before he can be crowned, which is not conferred vnto him by succession of his father, but by vertue of the law of the land" (sig. L2v). Bodin's treatise had a similar fate— whereas he meant to uphold the fundamental power of law, he makes statements that sound as absolutist as James's: "Sometimes things fall out, as that the law may be good, iust, and reasonable, and yet the prince to be no way subiect or bound thereunto" (sig. K5v). Both James and Bodin supply Duncan and Malcolm—but also Macbeth—with philosophical underpinning for their theatrically political practices.

In a Scottish context, James's theory makes good sense: he is establishing his right to divine rule to oppose and defeat the republican politics and theories of Buchanan that were promulgated by the kirk, first by John Knox and then by Andrew Melville and his followers. James wanted, in Roger A. Mason's words, "to establish an English-style royal supremacy over the Scottish kirk."[68] "Faced with the horrors of Buchanan and Huguenot resistance theory," Glenn Burgess adds, "James needed to demonstrate, not that kings were unlimited, but rather that their being limited did not imply that there was on earth any power superior to them."[69] But others saw things otherwise. Defining empire and imperialism, John Hayward also defined absolutism:

> The rights of Soueraignty or of maiesty, so termed by *Cicero;* and by *Liuie,* the rights of Empire, and of Imperiall Maiestie; by *Tacitus, sacra regni* . . . are nothing else, but an absolute and perpetuall power, to exercise the highest actions and affaires in some [cer]taine state. These are the proper qualities of Soueraigne or Maiesticall power: that it be both absolute and also perpetuall. If it be absolute but not perpetuall, then is it not soueraigne. . . .
>
> Againe, if it be perpetuall but not absolute, as either depending vpon some other, or else giuen either vpon charge, or with exception and restraint, then it is not soueraigne. (sigs. B2v–B3)

Playgoers in 1606 could argue, then, that the very idea of government as perpetuated by James involved tyranny; insofar as it meant absolute rule, it was potentially a dangerous matter. Yet in 1567 John Fortescue had written in *A Learned Commendation of the Politique Lawes of Englande* that "a People . . . without a heade, is not worthye to be caled a bodie" (sigs. D7–D7v), and in *The Interpreter: Or Booke Containing the Signification of Words* (1607) John Cowell records that "the Saxon word *Cyninge* signifi[es] him that hath the highest power & absolute rule ouer our whole Land. . . . And though at his coronation he take an oath not to alter the lawes of the land: Yet this oath notwithstanding, hee may alter or suspend any particular lawe that seemeth hurtfull to the publike estate" (sig. 2Q1).

At the same time that James assumed the mantle of Constantine, he tried to put off association with the blessed gift of Edward the Confessor whose crown he wore: the medieval *rois thaumaturges,* "his Cure" against scrofula—necessary, Shakespeare's English doctor tells Malcolm and Macduff, since his country's "malady conuinces / The great assay of Art. But at his touch, / Such sanctity hath Heauen, giuen his hand, / They presently amend" (4.3.142–45; 1972–75). This seems a strange shortcoming in a King so aware and so able at kingcraft. The disease was well known and widely feared. The Elizabethan physician William Clowes writes a book called *A right frutefull treatise of the artificiall cure of struma* (1602)

> to demonstrate and deliver unto the friendly Reader, the cure of a certain unnaturall tumor or Abscecse called in Latin. Struma; of the Arabians Steophala, but generally, in English. it is called, the kings or Queenes Evill: A disease repugnant to nature: which grievous malady is knowne to be miraculously cured and healed, by the sacred hands of the Queenes most Royall Maiesty, even by Divine inspiration and wonderfull worke and power of god, above mans skill. Arte and expectation. . . . Scrofula taketh the name of Scropha, which signifieth a Sow, that is a Gluttonous and Phlegmaticke beaste: and it groweth in them by reason of their overmuch eating. There be some againe which say, that it is called Scrophula, either because that Sowes which give sucke be subiect to this disease, and that is the reason of their needy eating: or else because the sow that giveth Milke brings forth many young ones at once.[70]

Indeed, unlike James, Francois Laroque writes, "The coincidence between Lady Macbeth's Circean powers to plunge men into a *swinish sleep* and the witches' use of sow's blood in their cauldron, on the one hand, and Edward the Confessor's powers to heal by touch, the sow's disease or king's evil, on the other, suggests that Shakespeare did go into what medical information was available about scrofula while he was writing *Macbeth*" (75).

This practice, which historically began with Edward the Confessor, was by 1606 centuries old. "Throughout medieval and early modern England," Carole Levin reminds us, "there was a strong belief in magical healers, and the king was the most magical of all."[71] If the practice came and went through the late-medieval years, it was firmly reestablished, with all its dignity, by Henry VII as an act that could only be performed by the Lord's anointed. His granddaughter Mary added the washing of the feet of the afflicted by the kneeling monarch, emphasizing the religiosity of the occasion; and Elizabeth I, though Protestant, continued the practice as part of her duties as sacred majesty (a title James also assumed). Each year on Maundy Thursday Elizabeth would wash the feet of the poor, drawing a cross on each foot; and touching for the King's Evil became more prominent. Where previous monarchs had executed the touch on particular occasions, Elizabeth I performed it whenever she felt a divine directive or whenever a sufficient number of the sick had applied to the royal surgeons and had been thoroughly checked to see that their illness was not a sham. The Queen usually performed the touch at St. Stephen's Chapel on Friday, Sunday, or a feast day; she also performed it on progresses through the countryside. And not only Clowes, but also Elizabeth's chaplain, William Tooker, wrote a book on it (1597).

But for James, the royal touch, begun by St. Edward, was associated with Catholicism and superstition, and he wanted none of it. "He said," according to a papal representative, "he could not see how he could heal the sick without a miracle; but miracles had ceased—they no longer happened."[72] Marc Bloch, in his comprehensive study of the royal touch, comments that James's own hesitation may have been due to Calvinist belief as well. An anonymous letter from London on October 8, 1603, to the Vatican—then especially anxious to test James's religious leanings as the son of a Catholic queen—notes that the rite was preceded by a Calvinist sermon. The King then pronounced himself in a dilemma: he could either perform the act he thought superstitious, which he himself did not believe in, or he could break royal tradition despite the benefits it might bring to his people. Although he consented to attempt the royal touch, he would, he said, consider it a prayer for healing the sick in which he invited all present to join him. At the point of actually touching, he glanced sideways at the Scottish ministers for approval or disapproval; after they were touched, he was content to hang—or request others to hang—a gold coin around their necks, but without making the sign of the cross. At the same time, James redesigned the coin, removing the cross and the word *mirabile*. John Howson, in *A Sermon Preached at St. Mary's in Oxford, the 17 Day of November* (1602), preached that "there is *divination in labii regis*, divination in the lips of the King, Proverbs 16" (26), but, Marc Bloch notes, James "does not seem always to have taken the matter very seriously" (192). Nevertheless, the ritual and its legacy are cruxes in act 4 of *Macbeth*. If this scene were played at the Globe in 1606—or even later at court—what might it mean? Was it a criticism of James? a warning? a plea? Was this latter-day Edward, reentering the play through reference to him, dissociated from English royal lineage he claimed? To fear superstition in Shakespeare's play here is not Malcolm's position; it is Macbeth's.[73]

James's sense of sacred tradition beginning with Constantine, his statements about imperialism, and his theories about the function of kingship all inherently permit a kind of absolutism that quickly leads to tyranny. That too is the real danger in *Macbeth*. "Let your Highnesse / Command vpon me, to the which my duties / Are with a most indissoluble tye / For euer knit," the complicit Banquo, James's legendary ancestor, tells Macbeth (3.1.15–18; 1000–1003); later turning aside from Lenox, Macbeth himself claims that "From this moment, / The very firstlings of my heart shall be / The firstlings of my hand" (4.1.146–48; 1699–1701). No statement could guarantee absolutism more. Macbeth is referred to as a tyrant fifteen times in the play; from 4.3 until 5.9, this label usually replaces his name in addressing or referring to him. But Macbeth's behavior is closely aligned with remarks James made in Parliament in his early years, drawing especially angry responses from members of the House of Commons. "It was in this intellectual and political environment that Gentili wrote his *Regales disputations tres* in 1605," Levack comments.

> It would not be an exaggeration to claim that it was the most absolutist piece of writing that appeared in England in the early seventeenth century. Armed with quotations from the *Corpus juris civilis,* including the famous "quod principi placuit" and "legibus solutis est," Gentili identified the sovereign power of the state or *majestas* with the king's prerogative, an extraordinary power that was free from the law. Gentili did not free the king from natural or divine law, but no one, either in the civil law or common law traditions, had ever done that. Parliament, which figured so prominently in [Sir Thomas] Smith's [*De Republica Anglorum,* published in 1583, 1584, 1589, 1594, and 1601 before it was revised in 1607] as the most high and absolute power of the kingdom, was relegated to the subordinate status of a consultative body.[74]

In fact, James seemed to put aside the very form of Parliamentary government that he had once hoped to use in Scotland to overcome the fragmentation caused by the home rule of various kirks; he turned instead to the singular rule of king with the advice of counselors who themselves had little power. This he coupled with his later insistence on the mysteries of state, the *arcani imperii,* that God revealed only to kings. Both were utilized, as he tells Prince Henry in the opening of Book 3 of the *Basilicon Doron,* by performance: "IT is a trew old saying, That a King is as one set on a stage, whose smallest actions and gestures, all the people gazingly doe behold: and therefore although a King be neuer so praecise in the discharging of his Office, the people, who seeth but the outward part, will euer iudge of the substance, by the circumstances; and according to the outward appearance" (sig. P6v).

Here were authentic, detailed means of political practice. According to the records in the *Calendar of State Papers, Scotland,* Lord Scrope reported to Francis Walsingham on February 21, 1587, that when James heard that "his mother was in truth put to death, he not only took that news very grievously and offensively, but also gave out in secret speeches that he could not digest the same or leave it unrevenged" (9:300). Elsewhere, in the Salisbury Papers, Pury Ogilive notes for Archibald Douglas, on March 2, "Last of all I will assure you that the King moved never his countenance at the rehearsal of his mother's execution, nor leaves not his pastime and hunting more than of before" (13:334). David Calderwood, in his *History of the Kirk of Scotland,* observes that "when the king heard of the executioun, he could not conceale his inward joy, howbeit outwardlie he seemed to be sorrowfull. . . . He said that night to some few that were beside him, 'I am now sole king.' "[75] James accepted Elizabeth's letter of condolence with her claim of innocence and put on black mourning clothes rather than the sword many had wanted him to exercise. In November 1596, Robert Bowes wrote to Lord Burghley, Elizabeth's principal secretary, that James "hath conceaved great offence" at Spenser's portrayal of his mother in *The Faerie Queene* but there was no—there could be no—direct or open protest because, at the same time, seeking to become Elizabeth's heir, he was calling himself in their correspondence her "brother and sonn," and addressing letters to her as "madame and dearest mother." No mention was made of the fate of his actual mother then.[76] Yet once he was safely on the English throne, one of James's very first acts was to send a velvet pall to cover the tomb of the woman once accused of treason; the second of the first seven articles he introduced in Parliament— the first was the formulaic one declaring him King—was, according to a manuscript recently found in the London Public Records Office, an "Act for Disannulling of the Sentence given against the late Prince of famous Memory, Marie, Queen of Scotland, and the Defacing of all Records and Memories thereof." In 1605 James named the first royal child to be born of the Stuart family in England Mary, honoring his mother and returning her name to his lineage. Finally, on September 28, 1612, six years after *Macbeth* was first staged at the Globe and a decade before its publication in the First Folio, James wrote to the dean and chapter of Peterborough Cathedral, ordering them to exhume her body. "For that we remember," he says there, "it appertains to the duty we owe to our dearest mother that

100

like honour should be done to her body and like monument be extant of her as to others her and our progenitors have been used to be done." Her body was instead buried in a splendid tomb in Westminster Abbey and given a more glorious monument than that of Elizabeth I. It was a matter of show, of outward gesture for the admiration of his people; and with it, James finally obliterated any traces of treason by exercising the divine right he said made him answerable only to God.[77]

From another perspective, James's behavior was Tacitean, what Markku Peltonen calls "authority . . . grounded on the exploitation of deceit, dissimulation and trickery [that] had, nevertheless, been the only real choice in the corrupt world."[78] Sir Philip Sidney had written his brother Robert on October 18, 1580, that Tacitus was dangerous to a ruler as "the pithy opening the venome of wickednes,"[79] and Gabriel Harvey notes in the margins of his books that Tiberius's "brave quality and most suttle property" was that he "altogither fayned to do that, which he meant not to do: and not to do that which in deade he meant to."[80] Following the portrayal of Nero's court in Tacitus (translated by Henry Savile in 1591 and reprinted in 1598 and 1602) and confirming the ideas of Machiavelli (through Gentillet's *Discourse* of 1602 as well as James's own treatises) Peltonen continues, James's court was seen as corrupt and wicked:

> According to Francis Bacon, the court abounded with men whose "Art" made "a flourishing estate ruinous & distressed" but who could at the same time "fiddell very cunningly" and gain "both satisfaction with their Masters, and admiration with the vulgar." The court was regarded as completely devoid of virtues. "The Courtier," Thomas Gainsford defined, "that is all for shew and complement, is the onely professor of humanitie, master of curtesie, vaine promiser, idle protester, servant of folly, and scholler of deceit." Nobody should be so foolish as to trust a courtier, for, in a word, "he neither performeth what hee commonly sweares, nor remembers in absence, what hee hath formerly protested: so that his oaths and words are like smoake and aire: and his deeds and actions meerly shadowes, and farre from substance." According to Henry Wright, the court was a place where "all credit, countenance, honors, and authority" were "for the most part slippery, and not to be trusted unto." (128)

It is little wonder that, in such an environment, James continued to have nightmares about Buchanan revisiting him, and the continuing belief that he, like his ancestors, like his father, would be murdered in his bed. As a consequence, James further protected himself—aside from his dagger-proof clothing—with a large number of Scots. Foreign, alien, they were distrusted, and part of the problem as well as part of James's Tacitean solution. Such cultural practices resonate widely. "It is Art to hide Art," Dinarco says in Nicholas Breton's *Dialogue* of 1603; Lady Macbeth tells her husband, "Looke like the time, beare welcome in your Eye, / Your Hand, your Tongue: looke like th'innocent flower, / But be the Serpent vnder 't" (1.5.63–65; 419–21), and he later tells her to "Away, and mock the time with fairest show, / False Face must hide what the false Heart doth know" (1.7.82–83; 565–66). But the most overt warning echoed in the play, the most telling byte in any ordered lexia, may be from the English translation of Gentillet: "It seemeth that *Tarquin* forgot nothing of all that a tyrant could doe" (sig. X5v; cf. 2.1.55–56; 635–36): grim indeed.

But Savile's Nero, out of Tacitus, could have served Shakespeare's Macbeth as ready exemplum:

> The great Monarch of the world, adored erewhile as a god, attended upon and garded by thousands of frendes, of souldiers, of seruants, now as a page knocking at dores findeth all shutte against his unfortunate state. Thus in aduersitie destitute of ayde, of counsell or comforte of frendes, he returneth home, where finding his chamber rifled, the chamberlaines fled, his box of poyson remooued awaie. (sig. p2–p2v)

Thus a comparison with what David Womersley calls "Savile's final, marmoreal judgment on Nero"[81] also resonates in *Macbeth*:

> Thus Nero, a Prince in life contemptible, and hatefull in gouernment, hauing thereby disarmed himselfe both of the loue and feare of his subiects, ended his daies the eighth of Iune in the one and thirtieth yeare of his age, and fourteeneth of his Empire, at the first hauing ruled the state with reasonable liking, insomuch that Traian was wonted to saie, that euen good Princes were short of Neroes fiue yeares: but after breaking forth into all infamous behauiour, and detestable oppressions and cruelties, and beeing withall a Prince weake in action, not of uertue sufficient to upholdes his uices by might, he was at the length thus ouerthrown. (sig. p3)

Savile's judgment might be easier to project forward in 1602 and 1606, since it has no known classical source. As one of these many lexias, it characterizes both Shakespeare's king—the actual James—and the dramatized Macbeth.

Lexias of Resistance

Centralized power—such as Macbeth and James both represent in 1606—aroused actively strong resentment in some quarters, and works of resistance theory were written, read, and studied in others: Macduff as Thane of Fife, the second most powerful lord in the Scotland of Shakespeare's Macbeth, and Malcolm, Prince of Cumberland, designated successor to Duncan in the play, together captured the cultural moment of 1606 in their own cultural practices. On the face of it, Shakespeare's *Macbeth* would seem itself redolent of such interrogations. The play shows Banquo as Macbeth's accomplice, initially, although later in the play (4.1) it is clear that he is also James's ancestor. James could hardly appreciate a play on regicide that displayed so openly the vulnerability of the king—killed in his bed at that—so closely on the heels of the nearly successful Powder Plot. Nor might he approve of a play that brings about peace by an invasion of ten thousand English soldiers (4.3.134; 1962). But resistance was by 1606 widespread. "It encompassed many juridified forms of dispute and resolution," Keith Wrightson notes; "public presentment; private litigation; mediation and formal arbitration. It extended also to more fugitive forms of political action: gossip; verbal abuse; anonymous threats; libellous attacks on the credit of opponents; the use of gestures and symbols; the cacophonous processional mockery of 'rough music'; insubordinate grumbling; footdragging; 'playing dumb.' "[82] Men were known for antienclosure riots and grain and food riots, but Bernard Capp records that "disorderly women" were also "found in riots over grain prices, enclosures, common rights and other issues."[83] They may have been encouraged by seditious works. "An advertisement towching seditious writings" dated around 1590 claims there are "evident digressions and excursions into matters of state, debating titles, and Jurisdictions, quarrelling with lawes, & actes of Parliamente, examyning Treatyes, and negotiations, & every way presuming to move question of the proceedinges both abroade and at home, aswell in the churche as in the civill estate."[84]

But the momentum in England had been building at least since the work of two Marian exiles, John Ponet and Christopher Goodman, whose radical political thought argued that disobedience could on occasion be justified. According to Ponet's *Short Treatise of Politic Power* in 1556, "A commonwealth may stand well enough and flourish, albeit there be no kings, but contrary wise without a commonwealth there can be no king. Commonwealths and realms may live, when the head is cut off, and may put on a new head, that is, make them a new governor, when they see their old head seek too much of his own will and not the wealth of the whole body, for the which he was only ordained" (sig. D7).[85] Kings for Ponet are always subject to laws that dictate state policies, and the laws are made for the good of the commonwealth foremost. Christopher Goodman's *How Superior Powers Ought to Be Obeyed,* published in Geneva in 1558, argues that docile followers of evil leaders are just as evil themselves: they "suffer themselves like brute beastes rather than reasonable creatures, to be led and drawen where so ever their Princes commandements have called" (145–46). By 1595, with the publication of *A Conference About the Next Succession to the Crowne of Ingland,* recusants joined in; there the Jesuit Robert Persons was urging the same thing: "Not only hath the commonwealth authority to put back the next inheritors upon lawful considerations, but also to dispossess them that been lawfully put in possession if they fulfil not the laws and conditions, by which and for which, their dignity was given them" (32). It was vox populi with a vengeance; such writers, Jenny Wormald sums, "made it terrifyingly clear that if the nobility did not advance God's cause, then they would go beyond them and appeal to the people."[86] Tyrannical pronouncements such as that of Shakespeare's Duncan (1.4), it was argued, brought about their own opposition.

Such resistance theory was even more pronounced in sixteenth-century Scotland where James spent his formative years. It is difficult now to say how well known Scottish historians of resistance such as John Major and Hector Boece were in England—although James would know them well enough, and so would many of the Scots who accompanied him to London—but it is clear that two Scottish writers of resistance theory, John Knox and George Buchanan, wrote works that were circulating in England before and during the time of *Macbeth.* One of Knox's many works, the *Admonition or warning that the faithful Christiās in London, Newcastel, Barwycke & Others, may auoide Gods vegeauce, both in thys life and the life to come* (1554), printed perhaps in Antwerp, perhaps in London, has a title-page woodcut that shows Crueltye in league with Tyrannye imprisoning Trueth. For plentiful illustration, Knox's *History of the Reformation in Scotland* detailed, in his actions, sermons, and interviews with Mary Stuart, his refusal to obey her when his conscience dictated otherwise. Knox taught that the authority of kings rests on the consent of the people; but as the head of the Scottish kirk he also pronounced that in matters of religion it was the church, and never the state, that was the final authority. Thomas McCrie, his biographer, summarizes Knox's position: "if rulers become tyrannical, or employ their power for the destruction of their subjects, they may lawfully be controuled by them, and, proving incorrigible, may be deposed by the community as the superior power; and that tyrants may be judicially proceeded against, even to capital punishment."[87] Mason notes that Knox found this theory at odds with his own fundamental belief in a covenant theology, but managed to write resistance theory anyway by introducing the idea of an inferior magistracy and by making a distinction between the office of a prince and the prince's person.[88]

As for Buchanan's account of history governed by resistance theory, he gives to Constantine a long oration rejecting the principle of hereditary kingship. He writes more generally that

> since the arbitrary will of kings supplanted the laws, and men invested with unlimited and undefined powers did not regulate their conduct by reason but allowed many things because of partiality, many because of prejudice, and many because of self-interest—the arrogance of kings made laws necessary. For this reason, therefore, laws were devised by the people, and kings were forced to employ the legal authority, conferred upon them by the people, and not their arbitrary wills, in deciding cases. The people had been taught by long experience that it is better to trust their liberty to the laws than to kings; for the latter can be drawn away from justice by a great variety of forces, but the former, being deaf to both entreaties and to threats, pursues the one, unbroken course. . . . All the Estates of Scotland, in public assembly, gave judgment that James the Third was lawfully put to death, for his extreme cruelty toward his people and his shameful wickedness. And they made sure that none of the persons who banded together, plotted, and contributed money or effort in connection with the slaying should suffer because of it. They judged this act, then, to have been right, and done with due regard to legal form; nor is there any doubt but that they wished to set a precedent for posterity.[89]

But even as early as 300 B.C. with Fergus I, the monarchy was elective; in the instance of the debauchery of Durstus during the reign of Scotland's eleventh king, his very luxuriousness caused the nobility to rise against him and kill him in battle. Both Knox and Buchanan thus lay the groundwork for attacking Mary Stuart's luxuriousness and justifying the deposition of James's mother; in fact, Buchanan designed a special coin after the deposition that shows a crown balanced on the point of a sword, the republican symbol, with the motto, "pro me (se mereor) in me," "if I deserve it the blade will be used in my defense, if not it will be turned against me." As for the story of Macbeth, Buchanan argues that Duncan's faults required his removal from office and that Macbeth's tyranny resulted from his extraordinary clemency during his early years as king.

Such claims necessarily instigated a counternarrative, a revisionary history by James himself. It is found in the *Basilicon Doron,* where he writes to Prince Henry that

> the reformation of Religion in *Scotland,* being extraordinarily wrought by God, wherin many things were inordinately done by a popular tumult and rebellion, of such as blindly were doing the worke of God but clogged with their owne passions and particular respects, as well appeared by the destruc-tion of our policie, and not proceeding from the Princes order, as it did in our neighbour countrey of *England,* as likewise in *Denmarke,* and sundry parts of *Germanie;* some fierie spirited men in the ministerie got such a guiding of the people at that time of confusion, as finding the gust of government sweete, they begouth to fantasie to themselues a Democraticke forme of government: and having (by the iniquitie of time) beene overwell baited vpon the wracke, first of my Grandmother, and next of mine owne mother, and after vsurping the libertie of the time in my long minoritie, setled themselves so fast vpon that imagined Democracie, as they fed themselues with the hope to become *Tribuni plebis:* and so in a popular gouernment by leading the people by the nose, to beare the sway of all the rule. (*Workes,* sig. O2v)

He returns to this matter again in advising Henry of the importance of law:

> And next the Lawes, I would have you to be well versed in authentick histor-ies, and in the Chronicles of all nations, but specially in our owne histories (*Ne sis peregrinus domi*) the example whereof most neerely concerns you: I meane not of such infamous inuectiues, as *Buchanans* or *Knoxes* Chronicles. . . . But by reading of avthenticke histories and Chronicles, yee shall learne experience by Theoricke, applying the bypast things to the present estate, *quia nihil nouum sub sole:* such is the continuall volubilitie of things earthly, according to the roundnesse of the world, and reuolution of the heauenly circles: which is expressed by the wheeles in *Ezechiels* visions, and counter-feited by the Poets *in rota Fortunae.* (sig. P4v)

The book he eventually prescribes is Caesar's *Commentaries.*

But in England, as the century came to its close, it was hardly the Reformation alone that was the issue, or the "false histories" it inspired. There was also in circulation, for instance, the Latin treatise *Vindiciae con-tra Tyrannos* (1581) by the Huguenot Philip de Plessis-Mornay, who argues (in an English translation as *A Defence of Liberty*) that

> the law of nature teaches and commands us to maintain and defend our lives and liberties, without which life is scant worth the enjoying, against all injury and violence. . . . In the receiving and inauguration of a prince, there are covenants and contracts passed between him and the people, which are tacit

and expressed, natural or civil; to wit, to obey him faithfully whilst he commands justly, that he serving the commonwealth, all men shall serve him, that whilst he governs according to law, all shall be submitted to his government, etc. The officers of the kingdom are the guardians and protectors of these covenants and contracts. He who maliciously or wilfully violates these conditions, is questionless a tyrant by practice.[90]

Mornay and others like him were undoubtedly influenced by the ideas of La Boétie, praised at length in Montaigne's essay "On Friendship" translated by John Florio into English in 1603. In *Slaves by Choice* (1548), LaBoétie argues that tyranny suppresses man's rights, and continues, "There are three types of tyrant. Some are king by democratic election, others by force of arms, others by inheritance. . . . They come to power by different methods, but the way they govern is always virtually identical. Elected monarchs treat the people like bulls to be tamed, conquerors treat the people as their prey, inheritors treat the people as their natural slaves."[91] "We seem to be traveling the path toward Parliament's assertion in the Apology of 1604," George L. Mosse observes, that " 'The voice of the people in things of their knowledge is said to be as the voice of God.' "[92]

Such anxiously polemical concerns were sharply refocused in 1606, the year *Macbeth* played at the Globe, with the English translation of Jean Bodin's *Sixe Bookes of a Commonweale.* Like Knox, Bodin was grounded in covenant theology similar to that in Scotland, and he argued for an efficient and successful government that relies on counsel, execution, and assent: "The greatest difference betwixt a king and a tyrant is, for that a king conformeth himselfe vnto the lawes of nature, which the tyrant at his pleasure treadeth vnder foot: the one of them respecteth religion, iustice, and faith; whereas the other regardeth neither God, faith, nor law" (trans. Richard Knolles [1606], sig. T4v). For Bodin, sovereignty was indivisible. So it follows that

> if the prince be an absolute Soueraigne, as are the true Monarques of Fraunce, of Spain, of England, Scotland, Turkie, Moschouie, Tartarie, Persia, Aethiopia, India, and of almost all the kingdomes of Affricke, and Asia, where the kings themselues haue the soueraigntie without all doubt or question; not diuided with their subiects: in this case it is not lawfull for any one of the subiects in particular, or all of them in generall, to attempt any thing either by way of fact, or of iustice against the honour, life, or dignitie of the soueraigne: albeit that he had committed all the wickednes, impietie and crueltie that could be spoken; For as to proceed against him by way of justice, the subiect hath no such iurisdiction ouer his Soueraigne prince. (sig. V3v)

Using some of the same premises—such as the nature of law in societies—Bodin proceeded to quite different conclusions.

But opposition to Buchanan, Knox, and other writers of resistance theory had already been contributing to the debate. In Scotland there were replies in the *Pro regibus apologia* of Adam Blackwood (Poitiers, 1581), the *Velitatio in Georgium Buchananum* of Ninian Winzet (Ingolstadt, 1582), and the *De regno et regali potestate* of William Barclay (Paris, 1600). According to Blackwood, "The Senate and People of Rome had a certain authority over [the emperor]: the Senate and People of Scotland have no authority over [their kings]."[93] Winzet makes kings analogous to priests, answerable only to God. Barclay in his turn built on Winzet: once a king was crowned, he was entitled to the full obedience and submission of his people, with due honor and reverence, and this by divine precept: to rebel against a king was to rebel against God. In England, the church added *An Homily Against Disobedience, and Wilfull Rebellion* (1570) to Book 2 of the state *Homilies* in 1571, following the Northern Rebellion of earls in 1569; it set forth the terms of allowable dissent. Preachers were instructed to read regularly in their parishes at the time of *Macbeth* the following:

> As in reading of the holy Scriptures, we shall finde in very many and almost infinite places, aswell of the old Testament, as of the New, that Kings and Princes, aswell the euill as the good, doe raigne by Gods ordinance, and that subiects are bounden to obey them: that GOD doth give Princes wise-dome, great power, and authority: that GOD defendeth them against their enemies, and destroyeth their enemies horribly: that the anger and displea-sures of the Prince, is as the roaring of a Lyon, and the very messenger of death: and that the subiect that prouoketh him to displeasure, sinneth against his owne soule. (1633 ed., sigs. 226v–34).
>
> What shall subiects doe then? Shall . . . they obey valiant, stout, wise, and good Princes, and contemne, disobey, and rebell against children being their Princes, or against vndiscreete and evill gouernours? God forbid. (sig. 3A2)

In 1605, I. R.'s Ramist Latin treatise *Orion republicae* raised the stakes. In this work, translated almost at once into English by Edmund Sadler, I. R. contends that rather than being controlled by eternal laws, govern-ment was usually the uncertain business stemming from "the fraile nature and unconstant minde of men." A commonwealth, the author argues, is an active community of citizens who have special abilities to contribute to the common good, but these abilities and talents are at once indispensable and vulnerable to the "divers perils of things."[94] The tract is both humanist and disturbing, echoing in plays at the Globe like *Julius Caesar*.[95] Naomi

Conn Liebler reminds us that in 1606 the playgoers would also focus on rebellion: "At the beginning of *Macbeth*, the external threat posed by the Norwegian invasion is compounded by the interior treasons of Macdonwald and the Thane of Cawdor" (196). The daggers of Brutus and the other conspirators in their republican revolution are taken up by Macbeth; but in calling on this conventional republican symbol, Shakespeare embeds in the play the cultural memory of the assassination (with Brutus) that temporarily brought down Roman imperialism and (in Macbeth's reference to Tarquin) the Roman ravishing and rape that led to the fall of the Roman monarchy.

In answer to such growing sentiment, James pulled back into a role of mystification. For him, "The holiness of power creates the power of holiness," as Debora Kuller Shuger has recently claimed. Both "the mysterie of the Kings power," as James himself put it, and his "absolute Prerogative" stemmed from the mystical knowledge that only divine rulers appointed by God came to have, the *arcana imperii*, or *secrets* of state, which surpassed discussion and dispute. "In James," Shuger adds, "this 'mystery' is equated with 'what a King may do in the height of his power,' that is with his *potentia absoluta* and perhaps also with the Tacitean *arcana imperii*, where it is implied that the prince's prerogative is not only sacred . . . but involves a disparity between 'declared policy and actual strategy.' "[96] In time, James would declare before Star Chamber, "It is Athiesme and blasphemie to dispute what God can doe; good Christians content themselues with his will reuealed in his word. so, it is presumption and high contempt in a Subiect, to dispute what a King can doe, or say that a King cannot doe this, or that; but rest in that which is the Kings reuealed will in his Law" (*Workes*, sig. 3A3).

In 1606 treason was defined broadly to encompass intentions, words, and deeds. Active conspiracies kept testing resistance theory; and in the years preceding 1606 at the Globe, there were many analogies to Macbeth's treachery and brutality. Those who had read the Scottish history in Holinshed's *Chronicles* knew it as a history of slaughter, beginning with the trap laid by King Durstus against those who wished for a more civilized government:

> Once signified abrode in their countreys amongst their friendes and kinsfolke, [this] caused a new commotiõ so that within a fewe dayes after, many thousandes of men in furious rage came before the castell, and besieged the king moste straitly therein. Who perseyuing himselfe in suche daunger as he

knewe not well howe to escape, came foorth with suche companie as he had about him, and encountring with his enimies was straight wayes beaten downe amongst them, and so at once loste there bothe kingdome and life in the .ix. yeare of his reygne. (1577 ed., sig. B3v)

Such treachery also pursued the Stuart government until the time of Shakespeare's play. First there was the matter of David Rizzio, the Queen's personal secretary. Convinced that the child Mary was carrying was Rizzio's, King Henry, Lord Darnley, was persuaded by his companions to murder Rizzio in the Queen's presence during their private dinner on March 9, 1566, hoping to frighten her and terminate the pregnancy. In retaliation—or so it was believed—and in league with the Earl of Bothwell who had replaced Henry Darnley in her affections, Mary was thought to be implicated in the death of James's father the following February. He was strangled within the house where he was recovering from an illness; the house itself was blown up by gunpowder: the notorious event at Kirk o' Fields, attached to the collegiate church of St. Mary-in-the-Field, just inside the Edinburgh town wall and not far from the palace of Holyrood-house. Four months later, on June 19, 1566, James was born; on July 29, 1567, he was crowned king after his mother, deposed by the Scottish lords, had fled to exile in England. For the first twelve years of his life, James was king largely in name; the country was first ruled by the Earl of Morton as regent, then by the powerful Earls of Argyll and Atholl. Shortly before James's twelfth birthday they persuaded him to abolish the regency and proclaim his own "acceptance of the government." According to historian G. P. V. Akrigg,

> The triumph was somewhat dashed for Argyll when the young Earl of Mar managed to regain control of Stirling Castle from him by a sudden coup, brought Morton before the King, and secured for the deposed regent a place on the Council. The scene was a nasty one and might have turned murderous. James was awakened from his sleep by the tumult and rose to see swords and daggers drawn, and the son of his governor, the Master of Mar, trampled to death in the mêlée. About the young King swirled the violent ambitions and passions of the great lords. He must have been sick with fear for his own safety.[97]

This doubtless contributed to James's lifelong fear of his own assassination; and it may also have contributed to *Macbeth*, which, notes Maynard Mack, Jr., "confronts the full tragedy of *king killing;* religious, political, and personal dimensions combine to piece out the full meaning of regicide; emphasis falls evenly on the action, the actor, and the figure acted upon."[98]

110

The other side of king killing is self-preservation. Since the weird sisters on the heath near Forres accurately predict Macbeth's new title of Cawdor, he reasons he can win and protect the crown by eliminating Banquo's line so that it cannot succeed him; when that fails, he attempts to find Macduff, the rival thane of Fife who ritually bestowed the crown at the ceremony at Scone. First Banquo and then Macduff, therefore, are presented at the Globe Theater in 1606 as threats to Macbeth's rule. In contemporary history, the rival Ruthven family had the same relationship with James. John Ruthven, first Earl of Gowrie, came from a family long the enemy of the Stuarts. His grandfather Patrick, third Lord Ruthven, was a leader in the Lords of Congregation who rebelled against Mary Stuart's mother, Mary of Guise, and his son William and he had been present at Rizzio's death. William, in turn, as the fourth Lord Ruthven, helped Lord Lindsay to force Mary Stuart's abdication at Loch Leven Castle and was a leader of the Ruthven Raid on James himself in 1582. That year—notably the year of Buchanan's *History* attacking Mary, his "infamous invective"— the Protestant opposition to James, who saw him as the son of two Catholics, one the former Queen of France, kidnapped him. James was in the company of his closest companion, Esmé Stuart, Earl of Lennox, his Catholic first cousin from France and his sole remaining family member. Lennox allowed James to hunt near Perth relatively unguarded and, as the kirk accused the King of neglecting Christ's true Church, James was abducted by Mar, the Earl of Gowrie, chief of the Ruthvens, the Master of Glamis, and others and brought to nearby Ruthven Castle, known as Huntingtower. James was kept there for what M. C. Bradbrook has called "ten painful months,"[99] taunted and humiliated by the older men. "But," writes Nigel Trantor,

> the sixteen-year-old monarch did more than weep. He perceived the uneasy alliance of his captors, their weaknesses and rivalries, and worked on them to cause dissention. Apparently accepting his state, he schemed to end his detention. He had messages smuggled out to other lords and factions, especially the Catholics, amongst them the Lord Seton who had once rescued his mother. And, at length, using his very fondness for the chase which had led to his capture as a means of ending it, he contrived a hunting expedition eastwards in which he got away from most of his guards and into the arms of those with whom he had been corresponding. They then all rode post-haste for St. Andrews and freedom.[100]

At liberty at last, James had learned to battle danger with dissimulation: he mocked his time with fairest show. He also learned that blood will have blood. In 1584, after a second attempt to capture him, James seized and executed the Earl of Gowrie. Subsequently, the house of Ruthven was restored to James, the son of William, named the second Earl of Gowrie. He died unexpectedly in 1588. His brother John, the third Earl of Gowrie, in alliance with the widowed Lady Gowrie their mother, by 1594 was involved in various attempts by Francis Stewart, the new Earl of Bothwell, on James's life. It was claimed that Bothwell (the "Wizard Earl," as he came to be called) convened a coven of witches at North Berwick who attempted to drown James and Anne of Denmark at sea and that he later attempted other acts of witchcraft. On the morning of July 24, 1593, the Earl of Bothwell actually entered James's palace. As D. Harris Willson narrates the event,

> the King awoke and was about to dress [when] he heard a strange commotion in the adjoining chamber. Rushing from his bedroom in a very dishevelled state, he was horrified to behold Bothwell on his knees with a drawn sword lying before him. By this symbolism the outlaw intended to convey the meaning that he was in possession of Holyroodhouse and had the King in his power yet would do no harm to the royal person. Naturally enough, however, James was more impressed by the sword than by Bothwell's suppliant position. Shouting "Treason," he made for the Queen's bedchamber but found it bolted. He then faced his enemy with a courage born of desperation [much as Macbeth faces Macduff in 5.8]. Bothwell might take his life, he screamed, but should not, like Satan dealing with a witch, obtain his immortal soul. . . . The tension of the melodrama was now relieved by the appearance of Lennox and other friends of the outlaw, and the King began to recognize a familiar pattern of Scots persuasiveness. He agreed to a parley. With rare presence of mind he pretended to be touched by Bothwell's show of contrition, questioned him sharply about his dealings with Elizabeth, and agreed to a compromise by which the rebel should withdraw from court until he stood trial for his old offence of witchcraft.[101]

Bothwell left court in shame and eventually disappeared; John, third Earl of Gowrie, went to Padua with his tutor to study and, it was rumored, converted to Catholicism in December 1598.

But then all was not well again. In August 1599 the Scottish kirk decided to recall Gowrie, who returned by way of London, opposing James's proposal for new taxes to reinforce an army in his quest for the English crown. What happened next, in the version overseen by the King himself, is reported in *The Earle of Gowries conspiracie against the Kings Maiestie of Scotland. At Saint Iohn-stoun* [Perth, the only walled city in Fife] *vpon Tuesday the fift of August. 1600,* printed in 1600 in Edinburgh and in

London by Valentine Simmes, who had printed several of Shakespeare's plays. Accompanied with the testimony before the Lord Chancellor and others of the friends and servants of Gowrie—John Welmys on August 9; William Rynd, the Earl's tutor, on August 20; and Andrew Henderson, who was in the turret, on August 20—the pamphlet tells the narrative of the time early on the morning of Tuesday, August 5, when young Master Alexander, "second brother to the late earle of Gowrie" (sig. A2), approached the King who was preparing to go buck hunting at Falkland Palace. Ruthven told of meeting "a base like fellow, unknowne to him, with a cloke cast about his mouth" (sig. A2v), who, upon examination, was found to have "a great wide pot to be vnder his arme, all full of coyned gold in great peeces" (sig. A2v). The King thought it might be papist money intended for Jesuits and agreed to come to Gowrie House to see it for himself. He was taken there where he was apparently unexpected, given dinner, and then led through a series of rooms, with each door shut and locked behind him. Finally he arrived at "a little studie, where he saw standing with a very abased countenance, not a bond-man, but a free man, with a Dagger at his girdle" (sig. B3). Master Ruthven then locked the study door in the turret of the house, removed his hat, picked up the dagger, and threatened to kill the King to revenge the death of his brother the second Earl. Just as suddenly, he left to consult with his living brother, the third Earl. Then "maister *Alexander* very speedily returned, and at his incomming to his Maiestie, casting his handes abroad in a desperate manner, saide, he could not mend it his Maiesty behooued to die" (sig. B4v). A struggle ensued and James called out the turret window for help. During the melee,

> the duke of Lennox, the Earle of Mar, and the rest of his maiesties traine, were striking with great hammers at the vtter [outer] doore, whereby his maiestie passt vp to the chamber with the said master Alexander, which also he had locked in his by-comming with his maiestie to the chamber: but by reason of the strength of the saide double doore, the whole wal being likewise of boordes, and yeelding with the strokes: it did bide them the space of halfe an houre and more, before they could get it broken and haue entresse. Who hauing met with his maiestie, found (beyond their expectation) his maiestie deliuered from so imminent a perill, and the sayde late Earle the principall conspirator lying dead at his Maiesties feete. Immediatly thereafter his maiesty kneeling downe, on his knees, in the midst of his owne seruants, and they all kneeling rounde about him: his maiesty out of his owne mouth thanked God of that miraculous deliuerance. (sigs. B4v–C2v)

Lennox and Mar pound on the door at Perth just as Shakespeare's Lenox and Macduff pound on the door at Inverness, the sound reinforced by the onomatopoetic words of the Porter: "Here's knocking indeede: if a man were Porter of Hell Gate, hee should haue old turning the Key. *Knock.* Knock, Knock, Knock" (2.3.1–3; 744–46).

Inwardly, James was said to think the escape a narrow one; outwardly, he proclaimed it a miracle that confirmed the divinity of his right to rule. He wrote his own account, encouraged like pamphlets with similar language concerning the miracle, and ordered public holidays and public thanksgivings. As for the conspirators, the King, having learned his bloody instructions once again (cf. 1.7.9; 483), executed all concerned with the plot and extinguished the Gowrie line. Ruthven was declared guilty of treason, hanged, and drawn and quartered so that his body could be exhibited, simultaneously, on poles fixed at Edinburgh, Perth, Dundee, and Stirling (cf. 5.8.25–27; 2465–67; and 5.9.20–21; 2504–7). The chief rival clan to the Stuarts was at last eliminated: "To know my deed, / 'Twere best not know my selfe" (2.2.72; 737–38). Stanley J. Kozikowski has pointed out that four features of *Macbeth* not in any other chronicle—the dagger, the appeal to conscience, the banquet, and the porter—are traceable only to this account and that Shakespeare and others who read the work broadly circulating in London made the analogy.[102] But in the King's account, the miracle of his salvation is contrasted to evidence of black magic connected to Gowrie:

> His maiestie hauing before his parting out of that towne, caused to search the said earle of Gowries pockets, in case any letters that might further the discouery of that conspiracy might bee found therein. But nothing was found in them, but a little close parchment bag, full of Magicall characters, and wordes of inchantment, wherein it seemed that hee had put his confidence, thinking himself neuer safe without them, and therefore euer caried them about with him: beeing also obserued, that while they were vpon him, his wound whereof he died, bled not, but incontinent after the taking of them away, the blood gushed out in great abundance, to the great admiration of all the beholders (sig. C2v),

bleeding afresh before the murderers, as Lady Macbeth fears Duncan might when he is discovered (2.2).

The "infamy which hath followed and spotted the race of this house" connects this attempted treason with the earlier acts of the Wizard Earl and to witchcraft (sig. C2v), to heresy. But this allusion to the occult annoyed members of the Scottish kirk, and the more outspoken preachers used their pulpits to denounce the story. They could not, and would not, believe that the King would allow himself to be taken alone into Gowrie House, nor, if he were, could they believe he would so easily be saved when the odds were so great against him. To them it seemed yet another dissimulation of the King, who, making his story a vizard to his heart, disguising his purpose (cf. 3.2.34–35; 1191–92), meant to annihilate the rival clan of Gowries as well as eliminate the Gowrie leadership of the Puritan opposition in the kirk. They "understood the use of propaganda as a political weapon far better than the monarchy," Jennifer M. Brown observes.[103] They were not alone. George Nicolson wrote to Sir Robert Cecil from Edinburgh on August 21, "I hear that the more the k[ing] dealeth in this matter, the greater do the doubts arise in the minds of the people as to what is the truth of the k[ing's] part."[104] Little more than two months later, on October 31, the Master of Gray wrote Cecil, "As for Gowrie's death, it is very strange for the Duke [of Lennox] says, he was there, and yet if he were on oath he could not say whether the deed proceeded from Gowrie or the king."[105]

Nevertheless, James went to Edinburgh, asked his chief prelate at St. Gile's Cathedral to preach on the miracle, and in time ostensibly won many to his side. He had had cause for concern. The Gowries had recently designed an unusual coat of arms: in the addition on the left of the sinister there was an armed man, in Gowrie livery, with his left hand grasping a sword, his right hand raised toward an imperial crown, hanging like a visionary dagger, suspended in air. From his mouth come the words "Tibi Soli," "for thee alone," but it is unclear whether the tribute is to the King or a sign of the Gowries' own "Vaulting Ambition, which ore-leapes it selfe" (1.7.27; 301). If John Chamberlain knew the Gowrie pamphlet the King issued, he is affecting a certain innocence in his letter about Shakespeare's company to Mr. Winwood on December 18, 1604, from London: "The Tragedy of 'Gowry,' with all the action and actors, hath been twice represented by the King's Players, with exceeding concourse of all sorts of people; but whether the matter or manner be not well handled, or that it be thought unfit that Princes should be played on the stage in their lifetime, I hear that some great Councellors are much displeased with it, and so 'tis thought shall be forbidden."[106] There is no extant evidence of the play otherwise; but perhaps part of it was preserved, refashioned as *Macbeth*.

Elizabeth I also suffered opposition, beginning with the Northern Rebellion of Catholic earls in 1569 and continuing with all the treasonous activity surrounding the captive Mary Stuart until her trial and execution at Fotheringhay in 1587: Shakespeare and his audience grew up to acts of resistance and rebellion. In addition there was the strange case of William Parry, who had sworn to murder Elizabeth, though he failed to do so on several occasions when he was given a private audience. As the matter is recounted in *A true and plaine declaration of the horrible treasons, practised by William Parry the traitor against the Queenes Maiestie,* printed in three editions in 1585,

> thou diddest confesse that thou haddest prepared two Scottish Daggers, fit for such a purpose and those being disposed away by thee, thou diddest say that an other would serve thy turne. And with all, *Parry,* diddest thou not also confesse before us howe wonderfully thou wert appauled and perplexed upon a suddaine at the presence of her Maiestie at Hampton Court this last Sommer, saying that thou diddest thinke thou then sawest in her, the very likenes & image of king Henry the seventh? (35)

This realizes the mystification that James would later urge. In addition, Curt Breight comments, "Some twenty years before Lady Macbeth's hesitation, contemporaries were thus asked to believe that a devoted and ruthless assassin (on numerous occasions) could not plunge the dagger into the royal person."[107]

Finally, in 1601 there was the fatal march of the Earl of Essex against the Queen at Whitehall, prompted at least in part, according to Mervyn James, by the urgent pleas of his sister, Penelope Devereux Rich, who acted on him as Mary Stuart had on Bothwell; her chief reason, much like that of the Gowries, was her sense of pride in the Essex lineage and her feeling that Elizabeth's actions had humiliated that line.[108] "To be a King, and weare a Crowne," Elizabeth told members of Parliament, as recorded in *Queene Elizabeths Speech to Her Last Parliament* (1601), "is a thing more glorious to them that see it, then it is pleasant to them that beare it" (sig. A3v).

John Stow records in his *Annales of England* (1605) a peculiarly haunting conjunction of events for 1603:

> The 27. of April being than wednesday in Easter weeke, by casualty of fire, taking hold of *18000.* weight of Gunpowder, and Salt petar, the powder mill and diuerse houses adioyning at Radcliffe in Surrie was there blowne vpp, and lost, and people slaine to the number of xiii or xiiii persons.
> The same 27 of Aprill proclamation was made for the apprehension of *William,* and *Patrike Ruthuen* brethren to the late Earls of *Gowrie.* (sig. 4S6)

This coincidence heralded the infamous Powder Plot in November 1605, but even before that as King of England, James had witnessed the Bye and

Main Plots against his policies. The Powder Plot, seen in the textual traces of the code name "farmer" and the doctrine of "equivocation"—both associated with the conspirator Father Henry Garnet and both found in the Porter's speech in 2.3—follows closely on Queen Anne's unexpected conversion to Catholicism sometime in 1604 and subsequent rumors in Paris and in Rome that the King was about to convert as well. To calm his Protestant supporters, James announced new practices against Catholics on February 10, 1604. He convicted 5,560 persons of recusancy; forced 112 to pay the full two-thirds of their annual rental as fines; and then, in a proclamation dated February 22, admonished and assured "all such Jesuites, Seminaries, and Priests of what sort soever, That if any of them shall be after the said nineteenth day taken within this Realme or any our Dominions, or departing now upon this our Pleasure signified, shall hereafter returne into this Realme or any our Dominions againe, that they shalbe left to the penaltie of the Lawes here being in force concerning them, without hope of any favor or remission from Us";[109] they were subject, that is, to capital punishment.

The small "cell" of Catholics who first conceived the Powder Plot was composed largely of Shakespeare's neighbors, Warwickshire gentry led by Robert Catesby, whose father held land in Stratford, Shottery, Bishopton, and Old Stratford; his cousins Tresham, Winters, and Throckmorton; and John Grant, who held property in Snitterfield, where Shakespeare's cousin still farmed on his grandfather's land. Under the pretense of hunting, they first met at Clopton Hall, then later in London at Catesby's lodgings in the Strand, and at the Mermaid Tavern. They enlisted the expert aid of Guy Fawkes, who knew about firearms and powder, and rented a basement next to Parliament House before renting the basement of Parliament House itself.[110] Over the course of the late spring and summer months, it is said they hid thirty-four barrels of gunpowder under faggots in order to blow up the royal family and the officers of church and state at the first gathering of Parliament, eventually set on November 5, 1605, while plotting to put a Catholic successor on the English throne. Fawkes, dressed as a porter, stood guard; he was also appointed to fire the powder when the time came. But the plan went awry. Someone—it is suspected to have been Tresham—sent a coded warning to Lord Mounteagle, the sole Catholic member on the Privy Council, to protect him from danger, and Mounteagle passed it on to Cecil, who, unable to decode it, passed it on to the King. James deciphered it only a day before the explosion was to take place. By the time of the discovery, the conspirators, for the most part, had fled to the Midlands to complete their plans to put in place a new government.

The first official word to reach London's playgoers was the King's own proclamation from Westminster on November 5 with its extraordinary heading of an imperial crown rather than the formulaic "By the King":

> Whereas one *Thomas Percy* a Gentleman Pensioner to his Maiestie, is dis-couered to haue bene priuie to one of the most horrible Treasons that euer was contriued, that is, to haue blowen vp this day, while his Maiestie should haue bene in the vpper House of the Parliament, attended with the Queene, the Prince, all his Nobilitie & the Commons, with Gunpowder (for which purpose a great quantitie of Powder was conueyed into a Vault vnder the said Chamber, which is this morning there found) the Chamber where they should bee assembled, which *Percy* is sithens fled: These are to will and comand all our Officers and louing Subiects whatsoeuer, to doe that which we doubt not but they will willingly performe, according to the former experience we haue had of their loue and zeale toward vs. That is, to make all diligent search for the said *Percy,* and him to apprehend by all possible meanes, especially to keepe him aliue, to the end the rest of the Conspirators may be discouered. The said *Percy* is a tall man, with a great broad beard, a good face, the colour of his beard and head mingled with white haires, but the head more white than the beard, he stoupeth somewhat in the shoulders, well coloured in the face, long footed, small legged. Giuen at our Pallace of Westminster, the fift day of Nouember in the third yeare of our Reigne of Great Britaine. (1609 ed., sigs. K4–K4v)

Broadsides, too, were soon everywhere, some with poems, many with pic-tures of Fawkes. Some showed the eye of God looking down on him; most showed him carrying a lantern or a lighted candle, making Macbeth's later remark that life itself was like a "breefe Candle" (5.5.23; 2344) especially haunting. Likening the Powder Plot publicly to the gunpowder plot that had occurred at the death of his father in Kirk o' Fields, James estimated the potential fatalities at thirty thousand. "That but this blow / Might be the be all, and the end all. Heere," Macbeth contemplates (1.7.4–5; 478–79); "Of dyre Combustion, and confus'd Euents, / New hatch'd to th'wofull time," Lennox comments on the discovery of Duncan's death (2.3.59–60; 807–8); "Strange Schreemes of Death" (2.3.57; 805). The Powder Plot was making the Gowrie conspiracy more credible.

We can still recover that cultural moment, at least in part, by the reports and practices that attended it, seeing even now how it called forth paralleling lexias in its own time. Some of them are these: in an unusually long and detailed letter to Sir Thomas Edmonds, the English ambassador to Brussels, Sir Edward Hoby comes at once to the point: "On the 5th of November . . . at one instant and blast to have ruin'd the whole State and Kingdom of England." Extended details follow. "Some say that Northumberland received the like letter that Monteagle did, and concealed it. . . . His Majesty in his Speech observed one principal point, that most of all his best fortunes had happened unto him upon the Tuesday; and particularly he repeated his deliverance from Gowry and others, in which he noted precisely, that both fell on the 5th day of the month; and therefore concluded, that he made choice that the next sitting of Parliament might begin upon a Tuesday."[111] John Chamberlain wrote Dudley Carleton on November 7: "Thomas Percy, that you suspected him to be a subtle, flattering, dangerous knave," was worse than "Nero and Caligula, that wished all Rome but one head that they might cut it off at a stroke; for he at one blow would have ruined the whole realm."[112] In *Great Britaines Resvrrection,* 1606, the King's chaplain, William Hubbard, made the point more tellingly: the traitors meant "to destroy roote, and branch: and fruite, parent, and childe in one day: to kill damme and young in one nest" (sig. B2), rather like Lady Macduff: "Poore Bird, / Thou'dst neuer Feare the Net, nor Lime, / The Pitfall, nor the Gin" (4.2.3435; 1751–53).

These were representative attitudes; Nicolo Molin, the Venetian ambassador in England, catches the mood in letters to the Doge and Senate:

> The King is in terror; he does not appear nor does he take his meals in public as usual. He lives in the innermost rooms, with only Scotchmen about him. The Lords of the Council also are alarmed and confused by the plot itself and the King's suspicions; the city is in great uncertainty; Catholics fear heretics, and vice-versa; both are armed; foreigners live in terror of their houses being sacked by the mob that is convinced that some, if not all, foreign Princes are at the bottom of the plot. The King and Council have very prudently thought it advisable to quiet the popular feeling by issuing a proclamation, in which they declare that no foreign Sovereign had any part in the conspiracy, God grant this be sufficient but as it is everyone had his own share of alarm. (November 21; p. 293)[113]

> Every day something new about the plot comes to light, and produces great wrath and suspicion. The result is that both Court and City are more than ever in a hubbub, nor can they quiet down; everyone is armed and ready for any event. Lately among the prisoners' effects a paper has been found, containing the list of all houses inhabited by Scots. When asked as to the meaning of this the prisoners said that it was intended, after the explosion of the mine, to massacre all the Scottish in this country, for they could not submit to the share which their natural enemies now had in the government.

119

The publication of this news has increased the hatred between the two nations, and rendered them quite irreconcilable. Many Scots are thinking of
returning home, for they fear that some day a general massacre may take
place. (December 22; p. 303)

Further proclamations also poured forth as more was learned or suspected—on November 7, 8, 18, and 19; January 15; March 22; April 10
and 27; June 10—relentlessly announcing aloud and posting a notice to
be read in each village square and at every market cross that potential
assassins remained at large or that new powers had been granted by the
King to locate them.

Then, just as he had done in the Gowrie affair, James described the
Powder Plot—first in an address to Parliament, then in published form in
1605 as the *True and Perfect Relation*—as proof of the divinity of his rule,
and thanked God "for the great and miraculous Deliuery he hath at this
time granted to me, and to you all, and consequently to the whole body
of this Estate" (sig. A4v). The Powder Plot, at first a personal salvation,
was now a national one. In 1606 he added to the statutes "An Acte for a
publique Thanksgiuing to Almighty GOD euery yeere on the Fift day of
November" and made it a special commemorative day in the *Book of Common Prayer*. In due course churchwardens bought books of special prayers
to commemorate the new religious state holiday and set aside money for
bellringers. The Earl of Northampton is said to have alluded to the shared
danger at the trial of Father Henry Garnet: "The circle of a Crowne Imperiall cannot be souldered, if it once receiue the smallest cracke" (sig. 2D4v).

And James's justice, like Macbeth's, "will haue blood they say: / Blood
will haue blood" (3.4.121; 1403–4). "Must they all be hanged, that swear
and lye? / Everyone" (4.2.51–52; 1771–72). Dissimulating himself, Sir
William Waad, Lieutenant of the Tower of London, trapped Father Garnet
into confession after (it was reported) he had been racked at least twenty-
five times; through sheer torture, Waad also learned from Guy Fawkes.
Once they were arrested, most of the conspirators were subjected to torture every bit as barbaric and savage as any cruelty Macbeth displays: they
were placed in "The Little Ease," a slit in a stone wall four feet by two feet
by eighteen inches in which they could neither stand nor sit; this was
followed by the rack, where their bodies were stretched with increasing
power by pulleys and levers until their joints might be torn from their
sockets; and by the "Scavenger's Daughter," rightly "Skeffington's Daughter," where an iron hoop compressed its victim who was doubled up in a
kneeling position.[114] Then, despite what Coke called "the admirable clemency and moderation of the King," each criminal was convicted. Another

Venetian ambassador, Zorzi Giustinian, wrote to the Doge and Senate on February 10, 1606, that there were executions in two different places on two different days "to extend the lesson to an infinite multitude of men. The object of this division was to feed the eyes of the mob for a longer period. The people were ablaze with fury and rage against the culprits, and this was fanned by the constancy which they displayed" (*Calendar of State Papers, Venetian,* 10:320). What happened the day of the execution is described and made into allegorical metaphor by Oliver Omerod in *The Picture of a Papist* (1605), following directions laid out by Coke:

> First they were drawne on hurdles from the prison to the place of execution, to shew howe they had beene drawne by brutish and *Cassian* affection. Secondly, they were hanged vp, to shew, that they were men vnworthie to tread vpon the earth. Thirdly, they were no sooner turned off the Ladder, but the Rope was cut, and they let fall downe, to shew the sequele and effect of treason, viz. how that they digge a pit for others, & fall into it themselues. Fourthly, they were noe sooner fallen downe, but the executioner snatched them vp, laid them on a blocke, cut of their secrets [genitals], and cast them into the fire, to shew that traytors are vnworthie to be begotten, or to beget others. Fiftly, their bellies were ripped vp, and there hearts torne out, & throwne into the same fire, because they were the fountaine of such an vnnaturall and vnhearde of treacherie. Sixtly, as they thought to haue cut off the head from the members in the ciuill bodie; so were their heads cut off from the members of their bodies, and their wickednesse turned on their owne heades. Seuently, their heads being cut off, their bodies were diuided into quarters, as they were diuided from the sound members in the ciuill bodie. Lastly, their quarters were set vpp vppon the gates of the Citie; that as their gracelesse attempts were an ill example to others: so their quarters there exposed to the eyes of all men, might be a good caueat to others. (sigs. Z2v–Z3)

"He vnseem'd him from the Naue to th' Chops," the Captain reports proudly of Macbeth's valor on behalf of his King (1.2.22; 41). "What I beleeue, Ile waile," says Malcolm; "What know, beleeue; and what I can redresse, / As I shall finde the time to friend: I wil" (4.3.8–10; 1823–25).

Yet here too, as with the Gowrie conspiracy, there were significant doubts; even Coke is said to have commented, "Quis haec posteris sic narrare poterit, ut facta non ficta esse videantur?" ("Ages to come will be in doubt whether it were a fact or a fiction").[115] The remark may have been deliberately amphibological; it was also meant to be prophetic. Joel Hurstfield speaks for many present-day historians, however, when he observes that "some of the confessions were obtained by torture or the threat of torture; and . . . parts of these confessions were never made public at all. . . . Apart from this, at various times writers have come forward to point out that from their examination of the topography of Westminster they consider it impossible for anyone to have carried the gunpowder without being seen."[116] Indeed, the relative transparency of the letter that Mounteagle, Cecil, and the Lord Chamberlain found impossible to decipher—

> MY Lord, Out of the love I beare to some of your friends, I haue a care of your preservation. Therefore I would aduise you, as you tender your life, to devise some excuse to shift off your attendance at this Parliament. For God and man haue concurred to punish the wickednesse of this Time. And thinke not slightly of this Aduertisement, but retire your selfe into your Countrey, where you may expect the euent in safetie. For though there be no apparance of any stirre, yet I say, they shall receiue a terrible Blow this Parliament, and yet they shall not see who hurts them. This counsell is not to be contemned, because it may doe you good, and can doe you no harme: for the danger is past so soone as you haue burnt the Letter. And I hope God will giue you the grace to make good vse of it: To whose holy protection I commend you. (sig. F3v)

—strains credulity, especially in the official report that continues for several pages to play with possible interpretations. Hurstfield further notes that "others have found mysterious callers at Salisbury's house who, they think, were his *agents provocateurs* among the plotters" (104) and adds that much of the attention has been given to Cecil, who, as Earl of Salisbury and James's principal secretary, was still somewhat uncertain of his future in James's government. Michael Drayton's poem "The Owl" (1603) may point to Cecil, who was said to have a special ability "To urge a doubtful speech vp to the worst / To broach new treasons and disclose them first." Another report, dated November 13, 1605, noted that the whole Powder Plot was being described in Paris as "a fable."[117]

In fact, discrepant documentation may cause each of us to reorder our individual sets of lexias concerning the Powder Plot as it relates to *Macbeth*. Christopher Devlin notes "the report of the member of the French Embassy, written the day after Fawkes's arrest, that the only powder discovered was a single small keg—and that, not in the vault under Parliament but in *Percy's house*."[118] Molin, writing to Venice on November 9, 1605, concerning the coming Parliament but yet unaware of the Powder Plot, provides another possible motive:

> The principal business before Parliament is the granting a subsidy, which the King greatly desires, but it is generally supposed that he will meet with serious difficulties, and that it will be refused: for many members openly declare

122

that as there is no war with Spain, no war in Holland, no army on the Scottish border—which they say cost the late Queen upwards of a million a year in gold—they cannot understand why the King, who has the revenues of Scotland, should want money. They add that the people are far more heavily burdened than under the late Queen, for the King stays so continually and so long in the country, where the peasants are obliged to furnish beasts and waggons for transporting the Court from place to place, and whenever he goes a-hunting the crops are mostly ruined. Further the Court is far larger than in the late Queen's time, and the peasants are forced to supply provisions at low prices, which is an intolerable burden. (*Calendar of State Papers, Venetian,* 10:285)

When Parliament was at last seated, their attention, like the King's opening speech to them, was on the danger James had averted and the miracle of his leadership, and their sympathy gave him the support he wished for new revenues. He had gotten the money he sought where before it had been uncertain. Meantime he had a special commemorative medal struck showing a serpent lurking among flowers; the inscription read "DETECTUS QUI LATUIT S.C." "Looke like th'innocent flower," Lady Macbeth tells her husband, "But be the Serpent vnder't" (1.5.64–65; 420–21).[119]

Anxiety continued well into 1606, as Shakespeare was writing (or rewriting) *Macbeth*. The anonymous author of *The returne of the Knight of the Poste from Hell* (1606) claims that "I had not taken about two or three turnes, ere I obserued this: that generally all men, whose talke I could ouer-heare, seemed onely to discourse of one Subiect, praysing God, that had reuealed a most horridde, and not to be imagined treason, & biterly cursing those monsters and monstrous men, whose diuelish braines could contriue a damnable Proiect, worse then euer the Diuell himselfe dreamde of" (sig. C1). Ironically, or unconsciously, Bacon was writing in *The Twoo Bookes of Francis Bacon: Of the proficiencie and aduancement of Learning, diuine and humane* (1605), "I haue often thought, that of all the persons liuing, that I haue knowne, your Maiestie were the best instance to make a man of *Platoes* opinion, that all knowledge is but remembrance, . . . such a light of Nature I haue observed in your Maiestie, and hath such a readinesse to take flame, and blaze from the least occasion presented, the least sparke of anothers knowledge deliuered" (sig. A2v). Countless related ballads were likewise circulating. Part of one of them, "*A forme of true Repentance, fit for* Traytors to Sing and vse now, and at all times *while life is in them,*" goes like this:

Heads of *Catesby,* and of *Percy,* / they were sent:

123

And sette vpon the vpper house, / of Parlyment.
Bravely plodding, yea and nodding, / each to other.
Thanking Pope, for Axe and Rope, for / them and other:
Such a downefall, to the Papall, / none alive:
But these Traytors, and their waytors, / could contriue (sig. B1)
Diuelish Treason, hath no reason, / night or day:
Proud ambition, makes sedition, / euery way.
Their aspiring, and their fyring, / comes from hell:
The vnkindenes, growes of blindenes, / most can tell. (sig. B1v)

It concludes: "Eightyeight yere, were in Gods feare, / may remember: / *Gowries* August, *Percies* uniusth, fift November" (sig. B3). Then too began the now-famous jingle: "Please to remember / The Fifth of November, / Gunpowder, treason, and plot; / I see no reason / why gunpowder treason / Should ever be forgot."

Surely playgoers did not, could not, forget. But those in the Globe who had read the account of the trials in the *True and Perfect Relation* might find lexias resurfacing in the play. There Catesby, like Macbeth, is said to pit regicide against conscience (sig. R3). Elsewhere, the report speaks of delusions and hallucinations. "But by evident confession it appeares, that the very night wherein the Powder should haue wrought the desperate effect; either the light of reason, the honor of vexation, or the power of reuelation, presented to *Robert Winter* in a dreame, the faces of his chiefe friends, and the highest Traitors that should haue acted execution vpon the bloody stage in such a gastly and oughly figure, more like to that *malus genius* which appeared vnto *Brutus* the night before his death" (sig. B3v): the comment links the Englishman and the Roman as republicans and traitors. Religion and rebellion are made synonymous. So we, as might playgoers in 1606, also hear the otherwise anachronistic Christian references in *Macbeth*.

LEXIAS OF JUSTICE

Corporal punishment was central and necessary to maintain state authority at the time *Macbeth* was performed at the Globe in 1606, providing a related but potentially different set of lexias leading out from or back to

the play. The most extreme form, execution, was the punishment for felony, as Nym is hanged for theft in 1600 in *Henry V* (4.4.71–75). As J. A.
Sharpe describes, the punishment was a ritual in which

> the condemned was expected to show obedience, penitence, and contrition
> on the gallows. He or she was also expected to make a speech, in which a full
> confession was usually made to the offence in question, and expressions were
> made of sorrow, of the hope that they would serve as a deterrent example to
> others, and that the monarch under whose laws death was being suffered
> would enjoy a long and prosperous reign. The speeches also customarily con-
> tained a long confession of youthful sin, which was seen as leading inevitably
> to the serious offence for which death was being suffered. The public execu-
> tion, so often treated by historians simply as yet more proof of the brutality
> of past ages, was in fact a highly structured ritual in which the authority of
> the state was demonstrated, in a dramatic fashion, to the public at large.[120]

"*Enter Macduffe, with Macbeths head*" (5.9.20 S.D.; 2504) is both expected
and satisfying, but in a society where the manner of dying was an important cultural practice, other parts of the ritual are present too. This is only
the conclusion of a set of actions which for playgoers could begin with
Macbeth's comment that

> I haue liu'd long enough: my way of life
> Is falne into the Seare, the yellow Leafe,
> And that which should accompany Old-Age,
> As Honor, Loue, Obedience, Troopes of Friends
> I must not looke to haue (5.3.22–26; 2239–43)

Macbeth's initial observation is followed by some of the play's most remembered lines,

> She should haue dy'de heereafter;
> There would haue beene a time for such a word:
> To morrow, and to morrow, and to morrow,
> Creepes in this petty pace from day to day,
> To the last Syllable of Recorded time:
> And all our yesterdayes, haue lighted Fooles
> The way to dusty death. Out, out, breefe Candle,
> Life's but a walking Shadow, a poore Player,
> That struts and frets his houre vpon the Stage,
> And then is heard no more. It is a Tale
> Told by an Ideot, full of sound and fury
> Signifying nothing (5.5.17–28; 2338–49),

seen as confession, followed by contrition and self-abasement, leading to the final pronouncement of an anticipated judgment: "Thou com'st to vse thy Tongue: thy Story quickly" (5.5.29; 2350).

Violent punishment and public mutilation insured a continuing consensual justice and continually set limits of behavior in Shakespeare's society. There was good reason for this: serious and petty crime was a common feature of life in 1606 and petty criminals jostled playgoers in the streets and in the playhouse. The aldermen of London complained in 1601 of "the great numbers of idle, lewd, and wicked persons flocking and resorting hither from all parts of this realm, which do live here and maintain themselves chiefly by robbing and stealing."[121] Preachers attacked vagrants as "the very filth and vermin of the common wealth . . . the very Sodomites of the land, children of Belial, without God, without minister; dissolute, disobedient, and reprobate to every good work."[122] Such statements were justifiable. William Fleetwood, the city recorder, recalls grimly that

only one quoted

> I did the same night send warrants out into the said quarters and into Westminster and the Duchy; and in the morning I went abroad myself and I took that day seventy-four rogues . . . and the same day toward night . . . took all the names of the rogues and sent them from the sessions house into Bridewell [the London house of correction]. . . . Upon Sunday . . . I conferred order for Southwark, Lambeth, and Newington from whence I received a school of forty rogues, men and women, and above. I bestowed them in Bridewell. I did the same afternoon peruse Paul's where I took about twenty cloaked rogues. . . . I placed them also in Bridewell.[123]

Ian Archer (239) has compiled statistics to show that whereas 467 cases were heard before the governors of Bridewell in 1559–60 and 722 in 1576–77, 954 were heard in 1600–1601.

There were many causes of crime: unemployment, dispossession, vagrancy, new waves of immigrants, disbanded soldiers, abandoned wives, the wandering jobless. The city was policed by the watch at night and the ward officials by day, by the hue and cry of citizens, and by presentments to court. The city marshalcy along with the Court of Aldermen were strengthened in 1603 by the appointment of a permanent provost marshal; in addition, the Privy Council looked into some disorders that seemed to be the concern of the state. John L. McMullan reports that "violence in the streets of London was apparently common. The fields about the city and the arterial roads were continual scenes of upper-class feuds. Pitched battles regularly occurred in Fleet Street and on the Strand. Armed affrays involving feuding nobles supported by their retainers sometimes went on for days" (91). Firearms officially replaced the bow in 1595, and as William Harrison points out, "Our nobility wear commonly swords or rapiers with their dagges as doth every common serving man also that followeth his lord and master. Some desperate cutters we have in like sort, which carry two dagges or two rapiers."[124] Law enforcement was difficult because fighting and crime were so frequent; it was made even more difficult because criminals—singly or in groups—would keep relocating. Prostitutes driven from one quarter of the city would soon be operating in another, or across the river near the theaters, associating with other petty criminals.

Local public and private punishment assigned at quarter sessions and assizes was therefore a central social practice. Criminals could be hanged, branded, or fined. Those who refused to plead guilty could be subjected to *peine forte et dure,* pressed slowly, to encourage a confession: this form was elected by some of the accused because if they did not confess there was a chance they could retain their property. Many punishments—the pillory, ducking, bridling, carting—were public acts of shaming, carrying religious overtones of penance with a recognition of guilt. Incarcerations, work discipline, and whippings characterized the practices at Bridewell. Vagrancy acts in 1593 and 1598 replaced ear borings and death with the lesser penalty of whipping, and in 1598, Ian Archer notes, whipping posts were set up in each London parish (220). At the time of *Macbeth,* petty crime was common and criminals thrived.

Associated with crime in 1606 was the frequent activity of spying; playgoers at the Globe would hear Macbeth instruct the hired assassins of Banquo and Fleance to waylay the two as if they were acquainted "with the perfect Spy o'th'time" (3.1.129; 1136). The world of *Macbeth* mirrors a world of suspicion and danger in Jacobean England where men and women were well aware that surveillance was practiced at every level of their culture, and on the innocent, suspected, and guilty alike. A courtier advises the Queen in Thomas Dekker's *The Noble Spanish Soldier* to place "Spyes amongst the people, who shall lay their eares / To every mouth, and steale to you their whisperings" (3.1.169–70). In *Pierce Pennilesse* (1592) Thomas Nashe likens a person in Paul's to "an Intelligencer" and finds *agents provocateurs* in Paul's Churchyard; Shakespeare's Hamlet had found such "sponges" in Rosencrantz and Guildenstern (4.2).[125] But, Curtis C. Breight writes, "The very structure of government was built upon human surveillance and its intended inducement of paranoia among servants of the crown," quoting Thomas Wilson in 1600:

> In all great offices and places of charge they doe allwayes place 2 persons of contrary factions and that are bredd of such causes, or growne to such greatness, as they are ever irreconcilable, to the end, each having his enemyes eye to overlooke him, it may make him looke the warilier to his charge, and that if any body should incline to any unfaithfulnesse in such charges of importance as concerne the publicque safety, it might be spied before it be brought to any dangerous head; which cannot be done all at once without many precedent actions conducing thereunto, whereof some must needs be perceived by a watchfull enemy, then which nothing is more vigilant and pearcing. (51)

But more subtle policing systems, as Albert H. Tricomi suggests, were "virtually ubiquitous. [Policing] underlay ceremonial occasions, as when marriage banns were proclaimed with the request to know if anyone possessed knowledge that might impede the joining of the engaged couple. . . . It appeared in communal supervision of heterodox spousal behavior [as well as in] parental supervision of children, husbands' supervision of wives, and householders' supervision of servants, not to mention guildmasters' superintendency of apprentices and pastors' stewardship of parishioners."[126] Playgoers watching a play must have been adept at clues; in 1625, when Francis Bacon came to describe his ideal commonwealth in the *New Atlantis,* it was, as John Michael Archer has it, "dedicated to the gathering of information."[127] But Bacon had long understood that knowledge was power, having participated in the spying network Essex established with the help of Bacon and of his brother Anthony. It was meant to rival, if not supersede, that already established by Walsingham and taken over by Burghley (and later Cecil).

In 1598, before his own brief excursion into France, Robert Cecil drew up a document that reveals a great deal about his own network: he had employed Peter Gerard in Lisbon at an annual salary of 400 ducats, the Dutch-speaking George Gilpin earned 500 ducats, one Palmer at St Jean de Luz was also paid 500 ducats, and Thomas Wilson was paid £150, Francis Lambert £109. Such amounts were customary. In the Low Countries Captain Ogle organized a ring of spies, as did George Kendall in the Spanish Netherlands and Lawrence Bankes in Middleburg. Stephen Lesiuer was his chief agent in the Hanse towns of northern Germany, Henry Lello reported from Constantinople, and even John Hawkins, imprisoned in Seville, made secret "drops."[128] The risks of spying were always great; but so was the excitement of the danger involved. Thus the spy Thomas Harrison remarked, in 1599,

> I have sundry times very dangerously adventured to have my throat cut as may appear. In the house of the Lord Seaton I lay in policy to discover Holt

the Jesuit fourteen days and caused him together with myself to be appre-
hended at Leith with all his packets for France and Spain. In Cochester, by
Mr Secretary's devise I was consorted with one Deane and Shelley a seminary
and lodged fourteen days in the outward prison to intercept all their letters,
which was also done to the discovery of a number of traitors.[129]

The spying organization Walsingham put in place to determine the connections of Mary Stuart during her incarceration were extended through
Elizabeth's reign and into that of James, just as foreign ambassadors in
London were keeping an eye on English affairs. Catholic invasion or rebellion, foreign attacks, or piracy were some of the key targets, but surveillance also promoted priest holes in country houses and secret alley
hideouts in London.

Indeed, McMullan writes that

> neighbors and tradesmen were encouraged to spy and turn evidence on each
> other. Forgers, thieves, robbers, highwaymen, and burglars were, from time
> to time, the subjects of specific legislation. Arrested suspects were urged to
> inform on their accomplices in return for a pardon or protection. The system
> was designed to give the informer partial or permanent immunity from legal
> penalties, and to create fissures within the world of crime. In particular, the
> fence was in a structural position to betray thieves and prostitutes. Law and
> enforcement were negotiable, and the maintenance of domestic order was
> characterized by perplexing ambiguity and contradiction. (143)

Moreover, he adds, "The Elizabethan and Stuart states were particularly
reliant on informers for the mediation of law. These agents were drawn
from a number of sources. Many were regular members of craft organiza-
tions who informed on a part-time basis. Others were licensed agents of
the state enjoined to form working groups of inspectors on a career basis.
Some acquired enforcement monopolies in specific territories or busi-
nesses" (147). Geoffrey Elton has told of one professional informer who
developed a kind of subnetwork of his own; with at least six accomplices
he covered the coast of England from Norfolk to Somerset.[130] Blackmailers,
false accusers, framers of evidence, sham-plotters, even sumners and jailers
were frequently employed. Nor, in the right circles, was this disgraceful.
Bacon once told James I with a certain pride that he served Elizabeth I as
"her watch-candle."[131] Hamlet lives in a world where all occasions inform
against him (4.4.32), and Siluius informs Agrippina in *Sejanus* that "euery
second ghest your tables take, / Is a fee'd spie, t'obserue who goes, who
comes, / What conference you haue, with whom, where, when, / What the
discourse is, what the lookes, the thoughts / Of ev'ry person there, they

doe extract, / And make into a substance" (2.4.44–49).[132] And what colors these plays shrouds the latter half of *Macbeth*. We sense it in Macbeth's every maneuver after the regicide; when Macduff, absent from the coronation at Scone, may not attend the coronation banquet either, Macbeth learns this too:

Macb. How say'st thou that *Macduff* denies his person
At our great bidding.
La. Did you send to him Sir?
Macb. I heare it by the way: But I will send:
There's not a one of them but in his house
I keepe a Seruant Fe'ed. (3.4.127–31; 1410–15)

The cultural practices of 1606 fostered a cultural moment redolent with distrust.

Economic Lexias

At a time of violence and uncertainty, the Porter on the stage of the Globe in 1606, subjected to a "diet" (the specific menu given laborers, which in the worst of times might devolve to bread and cheese or even oats),[133] feels keenly the situation of farmers who could not control harvests or prices, being especially vulnerable to uncertain weather. As Roger B. Manning has remarked, a number of crises in the years around 1606

> were characterized by a sequence of harvest failures, dearth, and food riots, as well as unemployment in the clothing trades; anti-enclosure riots occurred more frequently, and the government became more fearful of the problem of vagrants and masterless men. An epidemic of apprentices' riots, lasting nearly two decades, disturbed the peace of London, normally a well-governed city; an insurrection was attempted in Oxfordshire in 1596; and, finally, a rebellion spread across several midland counties in 1607.[134]

The weather, often unpredictable at best, turned bad in the late 1590s, epidemic increased, and the ravages of vulnerability and insecurity scarred the people. In 1598 and 1599—the years of Books 4–6 of Joseph Hall's *Satires* and Ben Jonson's *Every Man out of His Humour*—the bottom fell out of the wheat market. The average price for wheat per quarter in 1596 was 56s. 6¼d. and in 1597 25s. 4½d.; in 1598 it advanced to 31s. 1½d. but fell in 1599 to 29s. 8¾d. Then, the worst two famine years in the reign of Elizabeth I were followed by two harvests of relative plenty. By 1606 the situation had reversed once again; after low prices from 1601 to 1603, wheat began to rise to 29s. 7d. per quarter in 1604 before receding to 27s. 8½d. in 1605, or what would be its lowest price until 1619. The farmer who raised an abundance of grain the year *Macbeth* was performed, then, could be in serious straits.[135]

The years the playgoers had just survived had been very bad. Grain riots erupted in Norfolk, Essex, Kent, Sussex, Hertfordshire, Hampshire, and along the Thames valley, as well as in Gloucestershire, Wiltshire, and Somerset. There were marked consequences. In Elizabethan Essex, there was an annual average of 78.6 prosecutions for theft due to scarcity in the good harvest years (1592–94); in the bad years following (1595–97), the annual average was 178.3. There were food riots in Kent in 1595. That same year the magistrates in Norwich received an anonymous letter that read, "Some barbarous and unmerciful soldier shall lay open your hedges, reap your fields, rifle your coffers and level your houses to the ground"; it ended, "Necessity hath no law." A complaint was made in Essex that "yf victualls did not growe better cheape some wolde be plucked owte of their howses." The next year, 1596, rioters in Canterbury, learning from a lawyer's clerk that they should "not meddle with the corn," nevertheless prevented carriers from leaving the city with it. In Essex that year a weaver told a large crowd that "it would never be better untill men did rise & seeke thereby an amendment and wished in his harte a hundred men would rise and he would be their captain to cut the throates of the rich Churles & the Rich Cornemongers." In Somerest too it was said that "before the yeare went aboute ther wold be old threshing owt of mowes & Cuttynge of throats." In 1597 two-fifths of the nation's population fell below the poverty line, and in April that year food rioters at King's Lynn boarded a ship with a cargo of corn bound for Lincolnshire and unloaded her. In 1598 the vicar of Wendlebury, Oxfordshire, wrote in his personal register that "in the years of our lord god 1597 and 1596 wheate was sold for xis, barley for 7s, and beanes for vi⁵ viiiᵈ. This was a sorroful time for the poore of the land god grant that such a darth and famyne may never be sene agayn."

Wheat prices in Oxford more than doubled to five shillings in 1594 and rose again to eight shillings six months later. At nearby Bicester wheat was selling at nine shillings a bushel by that autumn. In 1596 a decision was made to put marginal land under the plow; in Oxford that year an attempt made to cut students' bread allowance stirred resistance in Christ

Church and local magistrates attempted to ban the taking of any grain out of the county. Resistance theory was taking root in a new and vital way. At a later hearing concerning the Oxford rising in 1595, one man told the examiners "that he hath hearde latelie divers poore people saie (as he tra-veilled in this Countie beinge a loader to Hampton Gaie Mill) That the prices of Corne weare so deere that there would be shortlie a risinge of the people, and more adoe than had been a greate while, ffor that the poore sorte of people could not telle howe to make shifte to compasse the years about." Another testified that he commonly "went to Marketts, [where] he heard poore people saie, that they were ready to famishe for want of Corne, and that they thought they should be enforced for hunger to take yt owt of men's howses." When told that grain was nine shillings a bushel at the Bicester market, one man asked "Then what shall poore men doe?" and was told, "Rather then they would be starved, they would ryse."[136] An abortive rising occurred in Oxfordshire in 1596 that alerted the local constabulary to heightened surveillance and brought a royal proclamation acknowledging the excessive dearth and extreme consequences.

Nor was Shakespeare's town of Stratford exempt. There the famine became so intense in 1597–98 that citizens petitioned local justices to impose the Privy Council's Book of Orders against hoarding, in order to break a cartel of local farmers who withheld corn from the market to inflate prices, although Burghley was calling them "wicked people more like wolves or cormorants than natural men." Richard Quiney, speaking for the "great corn-buyers," protested in turn to the Privy Council, noting that the ones most harmed would be the maltsters, whose brewing was the city's chief business. "Our town hath no other special trade, our houses fitted to no other uses, and many servants hired only for that purpose," he told them. On January 24, 1598, his partner Abraham Sturley pronounced the town's poor to be "malcontent," adding that they trusted "our country-man Mr. Shakespeare" to get them privileges for access to arable fields. On February 4, local authorities complied with the Privy Council's Book of Orders and returned an inventory of those with corn. One of the largest hoards was found to be at New Place, Chapel Street ward, in the name of William Shakespeare.

Still other economic factors—overpopulation, the decay of the guild system—were at the same time plaguing the city of London. A. L. Beier estimates that the overall metropolitan inhabitants numbered about 120,000 in 1550, 200,000 in 1600, and no fewer than 375,000 by 1650. "This rapid expansion caused serious social problems," he writes, "which grew even more quickly than the population. There was a threefold increase in City householders needing poor relief, c. 1550–c. 1600, although its population had risen by just a quarter. (The City grew much less rapidly than its suburbs.) Vagrancy arrests increased still faster, rising twelvefold from 1560 to 1625, a period in which the metropolitan population only quadrupled."[137] But even before 1600, Arthur J. Slavin notes, wealth was unevenly spread: "London was actually two cities—a mixture of poverty and parkland, of noxious air in the burgeoning slums and great houses in its western quarter. Even in the City the contrast was stark between the poor street howlers crying out their penny wares and the rich merchants whose shops ringed their guildhalls."[138] Ian Archer notes within the city's walls

> the distinction between background and crisis levels of poverty. . . . In St Martin in the Fields in 1603 the parish authorities reported that 52 parishioners received weekly alms, and that there were a further 123 householders with 265 dependents "that want relief and are more likely to come to have relief." The population of St Martin's at this date was about 2,950, so this represents 7.9 per cent of householders on regular relief and a further 18.8 per cent on the margins. The two groups together with their dependents account for 13.75 per cent of the population (153),

nearly identical to that of Southwark in 1618. Some migrants never left London, dying there penniless, having found it dirty, unhealthy, and inhospitable. Beier has found as entries for burials in the registers of St. Botolph's without Aldgate between 1593 and 1598, for instance,

> Edward Ellis a vagrant who died in the street.
> A young man not known who died in a hay-loft.
> A cripple that died in the street before John Awsten's door.
> A poor woman, being vagrant, whose name was not known, she died in the street under the seat before Mr. Christian Shipman's house called the Crown . . . in the High Street.
> A maid a vagrant, unknown, who died in the street near the Postern [Gate].
> Margaret, a deaf woman, who died in the street.
> A young man in a white canvas doublet . . . being vagrant and died in the street near Sparrow's corner being in the precinct near the Tower.
> A young man vagrant having no abiding place . . . who died in the street before the door of Joseph Hayes, a brazier dwelling at the

sign of Robin Hood in the High Street. . . . He was about 18 years old. I could not learn his name. (46)

Poor laws were passed and charity widely encouraged, and in the city funds were established to collect voluntary donations from householders with the proceeds used to distribute four thousand loaves of bread a week to the poor.

Discontent escalated. In 1595 alone "there were at least 13 insurrections, riots, and unlawful assemblies . . . in a dozen different parts of London and Southwark, of which 12 took place between 6 and 29 June," Manning tells us (208). He continues:

> The troubles began on 6 June when a silk-weaver and citizen appeared at the mayor's house and used "some hard speeches in dispraise of his government." The mayor assumed that the man was mad, and ordered him committed to Bedlam. Before the silk-weaver could be confined, a crowd of 200 or 300 persons gathered and effected his rescue. On 12 June there were anti-alien riots in Southwark and elsewhere. . . . On the 15th more crowds attacked the Counter Prison, and rescued prisoners on their way to the Counter. On 16 June leaders of the apprentices conferred with some discharged soldiers in the vicinity of St Paul's and, after discussing the assassination of the mayor, agreed to join forces. . . . On 27 June another attempt was made to break into the Counter and release prisoners. Twenty rioters were arrested on this occasion. The largest gatherings occurred in Cheapside and Leadenhall, where a crowd of 1,800, protesting the whipping of the butter-rioters, tore down the pillories and then proceeded to the lord mayor's house, where they erected a gallows in front of the mayor's door and dared him to come out. (209–10)

Two contingents of the garrison stationed at the Tower of London helped put the rebellion down, but it took many days to restore order. Double watches were assigned, and the Queen issued a proclamation of martial law on July 4. The trials of the leaders, held at Guildhall on July 22, resulted in five executions for treason.

But apprentices, vagrants, and the disaffected were a continual powderkeg. John Strype writes that

> The Apprentices of London are so considerable a Body, that they have sometimes made themselves formidable by Insurrections and Mutinies in the City, getting some Thousands of them together, and pulling down Houses, breaking open the Gates of Newgate, and other Prisons, and setting the Prisoners free. And this upon Occasion sometimes of Foreigners, who have followed their Trades in the City, to the supposed Damage of the Native Freemen, or

134

when some of their Brotherhood have been unjustly, as they have pretended, cast into Prison and punished.[139]

Aliens and foreigners who practiced crafts in London disrupted the guild system by refusing to acknowledge their customs and regulations, hiring cheaper labor, not keeping to required terms for apprenticeship, and making, said the guildsmen, shoddy goods so as to undersell them. Members of the Armourers Company accused strangers of engrossing; the Cutlers charged aliens with counterfeiting their very trade marks to pass off substandard goods. Alien clothiers undersold the traditional heavy, durable, high-quality woolens, the "Old Draperies," with the slightly lighter and cheaper worsteds and kerseys and the substantially lighter and cheaper New Draperies. "Towns sought to incorporate Dutch, Flemish, and French textile workers into their local economies, primarily desiring the establishment of bay and say weaving," Laura Hunt Yungblut comments, while the *Calendar of State Papers, Domestic* records that in addition to inviting skilled weavers for the making of seventeen different varieties of cloth, the ambitious officials in Maidstone sought workmen producing "Spanishe lether, fflauders potts, pavinge tyle and bricke, Brasiers, white and browne paper, corseletts and hedde peces and all kynde of armo^r, Gonne pouther, and many other artes and sciences which are not there knowen beinge both necessary and profittable for the comon Wealthe.' "[140] When John Parker, a plasterer in Southwark, was sued in Star Chamber by the Plasterers Company and shown the letters patent, he replied, "Letter me noe letters nor patent me noe pattentes. I care not a Turde for your letters nor patentes."[141] Persistent economic diversity, coupled with a tight market and an excess workforce, fissured by 1606 with the rich getting richer, the poor poorer.

By 1603 the riots had moved almost entirely to Southwark, since that was increasingly the poorest area. Population soared. So did cheap entertainment, houses of prostitution, gaming houses and sports, and crime. Here is where the low-income and the marginal settled, or kept moving, unsettled: musicians, jugglers, bearwards, actors, thieves, petty criminals, dealers of used goods, pawnbrokers. It was the home of the Paris Garden, the Mint, and the Clink, a half mile of tenements squeezed along major streets linked by webs of narrow alleyways, small gardens, and courtyards used as makeshift shelters. Eighteen alley paths ran from Bankside to Maiden Lane. There were masterless men in growing numbers by 1606 at gambling dens, bowling alleys, taverns, brothels, thieves' dens, and playhouses. Impoverishment and epidemics of plague began or spread around, even within, the Globe Theater. For those watching Shakespeare's play in 1606 who felt generally deprived or without hope, Macbeth's accomplishments and dreams would have seemed very distant, his frustrations agonizingly close. At least some playgoers would know life too as something "full of sound and fury / Signifying nothing" (5.5.27–28; 2348–49). When the drunken Porter came onstage, they found at last a character they actually knew. It may have been true comic relief. But the laughter might also have been nervous; there might have been no laughter at all. As for Shakespeare, who in the Porter would replicate the very opposite of his own landholdings and wealth in the Midlands and his share in the playing company, he found a character who could, at the heightened moment of discovering an assassination, fuse political and economic unrest at the very center of his play.[142]

Social Lexias

The social divisions that caused such dissension in 1606 resonate in *Macbeth* too: "O valiant Cousin, worthy Gentleman" (1.2.24; 43), Duncan greets Macbeth as he arrives from the battlefield, at once taming, classifying, and appropriating him. For Graham Holderness,

> The inadequacy of Duncan's comment, which translates a description of savage butchery into a decorously chivalric gesture of courtly compliment, testifies to a radical uncertainty at the heart of the play: since the very language with which the King seeks to unify his kingdom involves a systematic denial of its constitutive reality. . . . Duncan governs his thanes through his graceful and measured language of loyalty and gratitude, service and love; but he rules Scotland through the barbaric violence of those same professional warriors.[143]

The political and social strain that links public to private scenes in the play reflects the social unrest which in Shakespeare's day replaced the military code and the revenge code with more enforced if artificial codes such as those of honor and hospitality to hold together a society in transition.

We can measure the unrest to some degree in the insistence on social order by writers whose works were then in circulation. In the "Description of England" added to Holinshed's *Chronicles,* William Harrison discusses four degrees of people: gentlemen, the citizens and burgesses of cities, the yeomen of the countryside, and those who have neither voice nor authority.[144] Thomas Wilson, in "The State of England Anno Dom. 1600," lists nobles, gentry, citizens, yeomen, artisans, and rural laborers, and proudly cites some numbers: there are "19 Erles and a Marquis . . . 39 Barons and 2 Visconts . . . [and] Bishops . . . deanes . . . and Canons." "These," he says, "are the States of the Nobility, both Clergy and laye, which are called *nobilitas maior;* there rests to touch those of the meaner nobility which are termed *nobilitas minor* and are eyther knights, esquyers, gentlmen, lawe-yers, professors and ministers, archdecons, prebends, and vicars."[145] The distinctions he draws may be ideal, and somewhat misleading. Peers sat in Parliament, had some minor privileges in the law of debt, and advanta-geous ties to the universities for their families; gentry were those with landed property who could hold certain offices and wear the clothing des-ignated appropriate to their rank according to the sumptuary laws. But the sumptuary legislation was repealed in 1604, and classes began to blur. Elizabeth I had in a way helped to foster this by bringing the peerage and the gentry into her government at various positions (and at various times), co-opting them while rendering their social ranking more fluid, less pre-cise. Wilson himself senses the situation, adding that "the great yeomanry is decayed, yett by this meanes the Cominalty is encreased, 20 nowe per-haps with their labor and diligence living well and welthily of that land wich our great yeoman held before. . . . There are, moreover, of yeomen of meaner ability which are called Freeholders" (19).

But a threatened social ranking was maintained by various means. Peter Clark and Paul Slack have shown, for instance, that to qualify for alderman in London a man had to own considerable property; in the time of Elizabeth I, therefore, one-third of the aldermen were related and the aldermen's court was dominated by fifteen families.[146] The same was true in the country. Lawrence Stone observes that

> Town Charters were revised and reissued, in every case in order to place electoral power in the hands of a tiny minority. Where this was not done, the control of the town was restricted by mere governmental fiat, as at Sandwich in 1604, when the Privy Council ordered the electorate for the mayor to be reduced to the twenty-four of the Common Council. Similarly control of the parish was confined to the "better sort" by the device of the select vestry, while at religious worship the gradations of rank were publicly defined by the erection of private pews, the placing of which was the subject of continual friction and even violence. In the country local government was monopolized by a caucus of leading landed families, and in the national political institution of the House of Commons the same closing of ranks is visible. Not a single

merchant was made a J.P. in Essex after 1564, not a single clothier was returned as M.P. in the great cloth county of Wiltshire after 1603. . . . Within
the landed classes the hardening of the lines of social cleavage itself reflected
and was supported by a shift in the balance of economic advantage from the
yeoman leaseholder to the nobility and gentry landlords. The latter began to
cream off the agricultural profits in enhanced rents and fines [and enclo-
sures].[147]

As for the freemen, status distinctions came through membership in religious guilds and craft fellowships where identity was further made interdependent but not reciprocal: while apprentices could earn their way to
freedom, ordinary guild members were ranked lower than wardens and
liverymen, and artisan companies, such as the tanners or glovers, were
ranked beneath such prestigious guilds as the Mercers and Grocers. The
best-known differentiation was London's Twelve Great Livery Companies.

A statutory act (5 Eliz. vi) that set up the "several Commissions, to
limit, rate, and appoint the wages as well of such and so many of the said
Artificers, Handicraftmen, Husbandmen, or any other Labourer, Servant
or Workman, whose wages in times past hath been by any Law or Statute
rated and appointed" (sig. 5A3) was reprinted in 1603 and added new
ones. Not only was custom reinforced by the regulations and rules of
court, government, and guild, but private households too had their own
hierarchies based on lineage and on household responsibilities and duties.
A. J. Fletcher notes that "Every nuance of daily life and activity—clothes,
speech, modes of address, assumptions about social intercourse" was regulated.[148] Nobility especially continued to lay stock in tradition. Henry
Percy is certain to point out in *Advice to His Son* (1609), "There are certain
works fit for every vocation; some for kings; some for noblemen; some for
gentlemen; some for artificers; some for clowns; and some for beggars; all
are good to be known by everyone, yet not to be used by everyone. If
everyone play his part well, that is allotted him, the commonwealth will
be happy; if not then will it be deformed; but which is fit for everyone,
quaere?"[149] George Meriton, preaching before the King in February 1607,
draws the analogy between people and plants that is echoed in *Macbeth*—
there is "great difference of seeds and branches," and "it avayleth much
from what stock one descendeth." He painfully draws forth the implications: "Some are noble, some ignoble, some ingenuous, some base, some
quick of apprehension, some dull; some fit to rule, some to serve" (sigs.
B2v–B4).[150]

Such writers may protest too much: with a shifting economy, a newly
mobile population, and an expanding system of education, men of one

rank or station were seeking others. Ambition was not characteristic only of Macbeth: it was clearly the major characteristic of many in Shakespeare's audiences. Clark and Slack note this too: "Urban society in this period presents a picture both of a clear and relatively rigid social pyramid of wealth and status and of a social hierarchy whose individual members were constantly changing" (111). With James's accession, when arms of nobility gave way to titles, the gates opened. Elizabeth I had been parsimonious with the awarding of honors, allowing only 18 peerages and 878 knighthoods (because of Essex's rashness, in part) in her nearly half-century of rule. In contrast, James named 906 knights in the first four months of his reign; by 1642 there were 3,281 new knights, 364 baronets, and 103 peers exclusive of the Scots and Irish creations.[151] In *Roome for a Gentleman* (1609), Barnabe Riche claims that "Eyther a Knight or a knitter of Caps" is the fate of every man "for wee are now so full of Knights, that Gentlemen are had in little request" (29). Wallace MacCaffrey confirms that "in the intensely rank-conscious world of late Tudor England, there was an unceasing scramble to cross the dividing line which separated gentlemen (the 'common sort of nobility,' as Camden called them) from the mere yeoman or freeholder,"[152] while Ruth Kelso long before noted that "those who lacked the title of [gentlemen] were busy trying to acquire it."[153] In this, Shakespeare and his father were, seeking a coat of arms, not exempt. Frank Whigham argues that "the pressure from below of so many able young men attempting to enter the ruling elite, to 'serve the state' and to reap the fruits of such service, caused the established aristocracy much anxiety. What the humanist youth saw as public service (and opportunity), the established courtier saw as contamination and competition." Whigham cites two main channels in the universities and the Inns of Court where those with ability joined those with lineage.[154] Gabriel Harvey concurs: "You can not stepp into a schollars studye but (ten to on) you shall litely finde open ether Bodin de Republica or Le Royes Exposition uppon Aristotles Politiques or sum other like Frenche or Italian Politique Discourses."[155] Despite the difference in time and culture, they have their counterparts in the political and social ambitions of Lady Macbeth and Banquo.

Since appearance and behavior established, defined, and in a sense confirmed rank, a certain theatricality obtained outside the theater. Social performance was used to define, display, and apparently authenticate status—the ambitious, like Macbeth, wore borrowed robes. Attempting to transcend his position of battlefield champion to that of ruler and king, a

position for which he has not been trained as a Prince of Cumberland, Macbeth reverts to his military background when frustrated or uncertain:

> To be thus, is nothing, but to be safely thus:
> Our feares in *Banquo* stick deepe,
> And in his Royaltie of Nature reigns that
> Which would be fear'd. 'Tis much he dares,
> And to that dauntlesse temper of his Minde,
> He hath a Wisdom, that doth guide his Valour,
> To act in safetie. (3.1.47–53; 1038–44)

Macbeth's understanding of his situation—"We haue scorch'd the Snake,
not kill'd it: / Shee'le close, and be her selfe, whilest our poore Mallice /
Remaines in danger of her former Tooth" (3.2.13–15; 1167–69)—now
demands a fighter's response: "There's comfort yet: they are assaileable"
(3.2.39; 1197).

Thus *Macbeth* is also a play deeply invested in status and rank. For
playgoers at the Globe in 1606 such matters would sharply distinguish
Lenox, Rosse, and Banquo from Cathnes and Angus and yet complicate
them. Lenox, for instance, the lineal ancestor of the cousin who fled James
at the Raid of Ruthven and whose successor knocked hard at the door of
Gowrie House, defends Macbeth at the discovery of Duncan's death and
provides the crucial testimony that allows him to be elected king:

> Those of his Chambers, as it seem'd, had don't:
> Their Hands, and Faces were all badg'd with blood,
> So were their Daggers, which vnwip'd, we found
> Vpon their Pillowes: they star'd, and were distracted,
> No mans Life was to be trusted with them. (2.3.101–5; 865–69)

When he appears again in 3.6 with an unidentified Lord, he claims to
have changed his mind, but clearly he is spying for Macbeth.

> My former Speeches,
> Haue but hit your Thoughts
> Which can interpret farther: Onely I say
> Things haue bin strangely borne. The gracious *Duncan*
> Was pittied of *Macbeth*: marry he was dead:
> And the right valiant *Banquo* walkd'd too late,
> Whom you may say (if't please you) *Fleans* kill'd,
> For *Fleans* fled: Men must not walke too late. (3.6.1–8; 1472–79)

140

He has cast his bait and reels in the information he wants about Malcolm. "Sent he to *Macduffe*?" he asks in false incredulity (3.6.39; 1513). That he is loyal still is seen in 4.1: he alone knows where Macbeth has gone when seeking the weird sisters in their cave; he probably accompanied Macbeth and waited outside; at least what he does when Macbeth rejoins him is to warn him:

Macb.	Saw you the Weyard Sisters?
Len.	No my Lord.
Macb.	Came they not by you?
Len.	No indeed my Lord.
Macb.	Infected be the Ayre whereon they ride.
	And damn' d all those that trust them. I did heare
	The galloping of Horse. Who was't come by?
Len.	'Tis two or three my Lord, that bring you word:
	Macduff is fled to England.
Macb.	Fled to England?
Len.	I, my good Lord. (4.1.136–43; 1686–96)

Before he finally changes sides, along with Cathnes and Angus (5.2.31; 2212), measuring for playgoers Macbeth's diminishing strength and effectiveness, Lenox has been Macbeth's most trusted thane, the successor to Banquo and Macduff, who has managed to rise higher in Macbeth's court than Rosse. Rosse did not expect this; *he* first hails Macbeth as Thane of Cawdor "for an earnest of a greater Honor" (1.3.104; 209); and he has confirmed Macduff's departure, but this messenger comes too late (4.2) in the knowledge of what Lenox has already told Macbeth; and the next we see of him (4.3), he has defected to Malcolm and Macduff in England. Banquo, too, seems to be angling for position at the new court. Macbeth has promised support of a silenced Banquo who will not reveal their meeting with the weird sisters—"If you shall cleaue to my consent, / When 'tis, it shall make Honor for you" (2.1. 25–26; 604–5)—and when he makes conditions—"So I lose none . . . I shall be counsail'd" (2.1.26, 29; 605, 608)—he keeps his own counsel. Playgoers alert to the language of dissimulation will be wary of Banquo, even though his staying on at court—and his not revealing any suspicions of Macbeth at the time of Duncan's death—might seem to argue that he too believes in the witches, and that their prophecy, while it does not dictate what he must do, dictates the end he wishes: that he will foster a line of kings. He is either loyal or biding his time. His one soliloquy (3.1–10; 982–91)—which should uncover his most honest thoughts—is itself open to more than one interpretation.

LEXIAS OF LINEAGE AND HONOR

To preclude social chaos at such a cultural moment, England in 1606 attempted to preserve itself as a "lineage society [which] gave primacy to the sense of 'blood' as the vehicle of the collective family genius and virtue," Mervyn James writes, "bringing these out of the past and carrying them into the future. . . . There was little sense of any loyalties which overrode those imposed by the intense and particularized world of the lineage."[156] The sense of identity and pride through ancestry is put forth in countless writings beginning with John Ferne's study of heraldry, his "Glorie of Generositie" (1586). "A great temporall blessing it is, and a greate heart's ease to a man," Sir John Wynn writes, "to find that he is well descended." Sir Simonds D'Ewes "ever accounted it a great outward blessing to be well descended, it being in the gift only of God and nature to bestow it";[157] Macbeth registers great anxiety over his "vnlineall Hand" (3.1.62; 1053). Yet insofar as ancestry provided rank and established a basis for authority and privilege it was also, as Gail Kern Paster has pointed out, ideological—a means of assuring power and importance.

Shakespeare is aware of James's descent, too, because it began with Robert II as the show of eight kings in *Macbeth* does (4.1). Shakespeare may have used "the fourth table for the Historie of Scotland" in the 1587 edition of Holinshed—as some playgoers would recognize—where he would find these references in "Stewards their descent":

> 168/b/40: Banquho the thane of Lochquhaber, of whom the house of the Stewards is descended, the which by order of linage hath now for a long time inioed the crowne of Scotland, euen till these our daies. . . .
>
> 245/a/67: Thus ye may perceiue how the Stewards came to the crowne, whose succession haue inioed the same to our time: queene Marie mother to Charles James [that now] reigneth, being the eight person from this Robert, that thus first atteined vnto it (of whose first originall and descent you shall see before in the life of Duncan),

royal descent, rather than tanistry, assuring Malcolm the throne, his present analogue James's son Prince Henry. Macbeth clearly thinks along bloodlines, too, as duplicative of clan lines; as Macduff approaches him near the end, he shouts, "Of all men else I haue auoyded thee: / But get thee backe, my soule is too much charg'd / With blood of thine already"

(5.8.4–6; 2441–43). But Macbeth has been clear about blood lineage all along. Confronting royal blood, he is, as a soldier hardened to slaughter, chastened with respect for Duncan's corpse:

> Here lay *Duncan,*
> His Siluer skinne, lac'd with his Golden Blood,
> And his gash'd Stabs, look'd like a Breach in Nature,
> For Ruines wastfull entrance. (2.3.111–14; 876–79)

C The sense of royal blood echoes throughout the play; for Macbeth especially, it holds magical charm:

> Will all great *Neptunes* Ocean wash this blood
> Cleane from my Hand? no: this my Hand will rather
> The multitudinous Seas incarnadine,
> Making the Greene one, Red. (2.2.59–62; 721–24)

Lady Macbeth has a similar respect for Duncan's position (and his bloodline) when she finds she cannot bring herself to murder him, for his royal blood (as well as his appearance) reminds her of her father (2.2.12–13; 662–63), and its charmed qualities help drive her mad: "Out damned spot: out I say . . . / . . . who / would haue thought the olde man to haue had so much / blood in him?" (5.1.34–39; 2127–32). Her madness may also result from dwelling on her denial of children ("make thick my blood, / Stop Vp th'accesse, and passage to Remorse, / That no compunctious visitings of Nature / Shake my fell purpose" [1.5.43–46; 394–97]), violating a basic Scottish (but not English) tenet: "Ilk moder was nurice to hir awin barne" ("Each mother was nurse to her child"), John Bellenden remarks in his *Hystory and Croniklis of Scotland* (1540?) (sig. D1). Pierre le Loyer in his *Treatise of Spectres* (translated by Z. Jones in 1605) believes that menopause could produce similar results: "The blood of [women's] monthly disease being stopped from his course, through the ordinary passages and by the matrix dooth redound and beate backe again by the heart. . . . Then the same blood, not finding any passage, troubleth the braine in such sorte, that . . . it causeth many of them to have idle fancies and fond conceipts, and tormenteth them with diverse imaginations of horrible specters, and fearfull sights . . . with which being so afflicted, some of them doe seeke to throwe and cast themselves into wells or pittes, and others to destroy themselves by hanging, or some such miserable end" (ff. 110–110v).[158]

The concept of blood as bloodline (as well as murder) reaches its highest pitch when Macbeth recognizes that "It will haue blood they say: / Blood will haue Blood" (3.4.121; 1403–4). The blood of legitimate royalty will overpower his own. That is why "I am in blood / Stept in so farre, that should I wade no more, / Returning were as tedious as go ore: / Strange things I haue in head, that will to hand, / Which must be acted, ere they may be scand" (3.4.135–39; 1419–23). This is no longer a matter of death or murder, but of regicide. After this, all murder even to this hardened soldier will be without function or purpose, while, as consequences of this horrendous act, they will no longer bear his watching. Royalty also recognizes itself in this play. Duncan's younger son differentiates between the royal bloodline and the blood of royalty. "Where we are, there's Daggers in mens Smiles," Donalbaine says, "The neere in blood, the neerer bloody" (2.3.140–41; 914–15). Harry Berger, Jr., has noted that

> literally and symbolically, the natural basis of the warrior society is blood. Blood is, first of all, the organizing principle of social relations, the foundation of kinship and lineage, place and name, and critics have rightly made much of this ascriptive bond between the social order and nature. But they haven't made enough of the fact that other meanings of blood tend to contradict this harmonious basis. For blood is also the principle of individual self-assertion; the source of vital function, of courage, passion, and excitement; and beyond that, the principle of aggression. Blood will have blood. Bloodshed is the proof of manliness and the source of honor and reputation. Bloodshed, bloodiness, bloody-mindedness quicken the pulse of the social order and sharpen its edge.[159]

Examining the blood in *Macbeth*, then, is a hypertextual exercise: it is not merely image-clustering but rather a vital network of kinship practices and of social formations that for 1606 have immediate and vital significance.

In the years preceding *Macbeth* at the Globe, a new emphasis on lineage was also leading to fraudulence. Henry VII had strengthened the Tudor lineage by forging descent from a mythical King Arthur; Burghley had invented a family genealogy when joining the Privy Council of Elizabeth I; and even James, on arriving in London in 1603, began to claim descent past the fictional Banquo to Brut. Lawrence Stone, studying the matter at length in *The Crisis of the Aristocracy,* says that such fictional or forged lineages "had in 1417 been placed in the hands of the College of Heralds, whose duty it was to smother new wealth beneath a coat of arms and a respectable pedigree. Since the heralds made their living by the issue of these certificates of gentility, and since the number of aspirants was increasing at a tremendous pace, it is hardly surprising if a large element of venality soon crept in. Indeed the profits were such that they tempted confidence tricksters into the business, who toured the country distributing worthless coats of arms to the gullible" (66). He cites such a confidence man from Cheshire who gulled ninety gentry by the time he was discovered (66–67).

While the College of Heralds set up a process of Visitations to protect their titles, rapid shifting of land ownership and the burgeoning numbers of claims—over 2,000 between 1560 and 1589, at least another 1,760 from 1590 to 1639—rendered this practice imperfect at best. In 1433 there were 48 families claiming gentry status; in 1623 there were 470.[160] Thus a procedure was initiated in 1583 in Staffordshire: "These names being writtne on a sheet of paper with fower great letters, was carried by the Bayliffe of the Hundred & one of the Heraulds men to the cheife towne of that Hundred; where in the cheife place thereof the heraulds men redd the names (after crye made by the Bayliffs and the people gathered) & then pronounced by the said bayley every mans name severally contayned in the said Bill; that done, the Bayley sett the said Bill of Names on a post fast with waxe where it may stand drye . . . in the cheifest place of the said towne."[161] But the practice was so rampant that not all bogus claims could be detected.

In such a context, Duncan's battlefield recognition of Macbeth as his "valiant Cousin, worthy Gentleman" (1.2.24; 43), confirming their kinship, carried clear overtones in 1606. Duncan's greeting could be read as formulary, as a sign of tribute, as an acknowledgment of family pride, or, more darkly, as clarification of his role as King and the soldier's more subordinate position. But "old rules of conduct," and especially those that invited bogus exploitation, "can lead the way towards a shattering of the old order, and an opening towards a new one," Victor Kiernan reminds us.[162] To help remedy what Stone calls "the inflation of honours," the government under Elizabeth and James attempted to displace lineage to some degree with an honor code that inherently linked the tenth-century events on the stage of the Globe with circumstances in which playgoers of 1606 were living. According to Norbert Elias, this has been the standard way of emerging civilization: to move from a warrior to a courtier code of behavior. Prestige may be won by distinguished actions rather than by inheritance or the accumulation of wealth.[163] Under Elizabeth this growing culture of honor took many forms. It displaced warfare with duels. It introduced a widespread learning of fencing; the first English fencing school was opened at Blackfriars in 1576 by the Italian Rocco Bonetti, and, notes J. A. Sharpe in *Early Modern England,* "the art of fencing rapidly acquired upper-class patrons" (97). And there were ceremonial tilts, in which courtiers vying for prestige through skill and honor, rather than bloodline, combined Machiavellian *virtú* with Castiglionian ability at arms. In 1561 Elizabeth I closed in the Whitehall tiltyard built by her father and the following year began an annual custom of tilting on November 17, her

Accession Day. These tournaments, where nobles and gentlemen broke their lances in the Queen's honor, were presided over by Sir Henry Lee, the Queen's Master of the Armoury.

A visiting German has left a description of a tournament staged in 1584.[164] "Surviving speeches evoke a picture that is wholly romantic in sentiment," Sir Roy Strong comments. "One is spoken by the Damsel of the Queen of Fairies on behalf of an Enchanted Knight, who cannot tilt because 'his armes be locked for a tyme.' There is a sonnet on behalf of a Blind Knight, who has been overcome by the Queen" (45). But beneath the ritual, elaborate in speech and costume, there was serious business going on: the establishment of honor, favor, prestige, and patronage. When Sir Philip Sidney died, his horse, draped in black, was led across the tiltyard. Elizabeth herself attended all but four of these annual occasions held from 1581 to 1603, and after her death James continued to invest heavily in lavish knightly ceremonies. Similar chivalric activity—no longer on a deadly battlefield but just as important a victory for those involved—centered around Prince Henry, culminating in a special *Barriers* written by Ben Jonson in 1610 in which the Prince himself participated. That such acts of honor are necessary to complete rather than simply to insure lineage and rank is central to the seating of thanes in the banquet in *Macbeth*: "You know your owne degrees, sit downe," Macbeth says in lines anachronistic to the historic Macbeth; "At first and last, the hearty welcome" (3.4.1–2; 1256–57), following elaborate stage directions for the entrance (1254–55). One mark of the disruption by Banquo's ghost is Lady Macbeth's untraditional dismissal: "Stand not vpon the order of your going, / But go at once" (3.4.118–19; 1398–99). But we can also measure her sense of maintaining family stature through family honor and service in her initial welcome of Duncan to Inverness: "All our seruice," she tells the King,

> In euery point twice done, and then done double,
> We are poore, and single Businesse, to contend
> Against those Honors deepe, and broad,
> Wherewith your Maiestie loades our House. (1.6.14–18; 450–54)

She has this partly in mind, too, when, alarmed, she exclaims, at hearing of Duncan's death, "Woe, alas! What! in our house?" (2.3.87–88; 846–47), although in 1606 there would also be overtones of *house* as lineage, as the House of Macbeth.

"The role of honour in revolts and rebellions cannot be explained without a consideration of its social dimension," Mervyn James argues. He continues,

The man of honour was not merely violent and self-assertive, he was also involved in strong solidarities, incorporated in a society with its own distinctive organization, legality and culture. As far as the latter is concerned, perhaps the most fundamental tenet of honour belief is that Fate, irrational, incomprehensible, and uncontrollable, rules over human history. Events were inevitable and their causes obscure; no explanation was possible why this rather than that should have come to pass. A number of symbols, concepts and personifications has been used to express this point of view, from the *Wyrd* of Anglo-Saxon epic to the Goddess Fortune.[165]

This cultural representation in *Macbeth* is in the *wyrds* as the weird sisters, whose unpredicted appearance to Macbeth and Banquo in 1.3 suggests a prophetic ordering of the future that erupts onto the uncertainty of the battlefield. This cultural belief in 1606 may contextually explain why an obsession with the three witches causes Macbeth to displace Lady Macbeth with their supernatural knowledge and why he leaves the castle to seek them out in 4.1. It may also explain why the duel with Macduff—a single combat in which both honor and the witches' prophecy are tested—is what drives Macbeth in 5.8: "Lay on *Macduffe*, / And damn'd be him, that first cries hold, enough" (33–34; 2474–75).

But for Mervyn James, the connection of honor and revolt has other cultural significance. He sees it as the chief explanation for the Essex revolt in 1601, an event still in vivid living memory for the playgoers of 1606 and so a potential lexia. According to James,

> The interest of the [Essex] revolt is . . . that it was the last honour revolt: and as such the conclusion of a series and a tradition which recedes far back into the medieval period. . . . His aristocratic lineage, his military career, and the tradition he inherited all helped to make the earl a paradigm of honour. At the same time, the various literary and philosophical influences which circulated in the 1590s, emphasizing the cult of the heroic, and the aristocratic *megalopsyche*, or great soul, added to the glamour which surrounded Essex. . . . All the sordid details of the planned *coup d'état* to seize control of the court, to enter London, and take the Tower were exposed by the conspirators themselves. Then, after his condemnation and return to his cell in the Tower, Essex himself executed a remarkable volte-face. He admitted the falsity of the stand he had taken at the trial, denounced his associates, and made a total and abject confession of all his faults.[166]

Partly because of this confession, partly because of his heroism in an age still wanting and needing heroes, partly because of cultural definitions of honor, Essex's public reputation was not permanently damaged. When James came to the throne and exonerated one of the accomplices, Southampton, and in the Main Plot did not execute others, Essex's reputation was slowly rehabilitated until, by 1606, he was one of the cultural heroes of the day—and because of his practices, not in spite of them. The support of the Lancaster herald Francis Thynne, who had written the Scottish history for Holinshed's *Chronicles,* was enlisted because his treatise on the Earl's office, that of Earl Marshal, Thynne found to be one of such "antiquity, honor, and credit" that "fewe other offices eyther for place or dignitye are preferred before yt eyther amongst us or forraine nations."[167] When in the early years of James's reign Essex's whole career was reexamined, he became a cultural paragon, an icon for the fallen hero, but a hero nonetheless.

Thus it is that parallels between Essex and Macbeth, as distant as they might seem to us, constituted live options in 1606 and in the great revival of Essex as hero in subsequent years. The impetuous young Essex, ramming his spear against the gates of Lisbon in 1589, and later attempting expeditions to Cádiz and the Azores, resembles the actions of Macbeth, who, "Disdayning Fortune, with his brandisht Steele, / Which smoak'd with bloody execution," ran on Macdonwald and "vnseam'd him from the Naue to th'Chops, / And fix'd his Head vpon our Battlements" (1.2.17–23; 36–42). Both Essex and Macbeth combined bravado with ostentation; both, acting instinctively, were fierce in battle. Essex, like Macbeth, possessed a lineage he felt had been overlooked; even William Camden, acknowledging that Essex "was accomplished with all virtues worthy a most noble man," added, "His Genealogy ancient and very noble."[168] Both Essex and Macbeth feel slighted by their rulers. "The Prince of Cumberland," says Macbeth of the appointment that undermines his own new title of Cawdor, "that is a step, / On which I must fall downe, or else o're-leap" (1.4.48–49; 336–37). Penelope Devereux Rich, annoyed at her brother Essex's house arrest following his sudden return from Ireland, persuaded him to resist and even rebel against the Queen much as Lady Macbeth urges Macbeth on. Essex as Earl Marshal, Macbeth as the leading soldier—both were publicly underappreciated. But like Essex, Macbeth was conflicted about whether to attack the monarch: "this *Duncan,*" says Macbeth,

> Hath borne his Faculties so meeke; hath bin
> So cleere in his great Office, that his Vertues
> Will pleade like Angels, Trumpet-tongu'd against
> The deepe damnation of his taking off:
> And Pitty, like a naked New-borne-Babe,
> Striding the blast, or Heauens Cherubin, hors'd
> Vpon the sightlesse Curriors of the Ayre,
> Shall blow the horrid deed in euery eye,
> That teares shall drowne the winde (1.7.16–25; 490–99):

his soliloquy is a striking mixture of a sense of honor and a sense of battle, of honorable cherubim turned into an opposing army for what would be a shameful act "in euery eye" but his own. This keen sense of an unholy combination of codes—the honor code and the military code, which together for him define manliness and integrity—taints not only his reputation but corrupts his very motive: "I haue no Spurre," he confesses to himself, "To pricke the sides of my intent, but onely / Vaulting Ambition, which ore-leaps it selfe" (1.7.25–27; 499–501). Such lines condemn the honor code of 1606 too. Whether or not Essex meant to capture the Queen or had passing thoughts of regicide when he marched on the palace on Sunday morning, February 8, 1601, he failed, and with his small band of followers was arrested for treason. Macbeth, conversely, succeeds in killing the King. Yet Macbeth and Essex share a genuine sense of contrition. The *Calendar of State Papers, Domestic* records that on the eve of his execution, "Between 10 and 12 o'clock [Essex] opened his window, and said to the guard, 'My good friends, pray for me, and tomorrow you shall see in me a strong God in a weak man; I have nothing left but that which I must pay the Queen tomorrow in the morning.' "[169] Beach Langston records that "the rest of the night he spent in prayer and meditation with the three divines, endeavoring to preserve that just tempering of humility and faith which on the morrow enabled him to walk to the scaffold with a behavior 'firm, modest, and constant.' The great Essex died according to the book, in sincere religious penitence and profound religious trust" (128). Macbeth also has regrets, realizing that "that which should accompany Old-Age, / As Honor, Loue, Obedience, Troopes of Friends, / I must not looke to haue" (5.3.24–26; 2241–43). Then for a second time the two diverge: Essex's private execution gave a limited audience to his penance; Macbeth, solitary, falls back on a resigned attempt to test skill with honor in his stubborn public battle with Macduff.

"It was through seeking honour," Anthony Fletcher comments, that "men lived out their manhood."[170] In a continuing examination of honor and its relation to lineage, *Macbeth* focuses relentlessly on the protagonist: as Theodore Spencer has commented, "*Macbeth* is a play that closes in."[171] "It gives the hero more exclusive attention," Michael Long adds.[172] In fact, Macbeth speaks over 30 percent of the lines in comparison to Lady Macbeth's 11 percent, a dominance unmatched in any other play by Shakespeare. Yet with fewer lines, Lady Macbeth, also conscious of her royal lineage, struggles to find her own sense of honor. Her difficulty is her gender. She confronts this early on: "Come you Spirits, / That tend on mortall thoughts, vnsex me here, / And fill me from the Crowne to the

Toe, top-full / Of direst Crueltie: make thick my blood" (1.5.40–43; 391–94). Thus emboldened, her sense of honor has become one of battle, her notion of manliness one of might. When Macbeth hesitates at the thought of regicide, she taunts him (1.7.35–45; 512–22). His attempt to counter her with a more refined sense of the honor code—

> Prythee peace:
> I dare do all that may become a man,
> Who dares no more, is none (1.7.45–47; 523–25)

—is a reply she cannot afford now to hear or to understand. So she persists:

> What Beast was't then
> That made you breake this enterprize to me?
> When you durst do it, then you were a man:
> And to be more then what you were, you would
> Be so much more the man. Nor time, nor place
> Did then adhere, and yet you would make both:
> They haue made themselues, and that their fitnesse now
> Do's vnmake you. (1.7.47–54; 526–33)

Her fierce insistence—"But screw your courage to the sticking place, / And wee'le not fayle" (1.7.61–62; 541–42)—at last connects with his sense of manly honor married with that of the warrior, and he replies in kind:

> Bring forth Men-Children onely:
> For thy vndaunted Mettle should compose
> Nothing but Males. (1.7.73–75; 554–56)

Lady Macbeth wins, as Macbeth will realize for himself later, a Pyrrhic victory. Despite her lineage, her cross-gendered sense of honor drives her mad. She cannot murder Duncan, because he reminds her of her father. In smearing the grooms with blood—a second attempt at masculinity—she freezes her mind in a moment she cannot erase. An easy task for Bellona's bridegroom is an impossible task for Bellona. Lady Macbeth dishonors herself because she invades an honor code in which women have no part.

Yet for some playgoers at the Globe in 1606 it was the very idea of an honor code that was at fault, that made victims of Essex, Macbeth, and Lady Macbeth. Sir Walter Ralegh says so in his *Historie of the World*:

> What is this honour, I meane honour indeed, and that which ought to be so deare unto us, other than a kinde of history, or fame following actions of vertue, actions accompanied with difficulty or danger, and undertaken for the

publike good? In these, he that is imployed and trusted, if he faile in the performance, either through cowardize, or any other base affection; it is true that he loseth his honour. But the acting of a private combat, for a private respect, and most commonly a frivolous one, is not an action of vertue, because it is contrary to the Law of God, and of all Christian Kings: neither is it difficult, because even and equall in persons and armes: Neither for a publike good, but tending to the contrary; because the losse or mutilation of an able man, is also a losse to the Common-weale. (5.3.17.12; 1652 ed., sig. 5G3)

Honor was being reevaluated in Scotland, too. Gavin Douglas, in "The Plaice of Honour," had identified the code with a warrior society, the "most valiant folk,"[173] "*Bellona's* Bridegroome, lapt in proofe" (1.2.55; 79). Such an attitude had led to such events as the Ruthven Raid on King James in 1582. In 1567 Robert Sempill had called instead for "gentilnes" and civility in his "Exhortatioun To the Lordis," and James too advocated a more peaceful code of manly honor. He asked that men stop carrying "Gunnes and traiterous Pistolets" and that they no longer wear armor beneath their clothing in self-defense. His position was furthered in 1587 when he collected rival heroic and sometimes barbaric clans for a banquet and urged reconciliation:

At this conventioun the King maid ane harang to his nobelitie and estaites, declairing, that seing he was now come to his perfect aige of twentie ane yeiris compleit, hafing mony wechtie effaires to be advysit, thocht it best first to reconceill his nobellitie, quharin his Majestie had teane no small travell, and to such poynt as all sould tend to the pleasour of God, his Majesties standing, the weill of the countrie, and their awin ease and tranquilletie; protesting befoir God that he loved nothing so mikle as ane perfyt unioun and reconcili- • atioun amangis his nobellety in hairtes and gif ony sould seime obstinat, that the remnant of his nobiletie sould hald hand to the repressing of theme, and the first brekkaris of that happie unioun persewit be all extremitie.[174]

The King worked hard to end feuds among the clans during the winter of 1595–96 and convened them in the summer of 1598 with an act to end all feuding, especially the traditional "blood feuds" for which Scotland was widely known in England. He made certain this peaceful effort was part of his record when he arrived in England in 1603.

According to Jenny Wormald, clan behavior and structure were upheld in Scotland from 1450 through 1600 by the practice of "bonds of manrent" by which lords, lairds, and burgh officers granted their personal service and that of their dependents to greater men in return for "maintenance" and protection. Such oaths were written. One of them, drawn up by Henry Darnley, had committed several men to press for him to receive the crown matrimonial after his marriage to Mary, and to persuade Elizabeth I of England to his favor. Later he was able to reinterpret the bond so that it might also punish those who opposed him, such as "a stranger Italian called David," and if necessary have them killed. Other political bonds included Ainslie's Tavern Bond of April 1567, which enabled Bothwell to carry off the Queen and marry her; an opposing bond, signed on May 8, 1568, by nine earls, nine bishops, twelve abbots and commendators, eighteen lords, and ninety lairds after Mary had escaped from Lochleven Castle, committed them to work together to restore her to power.[175] But she fled to England, cutting herself off from this power base and causing the young James to be made King, while the English, learning from this, formed a Bond of Association to protect Elizabeth I against Mary and any rebellion she might foster to take over England while imprisoned in their country. These bonds of manrent established honor in Scotland through oaths spoken and written; Macbeth alludes to this cultural practice when he tells his wife of "That great Bond, / Which keeps me pale" (3.2.49–50; 1208–9). He later makes an oath against Macduff:

> But yet Ile make assurance: double sure,
> And take a Bond of Fate: thou shalt not liue,
> That I may tell pale-hearted Feare, it lies;
> And sleepe in spight of Thunder. (4.1.83–86; 1624–27)

This oath, this bond of manrent, marks his demise, however, because he makes the agreement with the three witches.

Oaths spoken and unspoken are central practice to *Macbeth*. Duncan is not exempt from the code of military honor, for he relies on messengers to announce the success of his campaigns while he remains at the margin of the battleground: as Norbert Elias has pointed out, kings are dependent on their aristocracy (or soldiers) as the subjects depend on them for leadership and security (2:268). Macbeth takes as a bond the King's new title for him of Thane of Cawdor, and then hears the King effectively annul his oath when appointing Malcolm to a still higher position. It is the beginning of contested power. When in 1.6 Duncan leaves the battlefield at Forres and enters the courtyard at Inverness, he is no longer in his own territory. He may sense this, since he overlays the castle with an agreeable description that at once announces his authority and conditions Macbeth's castle to his own welcome:

> This Castle hath a pleasant seat,
> The ayre nimbly and sweetly recommends it selfe

Vnto our gentle sences. (1.6.1–3; 434–36)

The remark is made to his royal entourage; the stage direction of the First Folio asks that the entrance, to "*Hoboyes and Torches*," be composed of "*King, Malcolme, Donalbaine, Banquo, Lenox, Macduf, Rosse, Angus, and Attendants*" (1.6. S.D.; 431–33). Duncan's constructed scene is at once exposed when Macbeth violates the violated bond. He does not welcome the King; Lady Macbeth does. Once more, Duncan will not be deterred or lose face:

> See, see, our honor'd Hostesse:
> The Loue that followes vs, sometime is our trouble,
> Which still we thanke as Loue. Herein I teach you,
> How you shall bid God-eyld vs for your paines,
> And thanke vs for your trouble. (1.6.10–14; 445–49)

The contest of wills now devolves on Lady Macbeth. Having unsexed herself, she proceeds to replace her husband, and Duncan, sensing this challenge to his own honor, admonishes her:

> Where's the Thane of Cawdor?
> We courst him at the heeles, and had a purpose
> To be his Purueyor: But he rides well,
> And his great Loue (sharpe at his Spurre) hath holp him
> To his home before vs: Faire and Noble Hostesse
> We are your guest to night. (1.6.20–25; 457–62)

When she seems undisturbed, he grows more insistent:

> Giue me your hand:
> Conduct me to mine Host we loue him highly,
> And shall continue, our Graces towards him,
> By your leaue Hostesse. (1.6.28–31; 467–70)

It is a sharp rebuff; the commands that work so well on and off the battlefield continue to issue forth at Macbeth's castle. But Duncan has little or no charm; he has no behavioral code for women. His world is wholly that of noblemen and soldiers. In Inverness he is out of tune, limited in authority. Not surprisingly for playgoers at the Globe, these are his last words in the play.

Banquo too is caught between two honor codes—that of the King and that of his friend and battlefield companion. To both of them he owes fealty. "The code of honour required faithfulness to friends as well as to one's lord," Mervyn James tells us. "The notion of friendship commonly indicated a relationship between equals, and often arose out of 'chamber companionship,' that is, the sharing of lodgings by young men serving at court or in a great household."[176] Banquo admits to this early on when he refers to Macbeth as "My Noble Partner" (1.3.54; 154). As events unfold, he is shown gratitude by Duncan but is given no reward; he is likelier to get rewards, then, from Macbeth. He is also invested in the witches' prophecies for Macbeth coming true, so that in turn the prophecy that he will father a line of kings will come true too. His loyalty to Macbeth holds more promise for him than loyalty to the King; and yet it is to Duncan that he owes his primary allegiance because of Duncan's position as King. Momentarily, in leading Duncan to Inverness, he is able to serve both. But once he is at Inverness, his allegiance, and his oaths, are again in conflict. That conflict is in turn resolved when the two become one—when Macbeth becomes King. Again if he does not act, Chance may crown his son king as Chance crowned Macbeth (1.3.144–45; 255–56). Only when Banquo begins to sense that Macbeth "playd'st most fowly" for the crown (3.1.3; 984) does he feel the freedom to break his own bond with Macbeth and still keep his honor intact. Again the image of Essex may lurk behind events. Essex's followers—men like Blount, Southampton, Mountjoy, and Danvers—were unquestioningly loyal until Essex began, in their own mind, to become too obsessed with unseating the Queen. At that point they debated leaving him, for he had changed the conditions under which they held their own informal bond of association. In *Macbeth*, a similar reaction is shared by Banquo, followed by Macduff, Rosse, and Lenox.

In *Ways of Lying*, Perez Zagorin notes that "the sixteenth and seventeenth centuries were the age par excellence of the English state's use of oaths and subscriptions as compulsory tests of belief and obedience."[177] But

> men of honour could (and did) lie, cheat, deceive, plot, treason, seduce, and commit adultery, without incurring dishonour. Such activities were of course immoral, and might compromise the perpetrator's religious status, bringing his eternal salvation into question. But as long as they were not attributed to him in a public way, honour was not brought into question. The importance of "promise" was that this gave the essence of honour, will and intention, the public status which enabled both to be brought into question. By the symbolic rite of "giving one's word"—the word of honour—promise bound honour itself to a specified position or course of action. Once so bound, withdrawal was possible only at the price of public diminishment. For "steadfastness" required adherence to an honour commitment once taken up. Any other course suggested that the will had been overruled, and the autonomy of honour cancelled. Submission implied in fact cowardice, the extremity of dishonour.[178]

This provides another series of lexias by which playgoers might understand the delay of Banquo in departing from Macbeth and recast Macduff's immediate leavetaking. But it also shows how playgoers could find 4.3 a scene filled with the tension of anxiety, fear, and the stain of dishonor when Malcolm tests Macduff and Macduff tests Malcolm during a cultural moment when oaths were determinant of action and some oaths might engender dissimulation. It is in this scene that the code of honor, the system of oaths, and the definitions of integrity and manliness come to their greatest pitch. Malcolm may or may not be bluffing—or testing—when he says that "there growes / In my most ill-compos'd Affection, such / A stanchlesse Auarice, that were I King, / I should cut off the Nobles from their Land" (4.3.76–79; 1901–4). He deconstructs kingship and divides lineage from honor: "The King-becoming Graces, / As Iustice, Verity, Temp'rance, Stablenesse, / Bounty, Preseuerance, Mercy, Lowlinesse, / Deuotion, Patience, Courage, Fortitude, / I haue no rellish of them, but abound / In the diuision of each seuerall Crime" (4.3.91–96; 1917–22). When all codes of behavior are reduced thus to sophistry, Macduff has no grounds by which to function and no tradition to guide him: "Such welcome, and vnwelcom things at once / 'Tis hard to reconcile" (4.3.138–39; 1666–67). Lineage is succeeded by individual passion and luxuriousness. The code of honor is replaced by codes of power and vengeance. In this crucial debate about the honor system on which much activity in 1606 also rested, 4.3 can conclude a series of lexias inside and outside the play, functioning as a scene by which all previous action and commitments are to be judged and from which all subsequent commitments and actions will be determined.

MILITARY LEXIAS

One hypertexual set of lexias, then, is that pertaining to the honor code; another, in the largely male world staged in *Macbeth*, was the military code. Indeed, "the great majority of English military treatises were printed between 1590 and 1600," Barbara Hodgdon notes,[179] such as William Garrard's *Art of Warre* (1591) and Matthew Sutcliffe's *Practices, Proceedings, and Lawes of Armes* (1593). James had no standing army, but like Elizabeth he mustered recruits for practice, indentured soldiers, and fined or imprisoned those who failed to attend musters or accepted bribes; arms were regularly stored in city and town armories, manor houses, and even churches, often under the supervision of local sheriffs. This continuing readiness for battle may have helped to cause what Hodgdon calls "an astonishing profusion of military treatises" (332). "On the one hand" she writes, "these texts indicate a renewed interest in military *history* and in documenting the 'arts' and 'stratagems' of war and the traits of an ideal soldiery. On that basis alone, the knowledge they made available had considerable cultural value, particularly at a time of national military crisis. On the other hand, such treatises spoke to what some perceived as the diminished virility of the age" (332).

In 1602, William Segar, Elizabeth's Garter at Arms, her chief herald, tied the military code directly to the honor code in *Honor, Military and Civill,* arguing that the knightly soldier "should be of bold aspect, rather inclined to severity than softness. He should be sober, and discreet, not inclined to vain delights or effeminate pleasures; obedient; vigilant and patient; faithful and loyal; constant and resolute" (49–50); a subsequent listing of primary duties includes near the top of the requirements "To serve faithfully, and defend his Prince and country courageously" and "To forgive the follies and offenses of other men, and sincerely embrace the love of friends" (60). "It seemeth," he adds, "that all Military Offenses may be comprised in three, viz. Cowardice, Treason, and Disobedience" (16). Such principles echo those of Barnabe Riche, who, in his *Pathway to Military Practise* (1587), describes a captain as one who "should be loving and comfortable to his company, and as he is to correct and punish them for their faults, so he is to commend and encourage them in their well doings. . . . [A] Captain that can carefully consider of his Soldiers' necessities, and lovingly provide to furnish their wants, shall have both unfeigned love, and dutiful obedience of his Soldiers, without the which, he is not only assured to lose his credit but many times in more peril of his own company than of the enemy" (sig. G1). Sutcliffe's ordinances and regulations were read out to every soldier, anticipating actions in *Macbeth* by requiring that "no soldier nor other being, once placed in array either in marching or fighting, shall depart thence, without lawful cause. Whosoever either to run to spoil, or to fly away, doth abandon his ensign or standing where he is ranged to serve, shall suffer death" (317), while George Silver, in his *Paradoxes of Defence, wherein is proued the True Grounds of Fight to Be in the Short Auncient Weapons* (1599), praises the "sharp light Sword" as a weapon "to carry, to draw, to be nimble withal, to strike, to cut, to thrust both strong and quick" (sig. F1), while the dagger is useful only in close quarters, "borne out straight to make the Space narrow" (sig. F1v).

In Shakespeare's play this permits and even encourages lavish praise and loving response. When we first meet the seriously wounded Captain, he describes Macbeth as "braue *Macbeth* (well hee deserues that Name.)" (1.2.16; 35); Rosse calls him "*Bellona's* Bridegroome" who is "lapt in proofe" (1.2.55; 79). The Captain continues reporting the major battle, despite his exhaustion, but only in terms of Macbeth (1.2.17–23; 36–42). Earlier, he reports, Macbeth and "The mercilesse *Macdonwald*" (1.2.9; 28) shared a loverlike hold—"As two spent Swimmers, that do'e cling together" (1.2.7–8; 27)—but now that he has slaughtered Macdonwald he is for Duncan "valiant Cousin, worthy Gentleman" (1.2.24; 43). The effort that the Captain puts into Macbeth's exploits fails him when he turns more generally to the battle at large; then "I am faint, / My Gashes cry for helpe" (1.2.43; 62–63). For Rosse, too, victory depends entirely on Macbeth, for whom he has unbounded admiration:

> The *Thane* of Cawdor, began a dismall Conflict,
> Till that *Bellona's* Bridegroome, lapt in proofe,
> Confronted him with selfe-comparisons,
> Point against Point rebellious Arme 'gainst Arme,
> Curbing his lauish spirit: and to conclude,
> The Victorie fell on vs. (1.2.54–59; 78–83)

Once more the battle is a personal one, a hand-to-hand duel, and it is this love of war that makes Macbeth Bellona's bridegroom, Mars. He is not simply warlike, he is the god of war, and so the epitome of the military culture.

After such a battle the King pays tribute to the Bloody Sergeant in keeping with the military code: "So well thy words become thee, as thy wounds, / They smack of Honor both" (1.2.44–45; 64–65). When Duncan does meet Macbeth, his words of admiration soar beyond the title he bestows upon him, adding Cawdor to his inherited title of Glamis. "O worthyest Counsin," he exclaims, "Thou art so farre before, / That swiftest Wing of Recompence is slow" (1.4.14, 16; 297, 299–300). "I haue begun to plant thee, and will labour / To make thee full of growing," he says—pregnant language—before adding, "My worthy *Cawdor*" (1.2.28–29, 47; 313–14, 335). He must also embrace Macbeth, since he clearly embraces the lesser Banquo: "Let me enfold thee, / And hold thee to my heart" (1.4.31–32; 316–17). Like Coriolanus and Aufidius, Brutus and Cassius, Achilles and Patroclus, these soldiers embrace. The moment is similar to the battlefield death of Yorke, in which, as Bruce R. Smith observes, he and Suffolk "seal a mystical marriage"—

So did he turne, and ouer Suffolkes necke
He threw his wounded arme, and kist his lippes,
And so espous'd to death, with blood he seal'd
A Testament of Noble-ending-loue (*Henry V,* 4.6.24–27; 2508–11)

—like the better-known marriage of the soldiers Othello and Iago (*Othello,* 3.3). Love between men does not threaten the military code; it fulfills it. Conversely, Smith adds, "In the same imaginative universe, an aggressively masculine, staunchly patriarchal society in which women have only a peripheral place [we find] Hotspur's cavalier ways with Kate, Henry Bolingbroke's brusque wooing of Katherine, and Richard III's brutal mastery of Prince Edward's widow."[180]

Such clarity in gendered roles was not always the case. Indeed, cultural practice in England in 1606 did not differentiate gender in young children, dressing both boys and girls in skirts until about the age of seven, when the boys were "breeched" or moved out of the female-supervised world of childhood. Medical science was itself confused and inconsistent. Stephen Orgel notes that

> Helkiah Crooke, whose *Mikrokosmographia* (1615) was the most compendious English synthesis of Renaissance anatomical knowledge, provides a striking testimony to the ambiguities of the science of gender in the period. Writing for an audience of physicians, Crooke presents a detailed discussion of the homological sex thesis, which he accepts with minor reservations, and then follows it with an entirely contradictory thesis in which women are not inverted versions of men at all, but are genuinely different and have their own kind of perfection, providing the human animal with substance and nurture, as the male provides it with form.[181]

Thomas Laqueur has also traced studies of anatomy in this period, beginning with the work of Leonardo, which show female genitalia as the inversion of the male organs—one held within the body, one projected outward—which pursue the theory first proposed in a widely known ancient text, Plato's *Symposium,* that the fully natural form of mankind is hermaphroditic. Forceful women like Lady Macbeth or those of indeterminate sex like the witches were not unknown representations in 1606. Similarly, attitudes toward the practice of sodomy in 1606 were mixed, but suggestions of sodomy in a play about a Scottish king during the reign of James might not seem altogether inappropriate. In Scotland, Andrew Melville had noted James had found it unusually painful to be separated from his cousin Lennox: "His Maiestie tok the matter farther till hart than any man wold haue beleuit."[182] In England in 1606 James was largely keeping his own male court separate from that of Queen Anne and was thought by many to be primarily interested in men.

The Parliamentary statute that first recognized sodomy and made it a felony, 25 Henry VIII ch. vi, considers it heresy, a charge repeated in the "Act for the punishment of the vice of buggerie" (1533–34) and again in the Reformation Parliament where attacks on Catholics insisted that for them sodomy seemed more permissible. Capital punishment for sodomy defined subsequently in 5 Elizabeth ch. xvii was rarely invoked; instead of homosexual bonding, sodomy more frequently meant "the abuse of private property in the form of someone else's cow, sheep, servant, apprentice or prepubescent child," Bruce R. Smith reports, "(as witness the indictment hearings recorded for the Home Counties between 1559 and 1602)."[183] In early modern England, Alan Sinfield confirms, " 'Sodomy' was the term which most nearly approaches what is now in England called 'gross indecency'; it was condemned almost universally in legal and religious discourses, and the penalty upon conviction was death. Perhaps because of this extreme situation, very few cases are recorded."[184] The only conviction between 1558 and 1625 was that of Thomas Woodford, who was sent to jail in November 1606 for "being accused to have committed sodomie with William Wood his servant, a boye of xiii yeares."[185] James I, in advising his son on the ideal tenets of a prince in the *Basilicon Doron,* publicly labels sodomy (along with witchcraft, willful murder, incest, and counterfeiting) one of the "horrible crimes that yee are bound in conscience never to forgive."[186]

Alan Bray has argued that sodomy was in fact a natural consequence of the frequent cultural practice of late marriage. Generally men did not marry until they had saved enough money to begin a family (the average age was twenty-nine; women married somewhat younger); and this was also an indirect social method of birth control and a way to avoid economic dependency on parents or guardians. In the meantime, in the extended period of bachelorhood, men might find sexual relief by seeking out other men; this seems particularly true of the servant class.[187] Cultural practice divided between, as Bray puts it, "extreme hostility to homosexuality which one comes across when homosexuality was being referred to in the abstract and its reluctance to recognize it in most concrete situations" (77). As Sinfield notes,

> Friends shared beds, they embraced and kissed; such intimacies reinforced
> the network of obligations and their public performance would often be part

of the effect. So the proper signs of friendship could be the same as those of same-sex passion. In instances where accusations of sodomy were aroused, very likely it was because of some hostility towards one or both parties, rather than because their behaviour was altogether different from that of others who were not so accused.[188]

Moreover, certain sectors of cultural activity seemed more permissive. The language of patronage at court was often tinged with homosexual words, as was the love poetry: Shakespeare's sonnets are only one well-known example. Courtiers were admired for their lean, athletic, and attractive bodies often made more attractive through habits of dress and gesture.[189] The practice of male bonding and of manrent in Scotland also encouraged close relationships between men. And, as with the clan activity in Scotland, sodomy was often connected with the army. But this, too, engendered mixed response. Barnabe Riche writes in his *Farewell to Militarie Profession* (1581, 1591) that effeminization of military life was a reason he left it:

> It was my fortune at my last beyng at London, to walks through the Strande towardes Westminster where I mett one came ridyng towardes me, on a scoteclothe Nagge, apparailed in a French Ruffe, a Frenche Cloake, a Frenche Hose, and in his hande a greate fanne of Feathers, bearyng them vp (verie womanly) against the side of his face: And for that I had neuer seen any man weare them before that daie, I beganne to thinke it vnpossible, that there might a manne be founde so foolishe, as to make hym self a scorne to the worlde, to weare so womanishe a toye. But rather thought it had been some shamelesse woman, that had disguised her self like a manne, in our Hose, and our Cloakes: for our Dublettes, Gounes, Cappes, and Hattes thei had got long agoe. (sig. B2)

Riche himself gave up fighting as a soldier to write romances for women: "The Militarie profession, by meanes whereof menne were aduaunced to the greatest renowne, is now become of so slender estimation, that there is no accompt neither made of it, nor any that shall professe it" (sigs. B2v–B3). Sodomy was frequently associated with theaters like the Globe as well. In *Skialethia* (1598), Edward Guilpin talks of the playgoer who "is at euery play, and euery night / Sups with his *Ingles,* who can well recite" (sig. B1). As lexias, such factors encourage special attention to the manliness of soldiers such as Duncan or women like Lady Macbeth and can be seen together to isolate Macbeth from both the King's forces and his own marriage.

* * *

Moreover, in the military world of *Macbeth,* Macbeth's own language turns at the end, deprived of his wife, to charges of effeminacy: he refers to the enemy as "English Epicures" and to his own servant as a "cream-fac'd Loone" with "that Goose-looks"; a "Lilly-liuer'd Boy" (5.3.8, 11, 12, 15; 2222, 2226, 2227, 2232). He is deprived of Banquo, and the boy is a poor substitute. For Banquo, in turn, Macbeth is his "Good Sir," his "Noble Partner" (1.3.51, 54; 151, 154). Their relationship as fellow soldiers is companionate, a close one bordering on intimacy. As soon as Rosse proclaims Macbeth to be the new Thane of Cawdor, Banquo draws him aside for a private conference, a secret sharing: "That trusted home, / Might yet enkindle you vnto the Crowne, / Besides the *Thane* of Cawdor. But 'tis strange" (1.3.120–22; 230–32). Even when he subsequently engages Rosse and Angus, his attention remains fixed on Macbeth: "Looke how our Partner's rapt" (1.3.143; 254). Throughout act 1, Banquo vies with Duncan in thinking of Macbeth as his "partner." The next time we see him, in 1.6, he describes Macbeth's castle with obvious pride and pleasure, his tribute nearly three times the length of Duncan's. This is clearly a special relationship, a bonding on and off the battlefield that is analogous to that which Robert Cecil, secretary to James, defines in his "State and Dignitie of a Secretarie of State" where he says the secretary enjoys special confidence and intimacy.[190]

In fact, the next time Banquo appears he is once again in private and even secret conversation with Macbeth (2.1): it is dark and there is no starlight—"Their Candles are all out" (2.1.5; 578)—but only a torch (2.1.1 S.D.; 570) and without being asked he tells Macbeth that the King has retired. Macbeth shrugs off this information and the dream Banquo has had of the weird sisters. But he seeks further occasion to discuss the matter in private—"Yet when we can entreat an houre to serue, / We would spend it in some words vpon that Businesse, / If you would graunt the time" (2.1.22–24; 599–601). Macbeth is making their companionship conspiratorial. In time this will lead to Banquo's sense of betrayal: Duncan has been killed and, says Banquo to Macbeth, "I feare / Thou playd'st most fowly for't" (3.1.2–3; 983–84). Even so, "Let your Highnesse / Command vpon me, to the which my duties / Are with a most indissoluble tye / For euer knit" (3.1.15–18; 1000–1003). Banquo's devotion—the male bonding of soldier to soldier, servant to master—is analogous to that of Macbeth and Duncan in 1.4. But with Banquo there is not only his death but the near death of his vulnerable son, and he exchanges the honor code and military code for the code of revenge, as a Ghost come back from the dead to stand speechless before his former companion. Conversely, Macbeth slays those whom he should most love.

That the play of *Macbeth* means to signify the peculiarly strong male bonding that characterizes military life at discrete moments or lexias seems even clearer in the case of Macduff, who is willing to leave his wife and children to join Malcolm's forces in distant England. Malcolm's initial suspicion of him, followed by a stern rebuff, is therefore surprising to him and painful. Yet Malcolm initially preys on Macduff's emotions—

> As I shall finde the time to friend: I wil.
> What you haue spoke, it may be so perchance,
> This Tyrant whose sole name blisters our tongues,
> Was once thought honest: you haue lou'd him well,
> He hath not touch'd you yet. I am yong, but something
> You may discerne of him through me, and wisedome
> To offer vp a weake, poore innocent Lambe
> T'appease an angry God. (4.3.10–17; 1825–32)

It is an odd speech, packed with innuendoes seductive from several directions at once. "Why in that rawnesse left you Wife, and Childe?" he asks (4.3.26; 1844), and when Macduff replies that Macbeth's tyranny—his betrayal—has left Scotland drenched in blood, Malcolm seizes upon the metaphor as a menstrual one of violation and rape ("it bleeds, and each new day a gash / Is added to her wounds" [4.3.40–41; 1860–61]), and this coded exchange becomes a full-blown testing as Macduff is tried, courted, and won to a new military leader, a new battlefield companion. The language is especially charged: "I grant him Bloody, / Luxurious, Auaricious, False, Deceitfull, / Sodaine, Malicious, smacking of euery sinne, / That h's a name. But there's no bottome, none / In my Voluptuousness," Malcolm vows. "Your Wiues, your Daughters, / Your Matrons, and your Maides, could not fill vp / The Cesterne of my Lust, and my Desire," concluding, "All continent Impediments would ore-beare: / That did oppose my will" (4.3.57–65; 1880–88).

Macduff's return in the closing scenes to a single hand-to-hand combat with Macbeth not only returns us to the duels reported in 1.2— Macduff as the new Macbeth battling the traitor Macdonwald—but suggests that for Macduff the engagement with another man—as with Coriolanus and Aufidius—is what makes life particularly fulfilling. James himself was terrified of bloodshed yet drawn strangely toward contemplating it; and his own closest relationships—his male hunting parties the equivalent of the Scottish armies in Macbeth—were always monogamously male. Victorious at the last, Malcolm stands before his men with confidence and assurance: "We shall not spend a large expense of time, / Before we reckon with your seuerall loues," he says to them at the close, "And make vs euen with you" (5.9.26–28; 2513–15).[191]

LEXIAS OF FAMILY

Kinship ties at times seem less pronounced in *Macbeth,* but families and generation are central to the play performed at the Globe in 1606 and fundamental to the cultural moment that openly sought an ongoing reformation of manners. David Cressy writes that kinship practices

> sought and extended information and advice, craved and offered introductions and connections, sought and satisfied the demands of "love and duty." [Kinsfolk] gave each other counsel, provided assistance in developing careers, and even helped arrange marriages. Travellers could find shelter beneath their kindred's roof and food at their kindred's table [as Rosse seems about to do with Lady Macduff in 4.2]. Kinsfolk served as witnesses, executors and overseers of each other's wills and as guardians to their siblings' or cousins' minor children. They participated in family rites of passage, attended weddings, wakes and funerals, and sometimes found themselves beneficiaries (if only residual legatees) of an uncle's or cousin's will. Loans between kin were not uncommon, and a likelihood existed of such loans converting to legacies.[192]

But the institution lacked firm boundaries. Cressy cites the will in 1571 of Richard Man, a yeoman of Braintree, Essex, who "gave most of his property to his children" but also left property to his wife and "took pains to recognize a broad range of cousins, second cousins and relations by marriage" as well as a foster son and godson: "Man evidently understood himself to be embedded in and responsible to a dense matrix of kin" (62). Duncan links generation in his own mind to Macbeth ("I haue begun to plant thee, and will labour / To make thee full of growing" [1.4.28–29; 313–14]) but then reverts to his son for the greatest of gifts—

> We will establish our Estate vpon
> Our eldest, *Malcolme,* whom we name hereafter,
> The Prince of Cumberland: which Honor must
> Not vnaccompanied, inuest him onely,
> But signes of Noblenesse, like Starres, shall shine
> On all deseruers (1.4.37–42; 324–29)

—completing in his mind the single encompassing set of ritual announcements after a battle. That Malcolm understands this ritual in the way Macbeth does not is confirmed in his closing lines of the play:

> My Thanes and Kinsmen
> Henceforth be Earles, the first that euer Scotland
> In such an Honor nam'd: What's more to do,
> Which would be planted newly with the time,
> As calling home our exil'd Friends abroad,
> That fled the Snares of watchfull Tyranny,
>
> . . . .
>
>   This, and what needfull else
> That call's vpon vs, by the Grace of Grace,
> We will performe in measure, time and place. (5.9.28–33, 37–39; 2515–20, 2524–26)

Duncan thus plants the Prince; at the end, the Prince himself is planting. Macbeth, too, is keenly aware of the significance of titles; in one of his first lines, he refers routinely to his father before him as Sinell, Thane of Glamis (1.3.71; 171).

For marriage and childbearing were society's cornerstones. "Who will not commend honorable wedlock as a thing of great excellency?" asks Andrew Kingsmill rhetorically in his *Schoole of Honest and Vertuous Lyfe* (1579).[193] Marriage, according to the popular theologian William Perkins, was to be viewed as "the lawful conjunction of two married persons; that is one man and one woman into one flesh" and "ordained of God, in paradise" for four chief purposes: procreation, perpetuation of the Church, containment of desire, and mutual assistance and comfort. Marriage for Perkins was central to community: "the foundation and Seminary of an other sorts and kinds of life in the commonwealth and in the church."[194] By 1606 Reformation attitudes were common cultural belief: marriage according to the *Book of Common Prayer* was "an honourable estate, instituted of God in Paradise, in the time of man's innocency";[195] the church homily on marriage repeatedly ordained that the Holy Ghost ruled the hearts of man and wife and knit their hearts together, permitting no discord. Thomas Becon calls matrimony "an hie, holye and blessed order of life, ordayned not of man, but of God."[196] In an image that has telling resonance in *Macbeth,* the "Precepts of wedlocke" in the English translations of *The Morals* of Plutarch (1603) reads:

> Like as a mirrour or looking glasse garnished with golde and precious stones, serveth to no purpose, if it doe not represent to the life the face of him or her

that looketh into it; no more is a woman worth ought (be she otherwise never so rich) unlesse she conforme and frame her self, her life, her maners and conditions sutable in all respects to her husband . . . even so a wife should have no proper passion or peculiar affection of her owne, but be a partaker of the sports, serious affaires, sad countenance, deepe thoughts and smiling looks of her husband.[197]

The most common term for a happy marriage, says Keith Wrightson, was "quietness."[198]

Lawrence Stone records that the

sixteenth-century aristocratic family was patrilinear, primogenitural, and pa-triarchal: patrilinear in that it was the male line whose ancestry was traced so diligently by the genealogists and heralds, and in almost all cases via the male line that titles were inherited; primogenitural in that most of the property went to the eldest son, the younger brothers being dispatched into the world with little more than a modest annuity or life interest in a small estate to keep them afloat; and patriarchal in that the husband and father lorded it over his wife and children with the quasi-absolute authority of a despot. (591)

Barnabe Riche writes of the ideal wife in *The Excellency of Good Women* (1613): "A man that wanteth a friend for pleasure, a servant for profit, a counsellour to advise him, a comforter to cherish him, a companion to solace him, a helper to assist him, or a spirituall instructor to informe him, a good and vertuous wife doth supply all these occasions" (2). His long list builds on the premise of the homily on marriage, which states at the outset that a wife's chief duty is to see to the (undefined) pleasure of her husband. At the same time, Robert Tofte translated from Benedetto Varchi the corollary in *The Blazon of Iealousie* (1615):

Shee that seldome speakes and mildly then,
Is a rare Pearle amongst all other Women,
Maides must be seene, not heard, or selde or neuer,
O may I such one wed, if I, wed euer. (27)

The aristocracy, like all other classes, generally married in their own ranks, were endogamous; but for those of the higher classes especially, parity of age, status, wealth, reputation, and religion alongside personal attachment were important.[199] "Among the aristocracy, the urban elite and leading gentry families," Keith Wrightson confirms, "marriage was a matter of too great a significance, both in the property transactions which it in-volved and in the system of familial alliances which it cemented" (72). Although G. E. Mingay believes that "among the propertied classes gener-ally the individual's interest in marriage was subordinated to the interest of the family,"[200] Wrightson observes that on occasion "love, or at least personal attraction, could be the keystone in the structure of a good match. . . . The force of physical and personal attraction was recognized, but in conjunction with, rather than in opposition to, other aspects of parity in a good match" (82). In his influential *Christian Oeconomie* of 1609, Perkins writes that man and wife "are equally bound each to other and have also the same interest in one anothers body, provided always that the man is to maintain his superiority and the woman to observe that modesty which beseemeth her towards the man. . . . So much of the first way of perform-ance of due benevolence. The second way is by cherishing one another."[201] In his wedding sermon called *A Bride-Bush* (1617), William Whately notes that husbands and wives are physicians to each others' souls.[202] For play-goers in 1606, the Macbeths' marriage would also, even when under enor-mous strain, seem affectionate. This is especially true in their most intimate and personal scenes, 3.2. and 3.4, surrounding the misbegotten corona-tion feast, as Lady Macbeth's language makes clear:

> How now, my Lord, why doe you keepe alone?
> Of sorryest Fancies your Companions making,
> Vsing those Thoughts, which should indeed haue dy'd
> With them they thinke on: things without all remedie
> Should be without regard: what's done, is done.
>
> . . . .
>   Come on:
> Gentle, my lord, sleeke o're your rugged Lookes,
> Be bright and Iouiall among your Guests to Night. (3.2.8–12, 26–28;
> 1162–66; 1183–85)

After the interrupted banquet, she is equally concerned, equally solicitous: "Almost at oddes with morning, whiche is which" (3.4.126; 1409); "You lacke the season of all Natures, sleepe" (3.4.140; 1424). He too can re-spond in kind despite his distraction and anxiety; it seems natural, auto-matic: "So shall I Loue" (3.2.29; 1186); "deare Wife" (3.2.36; 1194); "Be innocent of the knowledge, dearest Chuck, / Till thou applaud the deed" (3.2.45–46; 1204–5). Connecting these particular bytes, we can under-stand her opening lines as ones of concern as well, involved more with her husband's ambitions than her own, and her own only through his.

> Glamys thou art, and Cawdor, and shalt be
> What thou art promis'd: yet doe I feare thy Nature,
> It is too full o'th'Milke of humane kindnesse,
> To catch the nearest way. Thou would'st be great,

166

Art not without Ambition, but without
The illnesse should attend it. What thou would'st highly,
That would'st thou holily: would'st not play false,
And yet would'st wrongly winne. (1.5.15–22; 361–68)

Such a partnership of mutual understanding was not unusual. Divorce in 1606 was uncommon on any grounds: a proper divorce took a private Act of Parliament.

"That women occupied a position subordinate to men," Russ McDonald sums, "is beyond dispute; that this was the 'natural' state of affairs was almost beyond dispute."[203] According to the cultural belief in 1606 in the Galenic theory of medicine, men were mostly composed of air and fire—warm, dynamic, and therefore masculine humors—whereas women were composed largely of earth and water, which were cold, moist, and feminine. Woman's subordinate position to men was promulgated by the *Book of Common Prayer,* the ceremony of marriage, and the *Homily on Obedience*—"Almighty GOD hath created and appoynted all things in heauen, earth, and waters, in a most excellent and perfect order . . . some are in high degree, some in low; some Kings and Princes, some inferiours and subiects, Priests, and Lay men, Masters and Seruants, Fathers and Children, Husbands, and Wiues" (1633 ed., sig. F5); such order is "profitable, necessary, and pleasant" (sig. F5)—and in the *Homily of the State of Matrimony,* where women should "apply all thy diligence to thine obedience to thine husband" (sigs. 2X2–2X2v); these state sermons were commanded to be read frequently in every parish church. A wide array of scriptural proof was also frequently enlisted: Genesis 3:16; 1 Corinthians 11:5–11; 1 Timothy 2:9–15; Ephesians 5:22–23; 1 Peter 3:7. But religious laws alone did not support male supremacy. Edmund Tilney argues (1568) that "reason doth confirm the same, the man [having] not only skill and experience to be required but also capacity to comprehend, wisdom to understand, strength to execute, solicitude to prosecute, patience to suffer, means to sustain, and above all a great courage to accomplish, all which are commonly in a man, but in a woman very rare."[204] Even a women's advocate like Juan Luis Vives could say, in the English translation by Thomas Paynell from the Latin around 1555, "There are certain things in the house that only do pertain to the authority of the husband, wherewith it were a reproof for the wife without the consent of her husband to meddle withal."[205] So too the popular jingle:

Now when thou art become a wife,
And hast an husband to thy mind,

> See thou provoke him not to strife,
> Lest haply he do prove unkind.
> Acknowledge that he is thine head,
> And hath of thee the governance,
> And that thou must of him be led,
> According to God's ordinance.[206]

Such unquestioning duty has apparently been embodied by Lady Macduff, who is baffled and bitter over her husband's unexplained departure. "His flight was madnesse," she tells Rosse; "when our Actions do not, / Our feares do make vs Traitors" (4.2.3–4; 1715–16). "What had he done, to make him fly the Land?" (4.2.1; 1712). Her anxiety centers on her off-spring: "Father'd he is, / And yet hee's Father-lesse" (4.2.27; 1741–42). Her words strike common chords. Children were often thought to be the great blessing of marriage: it is estimated that in 1606 about one-third of the brides would give birth within the first year of marriage, and between two-thirds and four-fifths would have a child within two years. In a local study of this cultural moment, the average family size was five children born at roughly three-year intervals.[207] "Children were a source of delight," Wrightson tells us, " 'pretty things to play withall' as one observer put it."[208] Parents took great interest and spent much time in rearing them. Yet children were also a troubling source of pervasive, deep anxiety because of illness, accident, and the high rate of infant mortality, Macbeth's "vnlineall Hand" (3.1.62; 1053). In a recent demographic study of this period, 34.4 percent of all deaths were of children under ten. This suggests how very familiar to the playgoers at the Globe Lady Macduff's own fears are. "Wise-dom?" she asks Rosse, "to leaue his wife, to leaue his Babes, / His Mansion, and his Titles, in a place / From whence himself do's flye?" (4.2.6–8; 1719–21). Despite her capacity to love, her condemnation of Macduff—of Macduff's very nature—is quick and sure:

> He loues vs not,
> He wants the naturall touch. For the poore Wren
> (The most diminitiue of Birds) will fight,
> Her yong ones in her Nest, against the Owle:
> All is the Feare, and nothing is the Loue;
> As little the Wisedome, where the flight
> So runns against all reason. (4.2.8–14; 1721–27)

The broken family signifies for her the chaos and upheaval of the country; treason against family and state are parallel sequenced lexias. To extend reason as she says one should, however, would argue that betrayal by the husband will also mean betrayal by other family members—such as Rosse—and even by the King. Her characterization, briefly put because commonplace in its ideas, urges that inherited belief unexamined can destroy as well as preserve. Her precocious son senses this too:

Son.	What is a Traitor?
Wife.	Why one that sweares, and lyes.
	. . . .
Son.	Who must hang them?
Wife.	Why, the honest men.
Son.	Then the Liars and Swearers are Fools: for there are Lyars and Swearers enow, to beate the honest men, and hang vp them. (4.2.46–47, 53–57; 1766–67, 1773–77)

The unnamed son's inversion of fundamental cultural beliefs and practices marks a sense of doom that is both unsettling and annihilating. Yet this conversation, and his death, at last openly acknowledge how generation and children have always been important to the play. Duncan's hasty defense of his lineage is succeeded by a woman's denying herself children; two sons, their lives threatened, are forced into exile; and a third son is ignominiously murdered by unknown assailants. At the end the play turns largely on an unnatural birth, on Macduff, who "was from his Mothers womb / Vntimely ript" (5.8.15–16; 2455–56): both his life and that of his mother were at risk at a time when a cesarian operation foreordained the mother's death. Now his survival has given him the job of regicide. Yet Macduff's bloody birth, overcoming at the end Macbeth's "bloody execution" in which, "Disdayning Fortune," he would unseam his enemy (1.2.18, 17; 37, 36), causes Macduff to undertake a bloody execution of his own. It is one of the important and most telling silences of the play that unlike Macduff, unlike his wife, Macbeth no longer has any thought of children or of a family line that will follow him as king. For playgoers at the Globe in 1606, believing strongly that society was based on children and childbearing even when infant mortality was so high, the fate of the children in *Macbeth*—and of cesarian births and of children aborted—is a powerful means of conveying an unnatural Scottish state that is itself at risk.

There are other important trails of lexias by which the play continually addresses social issues. "Fears of an impending breakdown of the social order have been common in many periods of history," D. E. Underdown writes, but "at no time were they more widespread." He finds that "the

flood of Jacobean anti-feminist literature and the concurrent public obsession with scolding women, domineering and unfaithful wives, clearly suggest that patriarchy could no longer be taken for granted."[209] Shakespeare
had already treated such scolds in *The Taming of the Shrew,* where the
broken code was one of patriarchy rather than of honor. "Husband dominance," Linda Woodbridge tells us, "is almost always connected with
shrewishness. It is not a necessary connection: domination by icy stare is
theoretically possible. But this is not the style of Renaissance wives, whose
aggressiveness ranges from shrill scolding to physical violence."[210] While
some shrews were thought to be naturally ill-tempered, others used a
shrewish manner to gain power or authority. Thomas Platter comments in
1599 that English women "have far more liberty than in other lands, and
know just how to make use of it."[211] *The Homily of the State of Matrimony*
notes "how few matrimonies there be without chidings, brawlings, taunt-
ings, repentings, bitter cursings, and fightings,"[212] and church court records at this cultural moment frequently cite the insubordination of women
as a reason for marital strife. William Whately addresses the problem directly in *A Bride-Bush:*

> First, in speeches and gestures vnto him. These must carry the stampe of feare
> vpon them, and not be cutted, sharpe, sullen, passionate, teechie; but meeke,
> quiet, submissiue, which may shew that she considers who herselfe is, and to
> whom she speakes. The wiues tongue towards her husband must bee neither
> keene, nor loose, nor countenance neither swelling nor deriding: her behaui-
> our not flinging, not puffing, not discontented; but sauouring of all lowlinesse
> and quietness of affection. (1619 ed., 38)

At Southampton in 1603, Underdown records, "the leet jury noted 'the
manifold number of scolding women that be in this town'; a year later
they complained of their constant 'misdemeanours and scolding,' lament-
ing that the mayor was 'daily troubled with such brawls' " (119). Quite
apart from aggressively manly women, such as Mary Frith, known as Moll
Cutpurse, scolds were occasionally punished by imprisonment but more
often by being displayed in the stocks or in a cage, by being made to stand
in public in a white gown such as Lady Macbeth wears in act 5, by ducking
("cucking"), or by bridles that pinned down the tongue: such punishments
were meant to provide both revenge and humiliation. There were also
more elaborate charivari—processions of the scold (and often her husband) through the streets in an open cart to rough music and scornful
shouts of onlookers.

In such a context, Lady Macbeth's practices would be problematic.

She is unnatural in her willingness to forego having children: "Come you
Spirits, / That tend on mortall thoughts, vnsex me here" (1.5.40–41; 391–
92). Surprisingly, she claims to "haue giuen Sucke, and know / How tender
'tis to loue the Babe that milkes me" (1.7.54–55; 533–34), for Shakespeare
has deliberately omitted all reference to her historical son Lulach by her
first marriage and the reference suggests that, unlike many aristocratic
women in 1606, she nursed the child rather than sending it out to be
weaned. Rather, emphasis falls on her strength in rebellion against Duncan
and her shrewish scolding of Macbeth—"High thee hither"; "I may powre
my Spirits in thine Eare"; "chastise with the valour of my Tongue"—in
which she combines an act of treason ("All that impeides thee from the
Golden Round") with an act of heresy ("Fate and Metaphysicall ayde")
(1.5.25–29; 372–76). In every way, this is an unholy set of thoughts,
placed in the play alongside Duncan's more innocent ones. Her shrewishness, once unleashed, would seem to know no bounds; even the castle
becomes her own: "The Rauen himselfe is hoarse, / That croakes the fatall
entrance of *Duncan* / Vnder my Battlements" (1.5.38–40; 389–91). At
Macbeth's arrival, her command is relentless. Duncan will not survive his
visit ("neuer / Shall Sunne that Morrow see") because she will manage
everything ("This Nights great Businesse into my dispatch"). Macbeth will
gain "soueraigne sway, and Masterdome" because he will leave "all the
rest" to her (1.5.60–73; 415–29). Like her command of dissimulation
here—"Looke like the time, beare welcome in your Eye, / Your Hand,
your Tongue: looke like th'innocent flower, / But be the Serpent vnder't"
(1.5.63–65; 419–21)—she provides strategy as well as purpose which he
will absorb into his own thinking (2.1.49–56; 629–36).

In Macbeth's own more twisted thoughts, Lady Macbeth becomes
Hecate, as he becomes Tarquin: he will ravish witchcraft by raping Scotland. The breakdown of the kingdom and of his mind begins here, with
the breakdown of his marriage. Macbeth's response, finally, to this partner
in greatness is to dismiss her altogether: "Be innocent of the knowledge"
(3.2.45; 1204). Privately shamed, she will in the course of the play retreat
into her own private world where she will continue to rule. But the perver-
sion of such behavior leads her to an inverted world, the world of madness. The fact is visibly registered for the playgoers of 1606: in a
nightdress, carrying a candle (5.1.17 S.D.; 2111)—"How came she by that
light?"; " 'tis her command" (5.1.20, 22; 2114, 2116)—she enacts a popular shaming ritual for shrews, but one often employed also for witches.
Thomas Ady records in *A Candle in the Dark* (1656) that just such a ritual
was "to keep the poor accused party from sleep many nights and days,

thereby to distemper their brains, and hurt their fancies," their perverted imaginations (sig. O2). Her sense of humiliation and dishonor, enacting such a shaming ritual, shows her driven mad. In the honor society of 1606, she condemns herself; and it lends an additional poignancy to Macbeth's later "Out, out, breefe Candle" coupled with "She should haue dy'de heereafter" (5.5.23, 17; 2344, 2338).

Pregnancy and childbearing for poor families in 1606 meant not only pain and fear for some but for many unwanted or unbearable expense. Yet in the upper classes where there was special need to produce a male heir, 19 percent of the landed families died childless, either because they never conceived or because all their children predeceased them.[213] A letter of 1623 from Lucy, Countess of Bedford, to Jane, Lady Cornwallis, suggests how fearful childbearing could be even with the fourth pregnancy:

> Itt trobels me more to hear how aprehensive you are of a danger itt hath pleased God to carry you so often safely through, and so I doubt not will againe, though you may do yourselfe and yours much harme by those doubtings and ill companions for all persons and worst for us splenetick creatures. Therefore, dear Cornwallis, lett not this melancholy prevale with you to the begetting or nourishing of those mistrusts (wich) will turne more to your hurt than that you feare, which I hope will passe with safety and end to your comfort.[214]

Erasmus's colloquy *Puerpera,* translated as *The New Mother* in 1606 by the Puritan preacher William Burton, points out that St. Paul assured women they would be saved through childbearing, instructing mothers that children must "continue in the faith and love, with holinesse and modestie" to be saved, "so that you have not yet done the part of a mother, unlesse you first frame aright his tender bodie, and then his mind as tender as that with good education."[215] Manuals also urged breastfeeding and maternal nursing, and there was a decreasing use of wet nurses, by which the English began adopting Scottish custom. It is Shakespeare's contribution; there is no historical record that Lady Macbeth breastfed her son Lulach.

Humoral medical theory supported breastfeeding by supporting the circulation and conservation of fluids associating milk with blood and lactation with menstruation; one substance was thought to turn into the other. John Sadler, a Norwich physician, writes in 1636 that a woman's milk "is nothing but menstruous blood made white in the breasts" and argues that experience demonstrates that "so long as the woman giveth suck to the child, and hath store of milk in her breasts, her terms be of little or no quantity . . . forasmuch as the ebbing of the one is the flowing of the other";[216] and the preacher John Cleaver confirms the desirability of such cultural belief: "God converteth the mother's blood into the milk wherewith the child is nursed in her womb. He bringeth it into the breasts furnished with nipples."[217] As David Cressy observes, "Medical and gynaecological manuals were generous with advice about how to stimulate the flow of milk or how to dry it up, and most of the herbals offered similar information."[218] Lady Macbeth enlists reaction to such beliefs when she asks the "Spirits, / That tend on mortall thoughts" and which will "vnsex" her to "make thick my blood" (1.5.40–41, 43; 391–92, 394); her unnatural attempt to deny her generative capacities—"Come to my Womans Brests, / And take my Milke for Gall" (1.5.47–48; 398–99)—complements her thoughts of her husband as unmanly: he is "too full o'th'Milke of humane kindnesse" (1.5.17; 363). Moreover, Reginald Scot notes that village women who experience "the stopping of their monthly melancholic flux or issue of blood" are frequently accused of witchcraft.[219] Lady Macbeth's crucial soliloquy in 1.5 as a lexia, then, looks back to the unnatural King Duncan, who will "plant" Macbeth and "will labour / To make thee full of growing" (1.4.28–29; 313–14), and forward to Macbeth's displacement of his wife for the witches in the cave when he seeks further counsel on the future (4.1).

LEXIAS OF HOUSEHOLD

"A man's home is his castle," Sir Edward Coke writes in the early seventeenth century.[220] But the house was actually a household—not simply one or more buildings but a vast community of people forming an autonomous social and economic unit that also resembled a political state. According to John Dod and Robert Cleaver in *A Godlie Forme of Household* Puritans. *Government* (1598), "A household is as it were a little commonwealth, by the good government whereof God's glory may be advanced: the commonwealth, which standeth of several families, benefited; and all that live in that family may receive much comfort and commodity."[221] The importance of such country households in 1606 is hard to overestimate. L. C. Knights says that, illustrated by that of the Verney family,

> a great house provisioned itself with little help from the outer world; the
> inhabitants brewed and baked, churned and ground their meal, they bred, fed

and slew their beeves and sheep, and brought up their pigeons and poultry at their own doors. Their horses were shod at home, their planks were sawn, their rough ironwork was forged and mended. . . . Within doors the activity of the family and household was as great and as multifarious as without. The spinning of wool and flax . . . the fine and coarse needlework, the embroidery, the cooking, the curing, the preserving, the distillery that went on, were incessant.[222]

• In such an environment, according to *The Servants Dutie* of Thomas Fosset (1613), "the servant is called to three things: to labor, to suffer, and to serve . . . to obey and to be in subjection, to have no will of his own nor power over himself, but wholly to resign himself to the will of his Master."[223] By 1600 the households of gentry averaged 65 servants, from ushers, butlers, and panters to nurses, cooks, laundresses, and chambermaids. Noble households were on a still grander scale. The household of the Earl of Derby had 115 to 140 servants aside from family members, moving "ponderously," as Mark Girouard has it, "from Knowsley to Lathom Castle, and from Lathom Castle to the New Lodge at Lathom." The chief servants had servants of their own:

The earl's treasurer was Sir Richard Sherborne, who built his own great house at Stonyhurst and was one of the biggest landowners in Lancashire. The earl's steward, William Farrington of Worden, was a member of a well-established Lancashire family, a substantial property owner, a magistrate, the deputy-lieutenant of the county, and the son of a former upper servant of the earl's. His gentlemen waiters were all members of the local gentry. His clerk comptroller, William Fox, came from his own tenantry but was to found a family of minor gentry, as was his clerk of the kitchen, Michael Doughty, who was elected M.P. for Preston in 1589, on the earl's nomination.[224]

In 1606, James's servants numbered in the thousands. By stark contrast, the grand castle at Inverness has only a stage complement of servants—a maid, a gentlewoman, a nurse, a manservant or two, two doctors, and a porter; what is important is not that all of them remain largely functionary but that all of them save the Porter fail at their jobs. Banquets do not run smoothly; Lady Macbeth cannot be cured; Macbeth merely finds them annoying and bothersome as Birnam Wood makes it way to Dunsinane. Both Inverness and Dunsinane are, in the terms of 1606, dysfunctional.

The exception is the Porter. His presence belies the Jacobean writing of this Scottish play putatively set in the eleventh century. In the cultural moment of 1606, porters were invariably associated in the popular mind with alehouses, as this porter is, and known for their drunkenness—in 1606, an occupational hazard of porters.[225] This was not a matter of being exceptional but of being excessive. Drink was normally built "into the fabric of social life," Keith Thomas notes, for beer was cheap to make and relatively nourishing.[226] The clergyman William Harrison was brewing two hundred gallons every month for his household in the Elizabethan period; it was the basic ingredient of the diet for adults and children alike. Thomas adds that "alcohol was also an essential narcotic which anaesthetized man against the strains of contemporary life" (22). John Taylor the Water Poet writes that ale "doth comfort the heavy and troubled mind; it will make a weeping widow laugh and forget sorrow for her deceased husband . . . it is the warmest lining of a naked man's coat; it satiates and assuages hunger and cold; with a toast it is the poor man's comfort; the shepherd, mower, ploughman, and blacksmith's most esteemed purchase; it is the tinker's treasure, the pedlar's jewel, the beggar's joy; and the prisoner's loving nurse."[227] But in 1606 James was finding alehouses especially troubling. He mentions them in Parliament as menacing, and at the first calling of Parliament passed a statute to regulate them (Statute IX).

> That if after fourty dayes next ensuing after the end of this present Session of Parliament, (1) any Innkeeper, Victualler or Alehouse-keeper within this Realme of *England*, or the Dominions of *Wales*, where any such Inn, Alehouse, or Tipling-house is or shall be, to remain or continue drinking or tipling in the said Inn, Victualling-house Timing-house or Alehouse, (2) other then such as shall be invited by any Traveller, and shall accompany him only during his necessary abode there; (3) and other then Labouring and Handicrafts-men in Cities and Towns Corporate, and Market Towns, upon the usual working days, for one hour at dinner time, to take their Diet in an Alehouse; (4) and other then labourers and Workmen, which for the following of their work by the day, or by the great, in any City, Town, Corporate, Market Town or Village, shall for the time of their said continuing in work there, Soiourn, Lodge or Victuall in any Inn, Alehouse or other Victualling-house, (5) other than for urgent and necessary occasions to be allowed by two Iustices of Peace, That then every such Innkeeper, Victualler or Alehouse-keeper, shall for every such offence, forfeit and lose the sum of Ten shillings of currant money of *England*, to the use of the Poor of the Parish where such offence shall be committed. (sig. 5a5v)

These regulations seem unusually restrictive, especially for a beer-drinking society, but they had point: in 1606 alehouses were known as places where plots of treason and sedition were hatched.[228] The drunken Porter, then, is not only a cultural stereotype; he is associated with those who might harbor secret knowledge of treachery. The Porter of Hell Gate, whose only

appearance, with thirty-four lines, opens 3.4, is both a conventional portrait and a potential marker of the household at Inverness. He may also be
a late addition to the play, since all the most recent topical references in
the play concerning the Powder Plot belong to him: farmer, equivocation,
trials, harvest. His joking may be, at some level, a delaying tactic to aid
Macbeth, as it surely allowed Macbeth to change costume. Yet he also
harbors regicide, a staged analogy, perhaps, to Guy Fawkes, who had taken
the role of porter beneath Parliament House.

Save for those of higher status such as Lenox and Rosse, the only other
person serving Macbeth who has an important role is Seyton. The sound
of his name recalls the Porter. It is Seyton who prepares Macbeth for final
battle, putting on his armor, taking it off again; it is Seyton who announces
in punching monosyllables, "The Queene (my lord) is dead" (5.5.16;
2337). That the manservant Seyton may have been given as important a
part as he has, while not implicated in either the regicide or the subsequent
tyranny, may be due to the fact that Alexander Seton, Lord Fyvie, his direct
descendant, councillor to James in Scotland, was from 1597 to 1604 the
personal guardian of Prince Charles and, on March 6, 1606, was newly
created Earl of Dunfermline.

"Magnificence," William Vaughan records in *The Golden Grove* (1600),
"is a virtue that consisteth in sumptuous and great expenses . . . so that
. . . it is peculiar to Noblemen" (1.53). In 1606 it was the badge of royalty
and nobility alike. Everywhere, claims Lawrence Stone, there was

> an insistence upon the aristocratic virtue of generosity. Though contemporar-
> ies lamented the decay of hospitality—and it undoubtedly did fall away dur-
> ing this period—this is less remarkable than the vigorous persistence of the
> ideal, and in some measure the practice, in direct opposition to Calvinist
> ideals of frugality and thrift. The prime test of any rank was liberality, the
> pagan virtue of open-handedness. It involved wearing rich clothes, living in
> a substantial well-furnished house, keeping plenty of servants and above all
> maintaining a lavish table to which anyone of the right social standing was
> welcome. This was the quality most admired by the leading squires and no-
> bles of England, and this that they were most anxious to impress upon poster-
> ity. When Robert Morgan built Mapperton Hall in the 1540's and 1550's, he
> had inscribed in the hall:

> What they spent, that they lent;
> What they gave, that they have;
> What they left, that they lost.[229]

The parsimonious Lord Burghley thus spent £363 to feast the French commissioners in 1581 and another £629 on the three-day celebration of his daughter's wedding in 1582. "At this vast party," Stone tells us, "there were consumed, among other things, about 1,000 gallons of wine, 6 veals, 26 deer, 15 pigs, 14 sheep, 16 lambs, 4 kids, 6 hares, 36 swans, 2 storks, 41 turkeys, over 370 poultry, 49 curlews, 135 mallards, 354 teals, 1,049 plovers, 124 knotts, 280 stints, 109 pheasants, 277 partridges, 615 cocks, 485 snipe, 840 larks, 21 gulls, 71 rabbits, 23 pigeons, and 2 sturgeons. By these standards, the Earl of Salisbury [Cecil] was behaving with conspicuous moderation when he spent a mere £97 in 1605 and £200 in 1611 on banquets for King James" (560–61).

Inversely, the hollowness of Macbeth's household culminates in the inadequacy of his hospitality, or what among gentry was called "neighborliness," a fact that would register on playgoers at the Globe in 1606 regardless of their station. There was, for instance, the elaborate ritual of gift-giving. Where Macbeth is not present to welcome Duncan ("See, see our honour'd Hostesse" [1.6.10; 445]; "Where's the Thane of Cawdor?" [1.6.20; 457]), the King reprimands his host by shaming him with his own generosity:

> the King's abed.
> He hath beene in vnusuall Pleasure,
> And sent forth great Largesse to your Offices,
> This Diamond he greetes your Wife withall,
> By the name of most kind Hostesse,
> And shut vp in measureless content. (2.1.12–17; 586–91)

Earlier, Lady Macbeth has shamed Macbeth by reprimanding him for not staying at the welcoming banquet for Duncan, a literalization of what Duncan had metaphorically called his soldierly service (1.4.56; 342): "He has almost supt: why haue you left the chamber?" (1.7.29; 304). For Macbeth there are greater matters now than mere form, mere hospitality. There is the matter also of fealty and honor, perhaps of the Scottish statute known as "Murder Under Trust" which ruled a host responsible for the lives and welfare of all his guests, regardless of rank.[230] His verbal opinion is as firm as his action, his thought at one with his departure. Now he likens his plan to a "poyson'd Challice" (1.7.11; 485):

> We will proceed no further in this Businesse:
> He hath Honour'd me of late, and I haue bought
> Golden Opinions from all sorts of people,
> Which would be worne now in their newest glosse,

Not cast aside so soone. (1.7.31–35; 507–11)

Thus *he* reprimands *her.* Lady Macbeth, who normally speaks declaratively, turns his metaphorical chalice into a question—"Was the hope drunke, / Wherein you drest your selfe? Hath it slept since?" (1.7.35–36; 512–13)—underscoring the fact that the declarative Macbeth had just begun with a hypothesis which he then denies (1.7.1–7; 475–81). Noticeably against their intense, conspiratorial conversation—"Art thou affear'd . . . / Prythee peace: . . . / If we should faile? / We faile?" (1.7.39–60; 516–40)—playgoers must hear the convivial, normalized sounds of the banqueting within: the clash and clatter of routine, the noise of innocence and ignorance. As host, Macbeth too would sense the awful chasm between the two spaces: "Away, and mock the time with fairest show, / False Face must hide what the false Heart doth know" (1.7.82–83; 565–66). He capitulates when he brings banquet and host together, giving Duncan's "two Chamberlaines" too much "Wine, and Wassell," as Lady Macbeth scripts for him (1.7.64–65; 544–45).

At the second banquet, Lady Macbeth again upbraids her husband. "My Royall Lord, / You do not giue the Cheere . . . the sawce to meate is Ceremony, / Meeting were bare without it" (3.4.31–36; 1293–98); and once more Macbeth turns a question declarative by way of response: "Which of you haue done this? / Thou canst not say I did it: neuer shake / Thy goary lockes at me" (3.4.48–50; 1316–19). In losing control of the critical Stuart host's attribute of magnanimity, he also loses his royal stature as King at his own coronation feast. Lady Macbeth's defeat as hostess and Queen leads to a private charge that also publicly charges Macbeth with treason: "O proper stuffe: / This is the very painting of your feare: / This is the Ayre-drawne-Dagger which you said / Led you to *Duncan*" (3.4.59–62; 1329–31). It is a startling admission; consequences, untrammeled now, begin to ensnare them both. He confesses as much. "If Charnell houses, and our Graues must send / Those that we bury, backe; our Monuments / Shall be the Mawes of Kytes" (3.4.70–72; 1341–43). To the playgoers at the Globe, who see the actor playing Banquo's ghost, it is the ghost to whom Macbeth speaks, but to those attending the feast, who see no ghost, he is speaking of Duncan himself. Macbeth's failure as host—"Hee's heere in double trust; / First, as I am his Kinsman, and his Subiect, / Strong both against the Deed: Then, as his Host, / Who should against his Murtherer shut the doore, / Not beare the knife my selfe" (1.7.12–16; 486–90)—is his initial undoing, and hers. Once the guests have left, Lady Macbeth too wanders off in her thoughts (3.4.140; 1424). "The Wine of Life is drawne, and the meere Lees / Is left this Vault, to brag of" (2.3.95–96; 856–57).

But one last banquet remains. It belongs to *"the three Witches"* (4.1.1 S.D.; 1527). "Round about the Caldron go: / In the poysond Entrailes throw" (4.1.4–5; 1531–32). Here the infernal menu mockingly inverts the grand feasts provided by lords like Burghley, or what Gervase Markham recommends more broadly in *The English House-wife* (1630): paste of quinces, ipocras, gingerbread, jumbles, biscuit-bread, Banbury cakes, and marzipan. The witches' recipe has only dead body parts:

> Fillet of a Fenny Snake,
> In the Cauldron boyle and bake:
> Eye of Newt, and Toe of Frogge,
> Wooll of Bat, and Tongue of Dogge:
> Adders Forke, and Blinde-wormes Sting,
> Lizards legge, and Howlets wing:
> For a Charms of a powrefull trouble,
> Like a Hell-broth, boyle and bubble. (4.1.12–19; 1539–46)

Unlike the generalized banquets of 1.7 and 3.4, this later scene, interpolated around 1610, is specific in terms of a deliberate antomy of the stew and of the creatures whose parts compose it. There has been one earlier anatomy. In the Captain's report we learn that Macbeth approached Macdonwald and "vnseam'd him from the Naue to th'Chops" (1.2.22; 41). Macbeth is even now racing toward the witches for a second meeting, but in a way he has already been there. This dreadful fact is partly measured by a string of banquets as lexias—a way of measuring much of Shakespeare's play—and marked by the most primitive forms of hospitality in tenth-century Scotland, in a culture of Jacobean London that revered magnificence.

Five of the twelve great livery companies of London dealt in cloth and clothing: the Mercers, who dealt in expensive cloths; the Drapers, who made and dealt with less expensive fabrics; the Merchant-Taylors; the Haberdashers; and the Clothworkers. Peter Stallybrass writes of the society of playgoers in 1606 that theirs was a "cloth society" both because England's "industrial base was the production of cloth and the circulation of clothing, and [because] cloth was a staple currency." He goes on:

> To be a member of any but the poorest of households was to wear livery. It was to be paid above all in cloth. And the companies of London were named to emphasize their central relation to clothes: they were *livery* companies. When a guild member was set free, he or she was said to be "clothed" and to

be a free member was technically called "having the clothing." To be incorporated into a household, to be incorporated into a guild, depended upon a transmission of clothes.[231]

According to Steve Rappaport, "Merchants shipped an average of 103,600 cloths overseas each year from London during the last four decades of the sixteenth century . . . the size of the labour force in London's cloth-finishing industry continued to grow throughout Elizabeth's reign: the number of men admitted each year into the Clothworkers' and Merchant Taylors' Companies, the major cloth-finishing companies to which nearly one-quarter of the city's freemen belonged, doubled from 1550 to 1600."[232] Every other year at Easter each member of Shakespeare's acting company, the King's Men, received as livery three yards of bastard scarlet for a cloak and a quarter-yard of crimson velvet for a cape. The bright colors indicated some of the most expensive clothing. But the troupe was clothes-conscious, not surprising for actors accustomed to costumes. Augustine Phillips, an actor and shareholder in the King's Men, left clothes to a boy he had trained: "Item, I give to Samuel Gilborne, my late apprentice, the sum of forty shillings, and my mouse-colored velvet hose, and a white taffeta doublet, and black taffeta suit, my purple cloak, sword, and dagger, and my bass viol."[233] The bequest is not unique: in 1604 Thomas Pope, another actor in the King's Men, left to Robert Gough and John Erdmans "all my wearing apparel, and all my arms, to be equally divided between them."[234] Indeed, clothing at court was costly—a single black suit could cost as much as £50, the annual rent of a London townhouse.

Lawrence Stone finds that clothes were "second only to hospitality as a status symbol and as a vehicle for conspicuous consumption."[235] The most common materials were linen and wool. Linen was easy to clean and quick to dry and was used for inner garments such as shirts, underwear, collars, cuffs, and hose; it was occasionally stiffened with a gum to make buckram. Some linen was produced domestically, but most of it was imported. Wool was used for the outer garments: it accepted dyes, resisted rain, and was warm in winter and cool in summer. Silk was imported for finer clothes yet, and leather, sometimes tooled, was used for gloves, belts, and men's hats, doublets, and occasionally breeches. Fashion in such materials was constantly changing. It could also be viewed as excessive.

> "It is a world to see the costlinesse and the curiositie, the excesse and the vanitie, the pompe and the braverie, the change and the varietie, and finallie the ficklenesse and the follie that is in all degrees; in somuch that nothing is more constant in England than inconstancie of attire," declared a rustic observer. Nor was this an unsophisticated view, for foreign observers like van

Meteren were also struck by the fashion-consciousness of the English. Tailors crouched anxiously behind the pillars in old St. Paul's watching for a new cut of doublet or a novel pair of hose displayed upon the gallants exhibiting themselves in the aisles. The Spanish slop and the Skipper's galligaskin, the Switzer's blistered codpiece and the Danish hanging sleeve, the Italian close strosser and the French standing collar, the treble-quadruple Daedalian ruffs and the stiff-necked rebatoes, all succeeded one another in bewildering variety, as foreign fashions flooded into London at breakneck and purse-emptying speed.[236]

In this clothing-centered world of 1606, sumptuary regulations passed in 1562, 1566, 1574, 1580, and 1597 attempted to regulate both the production of clothing and what each class might wear: clothes literally as well as theatrically made the man. But they could also, as with the actors, characterize the man. The complaints of preachers and critics for unnecessary ostentation were commonplace; the best known is that of Philip Stubbes, whose *Anatomie of Abuses,* first published in 1583, was augmented in 1585 and reprinted in 1595.

> They haue great and monsterous ruffes made either of Cambrick, holland, lawn or els of some other the finest cloth that can be got for money, whereof some be a quarter of a yard deep, yea some more, very few lesse. (sig. D7)
>
> Certaine I am there was neuer any kinde of apparell euer inuented, that could more disproportion the body of man than these Dublets w[t] great bellies hanging down beneath their *Pudenda* (as I haue said) & stuffed with foure, fiue or six pound of Bombast at the least: I say nothing of what their Dublets be made, some of Saten, Taffatie, silk, Grogram, Chamlet, gold siluer, & what not? slashed, iagged, cut, carued, pincked and laced with all kinde of costly lace of diuers and sundry colours, for if I shoulde stand vpon these particularities, rather time then matter would be wanting. (sig. E2v)

Such clothing was not only approved by but inspired by the court itself—by Elizabeth I, who liked fine clothes, and by an extravagant King James; Lord Sydney paid £220 to dress for the Christmas masque of 1603 and £250 for another new suit, covered in pearls, a short time later. As for King James, Stone writes, "Over a period of five years from 1608 to 1613 he bought a new cloak every month, a new waistcoat every three weeks, a new suit every ten days, a new pair of stockings, boots, and garters every four or five days, and a new pair of gloves every day. Silks alone were costing the King and Queen over £10,000 a year, and the wardrobe expense altogether was running at over £25,000 as early as 1610" (563).

Costs regulated purchases somewhat, so that a man's status could be recognized by the color of his clothes. Browns and grays, the least expensive, signaled the lower classes and the poor; blue, from the herb woad, and russet, from the plant madder, were also relatively inexpensive and might denote servants and apprentices. Bright colors, including bright red, scarlet, and crimson, were made with imported dyes and were expensive; black was the costliest color of all. Because the natural dyes for bright colors tended to fade quickly, however, most clothing was fairly muted, which might help to explain the exaggeration in cutting and shaping the fabric. Such tailoring, however, resulted in complaints that women often dressed like men. "The Women also there haue dublets & Jerkins as men haue heer, buttoned vp the brest, and made with wings," Stubbes remarks. "It is written in in the 22. of *Deuteronomie,* that what man so euer weareth womans apparel is accursed, and what woman weareth mans apparel is accursed also" (sigs. F1–F1v). This excessiveness may explain the repeal in March 1604 of the sumptuary laws regulating clothing that could be worn as dependent on a man's or woman's status. By 1606 at the Globe, fashions were blurring class distinctions. So was the ownership of clothes, for nobility would often will their clothing to servants (who sometimes wore it themselves), and hangmen were entitled to receive the clothing of those they executed. In 1604 James regulated dress by proclamation. It had become difficult to distinguish clothing from costumes: at Hampton Court in 1604 Elizabeth I's wardrobe was ransacked for costumes for Samuel Daniel's masque *The Vision of the Twelve Goddesses,* staged on January 8. "Why doe you dresse me in borrowed Robes?" Macbeth asks Rosse, metatheatrically (1.3.108–9; 215). For a cultural moment in which clothes might no longer be the primary sign of rank, it is a telling question.

"Macbeth's borrowed robes symbolize for him the trappings of an alien part, and his failure to learn to wear them comfortably erodes his sense of self until it nearly destroys his sense of reality entirely," Jonas Barish notes; "the role, once chosen, seems to possess the character instead of the other way around."[237] Actually, Macbeth's career at the Globe in 1606 begins and ends with clothing; having ripped apart the clothing of Macdonwald on the field resembling Golgotha, he is dressed by Rosse and Angus in Cawdor's robes metaphorically, and Banquo watches: "New Honors come vpon him / Like our strange Garments, cleaue not to their mould, / But with the aid of vse" (1.3.145–47; 258–60). Unlike Macbeth's direct questioning of the propriety of such an honor, Banquo is neither surprised nor envious. He has faith in "the aid of vse" even when the garments are "strange." Angus will not speak again after confirming this title in 1.2 until 5.2, when, in his only other speaking appearance, he returns, chorically, to judge Macbeth in borrowed robes:

> Those he commands, moue onely in command,
> Nothing in loue; Now do's he feele his Title
> Hang loose about him, like a Giants Robe
> Vpon a dwarfish Theefe. (5.2.19–22; 2197–2200)

It is not a robe of his giving but a stolen gift that is judged. Like the crown Macbeth had usurped from Duncan, like the twofold balls and treble scepters carried by the eight ghostly kings of his own conjuration with the witches, none of these is his, nothing lasts. "Vpon my Head they plac'd a fruitlesse Crowne, / And put a barren Scepter in my Gripe" (3.1.60–61; 1051–52). It is all appearance, all theatrical show.

It is quite the opposite with Lady Macbeth. The night of Duncan's murder, her nightgown became her disguise as well as Macbeth's: "Get on your Night-Gowne, least occasion call vs, / And shew vs to be Watchers" (2.2.69–70; 734–35). He is told to wash his hands, too, to play the role of the innocent (2.2.45–46; 703–4). But the nightgown was what the dead were buried in—what alone they took to their graves as dress—and it is this in which, tellingly, she reappears in 5.1. Where before she had used a costume to signify her innocence, she has now become that costume, a winding sheet, as a walking image of death.[238] Seeing this traditional emblem embodied on the stage before them, the playgoers at the Globe in 1606 will not be surprised to hear the cry of women that announces her subsequent demise.

MEDICAL LEXIAS

Surrounded by brothels and two reconstructed prisons, the Marshalsea and the Clink, the Globe Theater in 1606 stood alongside St. Thomas's Hospital, founded in 1569. Here was an alternative "wooden O," the celebrated operating theater where diseased parts of bodies were cut away from the healthy ones, while nearby on the stage playgoers learned that Macbeth had himself "vnseam'd" a man "from the Naue to th' Chops" (1.2.22; 41). The surgeons who performed at St. Thomas's were presumably more skilled than the barbers, also known as barber-surgeons, who performed minor operations as well as dentistry. But more trained than the surgeons were the physicians who specialized in the diagnosis of illness and the prescription of medicines, often simples made from herbs and sold by apothecaries. There was a short life expectancy in 1606 due to the large number of illnesses: smallpox, malaria stones, venereal diseases (especially syphilis), dysentery, influenza, and measles. Those living in congested areas came down with typhus; sailors were infected with scurvy. Even toothaches, for a culture that cared little for its teeth, were commonplace. Shakespeare's son-in-law John Hall, who lived and practiced medicine at New Place in Stratford, wrote in 1607 that "a worthy physician is the enemy of sickness, in purging nature from corruption. His action is most in feeling of pulses, and his discourses chiefly of the nature of diseases. He is a great searcher out of simples, and accordingly makes his composition. He persuades abstinence and patience, for the benefit of health, while purging and bleeding are the chief courses of his counsel."[239] Citizens as well as peers were expected to have medical books in their own libraries, for fevers and infections were so common that men and women frequently experienced friends and neighbors who were sick, delirious, even dying.

The primary physiological basis for medicine was still humoral, based on Galenic belief and practice. According to this ancient authority, man's life is based in heat and moisture, while cold and dryness are hostile to the forces of life. Digestion or "concoction" produces a viscid, whitish fluid known as chyle, which, conveyed to the liver, undergoes a second "concoction" and produces one of four humors: choler, which is hot, dry, yellow, bitter, thin, and volatile; melancholy, which is cold, dry, black, sour, thick, and heavy; blood, which is hot, moist, red, and sweet; and phlegm, which is cold, moist, colorless, tasteless, and watery. All people are dominated by an excess of one of these humors and are, consequently, choleric, melancholic, sanguine, or phlegmatic in temperament. An alternative theory, attributed to Aristotle, saw the right kind of melancholy as favorable to the imaginative and intellectual powers and, linked to the planet Saturn, was like Saturn potentially ambivalent. But the imagination was also a chief subject of a popular book republished in 1604, Thomas Wright's *The Passions of the Minde,* now *"Corrected, enlarged, and with sundry* new discourses augmented." For Wright the physical condition is initiated by the imagination:

> When we imagine any thing, presently the purer spirites flocke from the brayne, by certayne secret channels to the heart, where they pitch at the doore, signifying what an obiect was presented, convenient or disconvenient

184

for it. The heart immediatly bendeth, either to prosecute it, or to eschewe it: and the better to effect that affection, draweth other humours to helpe him, and so in pleasure concurre great store of pure spirites; in payne and sadnesse, much melancholy blood, in ire, blood and choller; and not onely (as I sayde) the heart draweth, but also the same soule that informeth the heart residing in other partes, sendeth the humours vnto the heart to performe their service in such a woorthie place. (sigs. D7–D7v)

In the following chapter, Wright extends his analysis to include and explain the will: "Without any great difficultie may be declared, how Passions seduce the Will: because the witte being the guide, the eie the stirrer and directer of the Will, which of it selfe, beeing blinde, and without knowledge, followeth that the wit representeth, propoundeth, and approveth as good: and as the sensitive appetite followeth the direction of imagination; so the Will affecteth, for the most part, that, the vnderstanding perswadeth to bee best" (sigs. B5–B5v). Thus passion, will, understanding, reason, and imagination are all indivisibly connected. "The will, by yeelding to the Passion, receyveth some little bribe of pleasure, the which moveth her, to let the bridle loose, vnto inordinate appetites, because she hath ingrafted in her, two inclinations, the one to follow Reason, the other to content the Sences: and this inclination (the other beeing blinded by the corrupt iudgement, caused by inordinate Passions) here she feeleth satisfied" (sig. E5v). "Furthermore," Wright adds, "the imagination representeth to the vnderstanding, not onely reasons that may favour the passion, but also it sheweth them very intensively" (sig. E2). Thus in a line of thought strikingly modern, Wright finds physiology and psychology inseparable as well. Still a third theory reached out even farther: derived from the Swiss alchemist Paracelsus, this understanding of medicine built on the notion of man as microcosm in a larger world, the macrocosm, and saw all sickness connected to external events. Paracelsus proposes, for instance, that "a knowledge of both the immediate and ultimate causes of earthquakes and thunderstorms is relevant to an understanding of inner storms in humans, like those caused by epilepsy, major upsets in the stomach or abdomen, or mental turmoil." Paracelsus's major principle was God's doctrine of signatures, by which human nature and the natural world had come from the same imagination, that of God. God worked with both the natural and human worlds as a carpenter might build a henhouse: "The carpenter is the seed of his house. Whatever he is, such will be his house. It is his imagination which makes the house, and his hand which perfects it."[240] At the Globe in 1606, Macbeth fuses all these medical lexias as he worries over his own state of health: "O, full of Scorpions is my Minde, deare Wife" (3.2.36; 1194). Such scorpions, moreover,

185

have affected his mind so that what should be metaphorical for him may also be physically real: "Will all great *Neptunes* Ocean wash this blood / Cleane from my Hand? no: this my hand will rather / The multitudinous Seas incarnadine, / Making the Greene one, Red" (2.2.59–62; 721–24). His imagination, mind, passion, and will all merge on his bloodied hands.

As with his sonnets and with *Hamlet,* Shakespeare may also have taken his information from Timothy Bright's *Treatise of Melancholie,* published in 1586, for it is melancholy in particular that seems to have infected Macbeth by the medical understanding prevalent in 1606. Melancholy, Bright says, is where "naturall and internall light is darkened, their fansies arise vayne, false, and voide of ground: euen as in the externall sensible darkenes, a false illusion will appeare vnto our imagination" (sig. G4). *The General Practise of Physicke,* published in 1605, Jacob Mosan's translation of the *Praxis medicinae vniuersalis* of Christoph Wirsung, calls such an illness, such a state of mind, a mania:

> This *Mania* is a dottage or madnesse, and therfore a disease of the mind, which no otherwise distempereth the mind, but as any other sicknesse of the bodie, whereby can be no health. . . . [A second kind of] *Melancholie* is a corruption of the iudgment and thoughts, altered from their naturall kind, with an vnnaturall and spoiled maner, tempered with feare and care: through which the blacke bloud causeth a troubled and changed spirit . . . they be so full of fantasies & maruellous imaginations. Otherwhiles they be weary of their life: neuerthelesse they shun death: they complaine not any otherwise but that they be persecuted and murthered, or that some wild beasts will deuoure them. (sigs. I1v–I2)

It is no coincidence that the two figures of Melancholia and Mania straddled the portals to Bethlem Hospital.

In his *Declaration of Egregious Popish Impostures* (1603, 1604, 1605), Samuel Harsnett, the assistant to Bishop Richard Bancroft in the persecution of witchcraft and exorcism, provides more sequencing lexias by seeing the melancholic as a demoniac. "Men of this duskie, turbulent and fantasticall disposition . . . are . . . full of speculations, fansies, and imaginations of spirits and devils."[241] Michael MacDonald, who has studied the records of the London physician Richard Napier, notes that melancholy was also a class-oriented disease in the popular belief of 1606, a courtier's illness that gentlefolk were often diagnosing for themselves.[242] At the same time, Thomas Nashe was democratizing such illness, making it classless and, more unsettling, apocalyptic. In *The Terrors of the Night Or, A Discourse of Apparitions* (1594), he argues that

186

this slimie melancholy humor still thickning as it stands still, engendreth many mishapen obiects in our imaginations. Sundry times wee behold whole Armies of men skirmishing in the Ayre, Dragons, wilds beasts, blood streamers, blasing Comets, firie strakes, with other apparitions innumerable: whence haue all these their conglomerate matter but from fuming meteors that arise from the earth? so from the fuming melancholly of our spleene mounteth that hot matter into the higher Region of the braine, whereof manie fearfull visions are framed. (sigs. C2v–C3)

The play of *Macbeth* makes melancholy contagious, too: such strange sights worry the air around Inverness. "On Tuesday last, / A Faulcon towring in her pride of place, / Was a Mowsing Owle hawkt at, and kill'd," the Old Man tells Rosse, and Rosse replies:

And *Duncans* Horses,
(A thing most strange, and certaine)
Beauteous, and swift, the Minions of their Race,
Turn'd wilde in nature, broke their stalls, flong out,
Contending 'gainst Obedience, as they would
Make Warre with Mankinde. (2.4.11–18; 937–45)

In such a world, why would Birnam Wood not move? And, as Wirsung is made to remark in 1605, melancholy can lead to anger or to despair. Exemplary cases of both are found in Lady Macduff—her sorrow at the loss of her husband and her anger at his betrayal. "He loues vs not, / He wants the naturall touch" (4.2.8–9; 1721–22), she tells Rosse; and then, to her son, "Sirra, your Fathers dead" (4.2.30, 1746).

Both Macbeth and Lady Macbeth, in their turn, suffer from the melancholic's sense of ambition and jealousy. Three chapters along, Wright remarks that "there is no man in this life which followeth the streame of his Passions, but expecteth and verily beleeveth to get at last a firme rest, contentation, and ful satiety of all his appetites: the which is as possible, as to quench fire with fuell, extinguish a burning agew with hote wines" (sig. F5v). For Thomas Walkington in *The Opticke Glasse of Humours* (1607), melancholics can be dangerous. "I confesse this, that oftentimes the melancholike man by his contemplative facultie by his assiduitie of sad serious meditation is a brocher of dangerous matchiavellisme, an inventor of strategens, quirks, and pollicies, which were never put in practice" (fol. 66). In chapter 23, *"Howe affections be altered,"* Bright claims: "Enuious they are, because of their oune false conceaued want, whereby their estate; seeminge in their owne fantasie much worse then it is, or then the condition of other men, maketh them desire that they see other to enioy, to better their estate: this maketh them couetous of getting, though in expence where their humour moueth them with liking, or a voydance of perill, more then prodigall" (sig. I3). The careers of both Macbeths in acts 4 and 5 spiral downward into the dissolution and ennui that melancholy brings. Bright says that contentious melancholy brings "mourning, rising of vaine feare, or counterfet miserie, solitarinesse . . . a negligence in their affaires, and dissolutenesse, where should be diligence" (sigs. I3v–I4). "This conceit causeth vs to hide our selues, and to withdraw our presence from the society of men, whom we feare doe view our faultes in beholding vs, and wherof our presence stirreth vp the remembraunce. . . . Now because the vewing of another causeth the like from his againe, therfore doth the guilty minde abstaine ther from: that it prouoke not the eye of another whome he doth behold" (sigs. L5v–L6). Whether melancholy— too much black bile; too thick blood and too clouded a mind; a human condition accompanying wild and stormy nights—was cause or effect or both, whether their acts were seen as selfish, ambitious, or demonic, Macbeth and Lady Macbeth could be, for playgoers at the Globe in 1606, both physically and mentally ill.

MacDonald says that Richard Napier and his patients resorted to scientific, religious, and even magical concepts to explain and treat disorders (7). The treatment also varied. Carol Thomas Neely notes that Napier's "cures, designed to fit the disorder, were eclectically magical, medical, astrological, and spiritual; to some patients he gave advice, to most purges, to a few amulets or prayers or exorcisms."[243] Witches' charms lure Macbeth back to them, now in their cave, and the warnings he receives from the three symbolic apparitions of Macduff, Lady Macduff's son, and Malcolm in his overwrought imagination, as with the earlier ghost of Banquo— "Beware the Thane of Fife"; "none of woman borne / Shall harme *Macbeth*"; "*Macbeth* shall neuer vanquish'd be, vntill / Great Byrnam Wood, to high Dunsinane Hill / Shall come against him" (4.1.72, 80–81, 92–94; 1610, 1621–22, 1635–37)—take on a willed talsimanic power, as Janet Adelman has it, to protect him.[244]

Lady Macbeth's melancholia takes other forms. Napier's manuscript notation on Alice Davys suggests one cultural practice of melancholics.

Extreme melancholy, possessing her for a long time, with fear; and sorely tempted not to touch anything for fear that then she shall be tempted to wash her clothes, even upon her back. Is tortured until that she be forced to wash her clothes, be them never so good and new. Will not suffer her husband, child, nor any of the household to have any new clothes until they wash them for fear the dust of them will fall upon her. Dareth not to go to the church for treading on the ground, fearing lest any dust should fall upon them.[245]

Lady Macbeth's exaggerated version, washing her cleansed hands clean, is a variant of this. Another characteristic of melancholics is somnambulance. The physician André Du Larens, in *A Discourse on the Preseruation of the Sight* (1599), reports that

> in melancholike persons, the materiall is wanting . . . the minde is not at rest, the braine is distempered, the minde is in continuall restlessness: for the feare that is in them doth continually set before them tedious & grieuous things, which so gnaw and pinch them as that they hinder them from sleeping. But if at one time . . . they be overtaken with a little slumber, it is then but a troublesome sleep, accompanied with a thousand of false and fearful apparitions, and dreams so dreadfull, as that it were better for them to be awake. (95)

Duncan Salkeld comments that

> Lady Macbeth takes to furtive and compulsive writing. She disseminates in script a terrible, secret knowledge, yet censors it and conceals her text before returning to sleep. What is striking about this process is that its cycle is entirely enclosed: she unlocks her closet, takes paper, folds it, writes, reads what she has written, seals it and retires. The unmitigated violence of the play is thus contained in the woman whose confinement to her chamber is broken only by an action which represents a confining of thought.[246]

"A great perturbation in Nature, to receyue at once the benefit of sleep and do the effects of watching," the Doctor tells Lady Macbeth's waiting-gentlewoman; "This disease is beyond my practise" (5.1.9–10, 56; 2103–4, 2150).

In tracing as lexias the cultural practices of 1606, we may sense that Lady Macbeth may have brought her illness on herself, when in 1.5 she asks to change her blood (and her milk) to gall. Blood was valued as the means of reproduction. Macbeth is keenly aware of this when he tells Malcolm of his father's death by remarking, "The Spring, the Head, the Fountaine of your Blood / Is stopt, the very Source of it is stopt" (2.3.98–99; 861–62). As Giovanni Battista Nenna writes in *Nennio, or a Treatise of Nobility* (1595), "the ingendring of children is permitted to man, by meanes of his own blood" (6). Blood was also the source of semen in men. Thomas Cogan writes in the *Hauen of Health* (1584, 1589, 1596, 1605) that "after the third and last concoction: which is doone in everie part of the bodie that is nourished, there is left some part of profitable bloud, not needefull to the partes, ordeyned by nature for procreation which . . . is woonderfullie conveighed and carried to the genitories, where by their proper nature that which before was plaine bloude, is now transformed and changed into seede" (240). Semen then is the result of heat making white blood. The body that has much blood and much heat will produce much seed. In *The Differences of the Ages of Mans Life* (1607), Henry Cuffs confirms that "the matter whereof we are all made" is *"semen and sanguis parentum,* both abounding with heat and moisture [blood]" (117). Youths were thought to have a great deal of blood in them, hence hot-blooded. But not the elderly. In *The English Phlebotomy* (1592), Nicholas Gyer, a surgeon, notes this as a precaution in treating old men with bloodletting: "because there is in them little bloud. . . . Olde men after 70 yeares are not [as a rule] to be let bloud . . . ; in these years, the powers of the bodie to be weake, & that bloud aboundeth not" (70).[247] Such lexias surround Lady Macbeth's unnatural and troubling vow to a husband whose "Nature . . . is too full o'th'Milke of humane kindnesse" (1.5.16–17; 362–63) that she would herself take a baby suckling her milk from her breast and having "giuen Sucke" even "while it was smyling in my Face, / Haue pluckt my Nipple from his Bonelesse Gummes, / And dasht the Braines out" (1.7.54–58; 533–37). It is a vow of sterility that is also a vow of self-destruction. Macbeth's own vowed "Partner of Greatnesse" (1.5.11–12; 357–58) would destroy both the personal and public foundations of that greatness. Macbeth would have no wife, no mother of his children, and no queen. It is an awful situation for him to contemplate. But it is also, in a sense, deceptive, as the playgoers at the Globe know, for Lady Macbeth has already asked to "make thick my blood, / Stop vp th'accesse and passage to Remorse," to become unsexed and therefore incapable of childbearing (1.5.43–44; 394–95). What is more, her vow, unnatural in itself, has been made to infernal "Spirits" (1.5.40; 391). But while her imagery is brutally direct, as Macbeth's will be about blood, her medical association of milk, blood, and gall suggests a poisoning of the whole system: of heart and mind and will. She would be seen, as early as 1.5, to be a walking emblem of death itself. Her sense, clearly, is that blood and milk distinguish her youth, vitality, and fertility. This complex reemerges in her final scene, when she stalks like Death itself through the chambers at Dunsinane, clothed only in her nightdress from the night of the murder and carrying only a taper for illumination. Blood then is present again, ineradicably so; and its source is not herself but Duncan. She is astonished and transfixed by the fact that "the olde man [would] haue had so much blood in him" (5.1.38–39; 2331–32). The walking emblem of Death is astonished that the aged would have such youthful vitality, might have seed left, might be powerful beyond the power of easy killing. Such thoughts, revealing her own sense of medicine as it was practiced in 1606, enclose her in the play. Shakespeare may have inserted Duncan's vital supply of blood since King James would trace his ancestry back to such royalty; but for the playgoers, Lady Macbeth condemns herself here of diabolism.

Madness is an urgent concern of the two main women in *Macbeth*. Macbeth's hesitation to murder Duncan and his inability to pray subsequently, as the grooms are apparently doing, arouses Lady Macbeth's anxiety: "Consider it not so deepely. . . . These deeds must not be thought / After these wayes: so, it will make vs mad" (2.2.29–33; 686–90). For Lady Macduff, her vision clearer and more monocular, her sense of reality unchanged, says of her missing husband to Rosse, "His flight was madnesse: when our Actions do not, / Our feares do make vs Traitors" (4.2.3–4; 1715–16). Patients who reported extreme melancholic states to Richard Napier were "designated by terms such as 'mad,' 'lunatic,' 'mania,' 'frenzy,' 'raging,' 'furious,' 'frantic,' " but such terms, Neely tells us, were "rare" (88). Only 5 percent of Napier's male patients and only 4 percent of his women patients were termed "mad"; only 3 percent of the men and 2 percent of the women were "lunatic." These low numbers correspond with the small number of patients at the other great hospital at the margin of London life in 1606: the old St. Mary of Bethlem Hospital, founded in 1247 beyond Bishopsgate and recently taken over by King James. Known as Bedlam, it "continued to attract, fascinate and frighten its curious visitors and trouble the common sense of quotidian rationality," Salkeld comments (124). "The stark, Bedlam madman," MacDonald adds, was generally considered to be "dangerous, inclined to murder and assault, arson and vandalism . . . his behavior and moods suggested that he was helpless to govern the wild energy of his passions" (142). But the population was small. Although a report in 1598 names twenty-one patients, there were more commonly fifteen or twenty living at Bedlam, usually for many years.

Of the two women, Lady Macbeth moves in this play inexorably toward madness: a rare state but one that playgoers, visiting Bedlam as one of London's popular attractions for entertainment, might recognize in 1606. In *The Method of Phisicke* (1583, 1590, 1596, 1601), Philip Barrough argues that people suffering from extreme melancholy "desire death, and do verie often behight and determine to kill them selves" (46). The words resonate in Pierre de la Primaudaye's *French Academie*, reprinted in 1602: "Some to grow so far as to hate themselues, and so fall despaire, yea many kil and destroy themselues."[248] And Timothy Bright in chapter 18: "When desperate furie is ioyned with feare: which so terrifieth, that to auoid the terrour, they attempt sometimes to deprive themselves of life." But Bright also contends that such despondency is the "conscience of sinne."[249] "Suicide was a terrible crime in Tudor and early Stuart England," MacDonald and Murphy confirm. "Self-killing was a species of murder, a felony in criminal law and a desperate sin in the eyes of the church" (15). "For the heinousnesse thereof," writes Michael Dalton in *The Countrey Justice* (1618), "it is an offence against God, against the king, and against Nature" (1626 ed., 234). Many Protestant divines, like the Catholics before them, were preaching of suicide as the extreme act of despair and faithlessness. George Abbott, later to become Archbishop of Canterbury, observes in *An Exposition upon the Prophet Jonah* (1600) that suicide is "a sin so grieuous that scant any is more hainous unto the Lord" (132). Committing the extreme of demonology, Lady Macbeth suffers as well from an extreme case of melancholy. Suffering from planning regicide, she goes mad.

Macbeth too arguably commits suicide in pursuing Macduff: "And thou oppos'd, being of no woman borne, / Yet I will try the last. Before my body, / I throw my warlike Shield: Lay on *Macduffe,* / And damn'd be him, that first cries hold, enough" (5.8.31–34; 2472–75). Desperate courage meets and mixes with melancholic despair. But the grounds for his illness—physical, mental, moral—were laid out in the play as early as 1.3. "Good Sir, why doe you start, and seeme to feare / Things that doe sound so faire," Banquo asks of him after the titles pronounced by the three weird sisters (1.3.51–52; 151–52). In the speech of 1606, *fear* and *fair* were homophones.[250] The same pairing reappears later in Banquo's soliloquy: "Then hast it now, King, Cawdor, Glamis, all / As the weyard Women promis'd, and I feare / Thou playd'st most fowly for 't" (3.1.1–3; 82–84). Such a confusion of terms, psychologically and physiologically, may lead to the wide mood swings that characterize Macbeth's last hours: "Throw Physicke to the Dogs, Ile none of it" (5.3.47; 2270);

> The time ha's beene, my sences would haue cool'd
> To heare a Night-shrieke, and my Fell of hairs
> Would at a dismall Treatise rowze, and stirre
> As life were in't. I haue supt full with horrors (5.5.10–13, 2331–34),

and, a moment after that,

> To morrow, and to morrow, and to morrow,
> Creepes in this petty pace from day to day,
> To the last Syllable of Recorded time. (5.5.19–21; 2340–42)

When fair and fear are no longer separable but *interchangeable,* that way madness lies. In the minds of the playgoers at the Globe, thoughts of the neighboring St. Thomas could be displaced by thoughts of Bedlam.

LEXIAS OF DISEASE

Duncan's plentiful supply of blood might strike playgoers in 1606 as unusual, too, since death permeated the cultural moment, not life. It was an age characterized by the "belief that all nature was decaying in its old age," according to Richard Foster Jones.[251] Indications began as early as Francis Shakelton's *Blazyng Starr* in 1580:

> It shall manifestly be proued that this worlde shall perishe and passe awaie, if wee doe but consider the partes whereof it doeth consist, for doe we not see the yearth to be changed and corrupted? Sometymes by the inundation of waters? Sometymes by fiers? And by the heate of the Sunne? And doe we not see that some partes of the same doe waxe old, and weare awaie euen for verie age? Doe wee not in some places also read, that mountaines haue falne doune, by reason of earth quakes? And Rockes haue been cracked, and broken so in peeces, that by the meanes thereof, certaine Riuers haue been (as it were) dronke vp, or els, haue had recourse an other waie? Also haue ye not read, that the seas haue rebounded backe, ouerwhelmed whole Cities, and vtterly drouned whole Prouinces? And what are these strange alterations els, but euident argumentes that the worlds shall one daie haue an ende? (sig. A4)

Shakelton goes on to use discoveries in astronomy, mathematics, and botany to substantiate this biblical view (sigs. A4–A5). In 1604 Christopher Sutton added *Disce Mori. Learne to Die,* subtitled *A religious discourse, mouing euery Christian man to enter in to a serious remembrance of his ende,* but this was one of dozens of such works still extant. The grim sense of universal mortality as inevitable is echoed by Rosse too in his description of Macbeth's Scotland:

> Alas poore Countrey,
> Almost affraid to know it selfe. It cannot
> Be call'd our Mother, but our Graue: where nothing
> But who knowes nothing, is once seene to smile:
> Where sighes, and groanes, and shrieks that rent the ayre

Are made, not mark'd: Where violent sorrow seemes
A Moderne extasie: The Deadmans knell,
Is there scarse ask'd for who, and good mens liues
Expire before the Flowers in their Caps,
Dying, or ere they sicken. (4.3.164–73; 2000–2009)

Not only the general mood of these lines but the specific reference to flowers in caps points directly to their use as preventatives in epidemics of plague, which struck with a vengeance in both 1603 and 1606. Memories of the Black Death still lingered; the terrible devastation of lives was sudden, unpredictable, random, and unavoidable, despite continual surveys of possible conditions and causes. It was one of the preoccupations of the cultural moment that cannot be overestimated. A century earlier Erasmus had complained about houses that had clay floors covered with thatch and cleaned by adding new layers of thatch, so that there remained, he said, a buildup of decades of spittle, vomit, the urine of dogs and men, the dregs of beer, the remnants of fish and other garbage.[252] In 1600 the condition still obtained, and in 1602 Elizabeth issued a proclamation that banned the building of new houses in London and supported the divisions of old ones in an attempt to prevent further congestion, thought to spread the plague.[253] In churches, too, the rood cross had been pulled down with the Reformation, but wall paintings of the Dance of Death remained, especially in East Anglia, and throughout the city and country sepulchres lined naves and chancels. "The art of Death lived on" there, Colin Platt has recently remarked.[254] Tessa Watt notes that images of death decorated even the alehouse and quotes a pamphlet by Samuel Rowlands, *A Terrible Batell Betweene the Two Consumers of the Whole World: Time and Death* (about 1606). There Time says to Death,

Thy picture stands upon the Ale-house wall,
Not in the credit of an ancient story,
But when the old wives guests begin to braule,
She points, and bids them read *Memento mori:*
Looke, looke (saies she) what fellow standeth there,
As women do, when crying Babes they feare. (sig. E4v)[255]

Not only sight but sound was a constant reminder, as in Rosse's pointed allusion to "The Deadmans knell." The tolling bell, the "passing bell," was notification that a person was dying and a signal for all who heard to pray for the dying person's soul; after the death, there would be one short peal and from the sound one could tell if the dead person was male or female. For nobility, laying out meant disembowelling before a

194

burial in the church graveyard or private cemetery; for the middling class and poor it meant being laid out at home and buried from the church gate. But the night watchman also rang a bell on his nightly rounds, and by 1580, Watt reports, "it was commonplace to suggest an equation between these two sounds" (113). Thus the jingle "The nightly Bell which I heare sound, / as I am laid in bed: / Foreshowes the Bell which me to ground, / shall ring when I am dead." "Two of the stock ballads, 'The bell-man's good morrow' and 'A bell-man for England,' " Watt continues, "took the metaphor a step further beyond death to describe the bell-man as waking the hearers from sin by calling them to the Day of Judgement" (114), the equivalent of Macbeth's "Heauens Cherubin" (1.7.22; 496). *cf Donne*

Death, always unavoidable, was also unavoidably a common topic in 1606. Life was always, continuously, fragile. The most fatal disease of all was bubonic plague beginning in the fourteenth century. The plague was carried by the flea *Xenospylla cheopis,* which normally used rats as its host. If the fleas transferred to humans, they might communicate the sickness by a rate of 50 percent; if the plague entered a person's pulmonary system, it became pneumonic plague, in which death was virtually certain. Epidemics usually came to the English from the Netherlands, arriving with the extensive cloth trade; this might help to explain the plague that hit Norwich in 1578–79 and killed roughly a third of the population. National epidemics occurred in 1563 and 1603 at their worst, but were fast approaching that again in 1606: demographic charts show that in the 1590s eight London and metropolitan parishes recorded a total of 3,818 baptisms and 5,390 burials. The baptisms are relatively constant, with a high of 408 in 1600; the rate of burials varies, with the greatest number— 1,163—in 1593. On July 18, 1603, James's coronation was delayed by an outbreak of plague; playgoing was also prevented, and more than 17,000 died within the next two months. Thomas Dekker notes that over 40,000 died in London within the year. Another 2,199 deaths were entered in mortality bills for 1606. I. W. describes this part of the cultural moment in *A Briefe Treatise of the Plague* (1603):

> The aire is corrupted and infected diuerse wayes as Astronomers say, by the influences, aspects, coniunctions, and opposition of all planets, the Eclipse of the Sunne and Moone, through the immoderate heate of the aire, where the temperature of the aire is turned from his naturall state to excessive heate and moisture, which is the worst temperament of the airs, vapors being drawne vp by the heate of the Sunne, remaining vnconsumed, doe rot, putrifie, and

corrupt, and so with the venome the aire becommeth corrupted and infected. (sig. A4)

By 1615 Gervase Markham was including treatment for plague in *The English Hus-wife*:

If you be infected with the plague, and feel the assured signs thereof, as pain in the head, drought, burning, weakness of stomach and such like: then you shall take a drachm of the best mithridate, and dissolve it in three or four spoonful of dragon-water, and immediately drink it off, and then with hot cloths or bricks, made extreme hot and laid to the soles of your foot, after you have been wrapt in woollen cloths, compel the sick party to sweat, which if he do, keep him moderately therein till the sore begin to rise; then to the same apply a live pigeon cut in two parts, or else a plaster made of yolk of an egg, honey, herb of grace chopped exceeding small, and wheat flour, which in very short space will not only ripen, but also break the same without any other incision; then after it hath run a day or two, you shall apply a plaster of melilot unto it until it be whole.[256]

"In time of plague," G. K. Hunter reminds us, "the 'knocking at the gate' signified the search for dead bodies; and the noise on the Globe stage [in 2.3] must have reinforced the fear of a mortal plague in the castle by carrying its original audience's minds back to the terror and the horror of their own visitations."[257] Perhaps that is why the Porter thinks he is at Hell Gate: with sin all about him he is called to the door to count up deaths. But there were also images involved. The doors of the dead had red crosses painted on them; the doors of the sick had words: "Lord have mercy on us." Macbeth himself "memorize[s] another *Golgotha*," the Captain remarks (1.2.41; 61); Rosse tells Macbeth, as if in confirmation, that the King "findes . . . / thy selfe didst make / Strange Images of death" (1.3.93–97; 199–201).

"One of the things that made the plague so psychologically shattering was that fear of contagion destroyed the bonds of family solidarity," Lawrence Stone contends.[258] Among the aristocracy, one child in three had lost a parent by age fourteen; in the middling and lower classes the figure was far greater (58). Perhaps the most indelible pamphlet on the plague of 1603 remains Thomas Dekker's wide-selling account of *The Wonderfull yeare. 1603* printed in two editions that year. His attempt to bury the horror in metaphor makes it even more terrifying.

Corne is no sooner ripe, but for all the pricking vp of his eares hee is pard off by the shins, and made to goe vpon stumps. Flowers no sooner budded, but they are pluckt vp and dye. Night walks at the heeles of the day, and sorrow enters (like a tauerne-bill) at the taile of our pleasures: for in the Appenine heigth of this immoderate ioy and securitie (that like Powles Steeple ouer-lookt the whole Citie) Behold, that miracle-worker, who in one minute turnd out generall mourning to a generall mirth, does nowe againe in a moment alter that gladnes to shrikes & lamentation. (sig. C2v)

His more specific projection of the life of the corpse has awful but distant echoes in the sights of the Old Man and Rosse in 2.4.

What an vnmatchable torment were it for a man to be bard vp euery night in a vast silent Charnell-house? hung (to make it more hideous) with lamps dimly & slowly burning, in hollow and glimmering corners: where all the pauement should in stead of greene rushes, be strewde with blasted Rosemary: withered Hyacinthes, fatall Cipresse and Ewe, thickly mingled with heapes of dead mens bones: the bare ribbes of a father that begat him, lying there: here the Chaplesse hollow scull of a mother that bore him: round about him a thousand Coarses, some standing bolt vpright in their knotted winding sheetes: others halfe mouldred in rotten coffins, that should suddenly yawne wide open, filling his nosthrils with noysome stench, and his eyes with the sight of nothing but crawling wormes. And to keepe such a poore wretch waking, he should heare no noise but of Toads croaking, Screech-Owles howl-ing, Mandrakes shriking: were not this an infernall prison? would not the strongest-harted man (beset with such a ghastly horror) looke wilde. (sig. C3)

Dekker's *The Seuen Deadlie Sinns of London* carries the subtitle *Drawne in seuen seuerall Coaches, Through the seuen seuerall Gates of the Citie Bringing the plague with them.*

Earlier, Shakespeare had caught such fear in Juliet's anticipation of the Capulet crypt (4.3), in Hamlet's meditation on "the dread of something after death, / The vndiscouered Countrey, from whose Borne / No Traueller returnes" (3.1.78–80; 1733–34), and, at the time of *Macbeth,* in Claudio's prolonged shudder in *Measure for Measure:*

I, but to die, and go we know not where,
To lie in cold obstruction, and to rot,
This sensible warme motion, to become
A kneaded clod; And the delighted spirit
To bath in fierie floods, or to recide
In thrilling Region of thicke-ribbed Ice,
To be imprison'd in the viewlesse windes
And blowne with restlesse violence round about
The pendant world. (3.1.117–25; 1337–44)

Macbeth's "Tale / Told by an Ideot" that "Creepes in this petty pace from day to day, / To the last Syllable of Recorded time" where "all our yester-dayes, haue lighted Fooles / The way to dusty death" (5.5.26–27, 20–23;

197

2347–48, 2341–44) echoes the time when "al our dayes are gonne; we bring our yeeres to an ende, as it were a tale that is tolde," the words from Psalm 90:9 incorporated in the order for burial in the *Book of Common Prayer.*

Puritan

To allay such fears, manuals such as *A Salve for a Sicke Man* by William Perkins (1595) provided a ritual for *ars moriendi,* the art or craft of dying. Ralph Houlbrooke has summarized Perkins's counsel this way:

> Three things are expected of the Christian as he finally draws close to death. First, that he die in faith, placing his whole reliance on God's special love and mercy, focusing his inward eye on Christ crucified. This inner faith is to be expressed by the outward signs of prayer or thanksgiving. In the pangs of death, it may be impossible to utter prayers. But the sighs, sobs and groans of a repentant and believing heart are prayers before God, as effectual as if expressed by the best voice in the world. Last words may proclaim faith with especial power. The second duty is to die readily, in submission to God's will, and the third to render his soul into the hands of God as the most faithful keeper of all. As the result of an afterthought, Perkins added a sort of appendix in which he pointed out that the last combat with the devil in the pangs of death is often the most dangerous of all. "When thou art tempted of *Satan* and seest no way to escape," Perkins advised, "even plainly close up thine eyes, and answer nothing, but commend thy cause to God."[259]

But death was not solitary. In the withdrawing chambers of the aristocracy and the more public rooms of the lower classes, ministers, kin, and neighbors were expected and welcomed, to provide comfort and to give testimony on how well the dying responded against Satan's final temptation and how well the dying prepared for death. In addition, Robert Pricke writes in *A Verie Godlie and Learned Sermon, treating of Mans Mortalitie* (1608), "It ministreth comfort to them that bestow and lay up the dead bodies of their friends in the graves; for why? they know they do not yield or deliver them up to destruction, but lay them up, as it were in soft beds, to the end that they may sleep quietly till they be awakened by the sound of the last Trumpet."[260] "The reference to 'sleep' was not just an evasive euphemism for death," David Cressy writes, "but part of a complex eschatological theology. It was comforting and commonplace to think of churchyards and sepulchres as 'the dormitories of Christians.' "[261]

Like Juliet and Claudio, the lonely Macbeth harbors only anxiety: staring at the ghost of Banquo with "Thy goary lockes" (3.4.50; 1319), he makes the connection swiftly and surely: "If Charnell houses, and our Graues must send / Those that we bury, backe; our Monuments / Shall be the Mawes of Kytes" (3.4.70–72; 1341–43). Earlier he had mused, "If th'Assassination / Could trammel vp the Consequence, and catch / With his surcease, Successe" (1.7.2–4; 476–78), juxtaposing *surcease* as death, or completion, with its near rhyme word *success,* meaning event or (in 1606) succession (to the crown). For him the success on the battlefield and the coronation meld into one, and this victory over men and over country melds into the triumph and completion of life. What it belies is not paradox but unity. He would be Dekker's man in the charnel house but also the King outside it. He can perhaps contemplate this because death has become epidemic to him. For Macbeth death is not only con-quest; it is commonplace. "Braue *Macbeth*," the Captain reports, "Disdayn-ing Fortune, with his brandisht Steele, / Which smoaked with bloody execution" (1.2.16–18; 35–37), was a grand sight to behold. Rosse agrees, also taking a certain pride in what he saw and what he tells.

> *Norway* himselfe, with terrible numbers,
> Assisted by that most disloyall Traytor,
> The *Thane* of Cawdor, began a dismall Conflict,
> Till that *Bellona's* Bridegroome, lapt in proofe,
> Confronted him with self-comparisons,
> Point against Point, rebellious Arme 'gainst Arme. (1.2.51–57; 76–81)

Reared in a war culture, Macbeth is its hero in warlike terms; trained to kill, his achievement is in killing large numbers and under great danger. His success is so saturated with such activity that once King, he knows no other means of rule and survival short of murder (3.1, 3; 984); but his own death, unlike most deaths in 1606, will consequently be a lonely one. Such dark imagery is not lost on Malcolm who later tells Macduff,

> When I shall treade vpon the Tyrants head,
> Or weare it on my Sword; yet my poore Country
> Shall haue more vices then it had before,
> More suffer, and more sundry wayes than euer,
> By him that shall succeede (4.3.45–49; 1865–69),

and is then picked up at the end by Macduff himself:

> Wee'l haue thee, as our rarer Monsters are
> Painted vpon a pole, and vnder-writ,
> Heere may you see the Tyrant. (5.8.25–27; 2463–67)

The awful fact of death in this play serves a plague-ridden public con-fronted, contained, defeated, and (naively?) eliminated. The only one who does not succumb to a death culture outside of Lenox and Cathnes is Banquo. But he is also the only one who, following Duncan's death, shows no sign of sorrow or remorse. Perhaps while reflecting on this, playgoers at the Globe in 1606 would move from the theater to work or to home, many of them past the heads of traitors spiked on London Bridge and rotting on the front of Parliament House.

ESCHATOLOGICAL LEXIAS

The discovery scene (2.3) is not a matter of death only; with the sight of a household coming anxiously together in nightclothes that resemble winding sheets, it is a remarkably vivid representation of the Day of Judgment when graves yawn up their living dead. It is another reason for the Porter's self-portrayal as the keeper of Hell Gate. The sounds of dialogue match the vision. When Macduff, Thane of Fife, returns to the entry hall at Inverness having just witnessed the slaughtered body of the King, he searches for ways to express what he has seen to those blissfully ignorant:

> O horror, horror, horror,
> Tongue nor Heart cannot conceiue, nor name thee (2.3.64–65; 816–17),

he says, the inconceivable conceived, the unvoiceable voiced. In union Macbeth and Lenox ask what is wrong, and his language, for playgoers in 1606, is telling.

> vp, vp, and see
> The great Doomes Image: *Malcolme, Banquo,*
> *As* from your Graues rise vp, and walke like Sprights,
> To countenance this horror. Ring the Bell (2.3.78–81; 832–35)

Banquo, Donalbaine, and Malcolm have been sleeping—"Deaths counterfeit" (2.3.77; 831)—and he turns to them, not to those who, awake, have interrogated him. His imagery and his actions all acknowledge that what he is thinking of is Doomsday, the Apocalypse when, at the end of the world as he knows it, bells are rung and the Last Judgment begins.

For the playgoers of 1606, Doomsday had been coming for some time; many had expected the world to end in 1600, and had grown up with that anxiety. A widely known prophecy which Bacon recalls in his essay on the subject,

> which I heard when I was a child, and Queen Elizabeth was in the flower of her years, was

When hempe is sponne
England's done:

whereby it was generally conceived, that after the princes had reigned which
had the principal letters of that worde *hempe* (which were Henry, Edward,
Mary, Philip, and Elizabeth), England should come to utter confusion; which,
thanks be to God, is verified only in the change of the name; for that the
King's style is now no more of England, but of Britain.[262]

The King's own sermon on the end of the world, *A Fruitfull Meditation,
Containing A plaine and easie Exposition, or laying open of the 7.8.9.10 verses
of the 20. chap. of the Revelation, in forme & maner of a Sermon,* now forgotten, had just been published in England in 1603. He returns to the image
of that sermon in his official account of the Powder Plot when he writes
what would happen had the conspirators succeeded: "And so the earth, as
it were opened, should haue sent forth of the bottome of the *Stygian* lake
such sulphured smoke, furious flames, and fearefull thunder, as should
haue by their diabolicall *Domseday* destroyed and defaced, in the twinck-
ling of an eye, not onely our present liuing Princes and people, but euen
our insensible Monuments reserued for future ages" (sig. E3v). Richard
Bauckham has located 231 books on the Apocalypse in this period still
extant.[263] John Davies of Hereford's account of the plague published in
1605 as *The Triumph of Death* is harsh and forbidding. In a marginal note
we find "Then said I, Lord, howe long? and he answered, vntill the Cities
bee wasted without inhabitant, and the houses without man, and the Land
be vtterly desolate Isai. 6.18 And the Cities that are inhabited, shal be left
void, the Land shall be desolate, ye shall know that I am the Lord Ezech.
12.20" (223).

George Gifford's recent *Sermons upon the Whole Booke of the Reuelation*
(1599) transported Scripture to England in his account of the Last Judgment:

This battle is fought upon the earth, otherwise, how do the beast and the
kings of the earth and their armies fight? Moreover, the armies of Christ are
man upon the earth, even the godly kings, princes, nobles, and worthy cap-
tains, which with the material sword defend the Gospel, and the ministers of
the truth, which with the spiritual sword fight Antichrist. Against these are
the armies of the beast and of the kings do fight. These are said to be the
armies in heaven, because their cause for which they fight, is from heaven,
and also the power with which they fight. These ride upon white horses, and
are clothed in fine white linen and pure. . . . The warriors of this world,
which war according to the lusts of their flesh in ambition, in pride and
cruelty: may be said to ride upon red horses, and to be clothed in bloody

garments. Put on that fine white linen and pure, ride upon that white horse among this blessed company, and follow this high captain: and then shall your Honour perform right worthy things to the glory of God, to the good of his people, and to your own eternal praise and felicity. (sigs. A5–A5v)

In Shakespeare's play the bloodied Macbeth is smeared in red; Malcolm's troops allied with the English, purified under the saintly King Edward the Confessor, oppose him. Macbeth is explicitly compared to the Antichrist. Malcolm calls him "blacke *Macbeth*" (4.3.53; 1873) and "Diuellish *Macbeth*" (4.3.117; 1945), while Macduff remarks more caustically, "Not in the Legions / Of horrid Hell, can come a Diuell more damn'd / In euils, to top *Macbeth*" (4.3.55–57; 1877–79) and young Siward says that "The diuell himselfe could not pronounce a Title / More hatefull to mine eare" (5.7.8– 9; 2406–7). For, once the regicide is accomplished, Marilyn French comments, "Shakespeare suggests that the entire character of the world is changed. When the texture of the inner circle is identical to that of the outer one, the connection between means and ends is broken. Instead of procreation and felicity, the end of power becomes more power alone, consolidation and extension of power: thus, life becomes hell. The porter announces the change."[264] That the end of history has been achieved was a commonplace fear especially at the turn of the century, particularly with devastating bouts of plague. Macbeth's mind dwells on this, as his language makes clear; he has failed to "iumpe the life to come" (1.7.7; 481). The death of the King—the death of all earthly kings and kingdoms—may be at hand in this play, and the survival Macbeth seeks is more than the mere continuation of his life, his rule, and his country. To the witches he says,

> I coniure you, by that which you Professe,
> (How ere you come to know it) answer me:
> Though you vntye the Windes, and let them fight
> Against the Churches: Though the yesty Waues
> Confound and swallow Nauigation vp:
> Though bladed Corne be lodg'd, & Trees blown downe,
> Though Castles topple on their Warders heads:
> Though Pallaces, and Pyramids do slope
> Their heads to their Foundations: Though the treasure
> Of Natures Germaine, tumble altogether,
> Euen till destruction sicken: Answer me
> To what I aske you. (4.1.50–61; 1580–91)

"Behind this wild apostrophe to the storm," James C. Bulman writes, there lies an "apocalyptic command."[265]

202

as one gets from reading Survey of London by Jn Stowe

Such language so permeates *Macbeth* that it becomes a Doomsday play, drawing on biblical imagery, the traditions of biblical prophecy, and the sense of a new order at the expense of the old: Stuarts replacing Tudors. Holinshed had pulled the story of Macbeth out of prehistory and made it the beginning of the Stuart line; Shakespeare wants to pull it out of the present of performance to suggest its wider implications. The "Butcher" Macbeth (5.9.35; 2522) of act 5 is the one who would "memorize another Golgotha" (1.2.41; 61) at the start: the play throughout is drenched in his bloodshed. Lady Macbeth commands him to wash his bloodied hands—

> Goe get some Water,
> And wash this filthie Witnesse from your Hand (2.2.45–46; 703–4),

she says, recalling Christ's words to Pilate that his death should bear witness unto the truth, while Macbeth's reply—

> no: this my Hand will rather
> The multitudinous Seas incarnadine,
> Making the Greene one, Red (2.2.60–62; 722–24)

—echoes Revelation 16:3. Later he is more direct:

> Renowne and Grace is dead,
> The wine of Life is drawne, and the meere Lees
> Is left this Vault. (2.3.94–96; 855–57)

Macduff insists on the other apocalypse at Golgotha:

> Confusion now hath made his Master-peece:
> Most sacrilegious Murther hath broke ope
> The Lords anoynted Temple, and stole thence
> The Life o'th'Building (2.3.67–70; 819–22),

echoing Matthew 27:51. Even Rosse remarks that

> Thou seest the Heauens, as troubled with mans Act,
> Threatens his bloody Stage: by th'Clock 'tis Day,
> And yet darke Night strangles the trauailing Lampe:
> Is't Night's predominance, or the Dayes shame,
> That Darknesse does the face of Earth intombe,
> When liuing Light should kisse it? (2.4.5–10; 930–35)

Earlier Macbeth had projected this vision before the murder, before the bell of the Day of Judgment rang at Lady Macbeth's bidding: "Now o're the one halfe World / Nature seemes dead" (2.1.49–50; 629–30). Later he

203

admits to seeing Duncan's "gash'd Stabs' " which "look'd like a Breach in Nature, for Ruines wastfull entrance" (2.3.113–14; 878–89). What remains is to realize the totality of the annihilation, for he once knew, had the firm premonition that, it would also apply to him: "This euen-handed Iustice / Commends the Ingredience of our poyson's Challice / To our owne lips" (1.7.10–12; 484–86).[266] For Duncan's virtues will "pleade like Angels, Trumpet tongu'd, against / The deepe damnation of his taking off" (1.7.19–20; 493–94), and "Heauens Cherubin, hors'd / Vpon the sightlesse Curriors of the Ayre, / Shall blow the horrid deed in euery eye" (1.7.22–24; 496–98), abroad like the horses of the Apocalypse with their fateful message.

Macbeth's "Bloody Instructions" (1.7.9; 483) can, through such lexias, become the play's prolonged but inciting event. For the playgoers at the Globe in 1606 this Doomsday play echoes the weekly sermons they were required to hear. The sounds and the sense were deeply familiar. "The sunne shalbe turned into darkenes . . . before the great and terrible daie of the Lord come" (Joel 2:31). There will be earthquakes, the sun and moon will be dark, and stars will fall (Mark 13:19, 24, 25). There will be voices, thunder, lightning, earthquake (Revelation 8:5).[267] Moreover, when Lenox describes the "vnruly" night of Duncan's death—

Where we lay, our Chimneys were blowne downe,
And (as they say) lamentings heard i'th'Ayre;
Strange Schreemes of Death,
And Prophecying, with Accents terrible,
Of dyre Combustion, and confus'd Euents,
New hatch'd to th' wofull time.
The obscure Bird clamor'd the liue-long Night.
Some say, the Earth was feuorous,
And did shake (2.3.55–62; 802–11)

—he recites eight of the traditional signs of the Last Judgment that were still pictured on church walls, in stained glass, in church sculpture, and, during the childhood of the playgoers of 1606, in the children's picture books of the Bible. They were also illustrated in the several editions of *Christian Prayers Meditations in English, French, Italian, Spanish, Greeken and Latine,* continuously published since 1569. Macbeth remains at the heart of the imagery, "in blood / Stept in so farre, that should I wade no more, / Returning were as tedious as go ore" (3.4.135–37; 1419–21), but the chief apparation is not Banquo but the horses who keep reappearing throughout *Macbeth,* like the wild couriers carrying cherubin. There are

Duncan's horses that "Turn' d wild in nature, broke their stalls, long out, / Contending 'gainst Obedience, as they would / Make Warre with Mankinde" and then did "eate each other" (2.4.16–18; 943–46). There are ghostly, deadly horses heard: by the murderers who fail to see them as they wait to kill Banquo and Fleance, the future Scottish royal line; and those Macbeth does not see when leaving the witches for the second time (4.1.138–40; 1690–92). There are Macbeth's own: the one sent to Lady Macbeth which initiates her complicity in Duncan's death (1.5.35–37; 384–86) and the horsemen Macbeth sends "to skirre the Country round" and to "Hang those that talke of Feare" (5.3.35–36; 2255–56). Together they echo another well-known part of the Scripture, the horsemen of the Apocalypse.[268]

The playgoer at this Doomsday play may be sensing what the end of the world would be like, or judging what it is that causes or signals the end of the world. But that the play was about the end of the world is inescapable. In the final act, at the final battle for Macbeth's earthly kingdom, Macduff calls for trumpets—"Make all our Trumpets speak, giue thē all breath / Those clamorous Harbingers of Blood, & Death" (5.6.9–10; 2391–92). The trumpet, as in George Gascoigne's *Droomme of Doomes Day* (1576, 1586), is the trumpet announcing the Last Judgment. The vision of that day, brought onstage in 2.3, remains inexorable, inescapable.

Religious Lexias

Although the church also provided the basic markers in individual and social life—christenings, weddings, funerals—"the Reformation did not produce a Protestant England," Christopher Haigh writes; "it produced a divided England."[269] The broad-based state-supported Anglican Church whose polity was developed by John Jewel early and Richard Hooker later in the reign of Elizabeth I attempted also to embrace the Puritan wing of Protestantism, which believed in parish autonomy and services stripped bare of unnecessary ritual, as well as small separatist groups such as the Anabaptists and Family of Love. The Catholics were also divided. There were the recusants who continued to practice their faith actively if secretly, the noncommunicants who attended Anglican services but did not take communion, and the schismatics who took Protestant communion while remaining Catholic in belief. Since nonconformity or plain speaking was tantamount to treason and considered a felony, men and women exercised caution. They also practiced dissimulation. For some this was not only a way of life; it was the only way of life their faith permitted. There was also a good deal of changing of faiths with the change of state religion under each of the Tudor monarchs beginning with Henry VIII. Lawrence Stone cites the case of Edward, Earl of Derby, who

> was brought up a Catholic, swallowed the monastic estates when the opportunity offered, raised no open protest against the Edwardian innovations in religion, was a loyal supporter of Mary and the Catholic reaction, and an equally loyal servant of Elizabeth and was fairly diligent as a magistrate in enforcing Anglican worship after 1559. His real views about the problem of salvation are obscure, to say the least: his policy was one of support for established authority and the maintenance of social and political order.[270]

Those who changed beliefs with a change of rulers were known disparagingly as "time-pleasers"—something Maria calls Malvolio in Shakespeare's *Twelfth Night* (2.3.148; 840).

Nevertheless, the national religion always followed the monarch's own practices under the Tudors, and James, who argued for the divine right and divine authority of kingship—he changed his title from "your royal sovereign" to "your sacred majesty"—was especially firm on such matters. He insisted that as King he was the head of the church, a tradition devolving from the time of Henry VIII's break with the Roman papacy. For James, parity or autonomy in individual Puritan churches was incompatible with both state and church polity. T.H. recalls a sermon by the Bishop of London at Paul's Cross on Monday, August 5, 1604, in which he declared

> that his Maiesty had made a protestation before God and his Angels, that he was so constant for the maintenance of the Religion publikely in England professed, as that hee would spend his owne dearest bloud in the defence therof, rather than the Truth should be ouerthrown: and that if he had ten times as many more kingdomes as he hath, he would dispend them all for the safety and protection thereof; and likewise, that if he had any childrē that should out-liue him, if they should maintayne or vp-hold any other Religion, he desired of God, that he might see them brought to their graues before him, that their shame might be buried in his life time, neuer to be spoken of in future ages.[271]

Preaching before the King at Whitehall on Coronation Day, March 24, 1606, Lancelot Andrewes put it in a slightly different way: "And to what end a King? *Quid faciet nobis?* 'What will a King do unto us?' It hath beene said already; he will look that euery one do not that which is good in his own, and evil in God's eyes."[272] State and church under James were thoroughly intermingled: the royal coat of arms displaced the holy rood in the chancels of the churches; the state appointed, directly or indirectly, the two archbishops, twenty-six bishops, and parish clergy that numbered eighty-six hundred in the seventeenth century; the liturgy was prepared by and approved by the state, and state-read homilies were required cultural practice. The Letanie of the 1605 edition of the *Book of Common Prayer* asks God to deliver men "From all sedition and priuie conspiracie, from all false doctrine and heresie, from hardnesse of heart, and contempt of thy Word and Commandement" (fol. B2). William Wilkes took such matters to the local level. "It qualifieth the *Magistrate* to rule with conscience, in the dread of his iudgement, whose prouidence is the producer of order; it maketh the subiect for conscience, willing to obay, fearing the seueritie of diuine reuenge, which followeth them that are wilfully disobedient vnto *order*," he writes in his *Obedience or Eeclesiasticall Vnion* (1605). "So conscience the daughter of Religion, keepes them both, awefall to swarue from that which is right, & makes diligent obseruers of all effectuall furtherances of the Churches peace, the sure conseruatorie of *kingdomes* happinesse" (sigs. D2–D2v).

Such firmness was vital. Elizabeth's speech to her bishops in 1585 is only an open admission of what remained residual turbulence in church affairs:

> You suffer many ministers to preach what they list and to minister the sacraments according to their own fancies . . . to the breach of unity: yea, and some of them so curious in searching matters above their capacity as they preach they wot not what—that there is no Hell but a torment of conscience. Nay, I have heard there be six preachers in one diocese the which do preach in six sundry ways. I wish such men to be brought to conformity and unity: that they . . . preach all one truth; and that such as be found not worthy to preach, be compelled to read homilies . . . for there is more learning in one of those than in twenty of some of their sermons. And we require you that you do not favour such men . . . hoping of their conformity . . . for they will be hanged before they will be reformed.[273]

James's own attempt to regulate the English church firmly was one of his first, and abiding, concerns.

James's own connections with the church began with the Scottish kirk on July 29, 1567, when, little more than a year old, he was crowned King James VI of Scotland in the Church of the Holy Rude, the parish church of Stirling: the first Protestant coronation in Scottish history. The sermon was preached by John Knox, the charismatic leader of the kirk who had been recalled from exile in 1560 and who, as the sole minister at St. Giles Cathedral in Edinburgh, was preaching twice each Sunday and three more times during the week to congregations that often numbered in the thousands. "I assure you," the English ambassador Thomas Randolph wrote to Sir William Cecil in 1561, "the voice of this one man, John Knox, is able in one hour to put more life in us than five hundred trumpets continually blustering in our ears."[274] Knox's leadership was uncontested. As the author of the Church Order and the Book of Discipline, which prescribed the organization of a kirk freed from Catholicism, and as an important instigator of the translation of Psalms and the Geneva translation of the Bible used in Scotland and England alike, he was widely known as the leading Calvinist in both countries. His force came from his unshaken belief that he had been called to serve the kirk by God and was God's chosen prophet: "God hath revealed vnto me secretes vnknowne to the worlde," he remarked in a sermon on 1 Timothy 4 preached in 1566 (sig. A2v). This is also the basis of the claim that he is a founder of Scottish resistance theory. In his *First Blast of the Trumpet against the Monstrous Regiment of Women* (1558) he likened his own pronouncements to those of Jehu and Daniel, prophets who had preceded him:

> The same prophets for comfort of the afflicted and chosen saintes of God, did lie hyd amongst the reprobate of that age (as commonlie doth the corne amongst the chaffe) did prophecie and before speake the changes of kingdoms, the punishments of tyrannes, and the vengeance which God wold execute upon the oppressors of his people. The same did Daniel and the rest of the prophets everie one in their season. . . . And further it is our dutie to open the truth reveled unto us, unto the ignorant and blind world, unlest that to our owne condemnation we list to wrap up and hyde the talent commited to our charge. (fols. 2–4v)

"Knox brought to mind Daniel before all other prophets," Katharine R. Firth observes, "because he wished to make it clear that the prophet had not only the power of moral exhortation but clearly also that of pre-science."[275] What was at stake was authority. Knox argued a hierarchy of spiritual grace and the kirk's organization by presbyteries that were independent of the state and in spiritual matters superior to it. Knox died on November 24, 1572, spending his last hours listening to Scripture; he was succeeded by an equally strong-minded Andrew Melville.

At times the swelling self-confidence of the kirk and the actions of its proponents breached the line separating church and state, as in the Raid of Ruthven in 1582. One consequence was the "Black Acts" of Parliament in 1584, restoring episcopacy and denouncing the first group of presbyteries set up in 1581. One of the "Black Acts" condemned those who made "contumelious spechis" denying the King and Council and instead "ratefies and apprevis and perpetuallie confirmis the royall power and auctoritie over all statis alsweill spirituall as temporall."[276] But James made a significant strategic error in 1587 when he annexed the Scottish benefices to the Crown to address a chronic shortage of money. By 1592 the extreme Presbyterians, led by Melville, succeeded in establishing presbyteries by law, and so eliminating the whole episcopal order de facto. Throughout the 1590s James worked mightily to restore the bishops whose form of episcopacy was similar to that of the Established Church of England. The Scottish kirk, led by Melville, continued to oppose him and in the process grew so proud and contemptuous that one day in 1596 at Falkland Palace Melville took the King by the sleeve and publicly called him "God's sillie vassal." Melville preached a religion that in Scotland robbed James of his claim of divine right. "There are two kings and two kingdoms in Scotland," Melville argued. "There is Christ Jesus the King and His kingdom the Kirk, whose subject King James the Sixth is, and of whose kingdom not a king, nor a lord, nor a head, but a member":[277] it was Knox's language with Queen Mary Stuart, James's mother, all over again. So intractable and so vocal was Melville, in fact, winning most of the ministers of the kirk to his beliefs, that in 1606, the year of *Macbeth,* James made Scottish business English: he summoned several of the kirk's leaders to London, attempted to negotiate with them, and sent those who remained recalcitrant to the Tower of London.

James was in the midst of his initial journey from Edinburgh to London when he was presented with the Millenary Petition reportedly representing the views of one thousand Puritan English clergy. Although respectful in tone and moderate in demands, this "humble Petition of the Ministers of the Church of *England,* desiring Reformation of certaine Ceremonies, and abuses of the Church" made their views clear enough:

> We the Ministers of the Gospel in this Land, neither as factious men, affecting a popular Parity in the Church, nor as Schismatics aiming at the dissolution of the State Ecclesiastical; but as the faithful servants of Christ, and Loyal Subjects to Your Majesty, desiring, and longing for the redress of divers abuses of the Church; could do no less, in our obedience to God,

service to Your Majesty, love to his Church, than acquaint Your Princely Majesty, with our particular griefs,

    I. *In the Church-Service.* That the Cross in Baptism, Interrogatories ministered to Infants, Confirmation, as superfluous, may be taken away. Baptism not to be ministered by Women, and so explained. The Cap, and Surplice not urged. That Examination may go before the Communion. That it be ministered with a Sermon. That divers terms of *Priests,* and *Absolution,* and some other used, with the *Ring in Marriage,* and other such like in the Book, may be corrected. . . .

    II. *Concerning Church-Ministers.* That none hereafter be admitted into the Ministry, but able and sufficient men, and those to Preach diligently, and especially upon the Lord's day. . . .

    III. *For Church-Livings, and Maintenance.* That Bishops leave their Commendams; some holding Prebends, some Parsonages, some Vicarages with their Bishoprics. That double beneficed men be not suffered. . . .

    IV. *For Church-Discipline.* That the Discipline, and Excommunication may be administered according to Christ's own Institution: Or at the least, that enormities may be redressed. As namely, That Excommunication come not forth under the name of Lay persons, Chancellors, Officials, etc. That men be not excommunicated for trifles, and twelve-penny matters. That none be excommunicated without consent of his Pastor. That the Officers be not suffered to extort unreasonable fees.[278]

To strengthen their case, they drew on James's own words in the widely circulated *Basilicon Doron:* "And that yee may the readier with wisedome and Iustice gouerne your subiects, by knowing what vices they are naturallie most inclined to, as a good Physician, who must first know what peccant humours his Patient naturallie is most subiect vnto, before he can begin his cure" (1616 ed., sig. O2). They were quickly answered not by the King at first, but in *The Answere of the vicechancelor, the Doctors, both of the Proctors and other the heads of houses of the Universitie of Oxford* in October 1603:

> *God hath appointed his Maiestie vnto this kingdome.* It is true and wee magnifie the goodnesse of God for it, and congratulate his Highnes in the prosperous possession of it, from the ground of our hearts. But that God hath appointed him to this kingdome *for such a purpose as they conceite,* what spirit of divination is in them, that they should forespeake it? Nay rather, seeing almightie God hath ordained him as the great Physition (next and immediately vnder himselfe,) to take care of the body politique, both of this Church, and Common-wealth; he will surely cure such diseases, as these men are sicke of. (For turbulent and discontented humors, whether in Papist, or in Puritans are like to breede very daungerous diseases in a civil state): And not to be perswaded

(as they fondly imagine) by such suggestions as these, to alter that state of the Church, which is acceptable to God, honourable to his Highnes, comfortable to many thousand Ministers, the Nurse of good learning, admirable to strangers, approved by our Opposites, envied of our enemies, distastfull vnto none, but such as know neither how to rule, nor how to obey. (sigs. D1v–D2)

The King responded in another way: he called the Hampton Court Conference in January 1604 to iron out the differences and establish ecclesiastical polity and doctrine.

The Archbishop of Canterbury John Whitgift and eight bishops headed the eighteen members of the conference representing the Anglican Church; James limited the Puritan representation, whom he feared might be similar to the Calvinists in the Scottish kirk, to four. He displayed his own considerable competence in doctrinal issues: he had studied theology, church history, and the Scriptures himself. After a long discussion about absolution and confirmation he declared himself satisfied "so that the manner might be changed and some things cleared."[279] He agreed, at the urging of the bishops, to allow only ministers to perform baptism, although there might be occasions where this would be performed in private houses. Excommunication was to be abolished. When they insisted on presbyterian government, James grew angry; such a form "as well agreeth with a monarchy as God and the Devil" (102). He claimed that a theology of "the necessary certainty of standing and persisting in grace" entailed a "desperate presumption."[280] "No bishop, no king."[281] Nor would James budge on marriage ceremonies without rings, and baptisms without signing the cross. He insisted on keeping the regulation that all ministers would be required to wear square caps and surplices in church and vowed his enduring commitment to a preaching ministry. When on the final day of three John Raynolds asked for a period of time for such a transition for many of the more strict Puritan preachers, James agreed; and in July he issued a proclamation giving ministers until the end of November 1604 to "resolve either to conform themselves to the Church of England, and obey the same, or else to dispose of themselves and their families some other ways."[282] "We do require all Archbishops, Bishops, and other Ecclesiastical persons, to doe their vttermost endeuours by conference, arguments, perswasions, and by all other wayes of loue and gentlenesse to reclaime all that be in the Ministerye, to the obedience of our Church Lawes," the King concludes in his proclamation of July 16 from Oatlands: "And the like aduertisement doe we giue to all Ciuill Magistrates, Gentlemen, and others of vnderstanding, as well abroad in the Counties, as in Cities and townes,

Requiring them also, not in any sort to support, fauour, or countenance any such factious Ministers in their obstinacie" (sig. G5). In his published report sold in St. Paul's Churchyard, the King's chaplain, William Barlow, praised James as "a Living Library, and a walking Study" (84); Thomas Bilson, Bishop of Winchester, in his coronation sermon, noted that he spoke before a "learned king" (sigs. C3–C3v), and Richard Martin, Master of the Middle Temple, in his "Speach . . . to the King" (1603), called James a living example of Plato's philosopher-king (sig. B2v). He was, as he wished to be, compared to Solomon, the wise ruler of the Old Testament, in works by Hugh Broughton in 1605 and John Dod in 1606.

But the King who would maintain absolute authority in government would also brook no opposition in his leadership of the church. In his inaugural speech to Parliament on March 19, 1604, James claimed "it is sedition in subjects to dispute what a King may do in height of his power."[283] He continued:

> At my first comming, although I found but one Religion, and that which by my selfe is professed, publikely allowed, and by the Law maintained: Yet found I another sort of Religion, besides a priuate Sect, lurking within the bowels of this Nation. The first is the trew Religion, which by me is professed, and by the Law is established: The second is the falsly called Catholikes, but trewly Papists: The third, which I call a sect rather then Religion, is the *Puritanes* and *Nouelists,* who doe not so farre differ from vs in points of Religion, as in their confused forme of Policie and Paritie, being euer discontented with the present gouernment. . . . As for mine owne profession, you haue me your Head now amongst you of the same Religion that the body is of. As I am no stranger to you in blood, no more am I a stranger to you in Faith, or in the matters concerning the house of God. And although this my profession be according to mine education, wherein (I thanke God) I sucked the milke of Gods trewth, with the milke of my Nurse: yet do I here protest vnto you, that I would neuer for such a conceit of constancy or other preiudicate opinion, haue so firmly kept my first profession, if I had not found it agreeable to all reason, and to the rule of my Conscience.[284]

After Whitgift's death in 1604, James's new Archbishop of Canterbury, Richard Bancroft, continued to impose uniformity and eliminate any irregularity. In 1606 Bancroft issued a new set of Canons, admittedly Calvinist in doctrine but supporting Anglican liturgy, especially where the Puritans were objecting the loudest. They largely sidestepped the most troubling issue, that of predestination, noting that it was a difficult term and best left alone; clergy were warned against discussing it in sermons but leaving it rather to the debates of learned men. The Canons of 1604 were the first complete codification of Stuart ecclesiastical life. They were passed by convocation in June 1604 and confirmed by the King in September. They spelled out the power of excommunication as resting solely in the governor of the church—the King himself—to be issued to anyone refusing to comply with the legislation. It provided efficient machinery, too, for the deprivation of ministers who failed to comply with the laws. Although the King at first thought all Puritans were subversive Presbyterians of the kind he had fought against so long in Scotland, he softened when, in the course of investigating the Northamptonshire petitioners, he found "good and loving subjects, rather blinded . . . with indiscreet zeal than otherwise carried by any disloyal intentions,"[285] but nevertheless proceeded: in 1604–5 a record number of clergy were deprived of their parishes. Some of them must have been known to some of the playgoers in 1606. Then the English Solomon set about to complete a set of actions that made him the final authority for the complete and immutable law of the church and its practices. He ordered a new translation of the Bible, completed and given his name in 1611, that would displace the current Geneva Bible with its Calvinist glosses, especially to those passages on which he had established his divine right (1 Samuel 11 and Jeremiah 29), glosses he found "very partial, untrue, seditious, and savouring too much of dangerous and traitorous conceits."[286] Finally, with a proclamation from Westminster on March 5, 1604, he declared the authorization and uniformity of a new *Book of Common Prayer* "to settle the affaires of Religion, & the Seruice of God" (sig. F3).

The force of James's stand on church matters and the swiftness with which he acted caused widespread dissension, upheaval, and anxiety. Nor were the Catholics exempt for long. Nicolo Molin wrote to the Venetian Doge and Senate on March 11, 1604:

> Just as the Catholics were beginning to hope for a satisfactory solution of the religious question, encouraged by the liberation of so many ecclesiastics, which they attributed to a good disposition on the part of the King and Council, a Proclamation was issued, ordering the Jesuits and priests to leave the kingdom by the 19th–29th of this month under pain of the laws already in force against them. Some think that this step is taken against the priests because in all recent conspiracies they have had a great share, and that the King will use rigour with ecclesiastics only, and will treat the lay Catholics gentle. The tone of the Proclamation makes this clear; besides the King has remitted the recusancy fines, which were an insupportable burden, amounting to thirty per cent. of the income. Others think that the King and Council, knowing how many Catholics there are in the country, do not wish to drive both

213

lay and ecclesiastics to desperation at one and the same moment, but that after the clergy have been expelled the laity will gradually be crushed.[287]

A year later, on March 2, 1605, while Shakespeare was writing *Macbeth,* Molin wrote to Venice about the Puritans who, he said, "are firmly resolved not to submit to the Bishops":

> Eight days ago, in Saint Paul's, the Cathedral Church of this city, the Archbishop of Canterbury, the Bishop of London, and other Bishops held a meeting, and summoned to their presence all the Puritan ministers and preachers. They called upon them to swear to observe the constitutions recently published by the Bishops, and to promise to recognize the Bishops as their superiors. As the Puritans resolutely and boldly refused, the more audacious were deprived of their benefices and ordered to leave the kingdom within a month, others have been suspended, others granted twenty days to make up their minds. This has caused a great turmoil in this city, which is full of people who belong to the Puritan sect. Daily meetings are held in private houses. The party shows a determination not to yield, but to take every step for the preservation of their freedom and authority. The King thinks of nothing else than of humbling the pride and audacity of this party; but he meets with much opposition, for among his Council are certain members of the sect, who while seeking to protect their fellows, point out to the King that it is unwise to raise such a hubbub about a matter of so small moment, for after all it is merely a question of ceremonies . . . in fact . . . it is desirable that his Majesty should favour the Puritans, for nothing would give such encouragement to the Catholics as the persecution of Puritans, who are the King's most obedient subjects, wheras the Catholics, owing to their dependence on the Pope and other sovereigns, must always be the object of alarm and suspicion.
>
> The King, after listening to the arguments on both sides, displayed extreme annoyance and said he was amazed that a doubt should be raised as to his competence to punish either party if they showed themselves disobedient. He declared that he was resolved to proceed against the Puritans and their ministers, who refused to conform and swear obedience to the canons, and to deprive them of their benefices and expel them from the kingdom. (223–24)

Indeed, the Puritans mounted a strong counterattack that would have made George Buchanan and John Knox proud. They argued that James ignored the worship of other Reformed churches and that divines in England served not only the Church of England but also international Calvinism with headquarters in Geneva, where the Geneva Bible now widely used in England had originated. They cited the Second Commandment (Exodus 20:4–6) to refute the use of the sign of the cross in baptism and kneeling in communion, saying that when the King spoke in opposition to Scripture itself he and his advisers were endangering themselves to the wrath of God. They insisted on their original proposition that all parts of a service must have clear and pronounced biblical authority and not be the subsequent practices of men. The debate continued throughout 1605 and into 1606; no playgoer could have been ignorant of the large number of books cascading out of the bookstalls in St. Paul's Churchyard dealing with various matters of religion, theology, and church polity. Calvin's commentary on Hebrews was translated out of the French. A book circulated reviewing the canons. *Certayne Questions* interrogated church practices. *Certaine Demands with their grounds, drawn out of holy writ* examined copes, surplices, the use of the cross, and communion in both kinds. *A Learned Epistle of M. Iohn Fraser* questioned the authority of excommunication, especially with Catholics, and declared it foolish. Henoch Clapham defended the King.

While controversy raged about London, changes were nevertheless taking place there and elsewhere. Keith Wrightson and David Levine declare that "there was a steady improvement in the quality of the clergy."[288] Whereas only 19 percent of the clergy in the diocese of Worcester had graduated from the university in 1560, they found this had climbed to 23 percent in 1580 and would be 52 percent in 1620. While Ian Archer found church attendance and the taking of communion increasing in 1606, it was still a slow process, uneven across the parishes, and especially dilatory in the extramural parishes which, serving a thousand households, could not provide a single service for all of them. But two major developments were already taking root in 1606: James insured that Protestantism would be the national religion despite the fact that both his parents had been Catholic and there had been some doubt about his disposition (especially in Rome) when he arrived in England; and he began a widespread upgrading of the quality of the ministry and the sermons that were preached. In time, the hot disputes would settle down and the nation as a whole would benefit.

At such a cultural moment, a moral play like *Macbeth*, about the rise and fall of an evil man, could not help but project religious significance and point to contemporary references in the world of the playgoers as much as to the world on the stage. Macbeth's single-mindedness is resonant of King James's own firm policies on church and state. His sense of prophecy and destiny align Macbeth with the Calvinist belief in predestination; the communion feast in 3.4 as a Black Mass raises questions about

Catholic as well as social ritual, and his tortured conscience—recall "Thou sowre and firme-set Earth / Heare not my steps" (2.1.56–57; 636–37)— suggests as well the secrecy and continual anxiety of separatists. The bell that summons him to kill the King (2.1.63; 642) invites him like the sacring-bell at Holy Mass, but toward damnation; it peals like the Protestant bells that announce deaths in the parish. Macbeth's rising certainty of his course of action opposes Lady Macbeth's increased sense of remorse. Macbeth's decision to slaughter all rebels contrasts with the holy King Edward the Confessor and the "Grace of Grace" pronounced by the new King Malcolm (5.9.38; 2525), if somewhat less with what King James was saying absolutely about religious dissidents.

But the play is saturated with religious situations, ideas, and images. "If in the Christian sense the only true tragedy is to forfeit one's soul," Edward Wagenknecht remarks, "then *Macbeth* has a strong claim to be regarded as Shakespeare's Christian tragedy."[289] Macbeth sees winds "fight / Against the Churches" (4.1.52–53; 1582–83). He asks one of the murderers if he is morally prepared for Banquo's death: "Are you so Gospell'd to pray for this good man, / And for his Issue, whose heauie hand / Hath bow'd you to the Graue?" (3.1.87–89; 1087–89). He is concerned about giving his "eternall Iewell" to "the common Enemie of Man" (3.1.67–68; 1058–59). He calls the sacred majesty of Duncan "The Lords anoynted Temple" (2.3.69; 821). Banquo would rest his life in the "great Hand of God" (2.3.130; 899). In her progressive madness, Lady Macbeth is one who "More needs . . . the Diuine, then the Physitian" (5.1.71; 2166). Even the famous speech of despair, "To morrow, and to morrow, and to morrow, / Creepes in this petty pace from day to day" (5.5.19–20; 2340– 41), is redolent of Scripture, drawing on the dusty death of Psalm 22:15, the candle of Job 18:6, the walking shadow of Psalm 39:6, and the idiot's tale of Psalm 90:9. *Macbeth* is a play, Victor Kiernan says, about a man who "is anguished by knowing he has bartered the gold of men's esteem for the tinsel of sovereignty."[290] *Macbeth* is a play about good and evil, grounded in anachronistic Scriptures, but its exfoliation of possible meanings fans out to a variety of ordered sets of religiously oriented lexias.[291]

PURITAN LEXIAS

The term *Puritans*, Patrick Collinson has said on several occasions,[292] has no specific content at this time but is an abstract and generalized form of abuse. Nonconforming Protestants preferred to be called "the godly," but the English by 1606 had others words for them: "precisians," "saints," "scripture men," "gospellers," even "hot gospellers," all derogatory. These Protestants believed in the application of Scripture to individual lives and condemned rituals and liturgy as papist (and therefore human) contamination of the Holy Word. In doctrine, they believed in justification by faith alone; it both freed them to talk personally to God and kept them free of graft and even simony. They believed in the doctrine of predestination, Calvin's addition to Luther's thought, which assured the elect of their salvation and "gave coherence and confidence," as Christopher Haigh has it, "to the godly congregation."[293] To demonstrate their election rather than reprobation, they were formidably strict in their behaviors. For them, all acts were moral. Their thought was all-inclusive and absolute.[294] The practice of faith for them consisted of private prayer and meditation; the reading of Scripture, often aloud to the family or in small groups or cells; and in attending church, where the exegesis of the Scriptures by the minister was helpful guidance for their own thoughts. In 1604, in a book aimed at James, Bacon writes that nonconformists did not want any special display in the delivery of sermons; they "would bee offended at one that comes into the pulpit, as if he came vpon the Stage, to play parts of prizes" (sig. E1). He goes on to describe their practice of prophesying in his *Certaine Considerations touching the better pacification and Edification of the Church of England*:

> The ministers within a Precinct, did meete vppon a weeke day, in some principall Towne, where there was some ancient graue Minister, that was *President* and an Auditorie admitted of Gentlemen, or other persons of leasure; then euery Minister successiuely, beginning with the yongest, did handle one and the same piece of Scripture, spending seuerally some quarter of an houre or better, & in the whole, some two houres; and so the Exercise beeing begun and concluded with prayer, and the *President* giuing a Text for the next meeting, the Assembly was dissolued. And this was as I take it, a fort-nights Exercise, which in my opinion was the best way to frame and traine vp *Preachers* to handle the Word of God as it ought to be handled, that hath been practised. (sigs. E1–E1v)

For Bacon such meetings were instructive and practical, but for James and his followers it made Scripture relative, open to Puritan interpretation. This he considered heresy and treason.

Protestants also resisted more openly. The *Vindiciae Contra Tyrannos*, for example, variously ascribed to de Mornay and Languet, earnest but not seditious Protestants, argues that the authority of Scripture and the examples of martyrs direct men to obey the commands of God before any earthly ruler. Although the King is elected to enforce the nation's laws, to avoid chaos when each man attempts to make his own, he serves at the pleasure of the people. They found cultural beliefs and practices in works other than the King's. The Bible, the most popular and most widely owned book in England in 1606, provided sacred Scripture; vernacular scripture was found in the second most popular book, John Foxe's *Actes and Monuments* (1563, 1596), known as the *Book of Martyrs,* stuffed with gripping stories of martyrs who resisted the government when it became oppressive and illustrated with passionate woodcuts showing men under arrest, or on trial, or—far the commonest—being burned at the stake for their beliefs. One striking series of woodcuts shows the same man slowly burned, the flames progressively higher, as in time men might have been burned had the Powder Plot proven successful.

Both on stage and off, however, this highly serious, self-conscious, and self-centered practice of Christian faith was ridiculed. In 1605, as just one example of many, Oliver Ormerod published *The Pictvre of a Puritane,* a dialogue between an Englishman and a German in which the Englishman tries to explain what a "Puritan" is really like:

> The Deuill (to disturbe this worke) stirred vp certaine hot-brained, inconsiderate, & Importune Preachers, who neither liked of the Pope, nor of the present estate of the Church, for want of some puritie, as they fancied. . . . Our Admonitors vsed the same Diabolicall Sophistrye for to prooue that there ought to bee a paritie of Ministers. . . . And thus by their plotting & plodding together, they (being few in number at the first) are growne to such a multitude, as that one of their owne preachers said openly in a Pulpit, he was *perswaded that there were 10000. of thē in England, & that the number of thē increased daily in euery place of al states & degrees.* . . . And although our gracious Soueraigne hath continually laboured since his Maiesties entrie into his Realme, vntil this present time, by what meanes he possibly could deuise, to extinguish and quenchth in raging heate: yet so fierie are many of these factious spirits, as that no liquor will quench their furious flames. (sigs. B3–B3v, H1, C2)

While nonconformists felt confident and in many cases chosen to act as they did, using the authority of their own belief and understanding of God to promote what could be viewed as pride and ambition, to others, the conforming Anglicans, they represented an ongoing, potentially rebellious danger invulnerably cloaked in their own religiosity. No playgoer in 1606 could be ignorant of such religious ideas and practices, nor their impregnable ideas of righteousness and resistance, no matter how he or she interpreted them.

A Puritan sense of predestination pervades Shakespeare's play. Robert G. Hunter writes:

> In *Macbeth* the suspicion that the events of the play are preordained is always present, and that suspicion is a logical inference from the witches' knowledge of the contents of future time. This possibility is given poetic expression by Macbeth's last great speech. There Macbeth's sense of himself as poised between meaningless yesterdays and meaningless tomorrows comes into focus on the enigmatic phrase "recorded time" [5.5.21; 2342] with its implication that all time, future as well as past, is history, a matter of eternal record. . . . His psychomachies are scimachies, the struggles of a walking shadow. The literary metaphor that concludes the speech is an answer to and a development of Rosse's early theatrical metaphor for the intervention of divine providence. (2.4.4–6; 929–31)[295]

Macbeth's lines have an eerie resemblance to the words of Henry Smith in his *Sermons* (1592) on the wicked, reprinted in 1601 and again in 1604: "All his lights are put out at once: he hath no soul fit to be comforted. . . . Our fathers, marvelling to see how suddenly men are and are not, compared life . . . to a player which speaketh his part upon the stage, and straight he giveth his place to another. . . . If any of you go away no better than you came, you are not like hearers, but like ciphers, which supply a place but signify nothing."[296] Such comments address the Calvinist doctrine of covenant theology, a defense against the Arminian abyss of uncertainty about a man's fate—what Lancelot Andrewes called a "great mystery." The understanding of election (and of reprobation) could be learned from Scripture, notably in God's promise to Abraham, and (as the covenant of grace) in the teachings of Christ, so that those who wished to assure themselves or confirm to others their salvation could find ready authority. Such a sense of an individual covenant with God could put everything into perspective.[297] While a discussion of predestination could be found in Calvin's *Institutes of Christian Religion* (1536; reprinted in 1599) and in his catechism (1561, reprinted in 1597 and 1602), John Knox defined it for the Scottish church at length in his *Answer to a great nomber of blasphemous cauillations* in 1560, reprinted in 1591 (sigs. B3–B3v). Reassigning it as the "pauline doctrine of assurance" rather than "the Calvinist interpretation of certainty,"[298] the Elizabethan Archbishop John

Whitgift and the ecclesiastical commissioners adapted this in the Lambeth Articles (named for the Archbishop's London palace) in 1595:

I: God from eternity has predestined some men to life, and reprobated some to death.

II: The moving or efficient cause of predestination to life is not the foreseeing of faith, or of perseverance, or of good works, or of anything innate in the person of the predestined, but only the will of the good pleasure of God.

III: There is a determined and certain number of predestined, which cannot be increased or diminished.

IV: Those not predestined to salvation are inevitably condemned on account of their sins.

V: A true, lively and justifying faith, and the sanctifying Spirit of God, is not lost nor does it pass away either totally or finally in the elect.

VI: The truly faithful man—that is, one endowed with justifying faith—is sure by full assurance of faith of the remission of sins and his eternal salvation through Christ.

VII: Saving grace is not granted, is not made common, is not ceded to all men, by which they might be saved, if they wish.

VIII: No one can come to Christ unless it be granted to him, and unless the Father draws him: and all men are not drawn by the Father to come to the Son.

IX: It is not in the will or the power of each and every man to be saved.[299]

Such a harsh set of beliefs was understandably softened by a number of religious writers interpreting Calvin. Richard Field, in *Of the Chvrch, Fiue Bookes* (1606), for example, comments that

> the *elect* and chosen of God are of two sortes; some elect onely and not yet called some both elect and called. Of the latter there is no question but they are the most principall parte of the Church of God: Touching the former they are not actually of the Church, but only *secundum praescientiam. & praedestinationem,* in Gods prescience, and predestination, who hath purposed what they shall bee, and knoweth what they will be. (sig. D1)

This follows H. Holland's *Aphorismes of Christian Religion* (1596), a popular epitome of Calvin's *Institutes,* which sets forth the Calvinist idea of double predestination:

> IX. Neither yet may any rashly define or pronounce, that he is in the number of the reprobate, if the signes of election as yet appeare not in him,

220

for some are called, later then others, yea the theefe on the crosse was not before the end of his life called: wherefore we may despaire of none vnlesse manifest signes be shewed, that he hath sinned to death: that is, against the holy spirite, neither yet may any securely sinne in hope of mercy, but euer remēber today, if ye heare his voyce harden not your harts: for God is not mocked. (sig. H7)

The scriptural bases given marginally are Matthew 20:3, Luke 23:40, 1 John 5:16, Hebrews 3:7, and Galatians 6:7. The most popular theologian in 1606, William Perkins, developed the same idea in *God's Free Grace and* ✔ *Man's Free Will* (1602). Thomas Tuke, in a letter prefacing Perkins's *Christian and Plaine Treatise* (1606), defines the understanding and actions of the reprobate:

And as for the Reprobate, they haue no more to do with this certainty, then they haue with saluation. As it is impossible for them to be saued, so it is possible for thē to be truly assured of their saluation. He that dreameth, may think he walketh, eateth, talketh, seeth, whē he doth not: and he may think he is awake, whē he is not. So these dreamers may think that they shalbe saued, and may sooth vp themselues as if they were cock-sure, but they are deceiued. He that is in a swoone, doth sometimes perswade himselfe that he seeth many strange sights, but his perswasion is false: so the Reprobates may thinke all things runne round, they may perswade themselues they are in Gods fauour and shall be saued: but as the things are false whereof they do perswade themselues: so their perswasion must needs also be as false. It is but a spirituall swoone, or diuelish dreaming, or dizzinesse, that doth so blinde their eyes, and beguile them. (sigs. E6–E6v)

For the Christian of 1606, the signs sought to guarantee election and the delusions of the reprobate could be indistinguishable.

Playgoers in 1606, then, might focus intensely on Macbeth's thoughts and behavior for signs of election, early or late, in the face of the deterministic prophecy of the weird sisters. Depending on which lines or moments become the lexias in their ordered sets of thought or interpretation, their judgments might vary. If Macbeth's murder of Macdonwald did indeed "memorize another *Golgotha*" (1.2.41; 61), he could be doing God's business to protect the royal state, and so the Captain would have it; if he is instead "*Bellona's* Bridegroom," as Rosse puts it (1.2.55; 79), he is the slaughtering god of war who has no Christianity in him. But the verdict might still be out: the Captain is describing Macbeth's Christlike actions against Macdonwald; Rosse is describing his brutality in punishing Cawdor. Since they are separate battles, they may suggest that Macbeth is subject to double predestination, and that we are unable to tell, so early on, the fate of his soul. While the three sisters in the next scene (1.3) suggest by the coincidence of their prediction and Macbeth's own premature yearning the fact that he will become King, his pride and his unspoken demonic pact with them suggest he is reprobate; but his astonishment at the awarding of the first of the two new titles, Cawdor (1.3.108–9; 214–15), argues that he is at the moment among the elect. His own deliberative understanding supplied through the privilege of soliloquy does not go far to answer the question.

> This supernaturall solliciting
> Cannot be ill; cannot be good.
> If ill? why hath it giuen me earnest of successe,
> Commencing in a Truth? I am *Thane* of Cawdor.
> If good? why doe I yeeld to that suggestion,
> Whose horrid Image doth vnfixe my Heire,
> And make my seared Heart knock at my Ribbes,
> Against the vse of Nature? Present Feares
> Are lesse then horrible Imaginings:
> My Thought, whose Murther yet is but fantasticall,
> Shakes so my single state of Man,
> That Function is smother'd in surmise,
> And nothing is, but what is not. (1.3.130–42; 241–53)

He is correct in saying about the titles of Glamis and Cawdor that in announcing them "Two truths are told" (1.3.127; 238), but he deludes himself at the same time by thinking that the three sisters, in adding a third ("thou shalt be King hereafter" [1.3.50; 150]), are in fact "soliciting" him. Had they done so, they would have made an infernal pact, as Lady Macbeth does more willingly in 1.5, where her vows (1.5.40–51; 391–402) are an anti-hymn deliberately inverting the *Veni Creator Spiritus* of the Pentecostal service, her own Black Mass.[300]

But Macbeth is not yet prepared to commit himself: "That Function is smother'd in surmise"; and yet "nothing is, but what is not" and, therefore, what is not is, or should be. If his unfixed hair suggests moral revulsion, he is among the elect by nature and is at this point saved; if it results from the fears that the sisters have discovered his innermost longings, he is reprobate and their appearance, perhaps sent from the Devil, has proven it. Even so, they may instead serve as a warning; under the doctrine of double predestination, they may be providing him with an occasion on which he can change the direction of his will. Read one way, they are the Fates and his world is a deterministic one, as predestination assumes. Read another way, they are warnings of a charitable God who plans yet to save

222

Macbeth. Later, when Macbeth has his own Black Mass at the coronation banquet, he replaces the customary icon of a crucified Christ with the image of the bloodied Banquo. It is a clear sign of reprobation. Yet Macbeth's ability to be frightened by such a reminder and to confront it, moreover—"a bold one, that dare looke on that / Which might appall the Deuill" (3.4.58–59; 1327–28)—argues his ability to make moral judgments still. If he is uncertain about his status, there is perhaps reason to seek out the witches one more time (4.1), yet in "conjuring" up their meaning by commanding that they reveal their meaning—"Answer me / To what I aske you" (4.1.60–61; 1590–91)—he becomes complicit in their acts and in their spectral visions, agent as well as witness. When he learns that his wife too is past medical cure—"Therein the Patient / Must minister to himselfe" (5.3.45–46; 2268–69)—her reprobate status may seem to confirm his own. If we read these moments of the play in this way, Macbeth and Lady Macbeth are both, by Calvinist standards, reprobate, and their behavior is exemplary in telling us, as it would the playgoers of 1606, exactly what reprobation is and what it feels like. To those who felt in 1606 that Macbeth's destiny was to gain the crown and lose it, as brutally as he won it, by regicide, the issue is how, in a world of double predestination, one might determine his or her own status with God.

"As Fortunes man rides the Horse," Sir Walter Ralegh writes in the preface to his *Historie of the World* (1616), "so Fortune her selfe rides the Man" (sig. B3). Whether Macbeth is a criminal or a victim, whether or not he will be saved sooner or later, the issue was further compounded in 1606 by what Ralegh develops as the sense of two kinds of Providence—general Providence for the world at large, and special Providence, which is God's intervention into a historical moment (sigs. B4v–B5). At the cultural moment of *Macbeth*, one common way to confront such questions was by paying attention to prophecy—and for centuries in England, prophecies had always involved a political dimension. When the three sisters provide their predictions in 1.3 and their visionary spectacle in 4.1, the political element is central. At the same time, prophecies involved events within a providential frame; God's will was also involved. For the playgoers of 1606, prophecy was commonly where religion and politics intersected.

Prophecy also indicated a deep desire for change—political, social, or individual. Keith Thomas observes:

> It was the existence of rebellious feeling which led to the circulation of prophecies. . . . It was the rebels who read into them an application to current

events and they did so because they wished to do so. At times of stress, men scrutinized these ancient myths with a view to extracting from them some sanction for the dangerous courses of action upon which they proposed to embark. Under the pressure of change they most felt the need for reassurance that what was happening had been foreseen by their ancestors and was in some sense part of a larger plan. It was no accident that the periods when prophecies were most prominent in English life were precisely those of rebellion, discontent and violent change. . . . Prophecies disguised the break with the past,[301]

while offering a providential patina. Thomas finds all kinds of prophecies—written, pictorial, oral; hundreds of them—but the use made of them was often vital and crucial:

> To understand the need for such a validating charter it should be recalled that for sixteenth-century Englishmen the existing political order was not regarded as a matter of mere practical convenience, changeable at will. It was divinely ordained, and God's sanctions would fall upon the rebel wicked enough to challenge it. When a man embarked upon the drastic course of insurrection he was flouting all the moral teaching of the day and cutting himself loose from the whole social and political order in which he had been nurtured. At such times prophecy made its appeal by providing a sanction for such dramatic action. Ideally the prophecy was a divine one, indicating that rebellious activity was in accordance with God's will. (503)

Nevertheless, Richard Greenham warns in his *Workes,* reprinted in 1605, that belief in prophecy could be dangerous. "There are three kinds of false Prophets," he says. "The first teacheth false doctrine. The second teacheth true doctrine, but applieth it falsely. The third teacheth and applie well, but liue ill" (sig. 2N6). While Macbeth commits regicide, Lady Macbeth marks the act with an omen to verify it: "Hearke, peace: it was the Owle that shriek'd, / The fatall Bell-man, which giues the stern'st goodnight, / He is about it" (2.2.3–4; 650–52). The deed is shortly confirmed again by the Old Man: "On Tuesday last, / A Faulcon towring in her pride of place, / Was by a Mowsing Owle hawkt at, and kill'd" (2.4.11–13; 937–39). The second, specular prophecy, which seals Macbeth's doom with the presence of Banquo and his line of spectral kings, is confirmed by the visionary sound of horses. Now the man who was confident he would "iumpe the life to come" (1.7.7; 481) says to Lenox, "I did heare / The gallopping of Horse. Who was't came by?" (4.1.139–40; 1691–92). Lenox explains they were but "two or three my Lord, that bring you word: / *Macduff* is fled to England" (4.1.141–42; 1693–94), but for Macbeth they fulfill the apocalyptic vision of "th'cracke of Doome" (4.1.117; 1664). Judgement has come.

Time, thou anticipat'st my dread exploits:
The flighty purpose neuer is o're-tooke
Vnlesse the deed go with it. From this moment,
The very firstlings of my heart shall be
The firstlings of my hand. And euen now
To Crown my thoughts with Acts. (4.1.144–49; 1697–1702)

The analogy is with Macduff. When he learns that his family has been killed because he was not present to protect them, he takes this as heavenly judgment:

Sinfull *Macduff,*
They were all strooke for thee: Naught that I am,
Not for their owne demerits, but for mine
Fell slaughter on their soules: Heauen rest them now. (4.3.224–27; 2074–77)

But unlike Macbeth's fearful killing of Duncan when he overheard the grooms—

One cry'd God blesse vs, and Amen the other,
As they had seene me with these Hangmans hands:
Listning their feare, I could not say Amen,
When they did say God bless vs (2.2.26–29; 682–85)

—Macduff relishes in his vengeance: "Behold where stands / Th'Vsuprers cursed head" and sees the event heralding a providential time: "The time is free" (5.9.20–21; 2506–7).

In *The First Part of a Treatise concerning Policy and Religion* (1606), Thomas Fitzherbert proposes that God sometimes uses evil to good ends and, further, that "true Religion [is necessary] for the perfection of policy."[302] Like the world of *Macbeth,* where the law of tanistry is converted into primogeniture, the passing from Tudor to Stuart marked change where the relatively free, the self-made world of Elizabethan courtiers and adventurers, was giving way to the Jacobean insistence on unquestioned authority. Predestination was giving way to the Anglican dictates. When Banquo hears the same predictions that Macbeth does, his language takes on a different coloration in reply: "If you can looke into the Seedes of Time, / And say, which Graine will grow, and which will not" (1.3.58–59; 158–59). His sense of time is developmental and the prophecies mere nutrients to unfolding actions. Future events result from the germination of God and nature, not the intervention of man's choices and actions. He has no apprehension until Duncan later appropriates his thoughts in a more dangerous, perhaps more sinister, way: "I haue begun to plant thee, and will labour / To make thee full of growing" (1.4.28–29; 313–14). Macbeth gives his agency a developmental cast, too, to placate his anxiety:

> Besides, this *Duncane*
> Hath borne his Faculties so meeke; hath bin
> So cleere in his great Office, that his Vertues
> Will pleade like Angels, Trumpet-tongu'd against
> The deepe damnation of his taking off:
> And Pitty, like a naked New-borne-Babe,
> Striding the blast, or Heauens Cherubin, hors'd
> Vpon the sightlesse Curriors of the Ayre,
> Shall blow the horrid deed in euery eye,
> That teares shall drowne the winde. (1.7.16–25; 490–98)

Those who are guilty will be punished, and the wind, whirling while the grief of the informed swallows up the death in universal pity, is both more startling and sadder in the honesty of its recognition, but it too is seen as a natural and developing series of events in a world controlled by God. The passivity of Macbeth and Banquo subsequent to the prophecies in 1.3 are in sharp contrast to the more decisive opposition dramatized in acts 4 and 5. Malcolm's battle cry—"the Powr'es aboue / Put on their Instruments" (4.3.238–39; 2089–90)—declares a healthy faith in doing God's will, and young Siward's wounds "on the Front" (5.9.13; 2494) suggest that he too is one of the Church Militant fighting in the service of God. In the terms of the play, both are opposed to Macbeth, who began by "Disdayning Fortune, with his brandisht Steele" (1.2.17; 36); they turn instead to the kind of prophecy represented by Edward the Confessor: "He hath a heauenly guift of Prophesie, / And sundry Blessings hang about his Throne / That speake him full of Grace" (4.3.157–59; 1989–91). Malcolm returns to this sense of prophecy, where politics and religion intersect, by echoing it at the play's close: "This and what needfull else / That call's vpon vs, by the Grace of Grace, / We will performe in measure, time, and place" (5.9.37–39; 2524–26).

For a great many at the cultural moment of *Macbeth,* the way to determine God's will was by following the dictates of individual conscience. Holinshed first applies this possibility to King Kenneth, one of Shakespeare's models for Macbeth: "Shortly after, he beganne to shewe what he was, in steede of equitie practising crueltie. For the pricke of conscience (as it chaunceth euer in tyrantes, and suche as attayne to any astate by vnrightuous meanes) caused him euer to feare, least he should be serued of the same cuppe, as he had ministered to his predecessour" (sig. Q3v). William Baldwin's *A Treatise of Morall Philosophie containing the sayings of the wise,* published by Thomas Paulfreyman in an enlarged fourth edition in 1605, provides a common definition for 1606: "The conscience of man, is (in himselfe) a secret knowledge, a priuie opener, testimonie or witnesse, an accuser, an inward troubler, or tormentor, it is also a sacrificer or ioyfull quieter of the minde of man in all his doings" (sig. T1v), adding, "A troubled conscience tormenteth the minde" (sig. T5v). James gave an important place to conscience, too, in the *Basilicon Doron,* pointing out how it might go astray:

> Aboue all then, my Sonne, labour to keepe sound this conscience, which many prattle of, but ouer few feele: especially be carefull to keepe it free from two diseases, wherewith it vseth oft to be infected; to wit, Leaprosie, and Superstition: the former is the mother of Atheisme, the other of Heresies. By a leaprouse conscience, I meane *a cauterized conscience,* as *Paul* calleth it, being become senselesse of sinne through sleeping in a carelesse securitie as King *Dauids* was after his murther and adulterie, euer til he was wakened by the Prophet *Nathans* similitude. And by superstition, I meane, when one restraines himselfe to any other rule in the seruice of God, then is warranted by the word, the onely trew square of Gods seruice.
>
> As for a preseruatiue against this Leaprosie remember euer once in the foure and twentie houres, either in the night, or when yee are at greatest quiet, to call your selfe to account of all your last dayes actions, either wherein ye haue committed things yee should not, or omitted the things ye should doe, either in your Christian or Kingly calling. (sigs. N4v–N5)

For many, however, the most widespread and reliable source was William Perkins, the prolific Cambridge Calvinist whose eighteen collected *Works,* printed in 1603 and again in 1605, contained his popular *Discourse of Conscience.* His discussion of the stages of the corrupted or leprous conscience would seem to limn Macbeth's progress through the play. "The minde is the storehouse and keeper of al manner of rules and principles," Perkins begins. "It may bee compared to a booke of law, in which are set down the penall statutes of the land. The dutie of it is to preferre and present to the conscience rules of diuine law whereby it is to giue iudgement," adding, "Memorie serues to bring to minde the particular actions which a man hath done or not done, that conscience may determine of them" (*Works* [1605], sig. 3I2v). The evil conscience grows progressively troubled, according to Perkins, with its later stages producing shame, sorrow, and fear (sig. 3I3).

> The third [stage] is *feare,* in causing whereof conscience is verie soreible. If a man had at the delights and pleasures that heart can wish, they cannot

doe him any good if conscience be guiltie. . . . Yea the guiltie conscience will make a man afraid, if he see but a worme peepe out of the ground: or a sillie creature goe crosse his way; or if hee see but his owne shadow on a suddaine; of if he doe but forecast an euil with himselfe. . . .

Terrours of conscience, whiche are more vehement, cause other passiōs in the body, as exceeding heat, like that which is in the fitte of an ague, the rising of the entrals towards the mouth. . . .

The fourth is *desperation,* whereby a man through the vehement and constant accusation of his conscience comes to bee out of al hope of the pardon of his sinnes. . . .

The last is a *perturbation* or disquietnesse of the whole man: whereby al the powers and faculties of the whole man are forthe of order. Esa. 57.20. *The wicked is like the raging of the sea that can not rest, whose waters cast up mire and durt.* (sig. 313)

There is a simple test for Perkins: *"whatsoeuer is done with a doubting conscience is a sinne"* (sig. 313v). His views were widely influential among both conforming and nonconforming Protestants.

Later he discusses the dead conscience:

The causes why conscience lyeth dead in all men, either more or lesse, are many. I. Defect of reason or vnderstanding in crased braines. II. Violence and strength of affections, which as a cloud doe ouercast the minde, and as a gulfe of water swallow vp the judgement and reason: and thereby hinder the conscience from accusing; for when reason cannot doe his part, then conscience doth nothing. For example: some one in his rage behaues himselfe like a madde man, and willingly commits any mischiefe without any controlment of conscience: but when choller is downe, he beginnes to bee ashamed and troubled in himselfe, not alwaies by grace, but euen by the force of his naturall conscience, which when affection is calmed begins to stirre, as appeareth in the example of Cain. (sig. 3L1v)

The dead conscience, he continues, has two degrees: the slumbering conscience, which is benumbed to evil, and the seared conscience, which is terrified (sig. 3Llv).

Such a conscience is to be taken heede of, of vs as being most daungerous. It is like a wilde beast, which so long as he lies a sleepe seemes verie tame and gentle, and hurte no man: but when hee is roused, he then awakes and flies into a mans face, and offers to pull out his throat. And so it is the maner of a dead conscience, to lie still and quiet euen through the course of a mans life. . . . And heathen Poets knowing this right well, haue compared euill conscience to Furies pursuing men with fire-brandes. (sig. 3Llv)

He concludes his treatise, "Experience sheweth that men of excellent giftes by vsing badde conscience, lost them all" (sig. 3L4v). Perkins stresses that although a conscience can be benumbed, it cannot be totally extinguished. "Ile goe no more," Macbeth tells his wife after the slaying of Duncan (2.2.49; 708). "Hanged conscience will revive and become both gibbet and hangman to them either in this life, or the life to come," Perkins says in his dedication to William Piryam.[303] "As they had seene me with these Hangmans hands: / Listning their feare, I could not say Amen" (2.2.27–28; 683–84), Macbeth says, *listening* to their fear as if it were his own. "Me thought I heard a voyce cry, Sleepe no more: / . . . / *Macbeth* shall sleepe no more" (2.2.34, 42; 691, 700).

That conscience bothers both Macbeth and Lady Macbeth is evident in their initial shame at what they are about to do: "Starres hide your fires, / Let not Light see my black and deepe desires: / The Eye winke at the Hand; yet let that bee, / Which the Eye feares, when it is done to see" (1.4.50–53; 338–41); "Come thick Night, / And pall thee in the dunnest smoake of Hell, / That my keene Knife see not the Wound it makes, / Nor Heaven peepe through the Blanket of the darke, / To cry hold, hold" (1.5.50–54; 401–5). Evil for Macbeth troubles his conscience from the start, catches him up in its dilemma.

> If th'Assassination
> Could trammel vp the Consequence, and catch
> With his surcease, Successe: that but this blow
> Might be the be all, and the end all. Heere,
> But heere, vpon this Bank and School of time,
> Wee'ld iumpe the life to come (1.7.2–7; 476–81),

with the telling addition, "But in these Cases, / We still have iudgement heere" (1.7.7–8; 481–82). Following Perkins, Macbeth's conscience moves from terror ("I am afraid to thinke what I haue done: / Looke on't againe, I dare not" [2.2. 50–51; 709–10]) to desperation ("What Hands are here? hah: they pluck out mine Eyes" [2.2.58; 720]) to perturbation ("O full of Scorpions is my Minde, deare Wife" [3.2.36; 1194]). His remorse knows both envy of Duncan ("After Lifes fitfull Feuer, he sleepes well" [3.2.23; 1179]) and concern for his wife ("Cure her of that: / Can'st thou not Minister to a minde diseas'd, / Plucke from the Memory a rooted Sorrow, / Raze out the written troubles of the Braine, / And with some sweet Obliuious Antidote / Cleanse the stufft bosome, of that perillous stuffe / Which weighes vpon the heart?" [5.3.39–45; 2261–67]). "A mans conscience may be quiet for a season," Baldwin writes in his *Treatise of Morall Philosophie,* "but when the perseverance of gods terrible iudgements and the prick of sinne doe rise in our hearts, then such graceless & vaine trust is vtterly ouerblowne, and vanisheth away to naught" (sigs. T5–T5v). Macbeth's final words in confronting Macduff disclose a seared conscience battling a sense of futility:

> I will not yeeld
> To kisse the ground before young *Malcolmes* feet,
> And to be baited with the Rabbles curse.
> Though Byrnane wood be come to Dunsinane,
> And thou oppos'd, being of no woman borne,
> Yet I will try the last. Before my body,
> I throw my warlike Shield: Lay on *Macduffe,*
> And damn'd be him, that first cries hold, enough. (5.8.27–34; 2468–75)

The benumbed conscience, judge and jury, becomes its own final reward. Earlier in Edinburgh, in 1594, Alexander Hume wrote his own *Treatise of Conscience* which also registers the understanding of conscience at this later cultural moment. According to Hume, sinners with a bad conscience suffer fear, despair, lack of sleep, and evil dreams, and they seek relief by blaming others, consulting sorcerers, and looking for death.[304]

Catholic Lexias

"April 26, 1602: Here were three seminary priests hanged and quartered the last week," John Chamberlain writes in a letter, "but what is that among so many?"[305] The Catholic population had grown considerably during the years of Elizabeth I. In the diocese of Llandaff, for instance, there were 13 known recusants in 1577, 381 in 1603. In the North Riding there were 300 in 1580–82, 950 in 1590–95, and 1,150 in 1603. Part of the increase reflected in the statistics was no doubt Walsingham's and Cecil's elaborate system of informers, but many more held onto the old religion than were at first suspected and new Catholics were arriving from the Continent. Households would disguise priests as tutors, stewards, or (in one case) a gardener.[306] Lawrence Stone again provides an overview:

> In every county it was the peers and leading squires who took the initiative
> in breaking with the Anglican Church. For example, when recusancy began in
> Norfolk in the 1570s, it was headed by the three great families of Cornwallis,
> Bedingfield, and Silyarde. The utter dependence of the Jesuit mission of the

1580's upon these upper gentry and aristocratic hosts is admirably demonstrated by Father John Gerard's frank and vivid account of his activities. He first settled at Grimston in Norfolk, the house of Edward Yelverton. "I stayed openly six or eight months in the house of that gentleman. . . . During that time he introduced me to the house and circle of nearly every gentleman in Norfolk, and before the end of the eight months I had received many people into the Church, including one of my host's brothers, his two sisters, and later his brother-in-law." From Grimston Father Gerard moved to Lawshall in Suffolk, the house of Henry Drury, where he was kept safe for two years from persecution, provided with funds, and given opportunities for proselytizing the neighbouring gentry at hunting parties and other social occasions. Later benefactors were William Wiseman of Braddocks, Elizabeth Lady Vaux, and Anne Countess of Arundel. It was the Countess who for a long time sheltered Father Robert Southwell and his secret printing-press after he left Lord Vaux's house in Clerkenwell, who tried to obtain the release of Father Watson by bribery after his arrest, who paid for English girls to be placed in nunneries abroad, who founded the Tertianship for the English fathers at Ghent. She clearly played an extremely important role in the success of the Jesuit mission to England.[307]

The English College at Rome trained several recusants to reenter England as part of the underground priesthood, but there were other colleges, at Rheims and elsewhere. In his *Charge giuen at Norwich Assises* (1606), Sir Edward Coke notes that

you may then consider, that from the eleueth yeare of Queene *Elizabeths* Raigne, vntill the third yeare of our now Soueraignes gouernment, the Papists haue continually labored to aduance the supremacy of the *Romane Church,* which to accomplish they haue contended thirty foure yeares, in which time they haue not omitted to practise Treasons and Rebellions onely amongst vs here at home. But haue also complotted to bring vpon vs *Forraine Inuasions. . . .* [T]hese persons, and that Religion whereby *Iesuites* and *Seminaries* are receiued, protected and concealed, are equally to be accounted daungerous, for were there not such receiuers amongst vs, *Romes* state, Traytors would not so fast come, swymming from *Tyber* hither to arriue at *Tyburne.* Onely I conclude, therefore, that if in great *Brittaine,* there were no Papists, this *Monarchy* should be as free from treason as any Nation in the world. (sigs. F2–F2v)

From the nonconformists' perspective generally, the Catholic faith also represented a liturgy preventing the direct communication between the believer and his or her God; especially in the practice of absolution, Catholics disregarded and abolished "what ought to have been soterially advantageous bouts with doubt and discouragement."[308] Another Catholic practice, the casting out of devils (which Puritans took up as exorcism), was likened to witchcraft.

At the announcements of James's accession to the throne of England in March 1603, the King's own ancestry—both his father and mother were Catholic—caused considerable relief at first among English recusants and high hopes in many quarters. In June 1603 the English College at Rome celebrated James's accession with a Solemn High Mass and wished the King "a long life and happy reign." Only two months earlier, on March 24, the King had written Henry Percy, Earl of Northumberland, "As for the Catholics, I will neither persecute any that will be quiet and give but an outward obedience to the law, neither will I spare to advance any of them that will by good service worthily deserve it";[309] he was, after all, *rex pacificus*. The trouble with that was that he had already offered similar pledges to the English Protestants in 1600 in a bid to win their support for his succession to the crown of England, pledges that he would not only maintain and continue the profession of Gospel already practiced in England, but would not suffer or permit any other faith to be professed. The Puritan faction called him on such inconsistency. On February 22, 1604, James issued a proclamation from Westminster announcing the banishment of all priests from England:

> *Royal proc.* We doe hereby will and command all maner of Iesuites, Seminaries, and other Priests whatsoeuer, hauing Ordination from any authoritie by the Lawes of this Realme prohibited, to take notice That our pleasure is, that they doe before the nineteenth day of March next ensuing the date hereof, depart foorth of our Realme and dominions, And that for that purpose it shalbe lawfull to all Officers of our Ports, to suffer the said Priestes to depart from thence into any forreine parts, betweene this and the said nineteenth day of March: Admonishing and assuring all such Iesuites, Seminaries, and Priests of what sort soeuer, That if any of them shalbe after the said nineteenth day taken within this Realme or any our dominions, or departing now vpon this our pleasure signified, shall hereafter returne into this Realme or any our dominions againe, that they shalbe left to the penaltie of the Lawes here being in force concerning them, without hope of any favour or remission from vs (sig. F2);

they would, that is, be convicted of felony as traitors. It became, once more, an issue of governance for James. In his inaugural speech to Parliament on March 19, barely a month later, his language was tough and sure:

> Their point of doctrine is that arrogant and ambitious Supremacie of their Head the Pope, whereby he not onely claimes to bee Spirituall head of all

Christians, but also to haue an imperiall ciuill power over all Kings and Em-
perors, dethroning and decrowning Princes with his foot as pleaseth him, and
dispensing and disposing of all Kingdomes and Empires at his appetite. The
other point which they obserue in continuall practise, is the assassinates and
murthers of Kings, thinking it no sinne, but rather a matter of saluation, to
doe all actions of rebellion and hostilitie against their naturall Soueraigne
Lord, if he be once cursed, his subjects discharged of their fidelitie, and his
Kingdome giuen a prey by that three crowned Monarch. . . . [O]f one thing
would I haue the Papists of this Land to bee admonished, That they presume
not so much vpon my Lenitie (because I would be loath to be thought a
Persecuter) as thereupon to thinke it lawfull for them dayly to encrease their
number and strength in this Kingdome, whereby if not in my time, at least in
the time of my posteritie, they might be in hope to erect their Religion againe.
No, let them assure themselues, that as I am a friend to their persons if they
be good subiects: so am I a vowed enemie, and doe denounce mortall warre
to their errors.[310]

In the summer of 1604 he promised Parliament he would begin enforcing
penal laws against Catholics.

In 1603, one year earlier and two years before the Powder Plot,
Thomas Bell was claiming, in *The Anatomie of Popish tyrannie . . . of Secular
Priests and English hispanized Iesuites, with their Iesuited Arch-priest,* that
Jesuits "studie nothing but treason" and named those he knew: Persons,
Campion, Sherwin, Heywood, men "sent disloyally into this land from
Pope Gregory the 13" (3). In the index he calls Persons "an arrant Traytor,"
"a bastard," adding, "Parsons would be a Cardinall," "Parsons is a monster
of mankind," "Parsons is impudent and will affirme or denie anything."
He continues:

> Another thing also is much misliked by the secular priests, for it breedeth
> hatred to Catholics and danger, and that is the Jesuits equivocating, which
> you may term in plain English lying and cogging. For this amongst others is
> one of their rules; that a man framing to himself a true proposition, when he
> is asked a question, he may conceal thereof as much as he thinketh good. For
> example: one demanding of you whether, if the Pope should come in warlike
> manner to invade this land by force of arms, you would take his part or the
> Queen's; you framing this answer in your mind, "we will take the Queen's
> part if the Pope will command us so to do," may by their doctrine give this
> answer lawfully, viz. "we will take the Queen's part"—and conceal the rest;
> whereby he that asked the question is plainly deluded. (29–30)[311]

Equivocation, a device for Catholics, was redefined as an act of treason to
the Crown. The *Calendar of State Papers, Domestic* records some of the
surrounding events in 1603:

April 9. Fras. Tilletson, priest, to Sec. Cecil. Details a conversation with Capt. Fras. Burnell, about the feelings of the Jesuits and Papist on board his ship. They hope the speedy death of the King and his posterity, but mention no means of accomplishing it. (2)

June 25. Richard Bancroft, Bishop of London, to the King. Arrest of Dr. Cecill and other priests, taken at Gravesend. Creichton, a Jesuit, is at Calais. (17)

June? Declaration of the English Catholics to the King. Asserting their loyalty, and soliciting the free exercise of their religion. Fr. With a note that their request was granted. (18)

July. Tower. Lord Cobham to the Lords. Denies being concerned in Sir Griffin Markham's plot, or in any conspiracy against the King's life. (26)

Aug. 20? Note by Sir Griffin Markham, sent to Lord Cecil. The first motive that Watson used to engage him in the conspiracy to poison thē and his issue, was an assurance of the high rank of some of the conspirators. (33)

But the suspected opposition was only said to increase. In 1605, T. H. writes in *The Late Commotion of certaine Papists in Herefordshire* that the Lord of Star Chamber

began to shewe how certainly his Maiesty was informed, That the number of Papists in England was mightily increased, since his Maiesties comming, and that Popish Priests and Iesuites (factors for the Pope) lay lurking in many corners of this land, to seduce his Maiesties subiects from their due and lawfull allegeance vnto their rightfull Prince, to the acknowledgment of a forrain power and authority, namely, the Pope of Rome. Then also, that his Maiesty maruayled, how it happened, that Papists could so increase daily, or Priests and Iesuites be intertayned within his Kingdomes, considering, that his Lawes are in force against them . . . it being a thing impossible, that Priests and Iesuites should swarme so thick as they doe in any partes of England, or Wales, vnlesse Iustices of Peace in those parts where they frequented, were carelesse of their place and office. (sigs. B2–B2v)

In another work of 1605, *A Relation of the State of Religion,* Edwin Sandys reports that Scotland, Denmark, and Sweden "haue wholly cast off the Papacy" while in England there are still four thousand "sure Catholicks . . . with foure hundred English Roman Priests, to maintaine that *militia*" (sig. P2v).

The Catholics, meantime, still in hiding, found access to presses and replied at large to the government-inspired works circulating in London.

S. R., for example, in *An Answer to Thomas Bels Late Challeng* (1605), is biting in tone:

> Now let vs compare the practise of Protestants touching the deposition of Princes, with the practise of the Pope, since the tyme that Protestants began. They haue within this 70. yeares partly deposed partly attempted, as far as lay in thir power, one Emperor, three French Kings, two Kings of Spaine, one of Denmarke, one of Pole-land, one Queene of England, and one of Scotland. They haue slayne one King of Nauar, one of Denmarke, one Queene of Scotland, one Queenes husband, and burnt the bodies of two other Kings, & attēpted to murder one French King, two French Queenes, & one King of Scotland. Whereas the Pope neuer slew any Prince at al, but haue saued the liues, & kingdomes of many, & since Protestāts began, haue deposed one onely King Henry 8. and one Queene Elizabeth and spared both King Edward, the 6 & many Kings of Dēmark, & Sweuland, besids a great number of German Princes. And his Maiestie is so far from danger of being deposed by him, as he hath already censured al those that moleste, or disturbe his maiesty and his maiesty gratefully acknowledgeth him selfe *beholden to the Pope for his temporal cariage, and diuers kind offices towards him,* euen then when ther was lesse cause of such kindnes, then now is. (sigs. B5–B5v)

With a marginal note pointing to Knox and Goodman, S. R. sums, "Catholiques say, Kings may be deposed, Protestants say, they may be deposed and hanged" (sig. B2v).

Prior to the discovery of the Powder Plot on November 5, the entries on Catholics and treason increase in the *Calendar of State Papers, Domestic*. On June 15 it is learned that Father Garnet has told Catholics to lie low and that the Pope has prohibited them from doing harm for the present. On June 18 William Morgan is examined and his letters taken and read. On June 22 lists of the names of recusants are presented to the Crown, being taken down at such events as the funeral of Alice Wellington of Allensmore on March 21, helpers in the rescue of Leonard Marsh on May 24 (1603), and a mass celebrated at Whitfield and the Darren. Sometime in June, grants of recusants' lands were processed, awarding the property to those who convicted them. The Articles of Visitation for the archdiocese of Norwich (1605), doubtless representative, asks for the names of all religious dissidents (sig. A4). After the Powder Plot, Parliament passed "An Acte for the better discovering and repressing of Popish Recusants" (3. James I ch. iv), which notes that "pᵉʳsons Popishly affected doe . . . hide their false Hearts" (cf. *Macbeth* 1.7.83; 566) and attend the state church only as a cover. Marginalia meant to serve as an index begin with the notation of penalties of £20 the first year if those found are not taking communion, noting an increase to £40 the second year and £60 the third. But the notes show increasing paranoia. That for section 19 reads, "Penalty on Persons harbouring Recusants, or keeping Servants who do not attend Church, £10 per month." A note to the following act reads, "Recusants, &c. neglected to attend Divine Service for Three Months, shall not remain within Ten Miles of the City of London, and shall give their Names to the Lord Mayor, or nearest Justice of Peace, &c. Penalty £100."

In 1606 Shakespeare's elder daughter, living in Stratford, was prosecuted for recusancy.

Following the failed Powder Plot in November 1605, the Crown redoubled its efforts against Catholics. In 1606 the government "crafted an oath of allegiance," writes Linda Levy Peck, "that spoke directly to contemporary Catholic resistance theory" (87). The oath asked those who took it to "sweare, That I doe from my heart abhorre, detest and abiure as impious and Hereticall, this damnable doctrine and position, That Princes which be excommunicated or depriued by the *Pope,* may be deposed or murthered by their Subiects or any other whatsoeuer" (*Works* [1616], sig. X6). At the same time, Convocation drafted and passed canons supporting royal power and authority. Canon 2 declares it is a great error to make any claim that any "civil power, jurisdiction, and authority, was first derived from the people [and] is originally still in them, or else is deduced by their consents . . . and is not God's ordinance originally descending from Him."[312] There was also a renewed attack on the Catholics' cultural practice of equivocation. Frank L. Huntley has gathered some of the documentary evidence from the *Calendar of State Papers, Domestic:*

> Dec. 13, 1605. Examination of Richard Andrew, priest. "Thinks the Pope may absolve subjects from allegiance to a heretic King; equivocation is lawful where the right of the questioner is not acknowledged; has heard of the Book of Equivocation, but has not seen it."
>
> Feb. 5, 1606. Durham. "Arrest and examination of John Sicklemore, alias Ward, a priest; curious specimens of his equivocations. Salisbury's Exposure of Equivocations is greedily read."
>
> Feb. 14, 1606. "Reflections on the increasing power of the Jesuits,"

as well as the exasperated response of Coke: "their perfidious and perjurious Equivocating, abetted, allowed, and justified by the Jesuits, not only simply to conceal or deny an open Truth, but religious to aver, to protest upon Salvation, to swear that which themselves know to be most false;

and all this, by reserving a secret and private Sense inwardly to themselves; whereby they are, by their ghostly Fathers, persuaded, That they may safely and lawfully elude any Questions whatever."[313]

The work to which Coke refers is by Henry Garnet, Provincial for the Society of Jesus in England. It was originally written in defense of the priest and poet Robert Southwell, to whom it is dedicated, in 1598 but only came into the hands of the government in 1605. The original title of Garnet's manuscript was *A treatise of equivocation wherein is largely discussed the question whether a Catholicke or any other person before a magistrate being demaunded uppon his oath whether a Prieste were in such a place may (not w*th*standing his perfect knowledge to the contrary) without Periury and securely in conscience answere, No, with this secret meaning reserved in his mynde, that he was not there so that any man is bound to detect it.* Thinking better of this later, Garnet crossed out the title and substituted *A treatise against lying and fraudulent dissimulation . . . published for the defence of innocency and the instruction of ignorants.* Garnet discusses not only mental reservation but other strategies as well: using words true in one sense and false in another, obliqueness, ambiguity, amphibology. Equivocation for Garnet was to be used only for the health of the soul or body, piety, charity, just profit, or necessity, and not to be employed lightly lest it dishonor God. Perez Zagorin notes that

> Garnet further maintained that to protect themselves, Catholics would be justified in equivocating in an oath whether it was enforced or taken voluntarily. Even in the case of an oath containing an explicit reununciation of equivocation, he held that it was allowable to swear it with a mental reservation. In this instance, a lie would at most be a venial sin, whereas no lie could be as sinful as divulging the truth to the harm of other Catholics. In such a matter, he added, even plain lies without a true reserved meaning did not so offend by their falsity that he would not reward Catholics for their fidelity.[314]

The pamphlet was discovered by the government in the chambers of one of the accused conspirators in the Powder Plot, Francis Tresham; Coke, as Attorney General, is quoted in the official pamphlet about the conspiracy, *A True and Perfect Relation,* as saying equivocation was "a very labyrinth to lead men into error and falshood" (sig. I1). Zagorin notes that the doctrine may have been conceived first by William Allen and the Jesuit Robert Persons when they drew up exercises in casuistry at the seminary of Douai-Rhiems around 1586. They argued that a priest could change his name, clothing, and appearance, such pretense being lawful, and cited as an authority Christ's own disguise before his disciples at Emmaus (Luke 24:28).

Allen and Persons argued further that the responsibility for the deceit of equivocation rested with the questioner, not with the respondent: since he took the answer for a fact, he was actually deceiving himself (187).

Secular Catholics in England who chafed under Clement VII's order in 1598 to report to a Jesuit lashed out at this cultural practice. William Watson, in *A Deacordon of Ten Quodlibetical Questions concerning Religion and State* (1602), called equivocation "secret concealed treason" (32). A lay supporter, Anthony Copley, said in *An Answer to a Letter of a Iesuited Gentleman* (1601) that Jesuits were guilty of "lying legierdemaines, & dishonest dealings . . . consisting of mentall evasions in their speech . . . half-fac'd tearmes, tergiversations . . . whole and demie-dublings, the vulpecular fawne . . . holding it lawfull to be forsworne in too manie cases . . . of all which they have an Arte . . . whereby they take away . . . not onlie all good religion from amongst men, but also even morall honestie" (92–93). The leading Protestant critic was Thomas Morton, who writes a mock arraignment of mental reservation in *An Exact Discoverie of Romish Doctrine in the Case of Conspiracie and Rebellion* (1605) and in *A Full satisfaction, concerning a Double Romish Iniquitie* (1606) labels equivocation "lying falsehood" (47) and calls on the government to torture priests at the rack to wring the truth from them.

The Jesuit Superior Garnet was brought to trial on March 28, 1606, for complicity in the Powder Plot: he had known of it, although he did not actively participate in the preparation of the powder. According to Giustinian (writing the court at Venice, which was also at odds with the Jesuits), "His Majesty was present *incognito*," a spy, as it were, in his own house. Giustinian continues:

> The interrogation did not afford that satisfaction with Catholics expected, nay, he has scandalized the very heretics, and greatly disgusted his Majesty. For besides being on his own confession—not wrung from him by torture, as he affirms, but compelled by irrefutable evidence—cognisant of the plot, he further endeavoured to excuse his previous perjury, in affirming that he was ignorant of it, by a disquisition on equivocation, maintaining, a certain doctrine which has shocked the ministers, and especially the King, who is particularly versed is such matters, and has caused a great outcry against the Roman religion.[315]

This was an official report; the gossip about London held Fr. Henry Garnet to be an alcoholic. On March 27 John Chamberlain wrote Dudley Carleton from London that Garnet "comforts himself with sack to drown sorrow."[316] The execution set for May 1, 1606, was postponed to May 3, and Chamberlain writes, perhaps amused at his own wit, that Garnet "shifts, falters, and equivocates, but 'will be hanged without equivocation.'"[317] Arthur N. Stunz proposes that Shakespeare's drunken Porter, who seems obsessed with the word *equivocation* (2.3.9–13; 751–54), is a staged parody of Garnet and quotes a manuscript letter from John More to Ralph Winwood as evidence: "Garnet was executed on Saturday, on the west side of Paul's, ending his life in a reasonable constant manner, confessing his guiltiness of treason, but with many protestations endeavouring to clear the suspicion of his incontinence with Mrs. Vause [Vaux] wherein it is thought he served himself with his accustomed equivocation,"[318] incontinence being a charge the Porter makes of "Lecherie" (2.3.29; 771). The term stuck: in 1614 Ralegh applies it to Joshua in his *Historie of the World:*

> Out of the passage between *Josua* and the *Gibeonites,* the Doctrine of keeping Faith is so plainly and excellently taught, as it taketh away all evasion, it admitteth no intrusion nor leaveth open any hole or out-let at all to that cunning perfidiousnes, and horrible deceit of this later age, called *Equivocation.* . . . I say therefore, that if ever man might have served himself by any evasion or distinction, *Josua* might justly have done it. For he needed not in this case the help of *Aequivocation* or *Mentall Reservation.* For what he sware, he sware in good Faith. (sigs. 2D6–2D6v)

The government found its own metaphor. In the official *Answere to Certaine scandalous Papers, Scattered abroad vnder colour of a Catholicke Admonition,* printed in 1606 by the King's printer Robert Barker, it is said of the examiners of the conspirators, "All our actions are vpon the open stage, & can be no more hidden then the Sunne" (sig. E2).

The Porter in *Macbeth* indicates the widespread interest in equivocation in 1606. He may parody Garnet, or even embody him to a degree, but most importantly, he announces the play as a site of equivocation and, by extension, lying and treason. "Knock, knock," the "Porter of Hell Gate" (2.3.6; 74) says, "Who's there in th'other Deuils Name? Faith here's an Equiuocator, that could sweare in both the Scales against eyther Scale, who committed Treason enough for Gods sake, yet could not equiuocate to Heauen: oh come in, Equiuocator" (2.3.7–13; 750–54). The farmer and the tailor, one who suffers from an excessive harvest and one who makes others suffer by theft, are similarly made equivocators, justifiers of their own actions, and for a brief moment the Porter "had thought to haue let in some of all Professions, that goe the Primrose way to th'euerlasting Bonfire" (2.3.19–21; 760–61). In his world, everyone potentially equivocates—or lies, or feigns, as he does as an actor on the stage of the Globe professing his own dissimulating, and (by his own admission) damned.

In fact, the Porter wisely introduces a central scene of equivocation. The very concept of equivocation forms a set of lexias. Macbeth equivocates in describing Duncan's murder by using mental reservation:

> Who can be wise, amaz'd, temp'rate, & furious,
> Loyall, and Neutrall, in a moment? No man:
> Th'expedition of my violent Loue
> Out-run the pawser, Reason. Here lay *Duncan,*
> His Siluer skinne, lac'd with his Golden Blood,
> And his gash'd Stabs, look'd like a Breach in Nature,
> For Ruines wastfull entrance: there the Murtherers,
> Steep'd in the Colours of their Trade; their Daggers
> Vamannerly breech'd with gore: who could reframe,
> That had a heart to loue; and in that heart,
> Courage, to make's loue knowne? (2.3.108–18; 873–83),

a speech that deliberately misleads by insinuating a counternarrative. Lady Macbeth interrupts at this juncture and is seen to faint, halting Macbeth, who veers very close to the whole truth, from telling more. It is not at all clear that the faint itself is not a dissimulation. After all, she had entered with questions of innocence—"What's the Businesse?"; "Woe, alas: / What, in our House?" (2.3.81, 87–88; 837, 846–47)—suggesting that both her role as hostess and her own royal ancestry have been deeply offended by the chaos and regicide. Her interrogation is analogous to Macbeth's counternarrative.

Later, Macbeth's famous invocation to the powers of darkness is also deeply equivocal:

> Come, seeling Night,
> Skarfe vp the tender Eye of pittifull Day,
> And with thy bloodie and inuisible Hand
> Cancell and teare to pieces that great Bond,
> Which keepes me pale. Light thickens,
> And the Crow makes Wing toth' Rookie Wood. (3.2.46–51; 1205–10)

For the audience at the Globe, the homonym *seel/seal* could refer to seeling the eyes of a hawk, stitching them shut to tame it to a purpose while thus blinded. But it could also allude to sealing away from light deeds better attuned to (and performed in) darkness of night and of spirit; or, yet again, sealing in action the intentions of the regicide or the predictions of the witches and thus canceling out an earlier bond to his father, Glamis, his newly awarded title of Cawdor, his king, country, wife, or service. As light thickens he seems to be likening himself to the solitary crow, a cultural metaphor for a bird of carrion (killing, preying, feasting on dead bodies) and ill omen (acting out the prognostications of the weird sisters), while attacking the community that is the rookery. But Macbeth, able to hold different periods in his mind simultaneously—"If it were done, when 'tis done, then 'twere well, / It were done quickly" (1.7.1–2; 475–76)—is naturally given to equivocation, especially in the sense of amphibology. "This supernaturall solliciting / Cannot be ill; cannot be good" (1.3.130–31; 241–42); "To know my deed, Twere best not know myself" (2.2.72; 738–39). He engages in a kind of equivocal conversation with his wife again and again:

> **Mac.**   This is a sorry sight.
> **Lady.**   A foolish thought, to say a sorry sight. (2.2.20–21; 675–76)

The mood for such thought and language is contagious. Duncan is deliberately oblique in rewarding Banquo:

> I haue begun to plant thee, and will labour
> To make thee full of growing. Noble *Banquo,*
> That hast no lesse deseru'd, nor must be knowne
> No lesse to haue done so: Let me enfold thee,
> And hold thee to my Heart (1.4.28–32; 313–17),

and he gets a deservedly ambiguous answer: "There if I grow, / The Haruest is your owne" (1.4.32–33; 318–19). In point of fact, the Folio text is not clear itself: Duncan may be addressing Banquo; he may be addressing Macbeth. Once unleashed, equivocation seems to occur in a galaxy of examples throughout the play. "When the Battail'es lost, and wonne" (1.1.4, 1.2.69; 6, 94). "Faire is foule, and foule is faire" (1.1.11, 1.3.38; 12, 137). Banquo will be lesser than Macbeth and yet greater (1.3.65–66; 165–66). Duncan observes that "The Loue that followes vs, sometime is our trouble" (1.6.11; 446). Banquo wants to lose no honor in gaining more (2.1.26; 605). Lady Macbeth finds the night is "Almost at oddes with morning, which is which" (3.4.126; 1409). Macduff's son is fathered yet is fatherless (4.2.27; 1741–42). Lady Macbeth walks with her eyes open but her senses shut (5.1.23–24; 2117–18). Other matters remain even less clear than seeming paradox might make them. When Macduff charges "He ha's no Children" (4.3.216; 2065), does he mean Malcolm, Macbeth, or both? How do the characters judge Macbeth at the end? "Some say hee's mad: Others, that lesser hate him, / Do call it valiant Fury" (5.2.13–14; 2190–91). The greatest equivocation may come early and serve as the premise of the play. When the witches, like Macbeth, combine past

(Glamis), present (Cawdor), and future (King) in 1.3, are they making intuitive statements, guessing, prophesying, or making determining proclamations? When Banquo also takes their remarks about kingship as possible—after all, it does assure him a line of kings—he seems himself redefined. Near the end, Macbeth in a moment of apparent insight says,

> I pull in Resolution, and begin
> To doubt th'Equiuocation of the Fiend,
> That lies like truth (5.5.42–44; 2366–68),

but he also leads us to the play's conclusion. Macduff in killing the wicked Macbeth has defeated the enemy of Malcolm's Scottish state. But he has also killed a king, spilled royal blood, which James claimed could never be justified. And within the bounds of the play, Macduff has become a new Macbeth to Malcolm. Worst of all, such a matter of equivocation condemns the Protestant cultural practice of an inner conversation with God, thereby undermining much of the cultural moment's religious language.

LEXIAS OF WITCHCRAFT

"The Land is full of Witches," Sir Edmund Anderson, Chief Justice of the Court of Common Pleas, remarked at the trial of Mary Glover in London is 1602; "they abound in all places."[319] He went on to announce that he himself had hanged more than two dozen. There may be some truth in this. Samuel, in George Gifford's *Dialogue Concerning Witches and Witchcraft* (1593), reprinted the next year, says "there is scarse any towne or village in all this shire, but there is one or two witches at the least in it" (sig. A4v). In another work, his *Discourse of the Subtill Practises of Deuilles by Witches and Sorcerers* (1587), Gifford defined his understanding of a witch through communal response:

> Some woman doth fal out bitterly with her neighbour: there followeth some great hurt. . . . There is a suspicion conceived. Within fewe yeares after shee is in some iarre with an other. Hee is also plagued. This is noted of all. Great fame is spread of the matter. Mother W. is a witch. She hath bewitched goodman B. Two hogges which died strangely: or else hee is taken lame. Wel, mother W. doth begin to bee very odious & terrible unto many. her neighbours, dare say nothing but yet in their heartes they wish shee were hanged. (sigs. G4–G4v)

For Gifford, witches were identified through circumstances; but it did not help, especially in villages, that they were associated with cunning women whose medical practice demonstrated magical knowledge and unexplained cures. Indeed, such women may have served condemned witches as models and exacerbated local accusations. Earlier, in his *Discoverie of Witchcraft* (1584), Reginald Scot found witches to be of common physical appearance too for the most part, and easily recognized:

> ONE sort of such as are said to bee witches, are women which be commonly old, lame, bleare-eied, pale, fowle, and full of wrinkles; poor, sullen, superstitious, and papists; or such as knowe no religion: in whose drousie minds the divell hath goten a fine seat; so as, what mischeefe, mischance, calamitie, or slaughter is brought to passe, they are easilie persuaded the same is doone by themselves; imprinting in their minds an earnest and constant imagination hereof. They are leane and deformed, shewing melancholie in their faces, to the horror of all that see them. They are doting scolds, mad, divelish; and not much differing from them that are thought to be possessed with spirits so firm and stedfast in their opinions, as whosoever shall onelie have respect to the constancie of their words uttered, would easilie beleeve they were true indeed.
>
> These miserable wretches are so odious unto all their neighbors, and so feared, as few dare offend them, or denie them anie thing they aske: whereby they take upon them; yea, and sometimes thinke, that they can doo such things as are beyond the abilitie of humane nature.[320]

Scot felt such judgments usually premature, arguing that a need to fix responsibility for certain events led to a kind of scapegoating and that older and relatively vulnerable women were often made village targets. Gifford is not quite so sure, and the *Dialogue* allows him to portray his uncertainty. But he knows what they are often said to do:

> The witches raise tempests, and hurt corne and fruites vpon the trees, the witches bring the pestilence among men, and murraine among cattell: the witches send their spirits and make men lame, kill their children and their cattell: their spirits cannot bee taken heede of, nor kept out with doores and wals as theeues and murtherers, but come in when they be sent, and doe so many harmes: for this cause I thought it a maruellous good worke to put all suspected to death, though some of them were innocent, that so sure worke might bee made to haue not one left. (sig. H3)

Witches became a handy explanation for accidents or bad luck or elderly scolds. Like Lady Macbeth, they were prone to hallucinate; they might also be agents of the Devil, their witches' marks as indelible as her "damned spots" (5.1.34; 2127).

243

The cultural practices of witchcraft and magic were ecclesiastical offenses dealt with by ecclesiastical courts until Henry VIII made them statutory. His statutes were revised and renewed by Elizabeth and by James. "An Acte against Coniuration, Witchcrafte, and dealinge with euill and wicked Spirits" (1604) repealed the Elizabethan statute of 1563 and advanced a stronger position:

> Be it further enacted . . . That if any person or persons, after the saide Feast of Saint Michael the Archangel next comming, shall vse, practise, or exercise any Invocation, or Coniuration, of any euil and wicked spirit, or shall consult, covenant with, entertaine, employ, feede, or reward, any euill and wicked spirit, to, or for any intent or purpose, or take vp any dead man, woman, or child, out of his, her, or their graue, or any other place, where the dead body resteth, or the skin, bone, or any other part of any dead person, to bee imployed or vsed in any maner of Witchcraft, Sorcery, charme, or Inchantment, or shal vse, practise, or exercise any Witchcraft, Inchantment, Charme, or Sorcerie, whereby any person shalbe killed, destroyed, wasted, consumed, pined, or lamed in his or her body, or any part thereof; That then euery such Offendor or Offenders, their Ayders, Abettors, and Counsellors, being of any the sayd offences duely and lawfully conuicted, and attainted, shall suffer paines of death, as a Felon, or Felons, and shall lose the priviledge and benefit of Clergie, and Sanctuary. (sigs. C8–C8v)

The statute reflects James's own stern judgments in his *Daemonologie* (1597, 1603); there is also some evidence that copies of the *Malleus Maleficium*, arguing demonology and published in Germany in 1484, were still in circulation. The sternest witch-hunters, like Judge Anderson, held to witchcraft as a felony because it was a heresy. Thus Sir Matthew Hale, the Chief Justice of the King's Bench, thought one of the country's most learned and wisest of judges, remarked in 1604, "That there are such creatures as witches be in no doubt at all; for, first, the scriptures have affirmed so much. Secondly, the wisdom of all nations has provided laws against such persons, which is an argument of their confidence of such a crime. And such has been the judgement of this kingdom, as appears by that Act of Parliament which has provided punishments proportionable to the quality of the offence."[321]

But there may be other reasons lurking beneath such acts and such statements. One of the chief authorities on Scottish witchcraft, Christina Larner, has noted that witches work by charms, failed charms, and favorable and unfavorable prophecies, and that these are closely connected to the curse. All of them have in common attempts to gain and secure power.[322] If the church threatened the state at any point as a competing source of authority, witchcraft, which often inverted holy services in its own cultural practices, represented a similar threat. Larner notes that "the principal source of charms were the prayers of the pre-Reformation church" (140), such as the vow Lady Macbeth takes in 1.5; or the Mass itself, as it is given darker terms in 3.3. Keith Thomas adds holy water, holy candles, bells, consecrated herbs, or sacred words as other cultural practices.[323] If the witches turn the world of *Macbeth* into a world of evil, then both the bell which Lady Macbeth rings to summon Macbeth to kill Duncan (2.1.61 S.D.; 642) and the taper she carries when sleepwalking (5.1.17 S.D.; 2111) are diabolic. Her summoning of evil spirits of the night (1.5.40; 391) and Macbeth's conjuring in the witches' cave (4.1.50; 1580) announce their own intimacy with evil. Indeed, the word *conjure* was an especially powerful one in 1606, carrying a number of meanings: to swear together by a private arrangement or contract; to plan a conspiracy; to constrain by oath or appeal to something sacred, to abjure; or to entreat, plead, beseech, or implore. Especially in the second meaning, it carried political overtones—and overtones of resistance or rebellion. It also had strong religious meaning. Since the Puritans often used the word to denounce recusant priests (whose acts were conjurations, i.e., black art), *conjurors* became a synonym for both papists and Jesuits. So Reginald Scot:

> I SEE no difference betweene these and popish conjurations; for they agree in order, words, and matter, differing in no circumstance, but that the papists doo it without shame openlie, the other doo it in hugger mugger secretlie. The papists (I saie) have officers in this behalfe, which are called exorcists or conjurors, and they looke narrowlie to other cousenors, as having gotten the upper hand over them. And bicause the papists shall be without excuse in this behalfe, and that the world may see their cousenage, impietie, and follie to be as great as the others, I will cite one conjuration (of which sort I might cite a hundred). (252)

At the Globe in 1606, Macbeth stumbles across the witches as if by accident (1.3); later (in 4.1) he searches them out in their cave: "How now, you secret, black, & midnight Hags? / What is't you doe?" he asks, and when he is told "A deed without a name," he replies, "I coniure you, by that which you Profess / (How ere you came to know it) answer me" (4.1.48–51; 1577–81). Thus the first prophecy, giving him a royal title, is succeeded by a spectacle of eight kings with "two-fold Balles, and trebble Scepters" whose "Crowne do's seare mine Eye-bals" (4.1.121, 113; 1668, 1660). By this point, however, playgoers may see and hear what was only darkly hinted before: that the play of *Macbeth* makes indivisible witchcraft and politics, conjuration and conspiracy, imagination and ideology, and finds them at once both dangerous and delusory.

Holinshed associates Macbeth with three women, but he does not call them witches:

> It fortune as Makbeth & Banquho iourneyed towarde Fores, where . . . sodenly in the middes of a laūde, there met them. iii. women in straunge & ferly apperell, resembling creatures of an elder worlde, whom when they attentiuely behelde, wondering much at the sight. . . . This was reputed at the first but some vayne fantasticall illusion by Makbeth and Banquho, in so muche that Banquho woulde call Macbeth in ieste kyng of Scotland, and Makbeth againe would call him in sporte likewise, the father of many kings. But afterwards the common opinion was, that these women were eyther the weird sisters, that is (as ye would say) ye Goddesses of destinie, or els some Nimphes or Feiries, endewed with knowledge of prophesie by their Nicromanticall science, bicause euery thing came to passe as they had spoken. (sigs. Q2–Q2v)

Holinshed introduces his own uncertainty. While the three women are not called witches, he is unsure whether they are the Fates or merely fortunetellers, and he does not speculate on the source of their special knowledge or the extent of their powers. Shakespeare does not call them witches, either, although at one point in the Folio text the First Witch says she was addressed as one (1.3.6; 104) and the stage directions call them that. But at the time, Scotland and witchcraft had long been associated. In early Scottish history, Kenneth I, who ruled from 844 to 860, passed the first important statute against witches and sorcerers; those convicted of witchcraft were subject to death by burning. From that time forward, northern Scotland, especially Forres (near present-day Inverness), was connected to the practices of witchcraft, and in 968 witches at Forres attempted to kill King Duff by slowly melting waxen images of him. Buchanan comments on this in his *Rerum Scoticarum Historia*.[324] But there was also a history of witchcraft connected to the Stuart line almost within living memory of the playgoers at the Globe in 1606. In 1479 the Earl of Mar was accused of practicing magic to shorten the life of his brother James III. During the troubled reign of James V (1513–42), one daughter of a noble house, Janet Douglas, Lady Glamis, was killed at the stake, having been charged with an attempt on the King's life through evil charms and poison.[325] In the decade preceding Macbeth there had been a series of relatively fierce witch-hunts in Scotland and a number of women had been found guilty and executed. And there were at least two published accounts that circulated in England: *Newes from Scotland* (1592), an anonymous pamphlet quite possibly prepared by James or on his behalf, and James's own treatise on *Daemonologie* (1597).

"Prior to 1590," Larner writes, "there were no serious or consistent attempts to persecute witchcraft in Scotland and no sign of any interest among lawyers or theologians in the theory of the demonic pact. It is not therefore surprising that James had no interest in the subject of witchcraft. . . . The dramatic change in the climate of opinion in Scotland, and in James himself, became apparent during the massive trials for treason by sorcery of 1590–91."[326] A large coven of witches at North Berwick, at times thought to be encouraged by James Bothwell, the "Wizard Earl," who appeared at their meetings dressed at the Devil himself, claimed responsibility for raising the storms in the North Sea that threatened the lives of both James and Anne, delayed their marriage (ultimately transferred it to Elsinore castle in Denmark), and then delayed once more their journey home to Scotland as King and Queen. "What actually happened—whether there was a genuine conspiracy to kill the king, a scare that snowballed or a government plot to incriminate the earl of Bothwell," Larner continues, "it is now impossible to say. During the course of these trials it was alleged that over 300 witches had gathered at various times to perform treason against the king. . . . The trials lasted from November 1590 to May 1591; more than 100 suspects were examined and a large, but unknown, number were executed" (79). It was rumored that James appeared at some of the trials incognito. He had learned about the connection between witchcraft and diabolism in Denmark, where the court discussed the demonic pact that witches made, often for the overthrow of the king. The North Berwick trials were thus political; the charge was fundamentally treason.

A part of these trials is recounted in *Newes from Scotland,* a work that came to London and circulated as part of the cultural moment of *Macbeth.* There it was recounted that Agnes Sampson was said to have made a waxen image of the King and stuck it with pins. There were others:

> The said *Agnis Tompson* by her depositions since her apprehension saith, that if she had obtained any one peece of linnen cloth which the King had worne and fouled, she had bewitched him to death, and put him to such extraordinary paines, as if he had beene lying upon sharp thornes and endes of Needles. Moreouer she confessed that at the time when his Maiestie was in Denmarke, she being accompanied with the parties before specially named, took a Cat and christened it, and afterward bound to each parte of that Cat, the cheefest partes of a dead man, and seuerall ioynts of his bodie, and that

in the night following the saide Cat was conueied into the midst of the sea by all these witches sayling in their riddles or Ciues as is aforesaid, and so left the saide Cat right before the Towne of Lieth in Scotland: this doone, there did arise such a tempest in the Sea, as a greater hath not beene seene: which tempest was the cause of the perrishing of a Boate or vessell comming ouer from the towne of Brunt Iland to the towne of Lieth, wherein was sundrye Iewelles and rich giftes, which should haue been presented to the now Queen of Scotland, at her Maiesties coming to Lieth.

Again it was confessed, that the said christened Cat was the cause that the Kinges Maiesties Ship at his comming foorth of Denmarke, had a contrary winde to the rest of his Ships, . . . when the rest of the Shippes had a faire and good winde, then was the winde contrarye and altogither against his Maiestie.[327]

One of the leaders, "Doctor *Fian,* alias Iohn *Cunningham*" (18), is given the most detailed tortures and solitary confinement but refuses to admit any acts of diabolism:

> Wherevpon the kinges maiestie perceiuing his subborne wilfulnesse, conceiued and imagined that in the time of his absence hee had entered into newe conference and league with the deuill his master. . . . His nailes vpon all his fingers were riuen and pulled off with an instrument called in Scottish a *Turkas,* which in England wee call a payre of pincers, and vnder euerie nayle there was thrust in two needels ouer euen vp to the heads. . . . Then was hee with all conuenient speed, by commandement, conuaied againe to the torment of the bootes, wherein hee continued a long time, and did abide so many blowes in them, that his legges were crushte and beaten togeather as small as might bee, and the bones and flesh so brused, that the bloud and marrowe spouted forth in great abundance, whereby they were made vnseruiceable for euer. And notwithstanding al these grieuous paines and cruell torments hee would not confesse anie thing, so deepely had the deuill entered into his heart, that hee vtterly denied all that which he had before auouched. (26–28)

He is convicted nonetheless and then publicly carted, strangled, and burned in "a great fire" (28) on Castle Hill in Edinburgh in January 1591. James's obsession with demonology gave him good cause to make Bothwell an outlaw and to weaken his political support; it also allied him in some way with the Calvinists, even as he moved to reestablish the episcopacy and began to make a flanking attack on the presbyteries.

In 1597 James added witchcraft to the royal prerogatives, giving it the same status as treason. From that point on all cases of witchcraft were Pleas of the Crown. This was, for the scholar-king, a most serious matter, and in 1597 he wrote and published his own *Daemonologie*. In 1600 he demonstrated its truth by issuing a report of the Gowrie conspiracy in which a pouch of magic charms was found on the traitor's body. The *Daemonology,* drawing on the Continental ideas of demonology he had learned in Denmark, and insisting that such acts were both heresy and treason, was reprinted in 1603 in both London and Edinburgh. Because Reginald Scot's *Discoverie of Witchcraft* had essentially exonerated witches as elderly solitary women who had been blamed for misfortunes, James recalled Scot's work and substituted his own.

Any playgoer in 1603—or in 1606—who wished to know something of their new King from Scotland, then, would have as a primary source of information the *Daemonologie*. Many passages in the work serve as illuminating lexias for measuring ways in which playgoers might have interpreted *Macbeth* at the Globe in 1606. "Witches can," James says in the preface, "by the power of their Master cure or cast on diseases: Now by these same reasones, that proues their power by the Deuil of diseases in generall, is aswell proued their power in speciall: as of weakening the nature of some men, to make them vnable for women: and making it to abound in others, more then the ordinary course of nature would permit."[328] His first proof of witchcraft is scriptural. He cites 1 Kings 22 to show that God considered witchcraft heresy in the Old Testament, Exodus 7–8 to argue that witches imitate the miracles of Moses (i.e., God), and 1 Samuel 15—a commonplace—to link heresy with treason: "Disobedience is as the sinne of Witchcraft" (5). Recalling the hurly-burly that begins *Macbeth* in which the storm is likened to battle, James's discussion of witches at one point would seem to outline Shakespeare's play:

> The first by knowing thereby the powers of simples, and sickenesses, the course of the seasons and the weather, being ruled by their influence; which part depending vpon the former, although it be not of it selfe a parte of *Mathematicques;* yet it is not vnlawful, being moderatlie vsed, suppose not so necessarie and commendable as the former. The second part is to truste so much to their influences, as thereby to fore-tell what common-weales shall florish or decay: what persones shall be fortunate or vnfortunate: what side shall winne in anie battell: What man shall obteine victorie at singular combate. (13)

Later on, he defines sorcery as "the turning of the riddle" (31). The Devil himself, James informs his readers, "will make his schollers (witches and sorcerers) to creepe in credite with Princes, by fore-telling them manie great thinges; parte true, parte false" (22); he "oblices himself in some trifles to them [intended victims], that he may . . . obtein the fruition of their body & soule, which is the onlie thing he huntes for" (19).

Nor were James's observations limited to Scotland or to himself. Richard Napier has numerous references to people who thought they had met the Devil or been afflicted by him. In one such instance, in 1603, a miller from Foxley in Norfolk, while making his way from his water mill to his windmill, saw a man dressed in black going before him. He called to the man, hoping for companionship on his walk, and almost at once the man turned into a black dog. When the miller reached his destination, he saw the man again and again spoke to him. This time the man turned into a black bear and vanished.[329] "The devil was evidently firmly established in the popular consciousness," James Sharpe comments.[330] If the riddling witches, who likewise have mysterious shapes and mysteriously vanish, were thought to be demonic at the Globe in 1606—they likely appeared through the stage trap that served as the Hellhole—their initial enticement to win the bodies and souls of Macbeth and Banquo is, at least until the murder of Duncan, largely successful.

Many of the ideas in James's *Daemonologie* are taken from the *Malleus Maleficarum* (*The Hammer of Witches*) by Heinrich Kramer and James Sprenger (1484), which circulated in England as well as in Scotland, becoming a widespread fund of witch lore. There in Latin was a convenient list of the powers and activities of witches that affected thought in both countries. It reads in part in the modern translation of Montague Summers:

> They raise hailstorms and hurtful tempests and lightnings; cause sterility in men and animals; offer to devils, or otherwise kill, the children whom they do not devour. . . . [T]hey make horses go mad under their riders; they can transport themselves from place to place through the air, either in body or in imagination . . . they can bring about a great trembling in the hands and horror in the minds of those who would arrest them; they can show to others occult things and certain future events, by the information of devils, though this may sometimes have a natural cause . . . they can see absent things as if they were present; they can turn the minds of men to inordinate love or hatred; they can at times strike whom they will with lightning, and even kill some men and animals; they can make of no effect the generative desires, and even the power of copulation, cause abortion, kill infants in the mother's womb by a mere exterior touch; they can at times bewitch men and animals with a mere look.[331]

One fabliau that spoke to sterility was widely circulated orally in England:

> And what, then, is to be thought of those witches who in this way sometimes collect male organs in great numbers, as many as twenty or thirty members

250

together, and put them in a bird's nest, or shut them up in a box, where they move themselves like living members, and eat oats and corn, as has been seen by many and is a nature of common report? It is to be said that it is all done by devil's work and illusion, for the senses of those who see them are deluded in the way we have said. For a certain man tells that, when he had lost his member, he approached a known witch to ask her to restore it to him. She told the afflicted man to climb a certain tree, and that he might take which he liked out of a nest in which there were several members. And when he tried to take a big one, the witch said: You must not take that one; adding, because it belonged to a parish priest. (121)

Papistry, magic, and potency intertwine here and extend into the areas of power and manipulation based on men's sexual fears. Challenged by his wife's bewitching forcefulness, Macbeth's early reply is to claim with equal force, "I dare do all that may become a man, / Who dares do more, is none" (1.7.46–47; 524–25). Garry Wills has reported another common folk belief in England in 1606:

Battlefields were magnets for witches—for the same reason that shipwrecks were, or gallows, or prostitutes' lairs. They were all good places for collecting the most vital ingredient for witches' work—dead body parts, and especially dead bodies outside consecrated ground. All the body parts the witches name in this play—grease from a corpse hanging on the gallows, a whore's murdered newborn, a shipwrecked sailor's thumb—come from bodies either not buried yet (the gallows corpse) or not buried in consecrated ground (the drowned sailor), or unable to be buried in consecrated ground because unbaptized (like the whore's baby).[332]

The play of *Macbeth* helps to contain such horrors by placing both agents and victims on the stage before and apart from the playgoers.

Gifford's *Dialogue,* the work of a nonconformist clergyman from Maldon, Essex, reprinted in 1603, provides two discrete but parallel definitions of witchcraft, as Sarah Beckwith has put it: "The first posits it as an externalized manifestation of metaphysical evil—'the power of devils'—and the second places it in the 'hearts of men.' "[333] Both "supernaturall solliciting" and "Vaulting Ambition, which ore-leapes it selfe" come together in Macbeth as components of "the Imperiall Theame" (1.3.130, 1.7.27, 1.3.129; 241, 501, 240). They turn prophecy political. And "political prophecy in Britain had a venereble tradition," Howard Dobin writes. "The British believed that throughout history, God had expressed his will and revealed the future of the nation through his chosen prophets. The sixteenth-century English prophet came in every variety—contemporary doomsayer, religious fanatic, partisan propagandist, outright fraud."[334] Merlin was especially popular. Elizabeth was one who saw the power of making riddling prophecies political. Dobin notes that in the 1571 trial of Thomas Howard, Duke of Norfolk, in connection with the Ridolfi Plot that attempted to unseat Elizabeth for Mary Stuart, "an old blind Prophecy" (21) discovered lying beside Norfolk, even when the state had sufficient evidence against him, was added by the prosecution. The incident may have served James as a model for what he reports concerning the pouch of charms Gowrie was wearing in that conspiracy against Mary's son. The official position was that such prophecies and charms were mere "toys," yet treatises attacking them were also forthcoming. Henry Howard, the Earl of Northampton, writes in *A Defensative against the poyson of supposed Prophesies* (1583) that "Merlin's prophecies were cheyned to the deskes of many Libraries in Englande with great reverence and estimation" (n.p.). John Harvey, in *A Discoursive Probleme Concerning Prophesies* (1587), denounced them as "vain fables or idle rumors, or fond toyes or lewd practises or blasphemous hereies" (59). But a letter of February 18, 1601, recorded in the *Calendar of State Papers* notes that the government has suppressed an astrological prognostication of disaster by Regiomontanus because this "foolish prognositication" foretells "the unfortunate state of sundry great persons, great destruction of many mean ones, and threatens death to ecclesiastical persons, lawyers, rulers, &c. . . . This book is called in, though it be but a toy" (5:585).[335] In 1594, William West of the Inner Temple, in his *Symbolaeographie,* distinguishes "*Soothsaying Wizards*" who "divine and foretell things to come and raise up evil spirits by certain superstitious and conceived forms of words. And unto such questions as be demanded of them do answer by voice, or else set before their eyes in glass."[336]

But such answers were inevitably puzzling, obscure, or equivocal, the prophecies amphibological. For George Puttenham in *The Arte of English Poesie* in 1589, amphibology, the stuff of oracles, prophets, and witches, could mislead people and even incite rebellion, "as that of Iacke Straw, & Iack Cade in Richard the seconds time, and in our time by a seditious fellow in Norffolke calling himself Captaine Ket and others in other places of the Realme lead altogether by certaine propheticall rymes, which might be constred two or three wayes as well as that one whereunto the rebelles applied it."[337] Such varied attitudes complicate the more innocent prophecy which Dr. Matthew Gwinn had three children perform for King James in Oxford on August 27, 1605, the Latin *Tres Sibyllae,* in which the three sisters foretell to Banquo "*Imperium sine fine* tuae, rex inclyte, stirpis," "An *endless empire,* O renowned King, to thy descendants": for Shakespeare as for Macbeth, "Prologues to the swelling Act / Of the Imperiall Theame" (1.3.128–29; 239–40).[338]

Sometime before this Perkins had written a treatise on witchcraft (although no extant copy exists before 1608) on just how the Devil performed his evil through the agency of witches:

> The deuills wonders are of two sorts. Illusions, or reall actions. An illusion is a worke of Satan, whereby he deludeth or deceiueth man. And it is two-fold; either of the outward senses, or of the minde. An illusion of the outward senses, is a work of the deuill, wherby he makes a man to thinke that he heareth, seeth, feeleth or toucheth such things as indeede he doth not. . . . The second kind of illusion, is of the minde, whereby the deuill deceiues the minde, and makes a man thinke that of himselfe which is not true. . . . The second sort of the deuills wonders, are *reall workes,* that is, such as are indeede that which they seeme and appeare to be. These, howsoever, to men that knowe not the natures of things, nor the secret and hidden causes thereof, they may seeme very strange and admirable, yet they are no true miracles, because they are not aboue and beyond the power of nature. . . . [W]hat men doe ordinarily in the day time conceiue and imagine in their corrupt hearts, of the same, for the most part, they doe corruptly dream in the night. And this is the rather to be obserued, because though the wicked man shut his eies, and stoppe his eares, and harden his heart, and will not take notice of his enormities by the light of the Law; yet euen by his own dreames in the night, his wickednes shall be in part discouered, and his conscience thereby conuinced, and he himselfe left in the end inexcusable before God. (sigs. B3v, B5v–B6v, F8v)

So too Macbeth:

>   Present Feares
> Are lesse then horrible Imaginings:
> My Thought, whose Murther yet is but fantasticall,
> Shakes so my single state of Man,
> That Function is smother'd in surmise,
> And nothing is, but what is not. (1.3.137–42; 248–53)

"Both the Worlds suffer. / Ere we will eate our Meate in feare, and sleepe / In the affliction of these terrible Dreames," he tells his wife, "That shake vs nightly" (3.2.16–19; 1171–74).

In 1590 Henry Holland, in his *Treatise against Witchcraft,* could still lament "the continuall traffic and market which the rude people have with witches" (sig. B1). Witch trials had been a known fact of English life since the Chelmsford trial of 1566. Between the spring of 1585 and the summer of 1586 six demoniacs were exorcised by twelve Catholic priests, led by William Weston, alias Edmunds, S.J., in the houses of several recusants but mostly in the home of Sir George Peckham of Dedham in Buckinghamshire.[339] Beginning with accusations in 1589 and ending with a trial in 1593, the first possession of children, the five daughters of Francis Throckmorton, was investigated first by Dr. Barrow, a Cambridge physician, and later the Huntingdon Assizes; the account was published as *The Most Strange and Admirable Discoverie of the Three Witches of Warboys* (1593).[340] In 1586 John Darrell was able to exorcise the hysterical Catherine Wright of Derbyshire, although later it was proved that she faked her seizures; ten years later he performed the same rites on Thomas Darling, the Burton Boy, and, a month later, on seven members of the household of Nicholas Stark in Clayworth Hall at Leigh, Lancashire. Suspected of his practices by the church, Darrell nevertheless went on to exorcise William Somers, the Boy of Nottingham, who also proved to be dissimulating possession. At last, in 1599 Darrell was examined by Richard Bancroft and Samuel Harsnett at Lambeth, pronounced an imposter, and defrocked. Mary Glover's spectacular fits of possession, for which the physician Edward Johnson argued instead a natural medical case of hysteria, were a sensation in London in 1602.[341] Only an indictment remained in the case against John Banckes of Newport, who in 1603 was accused of bewitching to death the daughter of his neighbor Henry Nicholls because she refused his advances.[342]

The best estimate for the number of executions of witches in England from 1550 to 1650 is about five hundred, according to Joseph Klaits, fewer than half the number in Scotland for the same period. But torture was prohibited in England, and in the case of witchcraft (not demonology) the courts were often lenient. In the county of Essex, for instance, which was long the center of witch-hunts, only 24 percent of those indicted were ever executed.[343] Not only papists like Watson and conformists like Darrell were punished, however. John Garsett, a minister from Lincolnshire, was deprived in 1601 for conjuring and incontinency. John Knightley, vicar of Gilden Morden, Cambridgeshire, however, was acquitted of sorcery in 1599 by the Official of the Archdeacon of Ely, although his parishioners never stopped accusing him.[344] King James, like Macbeth, often thought of witchcraft. On January 26, 1605, the Earl of Mar wrote Robert Cecil from the King's hunting lodge at Royston, "We are here continually busied either at hunting or examining of witches, and although I like the first better than the last, yet I must confess both uncertain sports."[345] While visiting Oxford in August 1605, where he saw the show of the three sybills and heard disputations on the imagination, James became preoccupied with the case of Anne Gunter from a small village parish of North Moreton, twelve miles from Oxford. According to the account of Robert Johnson, a Scotsman from Edinburgh who had accompanied the King to England,

> a young girl about eighteen years of age excited the wonder of the people of Britain on account of her strange cleverness in deception, which imposed upon the astonished multitude. Whereupon James was seized with the desire of seeing one so celebrated in popular report. Therefore she was at once brought to the King. To the great wonder of the bystanders she lacked all sense of pain when she was stuck with pins. The strangeness of this created great astonishment. Not only was this wonderful in the eyes of those who were present, but she also cast out of her mouth and throat needles and pins in an extraordinary fashion. The King wondering whence she vomited forth so many pins so suddenly, plied her with repeated questioning but she remained firm, asserting that this happened to her by a miracle and that the sense of feeling taken away from her for the time being would soon return to her by divine providence. The King being skillful in untangling deceptions and considering the thing incredible, ordered physicians to determine whether this occurred by some natural cause or by human fraud. By recommendation of the theologians and the entreaty of the physicians, who differed widely concerning this novel and unusual thing, he committed the young girl and the investigation of the matter to the archbishop of Canterbury, in the hope of detecting the fraud. The archbishop, when he accomplished nothing by threats, warning and promises, called in the services of Samuel Harsnet, his chaplain, whom he honored above others. Led by a hint from the archbishop he induced a very proper youth in the retinue of the archbishop to entice the girl into love; who discovering the secret and promising marriage easily procured her favor. Thereafter he gradually neglected her on the pretext of her magical vanities, and the infamy of witchcraft, widespread through all Britain. But she (as is characteristic of womankind) inclined to lust, revealed all her tricks, committing fame and safety to the mastery of the youth. Thus was fraud laid bare and detected by the lack of self-control in a woman. In the end the glory of detecting the fraud was awarded the King, and ridicule for their vanity was awarded to its actors.[346]

Actually, the perpetrator was her father, Brian, who was using her to get vengeance on neighbors. One of Anne's early supporters, among a number of Oxford scholars, was John Hall, one of Shakespeare's later sons-in-law. James interviewed Anne Gunter four times between August 27 and October 10, but he was not convinced of witchcraft. Later she testified to the Archbishop of Canterbury and the Bishop of London at Lambeth. The trial went to Star Chamber in February 1606; when Gunter's house was searched, Darrell's book was found, as well as the account of Warboys that Brian and Anne had used for examples on how to dissimulate. Gunter was, then, thought to be associated with Darrell! The trial, putatively a trial of witchcraft, may have been yet another attempt by James to break the back of the Puritan opposition, to which Darrell and Gunter both subscribed. Thus Gunter is made a conspirator to witchcraft, as Macbeth conjuring witches is, by that word, a co-conspirator too.

Christopher Marlowe's *Doctor Faustus,* with its conjuror and its show of sins, was one of the most popular plays of the period. It was written by 1592, staged by Pembroke's Men at court during the Christmas season of that year, and taken over as a part of the repertoire of the Lord Admiral's Men at the Rose Theater by 1594. But the play was revived in 1602 following its publication in 1601 and was then reprinted again in 1604, apparently with the "adicyons" by William Birde and Samuel Rowley recorded in Philip Henslowe's *Diary* of company expenses. The vaulting ambition of Faustus, too, is a study in self-destruction, and the pageant of the Seven Deadly Sins may have suggested the eight kings of *Macbeth* to Shakespeare as well as to playgoers at the Globe in 1606. "Know that your words haue woon me at the last," Faustus greets Valdes and Cornelius, "To practice Magicke and concealed arts" (sig. A4), and adds, "Come shewe me some demonstrations magicall, / That I may coniure in some lustie groue, / And haue these ioys in full possession" (sig. A4v). When Faustus casts his own spell, as Macbeth will do in the cave in 4.1, a devil appears who calls him a "Coniurer laureate / That canst commaund great *Mephastophilis*" (sig. B1v). The power of that scene must have been incandescent, since there were rumors abroad that extra devils appeared in some performances and Edward Alleyn, playing Faustus, protected himself by wearing a black surplice with a white cross emblazoned on it.

In *Macbeth* the "Instruments of Darknesse" (1.3.124; 234) first amaze and yet communicate with Macbeth and bewilder Banquo before mysteriously vanishing. They speak directly to Macbeth's conditions, needs, and yearnings. Even though Banquo attempts to reassert his own authority with Macbeth by warning him of the illusory authority of the three sisters—

> oftentimes, to winne vs to our harme,
> The Instruments of Darknesse tell vs Truths,
> Winne vs with honest Trifles, to betray's
> In deepest consequence (1.3.123–26; 233–36)

—they have become secret sharers. Macbeth's partner in greatness shares this secret understanding, too: "Glamys thou art, and Cawdor, and shalt be / What thou art promis'd" (1.5.15–16; 361–62); to make certain she will

> powre my Spirits in thine Eare,
> And chastise with the valour of my Tongue
> All that impeides thee from the Golden Round,
> Which Fate and Metaphysicall ayde doth seeme
> To haue thee crown'd withall. (1.5.26–30; 373–77)

Her spirits replace those of the three sisters, and the conjuring—as secret planning, as conspiring, as plotting treason—shifts from them to her. From 1.3 on, it is a play of conspiracies: of Macbeth and the witches with their foreseen titles; of Macbeth and his wife; of Macbeth and Banquo complicit in silence; of Macbeth and Lenox, who supports his story at the discovery of the murder; of Macbeth and Rosse as he interrogates others and discovers Macduff's flight. Macbeth proceeds serially through the play, replacing one conspiracy with another, each one made inherently political and treacherous, old ones falling behind him as new ones are taken up. But then the play begins with a conspiracy: "When shall *we* three meet againe?" (1.1.1; 3), the first line of the first scene, which closes with all three sisters speaking in conspiratorial unison, as one.

The sisters' predictions in 1.3 are chorus-like and choric: all subsequent actions can be seen as lexias, to stem directly from them, the additional spectacles and words of 4.1 only supplementing their outline. James Calderwood thinks of the demonic quality of the play when he notes that "the regicidal act . . . takes on the aspect of a murderous 'black mass' in which Lady Macbeth plays acolyte arranging beforehand the poisoned chalices, and Macbeth himself takes the role of murdering priest advancing upon Duncan with Crosslike dagger upraised before him as the sleeping guards cry out 'God bless us' and 'Amen.' The black mass aspect of Duncan's murder is a radical extension of the sacralizing of violence on the battlefield"[347] and the sacred significance awarded the sisters' predictions. The infernal sacring bell that calls Macbeth to murder in time becomes the "Alarum Bell" warning others of "Murther, and Treason" (2.3.75; 829): the vision of a risen King has turned to the literal sight of a fallen earthly one. When Lady Macbeth reenters, she completes the inversion: "What's the Businesse? / That such a hideous Trumpet calls to parley / The sleepers of the House?" (2.3.81–83; 837–39), announcing the Last Judgment. Like the infernal services at North Berwick, like the allusions in James's *Daemonologie,* Macbeth and his Lady practice conjuring as witchcraft. And once their initial demonic Mass has been completed successfully, they move toward their infernal Eucharist, until a bloodied Banquo interrupts this feast of communion bringing Golgotha back to life (3.4.40 S.D.; 1299).

Had Macbeth entered 1.3 a few lines earlier, he would also have learned that the power of the three sisters had severe limits. A sailor's wife refuses a chestnut from the First Witch, but her revenge is hardly complete, nor can she make it so. She will "dreyne him drie as Hay" (1.3.18; 116), render him impotent (as she will Macbeth), and subject him to storms, but she cannot kill him. Throughout, the power of these strange creatures is strangely restricted. In 1.3 they can foretell titles for Macbeth but cannot by themselves guarantee them. In 4.1 the prophecies—to beware Macduff, to fear no man of woman born, to remain unconquered until Birnam Wood comes to Dunsinane Hill—are spoken by their apparitions but not by themselves. They can only say, in unison, "Seeke to know no more" (4.1.103; 1648). In such a context, the First Witch's grim warning of revenge, "Ile doe, Ile doe, and Ile doe" (1.3.10; 108), sounds remarkably like false bragging, hoping for more than she can deliver, just as Macbeth, in 4.1, will demand more of all three sisters than they are willing, or finally able, to provide. From the start, then, conjurations in the play are foreshortened, delusory. Having lost Banquo, about to lose the support of Lenox and Rosse, Macbeth visits the witches a second time and marks the midpoint of his downward course: by act 5 he loses Lady Macbeth and is totally alone. "I haue liu'd long enough," he will say, but only he will hear these words. His solitary physical life is matched by his co-conspirator's mental exile. Dressed in white with a taper, she resembles the shamed Duchess of Gloucester in 2 Henry VI and, following the Malleus Maleficium (184), the accused witch. Like Jane Shore in Thomas Heywood's contemporary 2 Edward IV (1599, 1605), she is "in a white sheet barefootd with her hair about her eares, and in her hand a waxe taper."[348] She had already reverted to the embodiment in 2.3 of the shamed shrew; now again she is the condemned witch, the incurable madwoman, the dead rising at the Day of Judgment. There is a sense in which the initial prophecies of 1.3 have conferred on the play of Macbeth all of the reality which it has; and all this reality is an illusion, double predestination erased by the falsity of double prophecies. In the hurly-burly of an unstable playworld, Macbeth at the Globe in 1606 profoundly catches up the fragmented ideas and anxieties that seem alive in each political, social, and religious dimension of that cultural moment, throughout its varied lexias of cultural practices.

SHAKESPEARE, *MACBETH*, AND THE COMMON UNDERSTANDING

Finding better questions to ask, and breaking old habits and traditions of asking, is a very difficult part of the grand human project of understanding ourselves and our world.

Daniel C. Dennett

The mind of man doth wonderfully endeavor . . . that it may light upon something fixt and immoveable . . . which may, in some measure, moderate the fluctuations and wheelings of the understanding.

Francis Bacon

Even sound authors are wrong in stubbornly trying to weave us into one invariable and solid fabric.

Michel de Montaigne

It does not follow that because a mountain appears to take on a different shape from different angles of vision, it has objectively no shape at all or an infinity of shapes.

E. H. Carr

The historian Peter Burke defines *culture* as an unofficial "system of shared meanings, attitudes and values, and the symbolic forms . . . in which they are expressed."[1] While it is also true that "the significance of an historical moment is always unknowable at that moment," as Eric S. Mallin has written, "just as the *originary* relation of texts to their contexts is indeterminate,"[2] we can compile facts, texts, and material from that culture to identify some of the concerns—some of the cultural presences— likely to be seen or recalled by those attending a play like *Macbeth* in 1606. We can recover some of the things they saw and heard given the stage conventions of the time. What they understood, however—what they thought or felt they were seeing and hearing—is a different and more complicated matter. For their cultural moment, like any cultural moment, was characterized by various forces, and their attendant practices were sometimes unrecognized, conflicting, or bewildering—like the "attitudes and values, and the symbolic forms" we have just reviewed. What was "most relevant" is hard to determine and may be beyond us in any event. Jean E. Howard has remarked that "the ideological consequences of play-going might be quite different for different social groups,"[3] but even that much is not altogether clear. While it is always helpful to distinguish among playgoers, a single social group might be constituted of Anglicans, Puritans, recusants, and radical nonconformists; what might appear a single belief system might have differing degrees of support for absolutism or divine right, the honor or military codes. The force and cultural importance of a play like *Macbeth* is that through its poetry it can manage so much, be (along with the ideas, values, and realized or unrealized intentions of the playwright) a matrix or containing experience for so many interests, desires, and needs. The effect of the play on the playgoers of 1606 might have been local (remembering only the Porter) or total, positive or negative, or each by turn; and their responses might have been interrogative, interpretive, or judgmental, just as the play itself deals directly, obliquely, or through absences—the actual killing of Duncan, the crowning of Macbeth, or the death of his wife, for instance—with multiple levels that touch at once on politics, society, and religion. Even Shakespeare's own acceptance, revision, or rejection of written sources such as those of Holinshed, Buchanan, or Knox, or such cultural resources as the witchcraft statute of 1604, the London food riots, or the Powder Plot, both locate and complicate matters. Again Mallin is helpful: "The sheared-off sense of history in texts may highlight the author's ability [or opportunity or need] to forge staggered, fractal, or composite images and understandings of material reality" (12).

In such a situation, lexias may not be random but rather informing matters. While each lexia, in *Macbeth* or suggested by it, is a discrete chain of information, combinations of lexias, always open to reformation, illuminate the database texts such as *Macbeth* by the use of a menu, derived from the play, from which and toward which the sequencing or grouping of lexias moves and coalesces. Marc Bloch worried about the fact that "the variety of historical evidence is nearly infinite";[4] Sir Walter Ralegh, corraling as much as he could within the received biblical framework of his own *Historie of the World,* still lamented "the disjointed and scattered frame of our English affairs."[5] The theater does not dismiss these problems; it plays to them. By fracturing a play like *Macbeth* into different scenes, different actors' parts, different lines, and differing performances at various venues, it anthologizes its story just as the earlier chronicles had. *Macbeth* is at once diffuse and multiple; to find in it a single, transcendent meaning is to impose willfully on the text something the text itself—and surely the text in performance—does not have. "A breach in Nature / For Ruines wastful entrance" (2.3.113–14; 878–79) signifies at once rape, tyranny, and the Apocalypse. Lady Macbeth seen in a nightgown, her hair down, carrying a taper, is for the spectators of 1606 a witch, a madwoman, a scold being punished, or a spectator awaiting the Last Judgment. The art of the play's language contains—holds together, however unstably—the epidemic of plague, the act of demonology, and the rise of an absolutist state. Thus meaning for the playgoers of 1606 depends on the selection and arrangement of data seen in or brought to the play. Whole sets of lexias can be rearranged, combined, or even scrambled together—those of conscience and equivocation, for instance, or of divine right and the military code—to address such issues as the play and its author seem to raise. Or spectators may willfully impose from beyond the play, as recorded playgoers did for *Gorboduc* and *Twelfth Night*. At the same time, the play interrogates what any concern means. Surely *Macbeth* is a play centrally focused on equivocation. But what does this mean? It could be a reflection on life, an extension or parody of a despised recusant practice, a study in treason, or a momentary faltering before the invitation to give an overriding truth or meaning to the play itself. Mallin rightly says that "just because a text interacts with its environment does not mean that it necessarily becomes culture's glassy essence" (2). Even the possibility of a glassy essence for *Macbeth* splinters, as George Puttenham observed concerning poetry: it is about 1040 seen through the eyes of 1606. Shakespeare, as well as his culture, has intervened.

Michael Heim writes in *The Metaphysics of Virtual Reality* that "for many today, networks and bulletin boards act as computer antidotes to the atomism of society. They assemble the monads. They function as social nodes for fostering those fluid and multiple elective affinities that everyday urban life seldom, in fact, supports."[6] It is this affiliation, this branching out from the text or database, that creates and constitutes hypertextual criticism—that permits multiple and individual meaning still governed within the authoritative range of a cultural moment and still initiated by and for a particular text. Such a means of analysis and eventual synthesis marks a clear paradigm shift in the management of texts, but one in which the possibilities and rewards can hardly yet be glimpsed. Hypertextual criticism, in its open admission and embrace of multiplicity and simultaneity in such branching—multiple but not tempest-tossed through its elective affinities or its constructed affiliations; simultaneous yet governed overall by the broader feature of text and culture—thus addresses a problem revisionist historians of the early modern period, such as Keith Wrightson and David Levine, have already identified. "England," they write, "has many histories":

> There is the history of court and cabinet, of high policy, politics, and diplomacy. There are the histories of the great institutions of national life, of churches, Parliament, and courts of law. In the world outside Westminster there are the histories of counties, towns and villages, of local administration, of trades and industries, of classes, of the land itself. Each of these histories has its own dynamics and its own integrity, its own elements of distinctiveness. Yet all are in a powerful sense interdependent, however much the degree of interdependence might vary with place and period,[7]

and, we can add, the cultural moment. Since no play—no work of art—ever floats entirely free of its time and place, no text is ever wholly innocent, we can better and more deeply understand that work of art by learning about and speculating on some of the concerns *Macbeth* could have held for various playgoers at the Globe in 1606. This is a job for hypertextual criticism.

Hypertextual criticism may also address at the same time the current crisis in literary studies. In an age of competing critical approaches to literary texts, when we no longer agree upon what is a text (anything that signifies or can be "read") or what is literary (anything using deliberately expressive or metaphorical language), the material practice of literary criticism and literary appreciation itself is fractured and specialized. We live in an age when as readers the sight of totally unrelated works seen at a glance, as in the pages of a newspaper, no longer seems unnatural; when as scholars we busy ourselves with the discrete entries in the plethora of encyclopedias and anthologies now being produced; when as a basic means of locating, distributing, or storing information we use a computer that allows us to recall what we have forgotten, to transform what we know, to erase or add or reconfigure information and conceptions on command. The newest emphasis on cultural criticism is clearly a response to such fissuring and such aporias. Past unrelated bytes as well as sequential lexias of knowledge can be reformulated as the study of national identities (the Spanish Empire), of historical and cultural development (postcolonialism), of personal behavior (gender studies), or of slices of time (the early modern era). All of these approaches to understanding the human condition—what, after all, is also a main purpose of poetry, of drama, of the humanities and the sciences generally—admit both sequencing and instability. They rest both on statement and conditionality. But, in this fundamental paradigm shift, they no longer hold in such high regard the shibboleths of past study: *progress, organicism, a history* (singular) *of ideas.* Cultural pressures on any idea are too forceful and too subject to change and complication. This does not, cannot, however, diminish the value of art; rather, it heightens it. As Robert N. Watson puts it, "Art exists for a reason," adding, "it is not mere decoration, but a necessary worker in the necessary business of a human culture."[8]

Such a common understanding of a variously signifying culture is what gives rise to sequencing information. When Charles Dickens's Mr. Gradgrind in *Hard Times* calls for facts and nothing but facts because they are all that is wanted in life, he parodies science, industry, and learning itself. We know from channel surfing (or surfing the Internet) that isolated facts, or informational bytes, are distracting and insufficient. They do not hold our attention because, isolated, they hold little or no meaning for us. Lexical chains, however, like the tree sets in algebra, pulsate with meaning. This too is part of our common experience. We have all read books hypertexually when we leave the page to check a footnote, or when we look up a word in the dictionary, or when we consult background materials or the writer's other works, or develop relationships between images, allusions, events, or passages: in each case, we temporarily suspend linearity to engage in another meaningful path of understanding in order to return to the text as database with an enhanced comprehension, its potentiality for us more fully realized.

Neuroscience has shown us that a similar procedure relates both learning and memory, too, since in both, some repetitive uses of certain synapses between neurons, the brain's building blocks, grow stronger and even store information to be retrieved on command and coordinated through the hippocampus. An area of the temporal lobe stores names; a part of the frontal cortex apparently holds verbs; and yet a third part of the brain assembles both nouns and verbs into sentences. This merging of observed and remembered facts re-members the present, calling on the past to help inform it, just as a playgoer might appreciate a play by reaching out to the surrounding culture referentially.

In *Descartes' Error,* Antonio Damasio argues that emotions and feelings are essential to the neurological process by which neurotransmitters speed along the axons to synapses; nerve branches are "organized in two large divisons, the sympathetic and the parasympathetic."[9] Visual images of "a favorite landscape," for instance, are processed inside the brain. He goes on to note that

> subcortical structures such as the superior colliculi are activated; so are the early sensory cortices and the various stations of the association cortex and the limbic system interconnected with them. As knowledge pertinent to the landscape is activated internally from dispositional representations in those various brain areas, the rest of the body participates in the process. Sooner or later, the viscera are made to react to the images you are seeing, and to the images your memory is generating internally relative to what you see. Eventually, when a memory of the seen landscape is formed, that memory will be a neural record of many of the organismic changes just described, some of which happen in the brain itself (the image constructed for the outside world, together with the images constituted from memory) and some of which happen in the body proper. (224–25)

Such reception is also conditioned by cultural forms and perceptions, what Ian Stewart and Jack Cohen call "extelligence."[10] "Contested memories," adds the sociologist Eviatar Zerubavel, result from a "cognitive repertoire" that arises from a mind's "tacit socialization" with others: "Each of us is a member of more than just one thought community."[11] Even fragmentary neural perceptions, then, draw on communal beliefs and even communal memories that distinguish a cultural moment: the persecution of Jesuits, for instance, or the fear of witches, or the Powder Plot. "Culture," writes Edward O. Wilson, arises "from the production of many minds that interlace and reinforce one another," a phenomenon he has named "consilience."[12]

Creation and comprehension are thus matters of accumulation but also accretion. There is, notes Debora Kuller Shuger, "some sort of deep structure or inner logic [that seems] discernible in the diversity and contradictions of the dominant culture."[13] The cultural yearning was embodied in Shakespeare's day in "learned exercises and conferences" known popularly as prophesyings, which represented, according to Patrick Collinson, "a method of searching out the true meaning of [a] text by bringing to bear the talents of a company variously schooled in the modern, humane studies: Greek and Hebrew philology, Greek and Roman history, comparative exegesis, as well as rhetoric and logic,"[14] as if a single best meaning might exist. But Shakespeare's age practiced creation and comprehension in just this way, too. The rhetorical handbooks that served as the basic textbooks for the grammar schools of Tudor and Stuart England taught various schemes and tropes, figures of speech and language, that were used to compose speeches as well as plays and sonnets.[15] Mary Thomas Crane has shown how commonplace books became a fundamental means, by collecting scraps of information, passages from ancient texts, and phrases from scattered reading in notebooks; this method of storage allowed bytes for ready retrieval to speak or write. "The twin discursive practices of 'gathering' . . . textual fragments and 'framing' or forming, arranging, and assimilating them created for English humanists a central mode of transaction with classical antiquity," she writes, "and provided an influential model for authorial practice and for authoritative self-fashioning."[16] Both the rhetorical handbooks and commonplace books were textual outgrowths of the earlier practice of the places or art of memory, by which ideas and images were stored in separate "rooms" of the house or mind for easy storage and easier retrieval. These domains of memory harbored not only facts and words but experiences and feelings and even various organizing schema, making the *places* of memory also a *process* of storage and recovery.

According to Mary J. Carruthers, "the activity of an educated mind" was one that centered "upon the notion of a *designed* memory as the inventory of all experiential knowledge,"[17] such as a ladder in Ramon Lull's *Liber de ascensu et descensu intellectus* (1512):

or the diagram of a tree in his *Arbor scientiae* (1515):

Such a practice has its cultural roots in the widespread Tudor study of Cicero's *De Oratore II,* where Antonius, Carruthers notes, "discusses with his friends the value of memory training. He recounts how Simonides first discovered the principles of the mnemonic technique of placing images (*imagines*) in an orderly set of architectural backgrounds (*loci*) in his memory because one day he had just left a banquet hall when the roof collapsed on it, killing all who were still there. He was able to reconstruct the guest list by recalling the location of each person's seat (*sedes*) at the table" (22). She further notes that "all accounts of the workings of memory written after Aristotle separate its activities into two basic processes: that of storage (in a strictly defined context, the activity to which the words *memoria* and *mnesis* are applied); and that of recollection (*reminiscentia* and *ananmesis*)" (46). Before neuroscience, that is, memory and knowledge were related. But the final principle was that of *patterning;* rhetorical *inventio* consisted of "finding" the places or passages and combining them to constitute a significant new whole. As Carruthers puts it, "Without the sorting structure, there is no invention, no inventory, no experience and therefore no knowledge—there is only a useless heap, what is sometimes called *silva,* the pathless 'forest' of chaotic material. Memory without conscious design is like an uncatalogued library, a contradiction in terms. For memory is most like a library of texts, made accessible and useful through various consciously-applied heuristic schemes" (33).

This cultural practice was first translated into English by William Fulwood in his *Castel of Memorie* (1573 and later) and added to by Giordano

Bruno's *Ars reminiscendi* (1583) shortly after he arrived in England. Visual images were thought to be the easiest and best retained—perhaps one reason drama was so popular in Shakespeare's day—and aural responses retained better when *attached* to images. Activated, conscious memory, according to Carruthers, is reminiscence, "an act of interpretation, inference, investigation, and reconstruction" (25). It is this sense of gathering and combining discrete information that Francis Bacon has in mind when he compares a scholar-scientist to a bee in the first chapter of his *Novum Organon,* and what Spenser's Eumnestes, of "Infinite remembraunce," does in *The Faerie Queene* when he records such facts in his "immortall scrine."[18] Dramatists attempted to shape their own patterns of fragmented images from Mr. S's *Gammer Gurtons Nedle* (1575) until well past Shakespeare's time by compartmentalizing images, speeches, and actions in the Donatan, Terentian stages of protasis, epitasis, and catastrophe, or background, conspiracy, and reversal.

Both Bacon and Spenser, Shakespeare's contemporaries, were poets. And it is most especially the poet who, Michel Foucault writes in *The Order of Things,* "beneath the named, constantly expected differences, rediscovers the buried kinships between things, their scattered resemblances."[19] But as the widespread undertaking in the early modern period to discover both buried and unburied kinships shows, this is not the function of the poet alone, but of anyone who wishes to know something. It is the way of knowledge itself. But this knowing, through assemblage, does not put either the knowledge or the one who would know into free fall. Despite the newly opened vista by the continual recombination of commonplaces in the Tudor and Stuart periods or hypertextual criticism today, we still remain bounded in, if only at a greater distance, by the need to establish patterns and by the database which is what we wish to illumine. A basic concern of computer scientists in artificial intelligence is to develop "narrativelike sequences," "data structures that are not just sequences of 'snapshots.' "[20] And the structures themselves "do not exist in a vacuum," as Elizabeth Fox-Genovese comments, but "remain hostage to available language, available practice, available imagination."[21] It is, after all, the imagination that creates the holding patterns that illuminate the database, and the variety of sequencing that we have seen that can make a text like *Macbeth* so varied and various while making sense. I have tried to show how this is possible, and how many combinations were possible, by citing numerous cultural documents and cultural practices that informed playgoers in 1606 and to which, more or less, they conformed and responded. For them doubtless as for us, Shakespeare's *Macbeth* was always disrupted, always renewed, by its constant negotiations and renegotiations of these documents and practices between the world of the play and the world it played to.

But Shakespeare's *Macbeth* not only reaches out to incorporate contemporary cultural practices; it also demonstrates how the play's characters do that and attempt to make sense by the powers and practices of their inquiring and amending imaginations reacting with data in the brain's first ventricle. Both Macbeth and his wife use their imaginations to heal their own fractured visions, divided between their present status at the beginning of the play and the apparent promises of the three weird sisters concerning their future. Both are blessed and cursed with imaginations of extraordinary fertility, vividness, and power. As if to hold together his fragmentary life by the sheer force of his will, Macbeth attempts to hold up the past, present, and future for comparison early in the play; his anticipation of what the sisters say and his later hallucinated dagger help us to realize what they suggest to the untrammeled consequence of his imagination. For Lady Macbeth time too collapses: as the play progresses, her own projected images seem to condense into the moments of Duncan's murder and its immediate aftermath.

If we take the powers of the imagination as the basic means for an ordered set of lexias outside the play as well as within it, we will find useful John Florio's 1603 English translation of Montaigne's *Essayes, or Morall, Politike Discourses,* a book popular with many of Shakespeare's playgoers in 1606 and, judging from close or exact verbal echoes, one Shakespeare himself knew. In his essay on the imagination, which Florio's title translates as "The Force of the Imagination," Montaigne writes that "*Fortis imaginatio generat casum*"—that is, "*A strong imagination begetteth chance . . .* I am one of those that feele a very great conflict and power of imagination. All men are shockt therewith, and some overthrowne by it. The impression of it pierceth me, and for want of strength to resist her, my endevour is to avoid it" (1.2., sig. E2v). Precisely what terrifies Montaigne, though, only attracts Macbeth: he takes chance, abstracts and personifies it, and then subjects it—or him, or her—to his own ends: "If Chance will haue me King," he says, "Why Chance may Crowne me, / Without my stirre" (1.2.144–45; 255–57). Even Duncan, far from any battlefield, real-izes, according to Rosse, that Macbeth is "Nothing afeard of . . . / Strange Images of death" (1.3.96–97; 200–201). But this is only one in a chain of images projected by Macbeth's ardent imagination. "This supernaturall solliciting / Cannot be ill; cannot be good," he remarks after *seeing* the unexpected three sisters (1.3.130–31; 241–42), and the three titles which they assign him force him to question not them but an imagined regicide that will concretize the "strange Intelligence" (1.3.76; 176) they have given him: his mind elides from an initial "suggestion" (1.3.134; 245) to a fully imaged "Murther" which "yet is but fantasticall" (1.3.139; 250). Since, as he says, "nothing is, but what is not" (1.3.142; 253), it may well follow that what is truly imagined, is. Later, to confirm his hallucinatory vision of a dagger, to make the mental image and the physical image collate, he draws his own dagger from his side: "I see thee yet, in forme as palapable, / As this which now I draw" (2.1.40–41; 620–21). Led by his imagination, making what is not is, he transforms the abstraction—murder—into a personification too, while he transforms his imagined look of horror into the image of the fierce Tarquin:

> Now o'er the one halfe World
> Nature seemes dead, and wicked Dreames abuse
> The Curtain'd sleepe: Witchcraft celebrates
> Pale *Heccats* Offrings: and wither'd Murther,
> Alarum'd by his Centinell, the Wolfe,
> Whose howle's his Watch, thus with his stealthy pace,
> With *Tarquins* rauishing st[r]ides, towards his designe
> Moues like a Ghost. (2.1.49–56; 629–36)

Regicide and rape become inseparable in his imagination of lexias and linkages, for both are politically imagined (the end of Roman law in the tyrant Tarquin as a self-projection); and the "supernaturall solliciting" is at one with his exterior and interior world, for when he hears a bell it is *his* bell, *his* signal, and yet, independently, an agent in regicide too: "the Bell inuites me. / Heare it not, *Duncan*" (2.1.62–63; 642–43). Macbeth's imagi-nation *invents* the murder of Duncan, just as later, in 3.2, he will imagine and so invent and cause the death of Banquo: "I will aduise you where to plant your selues, / Acquaint you with the perfect Spy o'th'time, / The moment on't, for't must be done to Night / And something from the Pal-lace" (3.1.128–31; 1135–38).

Lady Macbeth is not so often associated with such visual thinking, but she too displays an imagination by thinking through imagistic lexias:

Come you Spirits,
That tend on mortall thoughts, vnsex me here,
And fill me from the Crowne to the Toe, top-full
Of direst cruelties: make thick my blood,
Stop vp th'accesse and passage to Remorse,
That no compunctious visitings of Nature
Shake my fell purpose, nor keepe peace betweene
Th'effect and hit. Come to my Womans Brests,
And take my Milk for Gall, you murth'ring Ministers,
Where-euer, in your sightlesse substances,
You waite on Natures Mischiefe. Come, thick Night,
And pall thee in the dunnest smoake of Hell,
That my keene Knife see not the Wound it makes,
Nor Heauen peepe through the Blanket of the darke,
To cry, hold, hold. (1.5.40–54; 391–405)

Similar to her husband, Lady Macbeth pictures her desires and then turns those images into accommodating and acceptable components of her situation. Her ability to make images work for her and for her ends dominates act 1. "Looke like th'innocent flower, / But be the serpent vnder't" (1.5.65–66; 410–21). "Was the hope drunk, / Wherein you drest your selfe? Hath it slept since? / And wakes it now to looke so greene, and pale / At what it did so freely?" (1.7.35–38; 512–15). "When in Swinish sleepe, / Their drenched Natures lyes as in a Death, / What cannot you and I performe vpon / Th' vnguarded Duncan? What not put vpon / His spungie Officers? who shall beare the guilt / Of our great quell" (1.7.68–73; 548–53). "But screw your courage to the sticking place, / And wee'le not fayle" (1.7.61–62; 541–42). Often her words denote the visual act of the imagination: "sightlesse"; "looke." But in this play, no matter what we want our poetic, annealing imagination—or Shakespeare's—to do, imagination also disrupts: Lady Macbeth cannot kill Duncan because, in her imagination, he reminds her of her father. When Macbeth's imagination falters, it is before the murder and about possible consequences, not in the performance of the act itself. Both of these imaginings allow us to imagine the murder that we do not "see" (except in our mind's eye), and when it is finally given narrative, in Lady Macbeth's sleepwalking scene (5.1), she allows us to confirm our own earlier imaginings, lest we forget—before Shakespeare reminds us, through the words of the Doctor and the Gentlewoman and the horror of Macbeth—that this is also a delusion, a hallucination as surely, and as deadly, as his dagger was (2.1). The force of the imagination is also its danger, Montaigne has said, and the play promotes this idea through several lines we can link as lexias.

The annealing imagination, then, what is alien to the dispersal of hypertextuality, is very much a part of *Macbeth,* but the play shows us that that which might anneal can also delude, what might unify can as easily destroy. On the other hand, an ordered set of lexias about the imagination does have the annealing effect of providing member lexias that reinforce each other: Primaudaye's proposition that "*fantasie* is a very dangerous thing" (sig. K6) agrees with Bacon's distempers of learning, and they both gloss the events of *Macbeth.* Dispersing the passages about the imagination, as the performance of the play would disperse them at the the Globe in 1606, allows us—as it allowed performers and playgoers then—to find various lexias that might be joined to interpret, or evaluate, the use of imagination in *Macbeth.*

This play of textual fissures therefore invites, and even requires, an imaginative response in order to make any sense of it. The need is immediately apparent, for the central event of the play, the murder of Duncan, occurs outside our range of vision and *demands* our imagining. Not witnesses to the regicide, "we are obliged," Robert Hapgood has written, "to join Lady Macbeth in imagining it, in straining to see what we are not allowed to see, as Macbeth is 'about it.' "[22] The absent is made present, as James L. Calderwood has noted:

> It is one thing for us to know that Macbeth murders Duncan, but it is quite another for us to see him at it. Hence Macbeth's horrible but invisible imaginings must not be allowed to materialize on stage as a horrifying deed. But for Shakespeare to omit the deed entirely would be to break faith with his audience, who have been promised a regicide. The deed must be absent, but it must also be present. How is this managed? By substituting for the unstaged deed a speech by Lady Macbeth that mediates between us and it, obscuring and revealing it at once. For although Lady Macbeth is before us on stage, her own horrible imaginings are in the bedchamber with her husband. If Duncan had not resembled her father, she says, she would have done the deed herself. Now, in sense, she does do it.
>   And, alas, so do we.[23]

We must close this rupture with our own imagination, healing the rift of absence. Assuming the 1623 Folio text approximates the 1606 performance, the same demand was made then on playgoers at the Globe. The play confirms an imagined murder, if slowly: the absent murder of the King is followed by the murder, in half-light, of Banquo, and then by the murder, in full-light, of Macduff's son, and finally by the murder and mutilation of Macbeth himself. To heal this new rupture—a country without a king—Macduff initiates a verbal and swift election of Malcolm, who invites his followers to Scone to witness his investiture. We do not see that glorious scene, either; we are left to imagine it. We are left to imagine whether Malcolm is motivated more by reintegrating the kingdom or by consolidating and reestablishing personal power. But if our imagination is alert, we also recall another coronation we did not see: Macbeth's. And we realize the person creating this journey to Scone—Macduff—was characterized earlier (2.4.36; 972) as the one who refused to attend the coronation of Macbeth; we recall 4.3 and are alerted to the possibility that Macduff may become Malcolm's Macbeth. And where, now, is Donalbain, also eligible to contest the throne? Presences encourage us to recall, and contemplate, absences. Once more our amending imagination disrupts the narrative sequencing by attempting to understand it completely.

"When Shakespeare writes the culture that shapes his texts," Mallin reminds us, "he becomes more than merely an indifferent producer of cultural objects or a medium through which events are told; he is also reader, redactor, and rhapsode" (8). He realizes, as his Macbeth does, that "lies" or fictions or assumptions are "like truth" (5.5.44; 2368). What Shakespeare realizes that Macbeth fails to appreciate, however, is that metaphor, in John Kerrigan's pregnant phrase, "frees language into suggestion."[24] "Language," the semiotician Umberto Eco adds, "also says more than its unattainable literal meaning, which is lost from the very beginning of the textual utterance."[25] Metaphors have the power of condensation; they reduce expression but open up meaning. Like the imagination rightly used, they generate meaning—not, as Macbeth uses imagination, impose one imperially. *Macbeth* is full of metaphors for the cultural moment that produced it and which it produces in turn, that *make sense* of the culture while *making up* a representation of its forces, pressures, ideas, and values: a making up that elides thought and feeling. Both the playwright and playgoers in 1606 use the synecdochic power and the resonant force of metaphors (actually lies) to register—not merely to reflect but by extension and recombination to register—the perceived and recorded culture as well as it can be revealed, and as fully. The lying (by metaphor and metonymy) is not the truth; it is *like* truth. And it is *not unlike* truth. That is what *Macbeth* is doing, at the Globe and in the First Folio. But *like* is the sign of simile as well as of metaphor or metonymy; it is transparent. It yokes terms into analogies created out of similarity or parallelism or shared features as associative lexias might be linked; it yokes two terms or incidents or contexts at the moment of near-jointure. The trouble with analogies—and also their greatest strength and value—is that they can work reciprocally. The crowd scene in nightdress that is 2.3 looks (and feels) *like* the Last Judgment. And the Last Judgment, at least for this play, in its time and place, would look very much like an unexpected regicide through which God's voice on earth is somehow annihilated. This is not the only way to read 2.3, and it is not the customary way of reading that scene. But the visual metaphor, like the verbal obbligato by which the Porter introduces it, makes that possible. Metaphor and metonymy, then, produce the likeness in the comparison, a likeness that is not only multiple, but also provisional. It is also about-to-happen. It gains more, not less, from such characteristics, and gives such texts as *Macbeth* much of their power and poetry.

Still, Macbeth's observation concerning "lies like truth" comes to him (and to us) in a larger context. His full comment is this: "I pull in Resolution, and begin / To doubt th'Equiuocation of the Fiend, / That lies like truth" (5.5.42–44; 2366–68). Lying here for Macbeth is, first, equivocal; its full meaning is never wholly conveyed but partially *withheld,* and second, the work of fiends that are its agents. The witches, then, provide words for which the apparent meaning is deficient or, given the possibility of ambiguity, abundant, as he also realizes when, moments later, he says of the witches that they "palter with vs in a double sence" (5.8.20; 2460), revealing and withholding, saying and not saying. Either way, they render problematic for Macbeth the connections between the verbal and the phenomenological as well as the connections between intention and reception. In this way, the words of the witches, like similes, metaphors, and metonymies, draw attention to process. Hypertextually, they could open up to a large, indeterminate number of meanings, yet always the words on one side of the processing equation and the interpreter on the other side—the character Macbeth, the playgoer at the Globe, or the reader then and now—who must first focus on that chosen meaning. Hypertextuality also focuses on process, but it opens up the conjunction *like,* prying out unnumbered possibilities. As for the agency of the fiend, we are aware (even if Macbeth is not) that the fiend here is his own conjuration, his own creation, an extension of his own desire and understanding. The meaning of the matter (fiend) on the other side of the equation is what he makes of it on his side: the *like* of the simile is a transporting back and forth, not a one-way delivery system. Recognition of this causes us to open up, rather than shut down, meaning: it is the power of simile and metaphor that sustains dynamic meaning in such texts as *Macbeth.*

The words *equivocation* and *devil,* synonymous here with *fiend,* are conjunctive in one other scene in *Macbeth*—in 2.3 with the Porter, at the play's midpoint as well as at its close. The Porter finds equivocation in his own characterization of the farmer "that hang'd himselfe on th'expectation of Plentie" (2.3.4–5; 747–48) because he could not accept abundance. He lost sight of himself as agent and the sense of meaning as unending process and made it singularly fixed. The Porter knows better than that; he is, after all, a survivor by nature. Fixing a single meaning—something hypertextual criticism will not permit—defeated the farmer. But the Porter is not defeated; he can be "Porter of Hell Gate" (2.3.2; 745), and when that no longer serves his turn he will "Deuill-Porter it no further" (2.3.19; 759). He becomes a riddling jester to Macduff and Lenox, thereby offering new metaphors by which to interpret him and the play in which he resides. He knows the multiple meanings, one would guess from his behavior, of *lies like truth.*

"History is always being begun anew," Bloch's disciple Fernand Braudel writes; "it is always working itself out, striving to surpass itself. Its fate is shared by all the social sciences. So I do not believe that the history books I am writing will be valid for decades to come. No book is ever written once and for all, and we all know it."[26] What is true of the social sciences for Braudel is also true of the humanities. We learn because of the continuing need to learn. "The time has bene, / That when the Braines were out, the man would dye, / And there's an end" (3.4.77–79; 1350–52). As with Banquo's ghost, literary texts and hypertextual criticism of them know no end; metaphorically, associatively, they are always being rethought and reborn. As hypertext aids us in so many of our current projects, so it can inform our work of literary understanding. There is a built-in inconclusiveness to *Macbeth,* all right—what will happen when Donalbaine returns, for instance?—but there is no final authority, no single transcendent or "best" meaning. There are only discovered meanings that become invitations to know more, read more deeply, perform it once again, extend the possibilities, *imagine* a whole as in a house of memory. Hypertext reminds us, always, that this is so: our literary sensibilities stay alive because the text does. Robert Scholes has written that "interpretation is not a pure skill but a discipline deeply dependent on knowledge. It is not so much a matter of generating meaning out of a text as it is a matter of making connections between a particular verbal text and a larger cultural text [what I have called the cultural moment], which is the matrix or master code that the literary text both depends upon and modifies."[27] As I have said, and as Scholes seems to imply in *modifies,* that matrix too is subject to change as we recover more of it, perceive more in it. Hypertextual criticism, like the New Historicism and cultural materialism at their best, also makes metaphorical what the old historicism was content to leave documentary. That is what makes them new.

Appendix A:
The Text of Macbeth

When *Macbeth* was published in the First Folio of 1623, it was placed between *Julius Caesar* and *Hamlet,* Shakespeare's two other great tragedies of assassination and revenge. But unlike them, it is a play whose text is riddled with discrepancies. In fact, the Folio text disjoins itself, beginning with a character called both captain and sergeant. Just such an imperfect text irritated Dr. Johnson. He writes in his *Miscellaneous Observations on Macbeth* (1745):

> The incongruity of all the passages in which the Thane of Cawdor is mentioned is very remarkable. Ross and Angus bring the king an account of the battle, and inform him that Norway, assisted by the Thane of Cawdor 'gan a dismal conflict. It appears that Cawdor was taken prisoner, for in the same scene the king commands his present death. Yet though Cawdor was thus taken by Macbeth, in arms against his king, when Macbeth is saluted, in Scene iii, Thane of Cawdor, by the Witches, he asks, "How of Cawdor? the Thane of Cawdor lives, A prosperous gentleman," and in the next line considers the promises that he should be Cawdor and king as equally unlikely to be accomplished. How can Macbeth be ignorant of the state of the Thane whom he has just defeated and taken prisoner, or call him a *prosperous gentleman* who has forfeited his title and life by open rebellion? He cannot be supposed to dissemble, because nobody is present but Banquo, who was equally acquainted with Cawdor's treason. However, in the next scene his ignorance still continues; and when Ross and Angus present him with his new title, he cries out, "The Thane of Cawdor lives. Why do you dress," etc. Ross and Angus, who were the messengers that informed the king of the assistance given by Cawdor to the invader, having lost, as well as Macbeth, all memory of what they had so lately seen and related, make this answer:

> Whether he was combin'd with those of Norway,
> Or did lyne the Rebell with hidden helpe

And vantage; or that with both he labour'd
In his Countreyes wracke, I know not:

Neither Ross knew what he had just reported, nor Macbeth what he had just done.[1]

Daniel Amneus, who cites this passage from Johnson, himself notes that there are three schemes to murder Duncan—"mutually inconsistent" plans that are never addressed or reconciled—involving the plans of Macbeth alone, of his wife alone, and of the two of them together.[2] Kristian Smidt notes that in 3.1 Lady Macbeth is present during Banquo's departure because no stage direction indicates her exit, yet she does not know, in the following scene, that he has left the court. Furthermore, Smidt argues that her dialogue in 3.2 is more characteristic of "Macbeth's way of thinking than of hers" when she is alone (at 3.2.4–7; 1157–60), but is then at once contradicted when Macbeth appears (3.2.11–12; 1165–66).[3] He also finds it strange that once the guests have departed from the truncated coronation banquet, Lady Macbeth never questions Macbeth about what has happened or what he saw, and neither of them mentions their missing guest (160). Such minor lapses—which might be explained by the general anxiety Macbeth and his wife feel following the regicide—grow stranger in the apparent change of direction in the plotting of the play. Bertrand Evans has noted that

> if Acts I and II have prepared us to expect the remainder of the play to represent Scotland's search for unknown murderers, they have misled us, for after Act II, the dramatist turns quite away from this issue; indeed, except for passing allusions, Duncan's murder itself appears to have been forgotten by everyone but Lady Macbeth. . . . When Malcolm and Macduff raise an army to destroy Macbeth, it is not because he killed Duncan but because he has become a bloody tyrant.[4]

The Arden 2 editor, Kenneth Muir, has remarked that Lenox may likewise seem to be constantly reconceived:

> Lenox appears in III.vi as a savage critic of Macbeth and in IV.i. as an apparently loyal follower. Possibly his lines in IV.i were originally spoken by another character, or his feigned loyalty could exemplify the fact that Macbeth can trust no one. If III.vi is followed by IV.i it would be an effective means of expanding the brief announcement that Macduff has fled, without spoiling Lady Macduff's feelings of bewilderment in IV.ii;[5]

and the issue is compounded when we realize that it is Lenox who is Macbeth's warmest supporter in the discovery scene (2.3). The modern writer Garry Wills has even called attention to Macbeth's contradictory commands to Seyton in 5.3 to arm him, to remove his arms, to give him arms, anticipating the corrupted state of the single text in which Macbeth is killed by Macduff twice, first onstage (5.8.34 S.D.; 2476) and then off (5.9.19 S.D.; 2504).[6]

Critics too have found interpretation vexing. Characterizations are directly opposed to character descriptions (as in the case of Duncan), and loyalties are shifted for no apparent reason (Lenox, Rosse). One of the best examples of a troubled reader is Harry Berger, Jr. In "The Early Scenes of *Macbeth*: Preface to a New Interpretation," he remarks that "by the middle of 1.4 the Scottish king has run into two rebels, a foreign foe, and a budding regicide. These facts have to be set against the persistent praise of Duncan as an ideal king, the head of a harmonious state."[7] Indeed, for a King whose country faces an invasion from without and a rebellion from within, he seems curiously content to sit on the sidelines and determine the fate of battle from what may be conflicting reports, rather than to take charge himself. Yet Macbeth's slaughter wins only praise: Rosse would marry him as the war god Mars ("*Bellona's* Bridegroome" [1.2.55; 79]). Berger writes:

> It is Macbeth's "bloody execution" that evokes Duncan's "O valiant cousin! worthy gentleman!" But it isn't only that, for Macbeth is not alone in being carried away by this impulse. The speaker contributes to the overkill. He approves the violence. His salty phrases, his flamboyant verbal gestures, relish in the hero's carnage and add force to his brandished steel. Diminishing the rebel and enhancing the hero, he stands before the king as Macduff's ally. (77)

If Duncan forgoes military experience, he also here lacks political judgment. Not only does he appoint a second traitor as Cawdor and then undermine any force to that award by appointing his son Prince; he also gives lavish praise to Banquo—"Noble *Banquo*, / That hast no lesse deseru'd, nor must be knowne / No lesse to haue done so" (1.4.29–31; 314–16)—but then rewards him only by embracing him: "Let me enfold thee, / And hold thee to my Heart" (1.4.31–32; 316–17). Alternatively, Berger uses this early scene to contrast it with the play's end:

> Macduff's killing Macbeth recalls Macbeth's victory over Macdonwald: Macbeth also has Kernes fighting for him, and his head, Macduff threatens, will end up on a pole, if not on battlements. This may be viewed as poetic justice, the wheel come full circle. But it may also be simple recurrence, more of the same. In killing Macbeth, Macduff steps into his role. Will he become Malcolm's Macbeth? And in killing Macbeth he has killed not merely a tyrant but a properly appointed king, "nam'd" and "invested" at Scone (2.4.31); Malcolm's final reference to being "crown'd at Scone" may remind us that while Macbeth was a regicide he was not a usurper (which Macduff, at 5.9.21, wrongly calls him). . . . In purely political terms, Malcolm's leading the English army to Dunsinane is no less disloyal to the Scottish throne than is Cawdor's treacherous assistance to Norway. (73)

The soldier Macduff does turn political; by calling for Malcolm's election, confirming Duncan's oath, he aligns himself as Malcolm's chief supporter.

Language in the Folio text also falters. J. M. Nosworthy has counted a highly unusual series of nine metrically irregular lines in 1.2 alone:

(i)   Who like a good and hardie Souldier fought
'Gainst my Captiuitie: Haile braue friend . . . (1.2.4–5; 22–23)

(ii)   (Like Valours Minion) caru'd out his passage,
Till hee fac'd the Slaue:
Which neu'r shooke hands, nor bad farwell to him . . . (1.2.19–21; 38–40)

(iii)   As whence the Sunne 'gins his reflection,
Shipwrecking Stormes, and direfull Thunders:
So from that Spring, whence comfort seem'd to come,
Discomfort swells . . . (1.2.25–28; 44–47)

(iv)   Dismay'd not this our Captaines, *Macbeth* and *Banquoh*? (1.2.33–34; 53–54)

(v)   I cannot tell; but I am faint,
My Gashes cry for helpe (1.2.43–44; 63–64)

(vi)   Who comes here?
Mal. The worthy *Thane* of Rosse,
Lenox. What a haste lookes through his eyes?
So should he looke, that seemes to speake things strange. (1.2.46–48; 68–70)

(vii)   Where the Norweyan Banners flowt the Skie,
And fanne our people cold.
Norway himselfe, with terrible numbers . . . (1.2.50–52; 74–76)

(viii)   Assisted by that most disloyall Traytor,
The *Thane* of Cawdor, began a dismall Conflict . . . (1.2.53–54; 77–78)

(ix)   That now *Sweno*, the Norwayes King,
Craues composition:
Nor would we deigne him buriall of his men . . . (1.2.60–62; 85–87).[8]

But metrical irregularity is not all that plagues the state in which this text comes into the Folio. There are also prose passages that should clearly be poetry, as in the instances of Lady Macduff and her son (4.2) and the entire sleepwalking scene (5.1). There are mixed metaphors, as in Lady Macbeth's "Was the hope drunke, / Wherein you drest your selfe?" (1.7.35–36; 512–13) or Macbeth's "Put Rancours in the Vessell of my Peace" (3.1.66; 1057) and his more famous "Pitty, like a naked New-borne-Babe, / Striding the blast" (1.7.21–22; 495–96). There are other slippages and inaccuracies, too—such as Macbeth's entrance a line too early at 2.3.42, 784; Macbeth's lines apparently reassigned in 3.2; no disappearance and reappearance of the Ghost of Banquo in 3.4; Lenox's decision to defect (3.6) and then, inexplicably, return to Macbeth's court (4.1); the Doctor exiting one line too early at 4.3.145, 1975; and Seyton, who without an exit at 5.5.8, 2329, nevertheless reenters at 5.5.15, 2337. In many dimensions, then, this notably imperfect text denies the organicism desired by critics using the earlier New Critic paradigm of organicism; such basic coherence is not now available to any reader, student, or performer.

How did *Macbeth* get this way? Was it so popular a play that the company did not wish to make the script public? find that a Scottish play about a Scottish king was potentially dangerous to fix in any semipermanent form during the early years of James's rule? wish to keep it in a fluid state, changing it with alterations in company personnel or the occasion of performance on the road, in public and private theaters, at the court? And why was it finally issued in 1623? Were Heminge and Condell considering retirement? Was there danger that some of the plays would get lost or further mutilated over time? Was the company desirous of honoring their aging patron in the last years of his rule? With no authorial statements, prefaces, or commentaries, we can only rely on what we know about common playhouse practices: the King's Men, Shakespeare's company; and the conditions of printing in the early seventeenth century.

Jerome J. McGann has argued persuasively that such playtexts were sociocentric: they are "fundamentally social rather than personal or psychological products" and "do not even acquire an artistic form of being until their engagement with an audience has been determined."[9] More recently, G. Thomas Tanselle has elaborated on this observation:

> Over the past decade and a half there has been a notable shift of emphasis in the writing about textual matters, from a concern with authorial intention to an interest in the collaborative or social aspects of text-production. As the discussion has evolved, there has come to be an increased concern with textual instability and the significance of versions. All these concepts are naturally linked: for if texts are social products, then texts will take different shapes as they pass from one social milieu to another; and if authors are not the only source of validity in the constitution of texts, then all these variant texts carry their own authority as products of history. This attention to textual multiplicity extends backward into the initial creative process and forward into audience response (which is also a creative activity). Authorial versions—obvious emblems of textual instability—are studied both as products of particular moments and as parts of an endless process, which does not cease with the author's death; and readers, both during an author's lifetime and afterward, participate in this process by creating their own versions of the texts they encounter.[10]

Such textual practices of what Tanselle calls "composite creativity" (5) are direct responses to the fact that, as Bernard Cerquiglini has it, "Taking something and putting it into a book cuts into a continuous flow" of interpretation and significance.[11]

The original manuscript was owned by the company—in Shakespeare's case, the King's Men in 1606—and was subject to all the demands of active performers and vulnerable to all the conditions of the playhouse and company: scenes might be adjusted, lines added or dropped or delivered differently; even the size of the cast might change when performances at the public playhouse like the Globe, with 1,500 in attendance, was moved to a private theater like the Blackfriars that seated 600 or 700, or to the court with a more intimate audience. We can guess that a Scottish play about a Scottish king would have done well on the road, too, meaning that the company—probably reduced in size to save expenses—also performed the play in town halls and open innyards. Old and new performers might add suggestions of their own, and it might also be a reasonable guess that James I, always fearful of regicide and especially fearful of assassination in his own bed (as some of his ancestors had been killed), would not have wanted to see the regicide of Duncan performed, while the discussion in 4.3 that is a basis for unifying Scottish and English forces would have pleased the monarch who was urging the unification of the two countries as Great Britain in 1606. Humphrey Moseley, writing "The Stationer to the Reader" in the 1647 folio edition of the works of Beaumont and Fletcher, says that "One thing I must answer before it bee objected; 'tis this: When these *Comedies* and *Tragedies* were presented on the Stage, the *Actours* omitted some Scenes and Passages (with the *Authours'* consent) as occasion led them; and when private friends desired a Copy, they then (and justly too) transcribed what they *Acted*" (sig. A4v). Such fluid circumstances are another reason why it is not possible to argue a fixed organicism, or fixed meaning, on what was essentially an unfixed text.

Even if a potentially changing script reached a relatively stable form for the printer, or at least a form acceptable to Heminge and Condell as one which would honor and memorialize Shakespeare, W. W. Greg, Charlton Hinman, Stanley Wells and Gary Taylor, and others have found several corrupting practices in the preparation of the Folio text, including compositorial error or prejudicial habits that may affect spellings and even words; incomplete settings or revisions of type; the substitution in part of touring scripts; and rearranged lines. Authorities on the printing of the Folio of 1623 largely agree that *Macbeth* is one play set from a theatrical script, or the bookeeper's and typesetting habits indicate that of the twenty-one pages, nine were set by Compositor "A" and twelve by Compositor "B," with three of the pages appearing in some copies in a changed, corrected state. Hinman writes: "Both A and B made mistakes, but B made more than A and was especially given to particular kinds of aberration. Unlike A, Compositor B took frequent liberties with his copy."[12] Furthermore, Greg wrote in 1955 that "it is almost certain that the text as we have it has undergone at least some cutting. It has, for instance, many short lines; and while some of these may be, and probably are, original, others, either by their own awkwardness or by concomitant obscurity, suggest interference with the text, as for example at I.ii.20, 50, III.ii.32, iv.4,

IV.iii.28, 44. There are also some inconsistencies in the action which suggest that we have not got the whole story," and he goes on to suggest later that "at the time the Folio was printed James was still on the throne, and for a play so essentially his the editors may have thought it good policy to print a version prepared for court presentation."[13] This might mean recovering the script first used at court around 1606, or it might suggest editing the script presently in the possession of the King's Men to make it conform to what was thought to be the King's pleasure. If, however, we argue with some current theater historians that the King's Men was the more subversive of the public companies, there is some possibility that some inherent comments on King James that could be construed adversarial were retained.

Still, the text may be further contaminated by at least one other hand. *The Witch*, a short-lived play by Thomas Middleton that may have opened the Blackfriars Theater in 1610, has two songs that are imported into *Macbeth* at 3.5.35, indicated in the Folio by its first line—"*Come away, come away, &c*" (1467)—and at 4.1.43, "*Blacke Spirits, &c*" (1572). They are expendable; but having been added, they may also account for the expendable addition of all of 3.5, which also imports Hecate, and her reappearance in 4.1, where she remains unintegrated into the play as a whole. Andrew Gurr has suggested that the elaborate and expensive machinery built at the Blackfriars for the witches to fly in Middleton's play had been so expensive that, to cut their losses, Shakespeare's company used the machinery in subsequent productions of *Macbeth*.[14] This would have provided considerable spectacle and, like the Porter's scene, relieved tension in the main plot in performance. The script we have in the First Folio seems therefore to represent a layered text. Indeed, the fact that most of the references to the Powder Plot occur in the short scene with the Porter suggests in addition that this scene may have been added in 1606 to an earlier text—perhaps a topical updating of the earlier *Tragedy of Gowrie*.

There is only one record of an early performance that might help us to determine the actual performance script the King's Men had used prior to the 1623 Folio text. The astrologer Simon Forman, in his *Book of Plays and Notes thereof per Forman for Common Policy,* reports seeing a performance on Saturday, April 20, 1611.[15] He talks of Macbeth entering on horseback with Banquo, however, which seems more in keeping with an illustration in Holinshed than known stage practices of the time, and his brief report, largely on the first half of the play, seems as close to Holinshed's text as to any possible playtext. Our best guess now, then, is that Shakespeare began working on *Macbeth* around the time, or shortly after the time, James became King of England (and so raised interest in Scotland and in the King's ancestry), that it was modified or completed after the discovery of the Powder Plot in late 1605, and that subsequent performances and actors may have changed the script, most notably by 1611. The text thus naturally fissures if various parts of various periods of its development are put together for the Folio compositors. While there is no indication anywhere of an extant holograph copy by Shakespeare in 1623—a reliable authorial manuscript—there is a text that is itself sufficiently corrupt that it denies total reintegration without the participation of actors, spectators, or readers. The text of *Macbeth,* then, especially invites the exercise of hypertextual criticism, in which various parts of the play allow sequences outward from the script itself and where we must admit the necessity, to make sense of the play, of a reordering of parts and by our own amending imaginations.

Appendix B:
Gutenberg and Hypertext

At the Dalton School on the upper east side of Manhattan, Jacqueline D'Aiutolo has taught *Macbeth* to tenth-grade students since 1980. They begin "the epic journey into the dark heart" of the play by reading the entire text together closely. After that, in teams of three and four, they dig "deeper into the text" by using Macintosh computers linked to "an elaborate data base." Their investigations have not been directed to the cultural moment in England that we have been examining, although their work also includes that; rather, they have seen history diachronically, too, as process and duration as much as moment. For instance, three of them

> have been exploring the character of Lady Macbeth for a joint paper. What does she look like? How should she be imagined? A few keystrokes bring up a series of images: illustrations of the conniving noblewoman by a variety of artists, then a scene from Roman Polanski's 1971 film, *Macbeth*. As the action plays out in a window on the screen, the students discuss the lady's greed and her striking resemblance to a witch in the opening scene of Polanski's film. They can also look at scenes from the 1948 Orson Welles production and a 1988 staging for British TV. As they form theories about Shakespeare's intentions, they may consult any of 40 essays and hundreds of annotated bibliographies, as well as writings about the Bard's life and times.[1]

According to Claudia Wallis, the teacher "has been amazed to see how students can deploy this modern tool to plumb the depth of old texts. . . . The incisiveness of their work has stunned her" (49–50). The students in Room 608 of the Dalton School confirm what Sven Birkerts prophesied in 1994 in *The Gutenberg Elegies: The Fate of Reading in an Electronic Age:* "The societal shift from print-based to electronic communications is as consequential for culture as was the shift instigated by Gutenberg's invention of movable type";[2] indeed, he continues, "it is easy to imagine that in the near future a whole range of innovative electronic-based learning packages will be available and, in many places, in use. These will surely include the manifold variations on the electronic book. Special new software texts are already being developed to bring us into the world of, say, Shakespeare, not only glossing the literature, but bathing the user in multimedia supplements. The would-be historian will step into an environment rich in choices, be they visual detailing, explanatory graphs, or suggested connections and sideroads" (136). But he does not favor such a Kuhnian revolution; rather, he is in turn admonitory and elegiac. He is deeply troubled that assembling related documents and moving them alongside a base text is rapidly displacing Gutenberg's combinations of words made possible by his revolutionary invention of movable type in the mid-fifteenth century. To define hypertext, he quotes Robert Coover, "The End of Books" in the *New York Times* for June 21, 1992:

> With its webs of linked lexias, its networks of alternate routes (as opposed to print's fixed unidirectional page-turning) hypertext presents a radically divergent technology, interactive and polyvocal, favoring a plurality of discourses over definitive utterance and freeing the reader from domination by the author. Hypertext reader and writer are said to become co-learners and co-writers, as it were, fellow travelers in the mapping and remapping of textual (and visual, kinetic, and aural) components, not all of which are provided by what used to be called the author. (quoted 153)

At least two of Birkerts's unacknowledged premises are denied here: that the author must maintain control of the significance and interpretation of his work, and that that meaning (not polyvocal) is always singular. Both premises would astonish Gutenberg himself, who was more a transmitter or mediator than author.

But the wide sweep of Birkerts's title and his frequent appeal to "the book" are not exactly what he is talking about: he really means novels, works of the imagination where the author's imagination is to be shared (but never transformed) by the attentive and appreciative reader. Reading for Birkerts—although on several occasions he denies this, his illustrations never really do—is essentially passive, not active. The reader, for Birkerts, may dynamically involve him- or herself with the book, or actively (later) reflect on it; but it is largely a matter of sitting still and reading and then holding to the haunting afterlife of that author-controlled experience (see 38, 81, 95, 101). How taking sideroads is different from personal reflection (except that it uses other documents) and how the effects might be different are not actually addressed. In what has become the most substantial, emotional, and influential attack on hypertext among general readers, the price one pays with hypertext is divergence, plurality, co-learning, and co-writing. Turning for even a fraction of study from the kinds of books that constitute Gutenberg's legacy, we move from fixed meaning, controlled by the author, into enhanced meanings—what Birkerts calls supplementary and divergent, what he finds distracting and of questionable value.

Actually, *The Gutenberg Elegies* is itself polyvocal, since many of the chapters, in themselves freestanding essays, tend to repeat the same charges from different perspectives. Birkerts's best summary, however, comes early, in chapter 1, where he writes:

> We can think of the matter in terms of gains and losses. The gains of electronic postmodernity could be said to include, for individuals, (a) an increased awareness of the "big picture," a global perspective that admits the extraordinary complexity of interrelations; (b) an expanded neural capacity, an ability to accommodate a broad range of stimuli simultaneously; (c) a relativistic comprehension of situations that promotes the erosion of old biases and often expresses itself as tolerance; and (d) a matter-of-fact and unencumbered sort of readiness, a willingness to try new situations and arrangements.
>
> In the loss column, meanwhile, are (a) a fragmented sense of time and a loss of the so-called duration experience, that depth phenomenon we associate with reverie; (b) a reduced attention span and a general impatience with sustained inquiry; (c) a shattered faith in institutions and in the explanatory narratives that formerly gave shape to subjective experience; (d) a divorce from the past, from a vital sense of history as a cumulative or organic process; (e) an estrangement from geographic place and community; and (f) an absence of any strong vision of a personal or collective future. (27)

While the loss column is longer than the gain column, this is largely a matter of presentation: (a) and (f) are pretty such the same, as are (c) and (e). In another sense, measuring a novel against a play like *Macbeth* may itself be comparing apples and oranges, as surely a singular text certified by the author may be more integrated than a composite text found in the First Folio. But even Birkerts enjoys works made up of fragments: he finds a special and lasting pleasure in Virginia Woolf's *A Room of One's Own* largely because it is "a perfect demonstration of what might be called 'magpie aesthetics.' Woolf is the bricoleuse, cobbling with whatever is to hand; she is the flâneuse, redeeming the slight and incidental by creating the context of its true significance" (13). She is, we might say, *writing* (and composing) an early form of hypertext, "a method predicated not upon conclusiveness but upon exploratory digressiveness" (13), her own imagination the sole bonding force, just as the mind of someone reading hypertextually accepts some possibilities and discards others to construct his or her own sense of a basic text's meaning or significance. Someone looking at *Macbeth* from a perspective of Jacobean society may choose whether or not to admit matters of religion to his or her (finally singular) interpretation. Such a reader also practices "magpie aesthetics," just as Birkerts describes himself weaving a biography (or autobiography) out of the discrete stories and memories of his parents telling "of war and dispersal" or the independent (but potentially parallel or correlative) "artifacts" and "reminiscences" of his grandparents (22). Even Birkerts's method informing and shaping the observations of chapter 4, "The Woman in the Garden," is his own polyvocal approach to a single painting (77–86), what is later dismissed because it is "visual," and not a book. Chapter 4, in fact, permits the reverie he has earlier put on the loss side of his ledger, as do his family stories; and such fragments do not—as they never need not—result in "a reduced attention span." In Room 608 at Dalton School, "electronic postmodernity" allows tenth-grade students to *stay* with *Macbeth*, lengthen their "attention span" and establish "sustained inquiry." My design for this book, and in particular chapter 2, addresses (c) in the loss column directly: the shapes given to former institutions allow us to penetrate some of the inherent depths of *Macbeth whether or not* Shakespeare expected us to do so, just as in 1606 some spectators might well have *provided* depth by using multiperspectives to complicate the narrative line of the plot. (The play was always something more than the rise and fall of King Macbeth.) My same argument also addresses (d), although Birkerts does, too, in his appreciation of historical novels set in a particular time and place. What estrangement (e) allows is the "shadow life" (103) or alternative existence which Birkerts claims for good books—which transport us by their content and point of view—but with an added awareness, always, of the text as text. If loss (f) pertains, it is because a hypertextual reader chooses not to distill or combine his or her observations; but if they instead are employed toward the illumination of a base text (such as *Macbeth*), then a "strong vision" will obtain, one that is personal and historical and may be projected as its own grid for the future (as an awareness of kingly assassination of Duncan prepares the playgoer to project—imagine—the assassination of Malcolm as an event beyond the margins of the play, the future that Shakespeare declines to address). At one telling moment, Birkerts even announces that the long-range experience of books is not unlike the awareness of hypertext: "Our print memory is probably more like some indeterminate hyperspace filled with linked-up strands of coded matter, except that the matter is invisible—it is all impulse. The whole of our experience is there, disassembled, in saturated bits, ready for any of the myriad new formations that produce yet another version of the past" (111). He probably means to attack hypertext here—that the mind concerned with hypertext is left only with invisible matter and codes registering impulses, while the book holds together its singular, authorial vision to which a reader can always return. But he does not say that. And if he did, there would be another unstated premise: the *text* may stay the same, but the *reader* will have changed.

In chapter 8, "Into the Electronic Millennium," Birkerts proposes a different list of losses that are the legacy of hypertext (and electronic books). "1. *Language erosion*" (128). But as we have seen abundantly in chapter 2, the historic sense of language is, rather, brought back to life by returning to documents around 1606; and the students of Jacqueline D'Aiutolo practice the further advantage of different periods of language and (with film) different kinds of language. "2. *Flattening of historical perspectives*" (129), suggests that documents from different periods are smoothed out to the kind of singular authority that Birkerts wishes (through the author) all texts had. But in fact, as we have also abundantly seen, different moments of history in Room 608, putting Welles and Polanski alongside the Folio, show discrepancies that add up to duration, to historical changes, to historical relativity. The flatter historical perspective is that of single text, single meaning. "3. *The waning of the private self*" (130), the final objection of Birkerts in this chapter, is the natural consequence of the loss of silent reading, where the reader sits in isolation from the world around him or her, all of the reader's attention and feelings provided, from Birkerts's view, by the author of the text. But hypertext need not be a group process: one reader could match (more or less) what three or four students are doing in Room 608. That matching is done by an active self, not a passive one, and that private self is assembling meaning for which he or she (not the author, or not the author finally) is responsible. The involvement of the private self can only underscore and reactivate the activity of selving.

"The student may, through a program on Shakespeare," Birkerts tells us, "learn an immense amount about Elizabethan politics, the construction of the Globe theater, the origins of certain plays in the writings of Plutarch, the etymology of key terms, and so on, but will this dazzled student find the concentration, the will, to live with the often burred and prickly language of the plays themselves? The play's the thing—but will it be?" (138). It *has* to be, is the answer, if the play is what started the hypertextual exercise in the first place. What Birkerts never examines is the point of entry into hypertext: the reason for initiating it, employing it. As he seems unaware of the cause, so he ignores the consequence. "Wisdom has nothing to do with the gathering or organizing of facts—this is basic," he writes, rather grandly; instead, "Wisdom is a seeing *through* facts, a penetration to the underlying laws and patterns. It related the immediate to something larger—to a context, yes, but also to a big picture that refers to human endeavor *sub specie aeternitatis,* under the aspect of eternity. To see through data, one must have something to see through *to*" (75). What the hypertextual reader of *Macbeth* sees through to is—*Macbeth.* That is what those students in Room 608 are seeing through to and writing about. Uncaptured by some single dominant vision attributed to Shakespeare in the end, they are invited to consider, reflect on, perhaps even at moments of reverie imagine, what the play is *about.* Understanding it, through a selection of documents, a choice of viewpoints, and across time and space, they may well move closer to the Globe, and closer to meanings inherent in the play in 1606 that time, but not language, may have eroded. Like the spectators standing and sitting at the Globe, Shakespeare's play will have become their play.

As I have said, in a sense the analogy breaks down between Birkerts's concern over novels and our discussion of a play. In performance, Shakespeare's play is always public, never private. But Gutenberg's invention allowed Heminge and Condell to fix the performance text into a readerly text that is always potentially a private matter between the words and the reader of those words. At the same time, electronic study of such a play, polyvalent and essentially unending in possibility, has a much greater chance to take the students in Room 608—and us as well— back to the conditions of early performances at the Globe. It brings Shakespeare alive again.[3]

Carl Woodring's more searching and comprehensive examination of such matters as the use of hypertext and digitalized texts is both more sanguine and more conditional. "Make no mistake, the effect of digitalization on literature and literary study will be, not merely profound but the greatest in the history of the alphabet," he observes, and adds, "The question is whether those effects can be controlled or directed by humanists."[4] In the end, Woodring turns to remarks by Henry Louis Gates, Jr., who notes that "humanism"—itself a Renaissance "discovery," like movable type—"asks what we have in common with others while acknowledging the internal diversity among ourselves. It is about the priority of a shared humanity" (187). In that very basic sense, hypertext may not be the end (or the destruction) of the humanities as we know them, but their rebirth: their own Renaissance, and in our time.

Appendix C:
Literary Criticism and Hypertext

As with any Kuhnian paradigm shift, the transformation in literary analysis from examining the form and imagery of a text for its singular meaning to the new methods of hypertext can be wrenching. Those trained in or accustomed to an established canon of great works, the progressive history of ideas or of literary forms, or the verbal icons that established New Criticism during the fearful uncertainties of World War II find reading a text by first breaking it into fragments—even playtexts already divided into parts and susceptible to constant changes in performance—to be oppositional or even antagonistic to the imaginative and creative act that lies behind the making of literary texts. "The power of great literature is generated by its capacity to provide a model of human experience that engages us imaginatively and emotionally as well as intellectually," writes R. V. Young in one of the most recent treatises meant to attack postmodernism as ideological and nihilistic. "Like the other fine arts," he continues, "literature furnishes men and women with a knowledge of themselves that is immediate and concrete while at the same time, paradoxically, the object of disinterested contemplation."[1] As I have been at pains to show, in chapter 2 of this book especially, the most immediate means of understanding a literary text is to examine the concrete cultural practices at the moment of its inception; varied, they force contemplation as well as disinterestedness, while asking the reader (or playgoer) to make meaning by recombination of such actual data (or bytes) through meaningful sequences (or lexias). This prevents the overriding authorial voice from providing unquestioned meaning (what W. K. Wimsatt, Jr., one of the best of the New Critics, called the intentional fallacy), while the hypertextual method of working with historic data prevents the reader from imposing a foreordained response of his or her own (what Wimsatt called the affective fallacy). Hypertext employs data that arise from concerns of an imaginary text and are tested for their validity and utility by returning to that text.

291

What hypertext does to the text is to turn its expressions into lies like truth—similes and metaphors that hypertext illumines, enhancing local parts of a text and in turn the whole work. Its origin and conclusion are both literary, as with the examinations initiated by *Macbeth* in chapter 2. If "Literature is precisely man's imaginative ordering of his experience of the world," as Young goes on to say (16–17), it guarantees that such imaginative ordering is not a preordained, ideological, or imposed experience but one that grows *directly out of the implications of the text itself. Hypertext makes the most of the text.*

Young himself seems to agree: "Great literature . . . is constitutive" (131).[2] But he points to the danger of the initial deconstruction of texts by hypertextual associations when he notes, in discussing Derrida and his infinite deferral of meaning, Derrida's insistence on play for its own linguistic sake, for what becomes for Derrida and many deconstructionists and postmodernists "the priority of the signifier over the signified" (31). The answer, I have proposed, comes by making certain that the signifiers are all authentically historic, of the same broad cultural moment as the text itself. This agrees with, if it enlarges, the judgment of Joseph Sobran, whom Young admires and quotes at some length: "When I was a literature student in college," Young's Sobran remarks, "it was always stressed that the first thing you had to know about a text was what the words meant in their own time. Nobody cared what sublime emotions or fantasies the poet's words stirred in your own breast. The job of the scholar was to discover meaning, not to invent it or impose it" (117), just as hypertext does, the bytes drawn from the time, the lexias as sequential strings of bytes. This guarantees what Young wants and what he turns to in his reading of John Donne's poem "The Canonization": So many signifiers enrich the signified. It is true, of course, that as certain bytes enhance, others may distract, just as certain lexias illuminate and others, mistaken, digress or obscure. Establishing lexias that work—as the students are doing in Room 608 at the Dalton School—challenges, sharpens, and refines the imaginative, intellectual, and emotional responses of readers (just as it does playgoers whose memories are set into motion even during the course of performance).

Just as Young raises questions about the way texts are read, so he questions what is a text that can legitimately be read. New Historicists, he complains, call "works of literature . . . merely documents, not essentially different from any other printed material, products of the economic and cultural hegemonies of their society. As such, literary words are no more 'innocent' than other discourses; even the most personal lyric poem is implicated in the 'discursive formations' of the regnant ideology" (87). It would be difficult, and probably impossible, not to be, just as Young's whole argument is heavily influenced by the "discursive formation" of New Criticism. (His book is dedicated to Wimsatt.) But while this argument may be a telling one against some critical methods, hypertext works through a multiplicity of data—and not all of it is something written, though the observations and experiences are "read" textually—that serves us as mutually, continually self-corrective. That is one of the beauties of hypertext. Hypertext thus upholds what Young calls "the fundamental concept of liberal education," "the commitment to disinterested scholarship in the service of objective truth . . . of which a principal aim is to cultivate a faculty of critical inquiry and a spirit of dispassionate impartiality" (98). The students at Dalton School know the tasks and delights of disinterested inquiry, as they work out sequences of images and interpretations from ages not their own, although they may not remain—should not remain in the end—dispassionate. We applaud or hiss at plays, too.

Hypertext capitalizes on the frontiers of knowledge and practice, on the latest studies of cognitive science and neurology, and on the new programming possibilities of computers, none of which will go away. Conversely, those who insist on studying the literature of the Renaissance through the lens of a Western literary tradition, Tillyard's Elizabethan world picture (or Lovejoy's chain of being), Burckhardt's untrammeled consequences of a liberated individual, or Cleanth Brooks's well-wrought urn are declining to take advantage of the possible advances in literary criticism and our new ways of knowing how plays functioned by examining them through the cultural moment that inspired them and which they addressed. These more traditional critics would probably not retreat further back, to the time when literary criticism amounted to an appreciation of belles lettres, as Charles Lamb practiced it, or characterology, as his colleague William Hazlitt did. Priority in time does not guarantee a superior methodology. But as hyptertext does work toward objective grounding, impartiality through strings of historic data, and reflection on another cultural moment not seen (entirely anyway) through the peculiar filters of our own, so it helps make metaphors live as they once did—fresh, engaging, perhaps even at times overpowering—and helps us to exercise our historic imaginations and our abilities at historic recovery to see dimensions in earlier works, like *Macbeth,* that may have (temporarily, let us hope) been lost over time. We have, Steven Pinker writes at the conclusion of *How the Mind Works,* "a combinatorial mind that open[s] up a world of words and sentences, of theories and equations" by linking data, which are "the very things that make a mind worth having" (565).

Notes

PREFACE

1. Montaigne, Michele Eyquem de, "How One Ought to Gouerne His Will," in *Essays*, trans. John Florio (1603) III.xi., 262.

2. J. R. deJ. Jackson, *Historical Criticism and the Meaning of Texts* (London: Routledge, 1989), 7.

3. Ned Lukacher, *Daemonic Figures: Shakespeare and the Question of Conscience* (Ithaca: Cornell University Press, 1994), 189.

4. Lee Patterson, *Chaucer and the Subject of History* (Madison: University of Wisconsin Press, 1991), 422.

5. Raymond Williams, *Marxism and Literature* (Oxford: Oxford University Press, 1977), 120–22.

6. Garry Wills, *Witches and Jesuits: Shakespeare's "Macbeth"* (Oxford: Oxford University Press, 1995). Antonia Fraser, *Faith and Treason: The Story of the Gunpowder Plot* (New York: Doubleday, 1996).

7. Howard Felperin, *The Uses of the Canon: Elizabethan Literature and Contemporary Theory* (Oxford: Oxford University Press, 1990), 155.

8. Clifford Geertz, *Local Knowledge: Further Essays in Interpretive Anthropology* (New York: Basic Books, 1983), 21.

9. James Bailey, *After Thought: The Computer Challenge to Human Intelligence* (New York: Basic Books, 1996), 6.

10. George Johnson, "Think Again: How Much Give Can the Brain Take?" *New York Times,* section 4 (Week in Review), Sunday, October 24, 1999, p. 1.

CHAPTER 1:
MACBETH AND THE CULTURAL MOMENT

1. Michael J. Collins, "Macbeth and Its Audience," in *Shakespeare: Text, Subtext, and Context,* ed. Ronald Dotterer (Selinsgrove, Pa.: Susquehanna University Press, 1989), 94.

2. Graham Bradshaw, *Shakespeare's Scepticism* (New York: St. Martin's Press, 1987), 223.

3. References are to the New Arden *Macbeth,* ed. Kenneth Muir (Cambridge: Harvard University Press, 1957), and the First Folio Through Line Numbers.

4. Mary Augusta Scott, "The Book of the Courtyer," *PMLA* 16 (1901): 488.

5. John B. Harcourt, " 'I Pray You, Remember the Porter,' " *Shakespeare Quarterly* 12, no. 4 (1961): 394.

6. Graham Bradshaw, *Misrepresentations: Shakespeare and the Materialists* (Ithaca: Cornell University Press, 1993), 15. He is talking about *The Merchant of Venice.*

7. Beatrice Daw Brown, "Exemplum Materials Underlying *Macbeth,*" *PMLA* 50 (1935): 703–5.

8. Judith H. Anderson, *Words That Matter: Linguistic Perception in Renaissance English* (Stanford: Stanford University Press, 1996), 231.

9. T. S. Eliot, "Hamlet," in *Elizabethan Essays* (1934; reprint, New York: Haskell House, 1964), 61–62.

10. T. S. Eliot, "Tradition and the Individual Talent," in *Selected Essays* (New York: Harcourt, Brace, 1964), 3–11.

11. Eric Harth, *The Creative Loop: How the Brain Makes a Mind* (Reading, Mass.: Addison-Wesley, 1993), xxii.

12. The drawing is from Roger Penrose, *The Large, the Small, and the Human Mind* (Cambridge: Cambridge University Press, 1997), 126.

13. Gunnar Liestøl, "Wittgenstein, Genette, and the Reader's Narrative in Hypertext," in *Hyper/Text/Theory,* ed. George P. Landow (Baltimore: John Hopkins University Press, 1994), 87.

14. Daniel McNeill and Paul Freisberger, *Fuzzy Logic* (New York: Touchstone, 1994), 230.

15. Steven Pinker, *How the Mind Works* (New York: Norton, 1997), 83. This connection is, of course, also the basis for AI, artificial intelligence.

16. Terence Cave, *The Cornucopian Text* (Oxford: Clarendon Press, 1979), xi.

17. Mary Thomas Crane, *Framing Authority: Sayings, Self, and Society in Sixteenth-Century England* (Princeton: Princeton University Press, 1993), 4.

18. James Elkins, *The Poetics of Perspective* (Ithaca: Cornell University Press, 1994), 59.

19. I have taken this brief history from Espen J. Aarseth, "Nonlinearity and Literary Theory," in *Hyper/Text/Theory,* ed. Landow, 68.

20. George P. Landow, *Hypertext: The Convergence of Contemporary Critical Theory and Technology* (Baltimore: Johns Hopkins University Press, 1992), 2.

21. Roland Barthes, *S/Z* (Paris: Editions de Seuil, 1970), 11–12; trans. Richard Miller (New York: Hill and Wang, 1974), 5–6; quoted in Landow, *Hypertext,* 3.

22. Michel Foucault, *The Order of Things,* trans. A. M. Sheridan Smith (New York: Harper Colophon, 1976), 23; quoted in Landow, *Hypertext,* 4.

23. Peter Ramus, *La dialectique,* trans. Tom Sorell as *Dialectic in Descartes' Meditations: Background Source and Materials,* ed. Roger Ariew, John Cottingham, and Tom Sorell (Cambridge: Cambridge University Press, 1998), 2–3.

24. Rand J. Spiro, Walter P. Vispoel, John G. Schmitz, Ala Samarapungavan, and A. E. Boerger, "Knowledge Acquisition for Application: Cognitive Flexibility and Transfer in Complex Content Domains," in *Executive Control Processes in Reading,* ed. B. K. Britton and S. McGlynn, (Hillsdale, N.J.: Lawrence Erlbaum, 1987), 187–88; quoted in Landow, *Hypertext,* 122. Emphasis is in the original.

25. Jacques Derrida, *Speech and Phenomena,* trans. David. B. Allison (Evanston, Ill.: Northwestern University Press, 1973), 131; quoted in Landow, *Hypertext,* 8.

26. Thais E. Morgan, "Is There an Intertext in This Text: Literary and Interdisciplinary Approaches to Intertextuality," *American Journal of Semiotics* 3 (1985):1–2, quoted in Landow, 10.

27. Norman Jones and Paul Whitfield White, "*Gorboduc* and Royal Marriage Politics: An Elizabethan Playgoer's Report of the Premiere Performance," *English Literary Renaissance* 26, no. 1 (1986): 6. The full text is transcribed on pp. 3–4.

28. Marie Axton, "Robert Dudley and the Inner Temple Revels," *Historical Journal* 13 (1970): 365–78, cited by Jones and White, "*Gorboduc* and Royal Marriage Politics," 6 n. See also Axton, *The Queen's Two Bodies: Drama and the Elizabethan Succession* (London, 1977), chaps. 4 and 5, also cited by Jones and White.

29. This observation is made by Andrew Gurr, *Playgoing in Shakespeare's London* (Cambridge: Cambridge University Press, 1987), 108. He quotes the full text of Manningham's entry on pp. 107–8. A third extant account, by Simon Forman of a performance of *Macbeth* in 1611, concentrates on the plot of the first half of the play, and his indication that Macbeth and Banquo confront the witches while on horseback suggests he may have been consulting Holinshed in addition to, or even instead of, the play when recording his reactions (ibid.). The account is frequently reprinted; see, for example, Faith Nostbakken, *Understanding "Macbeth"* (Westport, Conn.: Greenwood Press, 1997), 122–23.

30. Vincent B. Leitch, *Cultural Criticism, Literary Theory, Poststructuralism* (New York: Columbia University Press, 1992), 167.

31. Pierre Bourdieu, *Outline of a Theory of Practice,* trans. Richard Nice (Cambridge: Cambridge University Press, 1977), 114.

32. Louis A. Montrose, *The Purpose of Playing: Shakespeare and the Cultural Politics of the Elizabethan Theater* (Chicago: University of Chicago Press, 1996), 20.

33. Quoted by John Nichols, *The Progresses, Processions, and Magnificent Festivities of King James the First, His Royal Consort, Family, and Court,* 4 vols. (London: Society of Antiquaries, 1828), 1:474.

34. Millar MacLure, *Register of Sermons Preached at Paul's Cross, 1534–1642,*

rev. P. Pauls and J. C. Boswell (Toronto: Centre for Reformation and Renaissance Studies, 1993), 85.

35. Paul Hentzner, *Travels in England during the Reign of Queen Elizabeth,* trans. Richard Bentley, ed. Henry Morley (London: Cassell, 1901), 83; Thomas Dekker, *The Seuen Deadlie Sinnes of London* (1606), 50; Dekker, *The Dead Tearme* (1608), 4. These passages and others are discussed by Bruce R. Smith, *The Acoustical World of Early Modern England: Attending to the O-Factor* (Chicago: University of Chicago Press, 1999), 52–64.

36. Recorded by G. B. Harrison in *A Jacobean Journal: Being a Record of Those Things Most Talked of during the Years 1603–1606* (London: Routledge, 1946), 279.

37. Quoted by Nichols, *Progresses,* 1:38.

38. *The Statutes of the Realm. Printed by Command of His Majesty King George the Third in Pursuance of an Address of the House of Commons of Great Britain. From Original and Authentic Manuscripts* (London, 1819), 4:1028.

39. *The Tyrannous Reign of Mary Stewart: George Buchanan's Account—Rerum Scoticarum Historia Books XVIII–XIX,* trans. and ed. W. A. Gatherer (Edinburgh: University Press, 1958), 111.

40. Alvin Kernan, *Shakespeare, the King's Playwright: Theater in the Stuart Court, 1603–1613* (New Haven: Yale University Press, 1995), 92.

41. Naomi Conn Liebler, *Shakespeare's Festive Tragedy: The Ritual Foundations of Genre* (London: Routledge, 1995), 222.

42. Michael Hawkins, "History, Politics, and *Macbeth,*" in *Focus on "Macbeth,"* ed. John Russell Brown (London: Routledge and Kegan Paul, 1982), 182.

43. Quoted by Janet Clare, *"Art Made Tongue-Tied by Authority": Elizabethan and Jacobean Dramatic Censorship* (Manchester: Manchester University Press, 1990), 98.

44. *The Essayes of Michael Lord of Montaigne Done into English by John Florio,* ed. Thomas Seecombe (New York: Dutton, 1908), 97.

CHAPTER 2:
CULTURAL PRACTICES

1. Curtis C. Breight, *Surveillance, Militarism, and Drama in the Elizabethan Era* (London: Macmillan, 1996), 89.

2. Ian Archer, "The Nostalgia of John Stow," in *The Theatrical City: Culture, Theatre and Politics in London, 1576–1649,* ed. David L. Smith, Richard Strier, and David Bevington (Cambridge: Cambridge University Press, 1995), 20–22, 41.

3. Howard Nenner, *The Right to Be King: The Succession to the Crown of England, 1603–1714* (Chapel Hill: University of North Carolina Press, 1995), 1.

4. Quoted in ibid., 22.

5. Historical Manuscripts Commission, *Calendar of the Manuscripts of the Most Honourable The Marquess of Salisbury Preserved at Hatfield House Hertfordshire* (London; Historical Manuscripts Commission, 1976), 24:282–83. I am indebted to Stuart M. Kurland for first calling these papers to my attention.

6. *Calendar of State Papers, Domestic Elizabeth,* 298–99.

7. Leeds Barroll, *Politics, Plague and Shakespeare's Theater: The Stuart Years* (Ithaca: Cornell University Press, 1991), 65–66.

8. *Dudley Carleton to John Chamberlain (1603–1624),* ed. Maurice Lee, Jr. (New Brunswick: Rutgers University Press, 1972), 51.

9. J. R. Tanner, *Constitutional Documents of the Reign of James I, A.D. 1603–1625* (Cambridge: Cambridge University Press, 1930), 338.

10. Patricia Parker, *Shakespeare from the Margins: Language, Culture, Context* (Chicago: University of Chicago Press, 1996), 256.

11. Thomas M'Crie, *The Life of Andrew Melville,* 2 vols. (Edinburgh: William Blackwood, 1819), 2:259.

12. G. Wilson Knight, *The Wheel of Fire: Essays in Interpretation of Shakespeare's Sombre Tragedies* (Oxford: Oxford University Press, 1930), 156–57.

13. Alvin Thaler, "The Players at Court," *Journal of English and Germanic Philology* 19, no. 1 (1920): 29.

14. I have chosen the text quoted in Virginia Cocheron Gildersleeve, *Government Regulations of the Elizabethan Drama* (New York: Columbia University Press, 1908), 36–37.

15. My text is from Andrew Gurr, *The Shakespearean Stage, 1574–1642,* 2nd ed. (Cambridge: Cambridge University Press, 1980), 197.

16. Roslyn Lander Knutson, *The Repertory of Shakespeare's Company, 1594–1613* (Fayetteville: University of Arkansas Press, 1991), 33.

17. Bernard Beckerman, *Shakespeare at the Globe, 1599–1609* (New York: Macmillan, 1962), 9, 130.

18. For additional speculations and drawings see Richard Hosley, "The First Globe Playhouse," in J. Leeds Barroll, Alexander Leggatt, Hosley, and Alvin Kernan, *The Revels History of Drama in English,* 4 vols. (London: Methuen, 1975), 3:175–96, but see also 121–74, 197–235.

19. *Calendar of State Papers, Venetian,* 10:206.

20. E. K. Chambers, *The Elizabethan Stage,* 4 vols. (Oxford: Clarendon Press, 1951), 1:7 n.

21. R. B. McKerrow, "The Elizabethan Printer and Dramatic Manuscripts," *The Library,* 4th ser., 12 (1931): 266.

22. Alan C. Dessen, *Elizabethan Stage Conventions and Modern Interpreters* (Cambridge: Cambridge University Press, 1984), 25–27.

23. Stephen Orgel, *The Illusion of Power: Political Theater in the English Renaissance* (Berkeley: University of California Press, 1975), 16–17, 19–20.

24. Ann Jennalie Cook, *The Privileged Playgoers of Shakespeare's London, 1576–1642* (Princeton: Princeton University Press, 1981); but see also Martin Butler, *Theatre and Crisis, 1632–1642* (Cambridge: Cambridge University Press, 1984), appendix 2, "Shakespeare's unprivileged playgoers 1576–1642," 293–306.

25. Gurr, *Shakespearean Stage,* 12.

26. John L. McMullan, *The Canting Crew: London's Criminal Underworld, 1550–1700* (New Brunswick: Rutgers University Press, 1984), 137.

27. Quoted from Thomas F. VanLaan, *Role-playing in Shakespeare* (Toronto: University of Toronto Press, 1978), 13–15.

28. Some of this paragraph is derived from David Bergeron, *Royal Family, Royal Lovers: King James of England and Scotland* (Columbia: University of Missouri Press, 1991).

29. Kernan, *Shakespeare,* 41.

30. G. P. V. Akrigg, *Jacobean Pageant; or, The Court of King James I* (Cambridge: Harvard University Press, 1962), 18.

31. "The King's Entertainment at Worksop and Newark" (1603), as reprinted in Nichols, *Progresses,* 1:88–89.

32. *The Manner of the Coronation,* ed. Christopher Wordsworth (London: Henry Bradshaw Liturgical Text Society, 1892), appendix 3, 80–83.

33. Kenneth Muir in his introduction to the New Arden *Macbeth,* rev. ed. (London: Methuen, 1972), xxxiv.

34. M. C. Bradbrook, "The Sources of *Macbeth,*" in *Aspects of "Macbeth,"* ed. Kenneth Muir and Philip Edwards (Cambridge: Cambridge University Press, 1977), 17.

35. R. Malcolm Smuts, introduction to Thomas Middleton, *The Magnificent Entertainment,* in *The Works of Thomas Middleton,* ed. Gary Taylor et al., forthcoming from Oxford University Press.

36. Thomas Dekker, *The Magnificent Entertainment Given to King James, and Queen Anne His Wife, and Henry Frederick the Prince,* as reprinted in Nichols, *Progresses,* 1:339.

37. David M. Bergeron, *English Civic Pageantry, 1558–1647* (Columbia: University of South Carolina Press, 1971), 76.

38. This account of the *Minerva Britannia* is adapted from Graham Parry, *The Golden Age Restor'd: The Culture of the Stuart Court, 1558–1647* (New York: St. Martin's Press, 1981), 23–24.

39. Graham Parry, *The Seventeenth Century: The Intellectual and Cultural Context of English Literature, 1605–1700* (London: Longman, 1989), 19.

40. From a manuscript titled *A Perfect Description of the People and Country of Scotland* by Anthony Weldon, as quoted in A. W. Beasley, "The Disability of James VI and I," *The Seventeenth Century* 10, no. 2 (1995): 153.

41. Brian P. Levack, *The Formation of the British State: England, Scotland, and the Union, 1605–1707* (Oxford: Clarendon Press, 1987), 61; his discussion is particularly useful.

42. Quoted by Akrigg, *Jacobean Pageant,* without source, as epigraph for chap. 5, p. 48.

43. Quoted in Maurice Lee, Jr., *Government by Pen: Scotland under James VI and I* (Urbana: University of Illinois Press, 1980), 36.

44. Pauline Croft, "Robert Cecil and the Early Jacobean Court," in *The Mental World of the Jacobean Court,* ed. Linda Levy Peck (Cambridge: Cambridge University Press, 1991), 136.

45. Quoted by Bruce Galloway, *The Union of England and Scotland, 1605–1608* (Edinburgh: John Donald Publishers, 1986), 18.

46. P. Hume Brown, *Early Descriptions of Scotland* (Cambridge: Cambridge University Press, 1908), 43, 60 (Major), 99 (Boece).

47. Quoted from William Carroll, *Macbeth: Texts and Contexts* (Boston: Bedford/St. Martins, 1999), 11. Carroll provides additional contemporary documents not cited here on sovereignty, treason and resistance, ideas of Scotland, witchcraft and prophecy, and women, pp. 185ff. But see also his introduction (1–20).

48. W. Croft Dickinson, *Scotland from the Earliest Times to 1603,* 3rd ed., rev. and ed. Archibald A. M. Duncan (Oxford: Clarendon Press, 1977), 387.

49. Jenny Wormald gives an especially helpful summary of anti-Scots sentiment in England, drawing on particular instances with apprentices (such as the members of Shakespeare's audience) in "Gunpowder, Treason, and Scots," *Journal of British Studies* 24 (April 1985): 159–60.

50. Galloway, *Union of England and Scotland,* 165.

51. Kenneth Fincham and Peter Lake, "The Ecclesiastical Policy of King James I," *Journal of British Studies* 24, no. 2 (1985): 169.

52. Quoted in Parry, *Golden Age Restor'd,* 21.

53. *An Epistle or exhoration, to vnitie & peace sent from the Lorde Protector, & others the kynges moste honorable counsaill of England: To the Nobilitie, Gentlemen, and Commons, and al others the inhabitauntes of the Realme of Scotlande* known as "The Complaynt of Scotland," ed. James A. H. Murray as appendix 3 (London: Early English Text Society, 1872), 243. I am grateful to Scott Lucas for sharing this text with me.

54. Roger A. Mason, "Introduction: Imagining Scotland: Scottish Political Thought and the Problem of Britain, 1560–1650," in *Scots and Britons: Scottish Political Thought and the Union of 1603,* ed. Mason (Cambridge: Cambridge University Press, 1994), 7.

55. Lori Anne Ferrell, *Government by Polemic* (Stanford: Stanford University Press, 1998), 42 (quote), 53.

56. Nichols, *Progresses,* 1:331.

57. I have taken these facts from Keith M. Brown, "The Vanishing Emperor: British Kingship and Its Decline, 1603–1707," in *Scots and Britons,* ed. Mason, 79.

58. Ibid., 63.

59. Wormald in *Scots and Britons,* ed. Mason, 19, cites these two poems and adds other works, pp. 19–23.

60. Cowper, Maxwell, and Russell passages are from Arthur H. Williamson, "Scotland, Antichrist, and the Invention of Great Britain," in *New Perspectives on the Politics and Culture of Early Modern Scotland,* ed. John Dwyer, Roger A. Mason, and Alexander Murdoch (Edinburgh: John Donald Publishers Ltd., n.d.), 44–45.

61. Wormald in *Scots and Britons,* ed. Mason, 22.

62. Quoted in Carole Levin, *"The Heart and Stomach of a King": Elizabeth I and the Politics of Sex and Power* (Philadelphia: University of Pennsylvania Press, 1994), 7.

63. Modern discussions of this begin with Frances A. Yates, *Astraea: The Imperial Theme in the Sixteenth Century* (London: Routledge and Kegan Paul, 1975); see especially 42–43.

64. Wormald in *Scots and Britons*, ed. Mason, 19.

65. Reprinted in Nichols, *Progresses*, 1:49.

66. Ernst H. Kantorowicz, *The King's Two Bodies: A Study in Medieval Political Theology* (Princeton: Princeton University Press, 1957), 496.

67. In conversation with Peter Blayney in April 1994.

68. *Scots and Britons*, ed. Mason, 10.

69. Glenn Burgess, *Absolute Monarchy and the Stuart Constitution* (New Haven: Yale University Press, 1996), 41.

70. As quoted in Francois Laroque, "Magic in *Macbeth*," *Cahiers Elisabethains*, no.35 (April 1989): 74–75.

71. Levin, *"Heart and Stomach of a King,"* 21.

72. Quoted in Marc Bloch, *The Royal Touch* (New York: Dorset Press, 1989), 188. Cf. Carroll, *Macbeth*, 224–25.

73. A good summary of these matters is F. David Hoeniger, *Medicine and Shakespeare in the English Renaissance* (Newark: University of Delaware Press, 1982), chap. 16, "The Royal Cure of Scrofula or the King's Evil in *Macbeth* and in Shakespeare's Time," 275–86. Carroll reprints part of Howson's sermon (*Macbeth*, 30), from which I have taken this excerpt.

74. Brian P. Levack, "Law and Ideology: The Civil Law and Theories of Absolutism in Elizabethan and Jacobean England," in *The Historical Renaissance*, ed. Heather Dubrow and Richard Strier (Chicago: University of Chicago Press, 1988), 228–29.

75. Lord Scrope, Pury Ogilive, and David Calderwood are all quoted in Bergeron, *Royal Family, Royal Lovers*, 44.

76. *Letters of King James VI and I*, ed. G. P. V. Akrigg (Berkeley: University of California Press, 1984), 63–72, 79–80, 84–85, 87–88.

77. Bergeron, *Royal Family, Royal Lovers*, 74; *Letters of King James*, ed. Akrigg, 326–27. "It was not until the last century that James' coffin was discovered, sharing the vault with Henry VII and Elizabeth of York beneath Pietro Torrigiani's superb monument for the founder of the Tudor dynasty and his queen": Irvin Leigh Matus, *Shakespeare: The Living Record* (New York: St. Martin's Press, 1991), 49.

78. Markku Peltonen, *Classical Humanism and Republicanism in English Political Thought, 1570–1640* (Cambridge: Cambridge University Press, 1995), 125.

79. Sir Philip Sidney, *Works*, ed. Albert Feuillerat, 4 vols. (Cambridge: Cambridge University Press, 1912, 1963), 3:132.

80. Gabriel Harvey, *Marginalia*, ed. G. C. Moore (Stratford: Shakespeare Head Press, 1913), 143 (to 461a).

81. David Womersley, "Sir Henry Savile's Translation of Tacitus and the Political Interpretation of Elizabethan Texts," *Review of English Studies* 52 (August 1991): 323. The passages from Savile's Tacitus are from pp. 322–24.

82. Keith Wrightson, "The Politics of the Parish in Early Modern England," in *The Experience of Authority in Early Modern England,* ed. Paul Griffiths, Adam Fox, and Steve Hindle (London: Macmillan, 1996), 12.

83. Bernard Capp, "Separate Domains? Women and Authority," in *Experience of Authority,* ed. Griffiths, Fox, and Hindle, 221.

84. Quoted by Breight, *Surveillance,* 90.

85. Quoted by Barbara Peardon in "The Politics of Polemic: John Ponet's *Short Treatise of Politic Power* and Contemporary Circumstance, 1553–1556," *Journal of British Studies* 22, no. 1 (1982): 45. Carroll (*Macbeth,* 237–38) reprints passages from Ponet.

86. Jenny Wormald, *Court, Kirk, and Community: Scotland, 1470–1625* (London: Edward Arnold, 1981), 113. Excerpts from Persons in Carroll, *Macbeth,* 191–200.

87. Thomas McCrie, *The Life of John Knox,* 2 vols. (Edinburgh: William Blackwood, 1813), 1:8.

88. Roger A. Mason, "Knox, Resistance, and the Moral Imperative," *History of Political Thought* 1, no. 3 (1980): 411.

89. George Buchanan, *De jure regni apud Scotos* (Edinburgh, 1579), trans. Charles F. Arrowood (1949) in Carroll, *Macbeth,* 242, 244.

90. *"A Defence of Liberty Against Tyrants": A Translation of "Vindiciae Contra Tyrannos"* by Harold J. Laski (New York: Burt Franklin, 1972), 190, 213.

91. Estienne de la Boëtie, *Slaves by Choice,* trans. Malcolm Smith (Egham Hill, Surrey: Runnymede Books, 1988), 47–48.

92. George L. Mosse, *The Struggle for Sovereignty in England from the Reign of Queen Elizabeth to the Petition of Right* (East Lansing: Michigan State College Press, 1950), 17.

93. Adam Blackwood, *Pro Regibus Apologia,* quoted in J. H. Barns, "George Buchanan and the Anti-monarchomachs," in *Scots and Britons,* ed. Mason, 149.

94. Quoted in Peltonen, *Classical Humanism,* 155.

95. Robert S. Miola, *"Julius Caesar* and the Tyrannicide Debate," *Renaissance Quarterly* 38, no. 2 (1985): 271.

96. Debora Kuller Shuger, *Habits of Thought in the English Renaissance: Religion, Politics, and the Dominant Culture* (Berkeley: University of California Press, 1990), 155–56.

97. Akrigg, *Jacobean Pageant,* 8.

98. Maynard Mack, Jr., *Killing the King: Three Studies in Shakespeare's Tragic Structure* (New Haven: Yale University Press, 1973), 148.

99. M. C. Bradbrook, *Muriel Bradbrook on Shakespeare* (Brighton, Sussex: Harvester Press, 1984), 145.

100. Nigel Trantor, *The Story of Scotland* (London: Routledge and Kegan Paul, 1987), 158–59.

101. D. Harris Willson, *King James VI and I* (London: Jonathan Cape, 1956), 112–13.

102. Stanley J. Kozikowski, "The Gowrie Conspiracy against James VI: A New Source for Shakespeare's *Macbeth*," *Shakespeare Studies* 13 (1980): 197–212.

103. Jennifer M. Brown, "Scottish Politics, 1567–1625," in *The Reign of James VI and I*, ed. Alan G. R. Smith (London: Macmillan, 1973, 1983), 29.

104. Quoted in Samuel Cowan, *The Gowrie Conspiracy and Its Official Narrative* (London: Sampson Low, Marston, and Company, 1902), 124–25.

105. Quoted in ibid., 129.

106. Nichols, *Progresses,* 1:470.

107. Curt Breight, " 'Treason Doth Never Prosper': *The Tempest* and the Discourse of Treason," *Shakespeare Quarterly* 41, no. 1 (1990): 12.

108. Mervyn James, *Society, Politics, and Culture: Studies in Early Modern England* (Cambridge: Cambridge University Press, 1986), 445–65; see esp. 447, 458.

109. Reprinted in *Stuart Royal Proclamations,* ed. James F. Larkin and Paul L. Hughes, 3 vols. (Oxford: Clarendon Press, 1973), 1:72.

110. Some of these details are taken from M. C. Bradbrook, *Shakespeare: The Poet in His World* (New York: Columbia University Press, 1978), 181–82. Cf. Antonia Fraser, *Faith and Treason: The Story of the Gunpowder Plot* (New York: Doubleday, 1996).

111. Nichols, *Progresses,* 1:584, 586–87.

112. *The Chamberlain Letters,* ed. Elizabeth McClure Thomson (London: John Murray, 1966), 57.

113. References are to the *Calendar of State Papers, Venetian,* vol. 10.

114. G. Abbott, *Tortures of the Tower of London* (Newton Abbot: David & Charles, 1986), 24–27.

115. Unidentified epigraph in John Gerard, S.J., *What Was the Gunpowder Plot?* (London: Osgood, McIlvaine, & Co., 1897), facing p. 1.

116. Joel Hurstfield, "Gunpowder Plot and the Politics of Dissent," in *Early Stuart Studies: Essays in Honor of David Harris Willson,* ed. Howard S. Reinmuth, Jr. (Minneapolis: University of Minnesota Press, 1970), 104.

117. Ibid., 105. William Barlow, bishop of Rochester, delivered the royal sermon on the first anniversary of the Powder Plot, using Psalm 18:50 as his text. See Ferrell, *Government by Polemic,* 77ff.

118. Christopher Devlin, *Hamlet's Divinity and Other Essays* (Carbondale: Southern Illinois University Press, 1963), 152.

119. Henry N. Paul, in *The Royal Play of "Macbeth"* (New York: Macmillan, 1950), 227, makes a similar observation.

120. J. A. Sharpe, *Early Modern England: A Social History, 1550–1760* (London: Edward Arnold, 1987), 111–12.

121. Merchant Taylors Court Minutes Books, 3:428; quoted by Steve Rappaport, *Worlds within Worlds: Structures of Life in Sixteenth-Century London* (Cambridge: Cambridge University Press, 1989), 65; also quoted in Ian Archer, *The Pursuit of Stability: Social Relations in Elizabethan London* (Cambridge Cambridge University Press, 1991), 204.

122. Quoted in I. Archer, *Pursuit of Stability*, 204.

123. Quoted from McMullan, *Canting Crew*, 85; a transcription of the original in old spelling may be found in *Tudor Economic Documents*, ed. R. H. Tawney and Eileen Power, 3 vols. (London: Longmans, Green, 1924), 2:335–37.

124. Harrison quoted in McMullan, *Canting Crew*, 91.

125. The examples are from Breight, *Surveillance*, 49–51.

126. Albert H. Tricomi, *Reading Tudor-Stuart Texts through Cultural Historicism* (Gainesville: University Press of Florida, 1996), 49–50.

127. John Michael Archer, *Sovereignty and Intelligence: Spying and Court Culture in the English Renaissance* (Stanford: Stanford University Press, 1993), 1.

128. Many of these details are from Alan Haynes, *Invisible Power: The Elizabethan Secret Services, 1570–1603* (Stroud, Gloucestershire: Alan Sutton, 1992), 140.

129. Quoted in ibid., 149.

130. G. R. Elton, "Informing for Profit," in *Star Chamber Stories*, ed. Elton (London: Methuen, 1958).

131. Quoted in J. M. Archer, *Sovereignty and Intelligence*, 125.

132. These examples are in Tricomi, *Reading Tudor-Stuart Texts*, 53,59.

133. Mark Kishlansky, *A Monarchy Transformed: Britain, 1603–1714* (London: Penguin, 1996), 17.

134. Roger B. Manning, *Village Revolts: Social Protest and Popular Disturbances in England, 1509–1640* (Oxford: Clarendon Press, 1988), 177.

135. These statistics are in Arthur N. Stunz, "The Date of *Macbeth*," *ELH* 9 (1942): 95–96.

136. Facts, statistics, and quotations have been assembled from manuscripts, public records, and from Keith Wrightson and David Levine, *Poverty and Piety in an English Village: Terling, 1525–1700*, 2nd ed., with a new postscript by Wrightson (Oxford: Clarendon Press 1995); John Walter and Keith Wrightson, "Dearth and the Social Order in Early Modern England," *Past and Present*, no. 71 (May 1976): 22–42; John Walter, "A 'Rising of the People'? The Oxfordshire Rising of 1596," *Past and Present*, no. 107 (May 1985): 90–143; John Walter, "The Social Economy of Dearth in Early Modern England," in *Famine, Disease, and the Social Order in Early Modern Society*, ed. John Walter and Roger Schofield (Cambridge: Cambridge University Press, 1989), 75–128; Buchanan Sharp, *In Contempt of All Authority: Rural Artisans and Riot in the West of England, 1586–1660* (Berkeley: University of California Press, 1980); and a talk by John Guy at the Folger Shakespeare Library on October 4, 1991.

137. A. L. Beier. *Masterless Men: The Vagrancy Problem in England, 1560–1640* (London: Methuen, 1985), 40.

138. Arthur J. Slavin, *The Tudor Age and Beyond: England from the Black Death to the End of the Age of Elizabeth* (Malabar, Fla.: Robert E. Krieger, 1987), 57.

139. John Strype in John Stow, *Survey of the Cities of London and Westminster*, quoted in Manning, *Village Revolts*, 192.

140. SP/12/43/19 quoted by Laura Hunt Yungblut, *Strangers Settled Here among Us* (London: Routledge, 1996), 102–3.

141. PRO, STAC, 5/P6/22 quoted in I. Archer, *Pursuit of Stability,* 137.

142. See also Jim Sharpe, "Social Strain and Social Dislocation, 1585–1603," in *The Reign of Elizabeth I: Court and Culture in the Last Decade,* ed. John Guy (Cambridge: Cambridge University Press, 1995), 192–212.

143. Graham Holderness, " 'Come in Equivocator': Tragic Ambivalence in *Macbeth,*" in *Critical Essays on "Macbeth,"* ed. Linda Cookson and Bryan Loughrey (London: Longman, 1988), 66.

144. For a good brief discussion, see A. J. Fletcher and J. Stevenson's introduction to *Order and Disorder in Early Modern England,* ed. Fletcher and Stevenson (Cambridge: Cambridge University Press, 1985), 1ff.

145. The MS of Thomas Wilson, "The State of England Anno Dom. 1600," as ed. by F. J. Fisher in the *Camden Miscellany,* vol. 16, 3rd series, vol. 52 (London: Office of the Camden Society, 1936), 22–23.

146. Peter Clark and Paul Slack, *English Towns in Transition, 1500–1700* (Oxford: Oxford University Press, 1976), 129.

147. Lawrence Stone, *The Crisis of the Aristocracy, 1558–1641* (Oxford: Clarendon Press, 1965), 31.

148. A. J. Fletcher, "Honour, Reputation, and Local Officeholding in Elizabethan and Stuart England," in *Order and Disorder,* ed. Fletcher and Stevenson, 115.

149. Quoted in L. C. Knights, *Drama and Society in the Age of Jonson* (London: Chatto and Windus, 1962), 148.

150. Quoted in Peltonen, *Classical Humanism,* 159.

151. The figures are reported in Cook, *Privileged Playgoers,* 40.

152. Wallace MacCaffrey, introduction to William Camden, *The History of the Most Renowned and Victorious Princess Elizabeth, Late Queen of England: Selected Chapters* (of the *Annals*) (Chicago: University of Chicago Press, 1970), xiii–xiv.

153. Ruth Kelso, *The Doctrine of the English Gentleman in the Sixteenth Century* (Urbana: University of Illinois Press, 1929), 18.

154. Frank Whigham, *Ambition and Privilege: The Social Tropes of Elizabethan Courtesy Theory* (Berkeley: University of California Press, 1984), 18.

155. Quoted in ibid., 26.

156. Mervyn James, *Family, Lineage, and Civil Society: A Study of Society, Politics, and Mentality in the Durham Region, 1500–1649* (Oxford: Clarendon Press, 1974), 276.

157. The remarks of Wynn and D'Ewes are in Stone, *Crisis,* 23.

158. Gail Kern Paster, *The Body Embarrassed: Drama and the Disciplines of Shame in Early Modern England* (Ithaca: Cornell University Press, 1993), 66. Bellenden and le Loyer are quoted in the introduction to *Macbeth,* ed. A. R. Braunmuller (Cambridge: Cambridge University Press, 1997), 38, 33–34.

159. Harry Berger, Jr., "The Early Scenes of Macbeth: Preface to a New Interpretation" in *Making Trifles of Terrors: Redistributing Complicities in Shakespeare,* ed. Peter Erickson (Stanford: Stanford University Press, 1997), 93.

160. The figures are from Stone, *Crisis,* 67.

161. B.M. Harleian MSS. 1173, fol. 85; in Stone, *Crisis*, 68.

162. Victor Kiernan, *Eight Tragedies of Shakepeare: A Marxist Study* (London: Verso, 1966), 138.

163. Norbert Elias, *The Civilizing Process* (*Uber den Prozess der Zivilisation*), trans. Edmund Jephcott, 2 vols. (New York: Pantheon Books, 1982), 2:259, 267.

164. Quoted without source in Roy Strong, *Splendor at Court: Renaissance Spectacle and the Theater of Power* (Boston: Houghton Mifflin, 1973), 45.

165. James, *Society, Politics, and Culture*, 314–15.

166. James, *Family, Lineage, and Civil Society*, 416–17.

167. B. L. Cotton MS, Vespasian 114, fol. 100, quoted in Richard C. McCoy, *The Rites of Knighthood: The Literature and Politics of Elizabethan Chivalry* (Berkeley: University of California Press, 1989), 90.

168. *The Farmer Chetham MS*, p. 189, quoted in James, *Society, Politics, and Culture*, 432.

169. *Calendar of State Papers, Domestic*, 592, quoted in Beach Langston, "Essex and the Art of Dying," *Huntington Library Quarterly* 13 (1949–50): 127–28.

170. Anthony Fletcher, *Gender, Sex, and Subordination in England, 1500–1800* (New Haven: Yale University Press, 1995), 322.

171. Theodore Spencer, *Shakespeare and the Nature of Man*. Lowell Lectures, 1942 (New York: Macmillan, 1942), 153.

172. Michael Long, *Macbeth*. Twayne's New Critical Introductions to Shakespeare (Boston: Twayne Publishers, 1989), 10.

173. Quoted by Keith M. Brown, *Bloodfeud in Scotland, 1573–1625: Violence, Justice, and Politics in an Early Modern Society* (Edinburgh: John Donald Publishers, Ltd., 1986), 203.

174. Quoted in ibid., 216; this account of James draws on ibid., 214–16. It is an extremely useful study in clan and blood honor in Scotland.

175. Jenny Wormald, *Lords and Men in Scotland: Bonds of Manrent, 1442–1603* (Edinburgh: John Donald Publishers, Ltd., 1985). This book is a singular and definitive study of a crucial Scottish tradition.

176. James, *Society, Politics, and Culture*, 330.

177. Perez Zagorin, *Ways of Lying: Dissimulation, Persecution, and Conformity in Early Modern Europe* (Cambridge: Harvard University Press, 1990), 224.

178. James, *Society, Politics, and Culture*, 339–40.

179. Barbara Hodgdon, *The First Part of King Henry the Fourth: Texts and Contexts* (Boston: Bedford Books, 1997), 333. The following texts by Segar, Riche, Sutcliffe, and Silver are on pp. 336–48.

180. Bruce R. Smith, *Homosexual Desire in Shakespeare's England: A Cultural Poetics* (Chicago: University of Chicago Press, 1991), 57–58.

181. Stephen Orgel, *Impersonations: The Performance of Gender in Shakespeare's England* (Cambridge: Cambridge University Press, 1996), 21.

182. Thomas Laqueur, *Making Sex: Body and Gender from the Greeks to Freud* (Cambridge: Harvard University Press, 1990). The case may be overstated, but

certain anatomical drawings of the early modern period suggest confusion. Melville quoted by Lawrence Normand, " 'What Passion Call You These?': *Edward II and James VI*," in *Christopher Marlowe and English Renaissance Culture,* ed. Darryl Grantley and Peter Roberts (London: Scolar Press, 1996), 183.

183. Bruce R. Smith, "L(o)cating the Sexual Subject," in *Alternative Shakespeares,* vol. 2, ed. Terence Hawkes (London: Routledge, 1996), 98.

184. Alan Sinfield, "How to Read *The Merchant of Venice* without Being Heterosexist," in *Alternative Shakespeares,* 2:130.

185. CLRO Rep. 27, fol. 319, quoted by Paul Griffiths in *Youth and Authority: Formative Experiences in England, 1560–1640* (Oxford: Clarendon Press, 1996), 271.

186. Quoted in Gregory W. Bredbeck, *Sodomy and Interpretation: Marlowe to Milton* (Ithaca: Cornell University Press, 1991), 5.

187. Alan Bray, *Homosexuality in Renaissance England* (London: Gay Men's Press, 1982), 47, 77–78.

188. Sinfield, "How to Read *The Merchant of Venice*," 134.

189. The case is persuasively made, with its social limitations, by Lois Banner, "The Fashionable Sex, 1100–1600," *History Today* 102 (April 1992): 37–44.

190. Robert Cecil, "The State and Dignitie of a Secretarie of State," Bodleian Ashmole MS 826, fol. 29, published in 1642 as *The State and Dignitie of a Secretarie of Estates Place. With the care and perill thereof.* The issue is discussed in Alan Stewart, "The Early Modern Closet Discovered," *Representations* 50 (Spring 1995): 76–100.

191. Lynda Boose has extended the image of blood in a letter to me, suggesting that "*Bellona's* Bridegroome, lapt in proofe" (1.2.55; 79), which associates blood in the man's lap area, or genital area, collates with the image of Tarquin in equating sexual penetration with the violence of war. The image may also collate with the bloody dagger Macbeth uses to penetrate Duncan; death and lovemaking were frequently related in the imagination and in conversation at this cultural moment.

192. David Cressy, "Kinship and Kin Interaction in Early Modern England," *Past and Present,* no. 113 (November 1986): 68.

193. Modernized and reprinted by Lena Cowen Orlin in *Elizabethan Households: An Anthology* (Washington, D.C.: Folger Shakespeare Library, 1995), 147.

194. Quoted in Keith Wrightson, *English Society, 1580–1680* (New Brunswick: Rutgers University Press, 1982), 67.

195. Quoted by Catherine Belsey, "The Serpent in the Garden: Shakespeare, Marriage and Material Culture," *The Seventeenth Century* 11, no. 1 (1996): 5.

196. Thomas Becon, *Worckes* (1560–1564), I, fol. Dcxvi, quoted by Belsey, "Serpent in the Garden," 5.

197. Plutarch, "Precepts of Wedlocke," in *The Philosophie, commonlie called The Morals* (1603), trans. Philemon Holland, 317–18.

198. Keith Wrightson, "The Politics of the Parish," in *Experience of Authority,* ed. Griffiths, Fox, and Hindle, 16.

199. See the discussion in Wrightson, *English Society,* 66–88.

200. G. E. Mingay, *The Gentry: The Rise and Fall of a Ruling Class* (1976), as quoted in Wrightson, *English Society,* 73.

201. William Perkins, *Christian Oeconomie* (1609), as reproduced in *Daughters, Wives, and Widows: Writings by Men about Women and Marriage in England, 1500–1640,* ed. Joan Larsen Klein (Urbana: University of Illinois Press, 1992), 171.

202. William Whately in *The Cultural Identity of Seventeenth-Century Woman: A Reader,* ed. N. H. Keeble (London: Routledge, 1994), 145.

203. Russ McDonald, *The Bedford Companion to Shakespeare: An Introduction with Documents* (Boston: Bedford Books of St. Martin's Press, 1996), 252.

204. Edmund Tilney, quoted in Suzanne W. Hull, *Women According to Men: The World of Tudor-Stuart Women* (Walnut Creek, Calif.: Sage Publications, 1996), 36.

205. Reprinted in *Daughters, Wives, and Widows,* ed. Klein, 132.

206. Reprinted in Hull, *Women According to Men,* 37.

207. The statistics are from David Marcombe, *English Small Town Life: Retford, 1520–1642* (Oxford: Alden Press for the University of Nottingham Department of Adult Education, 1993), 143–44. I have taken the figures of this local history as representative.

208. Wrightson, *English Society,* 208.

209. D. E. Underdown, "The Taming of the Scold: The Enforcement of Patriarchal Authority in Early Modern England," in *Order and Disorder,* ed. Fletcher and Stevenson, 116–17.

210. Linda Woodbridge, *Women and the English Renaissance: Literature and the Nature of Womankind, 1540–1620* (Urbana: University of Illinois Press, 1984), 193.

211. *Thomas Platter's Travels in England, 1599,* trans. Clare Williams (London, 1937), as quoted in Susan Dwyer Amussen, *An Ordered Society: Gender and Class in Early Modern England* (Oxford: Basil Blackwell, 1988), 49.

212. Quoted in Viviana Comensoli, *"Household Business": Domestic Plays of Early Modern England* (Toronto: University of Toronto Press, 1996), 21.

213. Patricia Crawford, "The Construction and Experience of Maternity in Seventeenth-Century England," in *Women as Mothers in Pre-Industrial England,* ed. Valerie Fildes (London: Routledge, 1990), as cited in Allison Sim, *The Tudor Housewife* (Montreal: McGill-Queen's University Press, 1996), 16.

214. *The Private Correspondence of Jane, Lady Corwallis, 1633–1644,* quoted in Sim, *The Tudor Housewife,* 18.

215. Quoted by Valerie Wayne, "Advice for Women from Mothers and Patriarchs," in *Women and Literature in Britain, 1500–1700,* ed. Helen Wilcox (Cambridge: Cambridge University Press, 1996), 61.

216. John Sadler, *The Sicke Womans Private Looking-Glasse* (1636), 10.

217. John Dod and Robert Cleaver, *A Godly Forme of Houshold Gouernment* (1630), sig. P5.

218. David Cressy, *Birth, Marriage, and Death: Ritual, Religion, and the Life-Cycle in Tudor and Stuart England* (Oxford: Oxford University Press, 1997), 87.

219. Quoted by G. R. Quaiffe, *Godly Zeal and Furious Rage: The Witch in Early Modern Europe* (New York: St. Martin's Press, 1987), 163.

220. Sir Edward Coke, *Report on Semayne's Case* (1605), trans. as *Reporte of Sir Edward Coke* (1658), sig. 2P3.

221. As quoted by Orlin, *Elizabethan Households,* 25.

222. *Memoirs of the Verney Family during the Seventeenth Century* 1:5–7, quoted in Knights, *Drama and Society,* 112.

223. Thomas Fosset, *The Servants Dutie: Or, The Calling and Condition of Servants* (1613), reprinted in Orlin, *Elizabethan Households,* 46.

224. Mark Girouard, *Life in the English Country House: A Social and Architectural History* (New Haven: Yale University Press, 1978), 82–83.

225. Peter Clark, *The English Alehouse: A Social History, 1000–1830* (London: Longman, 1983), 123.

226. Keith Thomas, *Religion and the Decline of Magic: Studies in Popular Beliefs in Sixteenth- and Seventeenth-Century England* (London: Weidenfeld & Nicolson, 1971; reprint, Harmondsworth: Penguin, 1982), 21.

227. Quoted in ibid., 23.

228. Sharp, *In Contempt of All Authority,* 41.

229. Stone, *Crisis,* 42–43.

230. Arthur Melville Clark, *Murder Under Trust, or the Topical Macbeth and Other Jacobean Matters* (Edinburgh: Scottish Academic Press, 1981), 58.

231. Peter Stallybrass, "Worn Worlds: Clothes and Identity on the Renaissance Stage," in *Subject and Object in Renaissance Culture,* ed. Margreta DeGrazia, Maureen Quilligan, and Stallybrass (Cambridge: Cambridge University Press, 1996), 289.

232. Rappaport, *Worlds within Worlds,* 101, 104.

233. Quoted in Stallybrass, "Worn Worlds," 311–12.

234. Quoted in ibid., 312.

235. Stone, *Crisis,* 562.

236. Ibid., 562–63.

237. Jonas Barish, *The Antitheatrical Prejudice* (Berkeley: University of California Press, 1981), 186.

238. This stunning observation is from Huston Diehl, "Horrid Image, Sorry Sight, Fatal Vision: The Visual Rhetoric of *Macbeth,*" *Shakespeare Studies* 16 (1983): 196.

239. As reprinted in J. Dover Wilson, *Life in Shakespeare's England: A Book of Elizabethan Prose* (Cambridge: Cambridge University Press, 1939), 231.

240. Quoted in James Patrick McHenry, "A Milton Herbal," *Milton Quarterly* 30, no. 2 (1996): 46.

241. Samuel Harsnett, *A Declaration of Egregious Popish Impostures,* chap. 21, ed. F. W. Brownlow (Newark: University of Delaware Press, 1993), 304.

242. Michael MacDonald, *Mystical Bedlam: Madness, Anxiety, and Healing in Seventeenth-Century England* (Cambridge: Cambridge University Press, 1981), 153.

243. Carol Thomas Neely, " 'Documents in Madness': Reading Madness and Gender in Shakespeare's Tragedies and Early Modern Culture," in *Shakespearean Tragedy and Gender,* ed. Shirley Nelson Garner and Madelon Sprengnether (Bloomington: Indiana University Press, 1996), 87.

244. Janet Adelman, *Suffocating Mothers: Fantasies of Maternal Origin in Shakespeare's Plays, "Hamlet" to "The Tempest"* (London: Routledge, 1992), 131.

245. Ashmolean MS 416 fol. 295 (Dwyer), quoted in MacDonald, *Mystical Bedlam,* 154.

246. Duncan Salkeld, *Madness and Drama in the Age of Shakespeare* (Manchester: Manchester University Press, 1993), 112.

247. These passages are quoted in David Shelley Berkeley, "Blood Will Tell in Shakespeare's Play," *Graduate Studies, Texas Tech University,* no. 28 (January 1984): 37–38.

248. Quoted in Lawrence Babb, *The Elizabethan Malady* (East Lansing: Michigan State University Press, 1951), 105, and in Michael MacDonald and Terence R. Murphy, *Sleepless Souls: Suicide in Early Modern England* (Oxford: Clarendon Press, 1990), 120.

249. Bright, *Treatise of Melancholie,* 111; quoted in Salkeld, *Madness and Drama,* 24.

250. This observation is taken from H. L. Rogers, *"Double Profit" in "Macbeth"* (Melbourne: Melbourne University Press on behalf of the Australian Humanities Research Council, 1964), 55.

251. Richard Foster Jones, *Ancients and Moderns: A Study of the Rise of the Scientific Movement in Seventeenth-Century England,* rev. ed. (St. Louis: Washington University Press, 1961), 22.

252. Erasmus is so quoted in James Chambers, *The English House* (New York: Norton, 1985), 73.

253. The proclamation is partly reprinted in Orlin, *Elizabethan Households,* 150–52.

254. Colin Platt, *King Death: The Black Death and Its Aftermath in Late-Medieval England* (Toronto: University of Toronto Press, 1996), 188.

255. See Tessa Watt, *Cheap Print and Popular Piety, 1500–1640* (Cambridge: Cambridge University Press, 1991), 163–65.

256. Reprinted in J. D. Wilson, *Life in Shakespeare's England,* 136.

257. G. K. Hunter, "Macbeth in the Twentieth Century," in *Aspects of "Macbeth,"* ed. Muir and Edwards, 11.

258. Lawrence Stone, *The Family, Sex, and Marriage in England, 1500–1800* (New York: Harper and Row, 1977), 76.

259. Ralph Houlbrooke, "The Puritan Death-Bed c. 1500–1600," in *The Culture of English Puritanism, 1560–1700,* ed. Christopher Durston and Jacqueline Eales (London: MacMillan, 1996), 125.

260. Quoted in Cressy, *Birth, Marriage, and Death,* 385.

261. Ibid.

262. Francis Bacon, "Of Prophecies," in *Works,* ed. James Spedding, Robert Leslie Ellis, and Douglas Denon Heath, 15 vols. (Boston: Brown and Taggard, 1860), 12:204–5.

263. Richard Bauckham, *Tudor Apocalypse* (N.p.: The Sutton Courtenay Press, n.d.), "Bibliography," 359–71.

264. Marilyn French, *Shakespeare's Division of Experience* (New York: Summit Books, 1981), 246.

265. James C. Bulman, *The Heroic Idiom of Shakespearean Tragedy* (Newark: University of Delaware Press, 1985), 186.

266. Some of this paragraph draws on Marion Bodwell Smith, *Dualities in Shakespeare* (Austin: University of Texas Press, 1966), 179–81.

267. See Paul A. Jorgensen, *"Our Naked Frailties": Sensational Art and Meaning in "Macbeth"* (Berkeley: University of California Press, 1971), 137.

268. *The Revelation of Iohn the Diuine,* 6:2–8, from *The Geneva Bible: A Facsimile of the 1560 edition* with an introduction by Lloyd E. Berry (Madison: University of Wisconsin Press, 1969), fol. 116v.

269. Christopher Haigh in *The English Reformation Revised,* ed. Haigh (Cambridge: Cambridge University Press, 1987), 209.

270. Stone, *Crisis,* 726.

271. T.H., "Preface to the Reader," *The Late Commotion of Certaine Papists in Herefordshire* (1605), sigs. A4–A4v.

272. Lancelot Andrewes, *Ninety-Six Sermons,* 10 vols. (Oxford: James Parker and Co., 1871), 5:181.

273. Quoted in Comensoli, *"Household Business,"* 10.

274. Quoted in Charles John Guthrie, *John Knox and John Knox's House* (Edinburgh: Oliphant, Anderson, and Ferrier, 1898), 123.

275. Katharine R. Firth, *The Apocalyptic Tradition in Reformation Britain, 1530–1645* (Oxford: Clarendon Press, 1979), 121–22.

276. Quoted in Jenny Wormald, "Ecclesiastical Vitriol: the Kirk, the Puritans, and the Future King of England," in *The Reign of Elizabeth I,* ed. Guy, 184.

277. Quoted by Dickinson, *Scotland from the Earliest Times,* 349.

278. The text is taken from *Images of English Puritanism: A Collection of Contemporary Sources, 1589–1646,* ed. Lawrence A. Sasek (Baton Rouge: Louisiana State University Press, 1989), 338–41.

279. Quoted in Roger Lockyer, *The Early Stuarts: A Political History of England, 1603–1642* (London: Longman, 1989), 101.

280. Quoted in H. C. Porter, *Reformation and Reaction in Tudor Cambridge* (Cambridge: Cambridge University Press, 1958), 334.

281. Quoted in Wormald, "Ecclesiastical Vitriol," 190.

282. Quoted in Lockyer, *Early Stuarts,* 105.

283. Quoted in John Marlowe, *The Puritan Tradition in English Life* (London: Cresset Press, 1956), 18–19.

284. The text is taken from *King James VI and I: Political Writings,* ed. Johann P. Sommerville (Cambridge: Cambridge University Press, 1994), 138. Part of this text is also in Carroll, *Macbeth,* 14–15.

285. Quoted in Lockyer, *Early Stuarts,* 109.

286. Quoted by Linda Levy Peck, "Kingship, Counsel, and Law in Early Stuart Britain," in *The Varieties of British Political Thought,* ed. J. G. A. Pocock (Cambridge: Cambridge University Press, 1993, 1996), 89.

287. *Calendar of State Papers, Venetian,* 10:138

288. Wrightson and Levine, *Poverty and Piety,* 11.

289. Edward Wagenknecht, *The Personality of Shakespeare* (Norman: University of Oklahoma Press, 1972), 129.

290. Kiernan, *Eight Tragedies,* 137.

291. For a detailed listing of scriptural echoes in *Macbeth,* see Naseeb Shaheen, *Biblical References in Shakespeare's Tragedies* (Newark: University of Delaware Press, 1999).

292. Most recently in conversation with me, but see his *Godly People: Essays on English Protestantism and Puritanism* (London: Hambledon Press, 1983), 1.

293. Haigh, *English Reformation Revised,* 212.

294. I am basing part of my definition on that first developed by M. M. Knappen, *Tudor Puritanism: A Chapter in the History of Idealism* (Chicago: University of Chicago Press, 1959).

295. Robert G. Hunter, *Shakespeare and the Mystery of God's Judgments* (Athens: University of Georgia Press, 1976), 180.

296. Quoted in John S. Wilks, *The Idea of Conscience in Renaissance Tragedy* (London: Routledge, 1990), 142; and by Peter Milward in *Shakespeare's Religious Background* (London: Sidgwick and Jackson, 1973), 133.

297. Porter, *Reformation and Reaction,* 355, also makes this observation, citing Andrewes.

298. The phrase is Porter's (ibid., 371).

299. For the text, translated from the Latin, see ibid., 371. See also *The Life and Acts of John Whitgift,* 3 vols. (Oxford: Clarendon Press, 1822), 2:250.

300. The observation is also made by Harry Morris, *Last Things in Shakespeare* (Tallahassee: University Presses of Florida; Florida State University Press, 1985), 171.

301. Thomas, *Religion and the Decline of Magic,* 505.

302. Quoted in Victoria Kahn, *Machiavellian Rhetoric from the Counter-Reformation to Milton* (Princeton: Princeton University Press, 1994), 91.

303. I have taken the comment from the dedication to Sir William Piryam from the text of William Perkins, *A Discourse on Conscience,* ed. Thomas P. Merrill (Nieuwkoop: G. DeBraaf, 1966), 3.

304. Hume's treatise is quoted and analyzed extensively in A. C. and M. K. Kistner, "*Macbeth*: A Treatise of Conscience," *Thoth* 13 (1973): 27–43.

305. *The Chamberlain Letters,* ed. Thomson, 30.

306. H. G. Alexander, *Religion in England, 1558–1662* (London: University of London Press, 1968), 99.

307. Stone, *Crisis,* 730.

308. Peter Iver Kaufman, *Prayer, Despair, and Drama: Elizabethan Introspection* (Urbana: University of Illinois Press, 1996), 62.

309. *Letters of King James,* ed. Akrigg, 207.

310. *James VI and I: Political Writings,* ed. Sommerville, 140–41.

311. All of these quotations are taken from the very useful essay by Frank L. Huntley, "*Macbeth* and the Background of Jesuitical Equivocation," *PMLA* 79 (1964): 390–400; A. E. Malloch replies in "Some Notes on Equivocation," *PMLA* 81 (1966): 145–46.

312. *The Convocation Book of MDCVI commonly called Bishop Overall's Convocation Book,* quoted in Peck, "Kingship, Counsel, and Law," 87.

313. Huntley, "Background," 396–97; references are to *Calendar of State Papers, Domestic,* 273, 286, 289. Some modifications were made in Huntley's statements by Malloch, "Some Notes," 145–46. Coke's remark is from the *Complete Collection of State Trials,* 6 vols. (London, 1742), 1:241; an excerpt is reprinted in Carroll, *Macbeth,* 265–66.

314. Zagorin, *Ways of Lying,* 196. My information on Garnet in this and the following paragraph is drawn in part on Zagorin's remarks (193–96). A portion of Garnet's *Treatise* is in Carroll, *Macbeth,* 266–68.

315. *Calendar of State Papers, Venetian,* 10:337.

316. Chamberlain quoted in Stunz, "Date of *Macbeth,*" 103.

317. Quoted in ibid., 101.

318. Quoted in ibid., 104.

319. Quoted by Michael MacDonald in his introduction to *Witchcraft and Hysteria in Elizabethan London* (London: Tavistock/Routledge, 1991), xviii.

320. Reginald Scot, *The Discoverie of Witchcraft,* with an introduction by Montague Summers (London: John Rodker, 1930), book 1, chap. 3, p. 4. Although not a facsimile text, the transcription is reliable. Other portions of Scot and Gifford are reprinted in Carroll, *Macbeth,* 307–12.

321. Matthew Hale quoted by Peter Haining in the introduction to *The Witchcraft Papers: Contemporary Records of the Witchcraft Hysteria in Essex, 1560–1700* (Secaucus, N.J.: University Books, 1974), 10. Carroll reprints the Jacobean statute on witchcraft (*Macbeth,* 328–30).

322. Christina Larner, *Enemies of God: The Witch-Hunt in Scotland* (Oxford: Basil Blackwell, 1981), 142.

323. Thomas, *Religion and the Decline of Magic,* 588.

324. See M. B. Smith, *Dualities in Shakespeare,* 172. Carroll publishes Holinshed's full account (*Macbeth,* 135–50).

325. Further discussion is in Montague Summers, *The Geography of Witchcraft* (London: Routledge and Kegan Paul, 1927), 207–8.

326. Christina Larner, "James VI and I and Witchcraft," in *The Reign of James VI and I,* ed. A. G. R. Smith, 78–79.

327. My text for *Newes from Scotland* is that edited by G. B. Harrison for the Bodley Head Quartos (Edinburgh: University Press, 1966), 10:16–17. Carroll reprints the entire text (*Macbeth*, 313–25).

328. My text for James's *Daemonologie* is that edited by Harrison for the Bodley Head Quartos, 10:xiii. Carroll prints other excerpts (*Macbeth*, 325–28).

329. Bodleian Ashmole MS 207, fol. 59v.

330. James Sharpe, *Instruments of Darkness: Witchcraft in England, 1550–1750* (London: Hamish Hamilton, 1996), 75.

331. *The Malleus Maleficarum of Heinrich Kramer and James Sprenger,* trans. Rev. Montague Summers (London: John Rodker, 1928), part 2, Qn. 1, chap. 2, p. 99.

332. Wills, *Witches and Jesuits,* 38.

333. Sarah Beckwith, "The Power of Devils and the Hearts of Men: Notes towards a Drama of Witchcraft," in *Shakespeare in the Changing Curriculum,* ed. Lesley Aers and Nigel Wheale (London: Routledge, 1991), 143.

334. Howard Dobin, *Merlin's Disciples: Prophecy, Poetry, and Power in Renaissance England* (Stanford: Stanford University Press, 1990), 20. Many of the citations that follow may be found on pp. 24–26, 110, 116.

335. Quoted in ibid., 24–25.

336. Quoted in Bradbook, *Bradbrook on Shakespeare,* 152.

337. George Puttenham, *The Arte of English Poesie,* ed. G. D. Willcock and Alice Walker (Cambridge: Cambridge University Press, 1936), 260–61.

338. See Paul, *Royal Play of "Macbeth,"* 163–68.

339. The details are given in D. P. Walker, *Unclean Spirits: Possession and Exorcism in France and England in the Late Sixteenth and Early Seventeenth Centuries* (Philadelphia: University of Pennsylvania Press, 1981), 43–49.

340. This work is summarized, among other places, in ibid., 49–52.

341. The full case, which is very problematic, is reproduced with facsimile texts in MacDonald, *Witchcraft and Hysteria.* See also James Sharpe, *The Bewitching of Anne Gunter* (London: Profile Books, 1999; Routledge, 2000), 150–52.

342. Haining, *The Witchcraft Papers,* 154.

343. Joseph Klaits, *Servants of Satan: The Age of the Witch Hunts* (Bloomington: Indiana University Press, 1985), 135.

344. These two cases are in Thomas, *Religion and the Decline of Magic,* 329.

345. Quoted in Paul, *Royal Play of "Macbeth,"* 114.

346. Quoted in ibid., 125–26. The entire case, with newly discovered evidence, is recounted by Sharpe, *The Bewitching of Anne Gunter,* but this outline, from a primary document, remains unchanged.

347. James L. Calderwood, *"If It Were Done": "Macbeth" and Tragic Action* (Amherst: University of Massachusetts Press, 1986), 99.

348. Thomas Heywood, *2 Edward IV,* in *Dramatic Works* (London, 1874), 9:165–66.

Chapter 3:
Shakespeare, *Macbeth*, and the Common Understanding

1. Peter Burke, *Popular Culture in Early Modern Europe* (London: Temple Smith, 1978), xi.

2. Eric S. Mallin, *Inscribing the Time: Shakespeare and the End of Elizabethan England* (Berkeley: University of California Press, 1995), 16.

3. Jean E. Howard, "Women as Spectators, Spectacles, and Paying Customers," in *Staging the Renaissance: Reinterpretations of Elizabethan and Jacobean Drama,* ed. David Scott Kastan and Peter Stallybrass (London: Routledge, 1991), 70.

4. Marc Bloch, *The Historian's Craft* (Manchester: Manchester University Press, 1954, 1963), 66.

5. Preface to Sir Walter Ralegh, *The Historie of the World* (1652 ed.), sig. A1v.

6. Michael Heim, *The Metaphysics of Virtual Reality* (New York: Oxford University Press, 1993), 100.

7. Wrightson and Levine, *Poverty and Piety,* 1.

8. Robert N. Watson, "Tragedy," in *The Cambridge Companion to English Renaissance Drama,* ed. A. R. Braunmiller and Michael Hattaway (Cambridge: Cambridge University Press, 1990), 300.

9. Antonio Damasio, *Descartes' Error: Emotion, Reason, and the Human Brain* (New York: Putnam, 1994; reprint, New York: Avon Books, 1995), 205.

10. Ian Stewart and Jack Cohen, *Fragments of Reality: The Evolution of the Curious Mind* (Cambridge: Cambridge University Press, 1997), esp. chap. 10.

11. Eviatar Zerubavel, *Social Mindscapes: An Invitation to Cognitive Sociology* (Cambridge: Harvard University Press, 1997), 13, 17, 16, 17.

12. Edward O. Wilson, *Consilience: The Unity of Knowledge* (New York: Knopf, 1998; reprint, New York: Vintage Books, 1999), 243.

13. Shuger, *Habits of Thought,* 255.

14. Patrick Collinson, *The Elizabethan Puritan Movement* (London: Jonathan Cape, 1967), 126.

15. Anderson, *Words That Matter,* 2–3.

16. Crane, *Framing Authority,* 34.

17. Mary J. Carruthers, *The Book of Memory: A Study in Medieval Culture* (Cambridge: Cambridge University Press, 1990), 3.

18. I have drawn these examples from ibid., 39.

19. Foucault, *The Order of Things,* 49.

20. Daniel C. Dennett, *Consciousness Explained* (New York: Little, Brown, 1991), 258, who cites the work of Patrick Hayes (1979), Marvin Minsky (1975), John Anderson (1983), and Eric Sandeval (1991).

21. Elizabeth Fox-Genovese, "Literary Criticism and the Politics of the New Historicism," in *The New Historicism,* ed. H. Aram Veeser (London: Routledge, 1989), 221.

22. Robert Hapgood, *Shakespeare the Theatre-Poet* (Oxford: Clarendon Press, 1988), 45.

23. Calderwood, *"If It Were Done,"* 52.

24. John Kerrigan in his introduction to William Shakespeare, *The Sonnets* (Harmondsworth: Penguin, 1986), 30; quoted in Charles Wells, *The Northern Star: Shakespeare and the Theme of Constancy* (Upton-upon-Severn: Blackthorn Press, 1989), 194.

25. Umberto Eco, *The Limits of Interpretation* (Bloomington: Indiana University Press, 1990), 2.

26. Fernand Braudel, *Afterthoughts in Material Civilization and Capitalism,* trans. Patricia M. Ranum (Baltimore: Johns Hopkins University Press, 1977), 115.

27. Robert Scholes, *Textual Power: Literary Theory and the Teaching of English* (New Haven: Yale University Press, 1985), 33.

Appendix A:
The Text of *Macbeth*

1. Dr. Samuel Johnson, *Miscellaneous Observations on Macbeth* (1745), reprinted in Daniel Amneus, *The Mystery of Macbeth* (Alhambra, Calif.: Primrose Press, 1983), 75–76.

2. Amneus, *Mystery of Macbeth,* 29–31.

3. Kristian Smidt, *Unconformities in Shakespeare's Tragedies* (New York: St. Martin's Press, 1990), 158–59.

4. Bertrand Evans, *Shakespeare's Tragic Practice* (Oxford: Clarendon Press, 1979), 192.

5. Quoted by Smidt, *Unconformities,* 154.

6. Wills, *Witches and Jesuits,* 136.

7. Harry Berger, Jr., "Early Scenes" in *Making Trifles of Terrors,* ed. Erickson, 73.

8. J. M. Nosworthy, *Shakespeare's Occasional Plays: Their Origin and Transmission* (New York: Barnes and Noble, 1965), 20.

9. Jerome J. McGann, *A Critique of Modern Textual Criticism* (Chicago: University of Chicago Press, 1983), 44.

10. G. Thomas Tanselle, "Textual Instability and Editorial Idealism," *Studies in Bibliography* 49 (1996): 1.

11. Bernard Cerquiglini, *In Praise of the Variant: A Critical History of Philology,* trans. Betsy Wing (Baltimore: Johns Hopkins University Press, 1999), 45.

12. Charlton Hinman, *The Printing and Proof-Reading of the First Folio of Shakespeare,* 2 vols. (Oxford: Clarendon Press, 1963), 1:10.

13. W. W. Greg, *The Shakespeare First Folio: Its Bibliographical and Textual History* (Oxford: Clarendon Press, 1955), 389, 395.

14. Andrew Gurr in a discussion about the relationship of the two plays with me in February 1993. I have also benefited from discussions with S. P. Cerasano.

15. Simon Forman, *The Book of Plays and Notes thereof per Forman for Common Policy,* is reprinted as appendix C in *The Tragedy of Macbeth,* ed. Nicholas Brooke (Oxford: Oxford University Press, 1990), 235–36, and elsewhere.

APPENDIX B:
GUTENBERG AND HYPERTEXT

1. Claudia Wallis, "The Learning Revolution," *Time,* Special Issue, Spring 1995, p. 49.

2. Sven Birkerts, *The Gutenberg Elegies: The Fate of Reading in an Electronic Age* (Boston and London: Faber and Faber, 1994), 192.

3. A more recent concern of Birkerts's, which he elides into hypertext, is the invention of electronic books. Steven Levy confronts this related but separate issue in "It's Time to Turn the Last Page":

> When Y3K pundits look back on our time, they'll remember it as the *Last* Century of the Book. Why? As a common item of communication, artistic expression and celebrity anecdote, the physical object consisting of bound dead trees in shiny wrapper is headed for the antique heap. Its replacement will be a lightning-quick injection of digital bits into a handheld device with an ultrasharp display. Culture vultures and bookworms might cringe at the prospect, but it's as inevitable as page two's following page one. Books are goners, at least as far as being the dominant form of reading.
>
> Most of the pieces are already in place: fast chips, long-lasting batteries, capacious disk drives and the Internet. Only two things, really, hold us back from having reading devices that are just as felicitous as the dust-jacketed packages we know and love. One is high-speed wireless bandwidth, so that the devices can be quickly loaded. Fixing that is a no-brainer. No one doubts that such a big digital transmission system will show up early in the millennium. The second is a screen whose output is as sumptuous as the current books, which engage not only our minds but our sense of touch. (*Newsweek,* January 1, 2000, pp. 96–97)

But of course we will read e-books as we read conventional books, and they will serve as the text from which we will practice hypertext. Here the more things change, the more they stay the same.

4. Carl Woodring, *Literature: An Embattled Profession* (New York: Columbia University Press, 1999), 139.

APPENDIX C:
LITERARY CRITICISM AND HYPERTEXT

1. R. V. Young, *At War with the Word: Literary Theory and Liberal Education* (Wilmington, Del.: Intercollegiate Studies Institute, 1999), ix. The book is particularly useful because it represents lectures and published essays delivered and written over a long period of time.

2. Young's sentence continues, "and interpretation can be a means of recruiting the powerful vision of the artist to one's own conception of the world." What Young actually means here is difficult to discern, since he has earlier denied the author absolute authority (that would be the intentional fallacy) and has argued strongly for critical judgment and dispassionate reflection. The word *recruiting* is especially troublesome.

Index

Cogan, Thomas: *Hauen of Health,* 54,
189–90
Cognition, 30–33, 41. *See also* Brain; Mind
Cognitive theory, 14, 30, 33. *See also* Neuro-
science
Cohen, Jack, 264
Coke, Sir Edward, 62, 90, 121, 173,
236–37; *Charge giuen at Norwich Ass-
ises,* 231
Collins, Michael J., 23
Collinson, Patrick, 216, 264–65
Color, 182
Commandment, 37
Commonplace book, 37, 265
Composition, 37
Computer, 14, 32, 34, 36, 41, 261, 267,
285, 286
Confession, 125, 126, 127, 147
Conjure, 245, 246, 257, 258
Conscience, 55, 114, 124, 192, 207, 216,
226–30
Consilience, 264
Constantine, 87, 92, 105
Contrition, 125, 126, 149
Cook, Ann Jennalie, 73–74
Copley, Sir Anthony, 47, 64, 65; *An Answer
to a Letter of a Iesuited Gentleman,* 238
Coppin, G., 61–62
Coriolanus, 162
Cornwallis, Jane, Lady, 172
Costume, 73, 182. *See also* Cloth/clothing
Court, 71, 145, 160, 181
Courtier, 101, 145, 160, 186
Cowell, John: *The Interpreter: Or Booke Con-
taining the Signification of Words,* 96–97
Cowley, Robert, 72
Cowper, William, 91
Craig, Alexander, 90–91
Craig, Sir Thomas: *The Right of Succession to
the Kingdom of England,* 61
Crane, Mary Thomas, 37, 265
Cressy, David, 163, 173, 198
Crime, 126–27, 183; and alehouses, 175;
and economy, 131; and James I, 78;
and London, 60; and nonconformity,
206; and witchcraft, 244, 248, 249.
See also Justice; Law; Punishment; Tor-
ture
Criticism, 14, 24, 261, 262, 291–93

Croft, Pauline, 84
Cromwell, Oliver, 78
Crow, 240, 241
Cuffs, Henry: *The Differences of the Ages of
Mans Life,* 190
Cultural materialism, 13, 275
Cultural moment, 13–14, 24, 43, 259–60,
262, 275
Culture, 13, 42, 43, 59, 74, 259–60, 262,
263, 264, 275
Cunningham, Iohn, 248
Curtain Theater, 69
Cutpurse, Moll, 170

Dagger, 46, 93, 109, 114, 115, 268, 269,
308n191
D'Aiutolo, Jacqueline, 285, 288
Dalton, Michael: *The Countrey Justice,* 192
Dalton School, 285, 288, 289, 292, 293
Damasio, Antonio: *Descartes' Error,* 264
Dance, of death, 194
Daniel, Samuel: *Certain Small Poems, Lately
Printed,* 56; *Cleopatra,* 56; "Panegy-
ricke Congratulatorie," 87–88; *The Vi-
sion of the Twelve Goddesses,* 90, 182
Darling, Thomas, 254
Darnley, Henry Stuart, Lord, 50, 51, 52, 53,
76, 77, 110, 118, 152
Darrell, John, 254, 256
Davies, John, of Hereford: *Microcosmos,*
83–84; *The Triumph of Death,* 201
Davys, Alice, 188
Death: and Banquo, 199–200; and bell, 46,
194, 195, 216; and children, 168;
dance of, 194; and disease, 184,
194–97; and *Julius Caesar,* 56; and
Lady Macbeth, 183, 190–91; and London, 60; and Macbeth, 196, 197–99,
216; and *Macbeth,* 56, 196; and melancholy, 191–92; and memorial, 45; and
nature, 193; and poverty, 133–34; and
ritual, 125; and sleep, 54
Deceit/dissimulation, 102, 141, 206, 240,
254; and James I, 66–67, 100, 101,
111, 115, 247. *See also* Disguise
Dee, John, 40–41
Dekker, Thomas, 46, 195, 199; *The Noble
Spanish Soldier,* 127; *Seuen Deadlie
Sinns of London,* 63, 197; *The Wonderfull yeare. 1603,* 196–97